D0986972

I SAW DEATH COMING

ALSO BY KIDADA E. WILLIAMS

They Left Great Marks on Me: African American Testimonies of Racial Violence from Emancipation to World War I

Charleston Syllabus (with Keisha N. Blain and Chad Williams)

I SAW DEATH COMING

A History of Terror and Survival in the War against Reconstruction

KIDADA E. WILLIAMS

BLOOMSBURY PUBLISHING
NEW YORK · LONDON · OXFORD · NEW DELHI · SYDNEY

BLOOMSBURY PUBLISHING
Bloomsbury Publishing Inc.
1385 Broadway, New York, NY 10018, USA

BLOOMSBURY, BLOOMSBURY PUBLISHING, and the Diana logo are trademarks
of Bloomsbury Publishing Plc

First published in the United States 2023

Copyright © Kidada E. Williams, 2023
Map created by Gary Antonetti

All rights reserved. No part of this publication may be reproduced or transmitted
in any form or by any means, electronic or mechanical, including photocopying, recording,
or any information storage or retrieval system, without prior permission in writing
from the publishers.

LIBRARY OF CONGRESS CATALOGING-IN-PUBLICATION DATA IS AVAILABLE

ISBN: HB: 978-1-63557-663-4; EBOOK: 978-1-63557-664-1

2 4 6 8 10 9 7 5 3 1

Typeset by Westchester Publishing Services
Printed and bound in the U.S.A.

To find out more about our authors and books visit www.bloomsbury.com and sign up
for our newsletters.

Bloomsbury books may be purchased for business or promotional use. For information
on bulk purchases please contact Macmillan Corporate and Premium Sales Department at
specialmarkets@macmillan.com.

For my family, with gratitude

CONTENTS

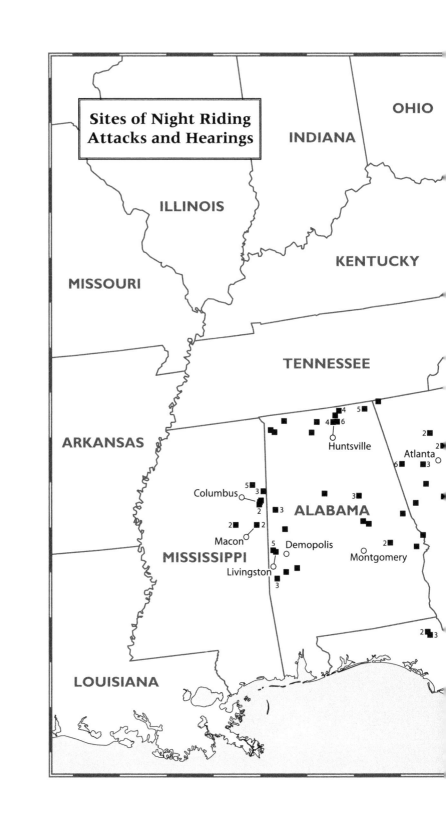

Sites of Night Riding Attacks and Hearings

OHIO

INDIANA

ILLINOIS

KENTUCKY

MISSOURI

TENNESSEE

ARKANSAS

2■

2■

Atlanta

6■ ■3

4■ 5■

4 6

Huntsville

5■

3

Columbus ○ 3 3■

2 ■3 ALABAMA

2■ ■2

Macon ○

5 Demopolis

MISSISSIPPI 2■

Livingston Montgomery ○

3

2■ ■

2■■3

LOUISIANA

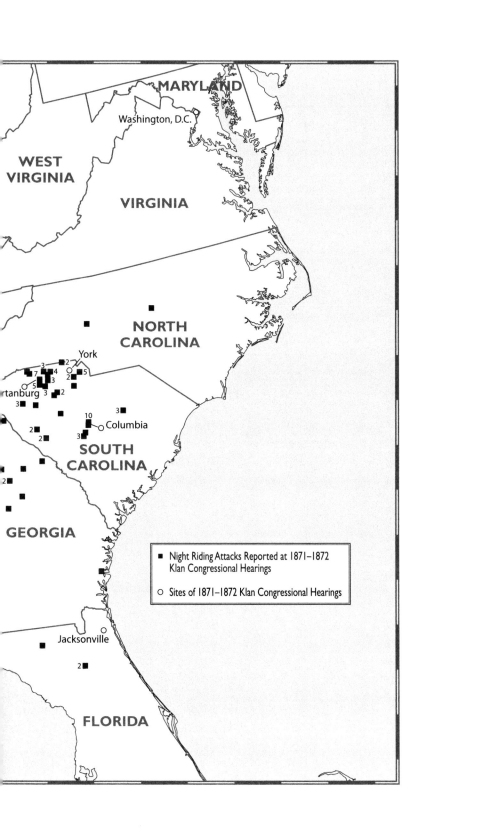

MARYLAND

Washington, D.C.

WEST
VIRGINIA

VIRGINIA

NORTH
CAROLINA

York

3
2
7   4
5   3
5
tanburg 3 2
3
2
2

10
3
3

Columbia

SOUTH
CAROLINA

GEORGIA

■ Night Riding Attacks Reported at 1871–1872
   Klan Congressional Hearings

O Sites of 1871–1872 Klan Congressional Hearings

Jacksonville

2

FLORIDA

INTRODUCTION

Question: Now, tell us whether the Ku-Klux raided on you.

Answer: Well, they came to my house about midnight—some time in March . . . When I saw death coming I got out . . .

—ABRAHAM BRUMFIELD, YORK COUNTY,
SOUTH CAROLINA, 1872

On a November night in 1871, some ten miles east of Aberdeen, Mississippi, Edward Crosby stepped outside to get some water for his thirsty child, when suddenly, he heard and felt the thunder of a team of horses. He gazed out, and by either moonlight or the glow of his torch, he saw about thirty disguised men descending on his home, their mounts draped by full-body cloth coverings.

Mrs. Crosby—who must have seen or heard the men approaching, too—asked Edward who and what they were. Edward had heard stories about armed white men on horseback galloping through the countryside and torturing and murdering Black families in the middle of the night during recent elections. The perpetrators and their apologists often referred to these raids euphemistically as "visits," masking their brutality behind the veneer of a friendly social call. Edward told his wife he reckoned the gang heading for them was what people in their community called "Ku-Klux," shorthand for the Ku Klux Klan.[1]

In the spring of 1866, ex-Confederates in Pulaski, Tennessee, formed social clubs in which they sometimes donned masks or elaborate costumes and performed musical entertainment. They called themselves the "Ku-Klux" after the Greek word *kyklos* (circle). Shortly after they organized, Klansmen's activities evolved to roaming armed through communities in the middle of the night conducting paramilitary strikes on Black and white southerners. According to one historian, Klansmen "harnessed nineteenth-century technology and organizational techniques" which allowed more Klan groups to spread across the South.[2] Klansmen's work gave rise to a racist movement that became so widespread that any white man or group of men who wanted to intimidate or kill their targets might be associated with it whether they were affiliated with the Klan or not.[3]

That is why when Edward saw the costumed men and horses he concluded they were "Ku-Klux." Worried that death was coming for *him* but hoping it would spare his wife and children, Edward slipped into his family's smokehouse. He thought the men might not think to look there, even if they decided to search the property for him.

When the posse arrived in the Crosbys' yard, several men got down from their horses and called out for Edward to present himself. Although terrified, Edward retained his composure and stayed in his hiding place. Mrs. Crosby calmly told the men she did not know where her husband was, but she thought he had gone to call on his sister. The men hung around for a bit, dithering about what to do, before accepting they would not catch their target and leaving.

The Crosbys survived the raid but did not emerge unscathed. Secession and the founding of the Confederacy were less than a decade in the past; barely five years separated them from the end of the bloody Civil War. These men's arrival revealed to the Crosbys that Monroe County's racially conservative whites had marked them as enemies. This terrified the family and left them afraid their lives would never be the same.

The "visit" was not Edward Crosby's first encounter with hostile white Mississippians. Before the war, enslaved people outnumbered free people in

Monroe County by about four thousand. The enslaving class had used extreme levels of violence to control the Black majority. Emancipation and Black male enfranchisement gave men like Edward the chance to create a more just world—a world they were ready to seize—and whites in Monroe County knew it. White landowners in the county collectively found ways to deny Black people's freedom and power wherever they could, including by imposing the system of sharecropping and tenant farming. This economic violence rendered families like Edward's vulnerable to retaliatory eviction; against organized white resistance, it would be hard for Edward to secure employment, shelter, and life's necessities anywhere else in the county. And as if threats of being unhoused were not enough, paramilitary gangs like the Klan had massed across the region. Edward and other Black people were "living like lost sheep," he later said, doing their best to survive.[4] Edward knew the only way he could break the grip the former enslavers still had on his life and his family's future was to help elect candidates who would advance his right to freedom.

In November 1871, African Americans in Monroe County tried to vote for progressive candidates and faced menacing opposition from whites who insisted that, if men like Edward cast ballots at all, they must be for white conservative candidates. Edward's landlord—the same man who had previously held him in bondage—even warned Edward that if he voted away white men's right to run Monroe County and rule over Black people as they saw fit, he would take Edward down. Edward dissembled, swearing to vote the way his employer wanted, but the suspicious white man promised he and his people would be on the lookout come election day.

Edward and other voters went to the polls, hoping to lift their preferred candidates to victory. They were part of a larger contingent of Black people working to make freedom real. Many of them had resisted or escaped slavery during the Civil War. For these Americans, the Emancipation Proclamation and Thirteenth Amendment were the first steps on the road to freedom, not the last. Freedom wasn't just about legal equality or the vote for them. It was about family and community. The franchise was a means to help Black families and communities achieve their goal: the end of any oppressive systems and practices that denied them their right to be free, equal, and secure.

Black freedom seekers had been behind the push for the civic, social, and political protections spelled out in the Fourteenth and Fifteenth Amendments and the Civil Rights Act of 1866.[5] That act said all persons born in the United States were citizens, and positively affirmed that all American citizens were equally protected by all the nation's laws. More specifically, the act said citizens, including Black people, had the right to make and enforce contracts and to inherit, sell, and hold property. In theory, at least, the Civil Rights Act granted Black people liberties denied to them in bondage and by racist restrictive laws. Men and women like the Crosbys saw themselves fine-tuning American freedom by making the nation live up to its creed and the promises spelled out in the founding documents.

At his polling place, Edward Crosby requested a Republican ballot, but he was told none were available. He waited, trying to figure out what to do and hoping an ally would show his face and give Edward the ballot he wanted to cast. None appeared. Edward hung around. Throughout the day, thirty to forty more Black men came to the polling place and asked to vote for the Republican ticket, all to be told the same thing.

Black men in Mississippi had read and understood the words "all men are created equal" in the Declaration of Independence; they believed in democracy and wanted to vote and run for office to secure their rights and advance their visions of freedom. These men knew the amended U.S. Constitution now recognized their right to do so. They also believed there should have been plenty of ballots available. But, locked in the southern planter class's viselike grip and fearing right-wing whites' unleashed fury, the eager voters could not risk making a fuss. Edward tried voting at another polling place without success. "I saw that I was beat at my own game," he said, "and I got on my horse and dropped out." Edward was down but not yet defeated.[6]

Frustrated by having his rights violated, and petrified his landlord and other white men would make good on their threats and continue to pursue him, Edward began planning to relocate. He did not know whether the man who had held him in bondage would have him whipped, like other Black men had been in his community, or drive his family off the land. He knew that if he resisted, the white man and his associates would kill him. "All of us live a little in doubt," Edward said of his social circle. "We didn't hardly know what to be at times."[7]

White men's threats to Edward's life and the night riders' "visit" to his home laid bare his family's precarious position. Edward's concerns were justified. When the men arrived at his door after he tried to vote, they brought with them white southern hate for who the Crosbys were and what their new lives and status as freed people represented. Whatever Edward and his wife thought they understood about surviving slavery and the Civil War was shaken that night, along with their faith in Reconstruction's reimagining of Black people's place in the nation. The "visit" exposed the freed family's disposability, dashing their postbellum dreams. The system of power that exposed Black families to this menacing violence infused the Crosbys' home and took up residence in the souls of each of its occupants.

Home ceased to exist—both the safety of their dwelling, where the Crosbys were supposed to be able to fortify themselves against the world, and the larger community in which they hoped they might live in peace. The cradle of their security in northeastern Mississippi—and in the Founding Fathers' ever more perfect Union—crumbled. The Crosbys' world had undergone changes unimaginable a decade earlier; laws had been passed that said they were to be treated as citizens and valued members of the American family. Nevertheless, that world appeared to be casting them out like refuse.

Although it may not seem like it, the Crosbys were lucky. Everyone survived the raid without sustaining physical injuries. They were terrified but alive and together. For the time being, at least, they had a place to call home and could still support themselves.

Other families were not as fortunate. White men "visited" them, too. But they were left undone by what happened to them.

———

Universal slave emancipation, the Civil Rights Act of 1866, and the Fourteenth and Fifteenth Amendments all increased Black people's odds of securing a more liberated future. But these transformations also set in motion forces that birthed a new era of violent conflict in the former slaveholding states. Black people like Edward Crosby played a central role in reconstructing American freedom and democracy, which is why white southerners targeted them—as was clear to any American policymakers who cared to see. While acknowledging the significance of the "social revolution" taking place after slavery was abolished, in 1865, retired U.S. Army general Carl Schurz advised Americans against indulging "in any delusions" about the real state of affairs in the South. But some white northerners and westerners were content to be deluded: they were exhausted from the war, grateful for peace, and—not having experienced the obscenity of slavery themselves— ignorant of the true depths of enslavers' capacity for depravity.[8]

Schurz had a better view of the postwar landscape, and he issued a warning. Traveling across the South at President Andrew Johnson's behest to assess conditions there, Schurz had observed among Confederates and other southern white conservatives what he called "an utter absence of national feeling." Secessionists and their allies had accepted slavery's end, but "the general spirit of violence" slavery fostered toward Black people had not dissipated, the general said.[9]

Right-wingers had only returned begrudgingly to the "more perfect Union" the Founding Fathers had created, and they clearly dismissed the terms of the peace when it came to respecting Black people's liberty. They were canny, biding their time until federal troops left. A specific sect, Schurz noted, "the incorrigibles," refused even the pretense of honorably accepting defeat.[10] Furious at losing some of their cherished privileges of political and racial supremacy, these Confederates revolted, unleashing their rage at accomplished and aspiring Black families.

White men—like those who denied Edward Crosby his vote and rallied the Klan to punish him—mobilized around the belief that, although seces-sionists had surrendered the battlefield to United States forces, the war to maintain complete mastery over Black people was still on. U.S. Army officials, like General Thomas Kilby Smith, observed that these southern whites were "disloyal in their sentiments and hostile to what they call the United States"; they waited to be "restored to independence" and left to manage Black people just as they had before the war.[11]

But Confederates did not merely wait passively. Unable to reclaim political power legitimately through the ballot box and the statehouse, and unwilling to confront their individual Black adversaries man-to-man, right-wingers organized into a shadow army of paramilitary gangs and attacked African Americans directly, waging war against anyone who threatened white people's social, economic, or political power. Killing and maiming large numbers of enslaved people had been unprofitable, but doing the same to *free* Black people, especially those actively trying to act on their new rights and privileges, was, as one government agent surmised, "nobody's loss."[12]

Some Confederates' indifference to free Black people's lives was reflected in unremitting waves of extremist violence. Enslavers' refusal to release Black people from bondage rippled across the South. First they retaliated by maiming and killing Black people trying to escape or rescue their kin. Then came the raging torrent of assassinations of Black voters and officeholders. When that wasn't enough to keep men like Edward from the polls, extremists unleashed the tidal force of Klan strikes on Black southerners generally. Reporting on conditions in Texas in 1868, Secretary of War Edwin Stanton wrote that the killings of Black people were so common as to "render it impossible to keep an accurate account of them." This violence could only occur, Stanton added, because it was "countenanced, or at least not discouraged by the majority of white people where it occurred."[13]

The coalescing violence that government agents and Secretary Stanton described was not the impulsive antics of defeated soldiers. It was the pursuit of the Confederate cause by other means. Many ex-Confederates remained united in their opposition to emancipation and to Black people enjoying any liberties and privileges. White Americans' resistance to Reconstruction was widespread. Most white northerners and westerners had only accepted emancipation to end the war, and many weren't any more thrilled by the prospect of legal equality than white southerners were.

Many white Americans seemed to take it for granted that former Confederates would be outraged by defeat and abolition. The *expected* nature of white southerners' reprisal against Black freedom allowed postbellum violence to remain normalized and institutionalized, just as it had been during slavery. But this was not merely a continuation; emancipation and Black people's fight for legal equality changed everything, incentivizing the all-out war white southerners waged on freedom during the Reconstruction period.[14]

The Crosbys were one of the many southern families subjected to terrorizing raids by armed and often disguised white men who rejected emancipation and the protections African Americans were supposed to enjoy. Victims reported the brutality to their local authorities often, to little or no avail. If white officials were not themselves involved in the attacks, then they were less than enthusiastic about bringing the culprits to justice. Even policymakers who were committed to upholding the law and maintaining order often found themselves overwhelmed by the intensity and diffused nature of these assaults, and by the lack of sufficient support from local citizens or higher-ranking state and federal officials. Impunity, in turn, encouraged more violence.

Receiving a flood of reports of disenfranchisement and Klan attacks on Black people across the South, U.S. senators and congressmen, in 1871, convened the Joint Select Committee to Inquire Into the Condition of Affairs in the Late Insurrectionary States. The "affairs" the twenty-one-member bicameral committee investigated were "the execution of laws, and the safety of the lives and the property of the citizens of the United States."[15] The committee's work became known as "the Klan hearings" because of how prominently violence like the "visit" the Crosbys received featured in the investigation. For the next year, lawmakers traveled to hot spots of southern disorder, where they solicited testimony from officeholders, voters, accused perpetrators, and their victims. Some witnesses the committee subpoenaed, but others stepped forward of their own accord, hoping to convince federal officials to take purposeful action to end the violence.

In mid-November 1871, Edward Crosby traveled some thirty miles from his home near Aberdeen to Columbus, Mississippi, one of the sites where the committee hearings were in session. Coming through the hilly north-eastern part of the Magnolia State, Edward likely tracked the curves of the Tombigbee River, passing farms and labor camps in various stages of wrapping up the season's production of corn, cotton, and sweet potatoes and tending to livestock. He may have felt secure taking the roads, or cut through the woods for greater stealth. He was charged with a personal mission, bearing the story of how white Mississippians upended his family's increasing stability and self-sufficiency.

Edward knew that Democratic and Republican lawmakers at the hearings cared most about election disorder and its consequences. But having lived through several harrowing events, and still facing the uncertainty of his family's future, he refused to stick to the investigators' restrictive script. Edward spoke to the committee about how white men told Black voters "they would drop us at once" for voting any ticket other than the Democratic one. The aspiring voters knew this was a deadly promise the armed white men at the precinct would be willing to keep. His testimony teems with the anxiety he endured after being visited. Edward certainly feared having his right to vote violated, but more than that he wanted the committee to understand how the white men's arrival at his home, and the possibility they would return, presented a far greater danger to his family's well-being and freedom. Edward told lawmakers Black Mississippians were still at the mercy of enslavers who had instigated the Civil War. Those white men were apoplectic about their defeat on the battlefield and emancipation, and they were overthrowing Reconstruction.

The congressional hearings yielded thirteen volumes of firsthand testimonies, including from Black victims. Edward Crosby stood shoulder to shoulder with several hundred Black southerners who told lawmakers, the nation, and the world that ex-Confederates were openly violating the U.S. Constitution. Targeted people's testimonies provide a counternarrative to the stories we're told about Reconstruction's supposed "failure." Speaking with one voice, they said white southerners were not attacking Black people impulsively or defending themselves from Black violence, as former Confederates and their apologists claimed. They were purposefully waging war on Black people's freedom. Witnesses like Edward wanted the nation to end the war and restore what Black people had lost.

———————

I Saw Death Coming pieces together the testimonies of survivors like Edward Crosby to take readers into the epic story of Black Reconstruction. It explores the history of Black people who leapt from the frying pan of slavery into the fires of freedom—as the novelist Attica Locke put it, "from the certainty of hell to the slow, hot torture of hope."[16] It does this by following Black families on their journey out of slavery, through their testimonies about the war white southerners waged on their freedom.

African Americans' stories about this *other* war challenge the "failure" narrative of Reconstruction—that bold experiment that expanded freedom and democracy. Confederates and their sympathizers spun a mythic tale of white southerners needing to protect their honor after northerners placed them and their families under the thumb of ignorant and predatory Black men. This interpretation of Reconstruction formed the basis of racist "Lost Cause" ideology that justified the slaughter of thousands of Black southerners. It rationalized lynching and the establishment of the Jim Crow system, which restored many of the social, economic, and political relations of slavery.

In the early twentieth century, white professional historians like William A. Dunning affirmed that narrative by portraying the Reconstruction era as a "tragic" one of misrule caused by the supposedly misguided decision to enfranchise Black men.[17] In his 1935 book *Black Reconstruction*, W. E. B. Du Bois criticized historians like Dunning for acting less as scientists, pursuing the facts as the historical records reveal them, and more as propagandists in service of the violent white supremacy of the Jim Crow era.[18] In recent years, other historians have unintentionally amplified the "Lost Cause" narrative by using the language of "failure" as a shorthand for what the historical records reveal: federal officials "failed" to aid freed people's hunger for self-sufficiency and self-determination, "failed" to redistribute land, "failed" to enforce Black people's civil and political rights, "failed" to punish whites who attacked and killed Black people. Government entities bear some responsibility for Reconstruction not living up to its promises, certainly. But this "failure" narrative erases the story Black Americans like Edward Crosby told about Reconstruction: it did not simply fail, white conservatives overthrew it.

I Saw Death Coming seeks to immerse readers in the immediacy of Black people's collective experience of living through the war *after* the Civil War. Seeing night-riding strikes through survivors' eyes challenges misconceptions about Reconstruction and about Klan violence. The testimonies create a vivid portrait of how much Black southerners accomplished with freedom. Survivors described how they picked themselves up from slavery by reassembling their families, securing autonomous homes, obtaining employment and land, and establishing thriving independent businesses, schools, and churches. They spoke of how they tried to protect these gains by voting and officeholding. White extremists attacked them for their success. Atrocities committed during Reconstruction, and the nation's betrayal, changed African American families and the course of American history.

The book starts with Black families' journeys out of slavery and their efforts to be free, equal, and secure. Then it uses targeted people's accounts and their astute insight into their attackers' aims and tactics to chart the evolution of the war on freedom, from daily emancipation resistance to massacres, political assassinations, and night-riding assaults. From there, the book recounts what victims said it was like to be a target of or a witness to the violence. Their testimonies reveal the life-threatening mayhem of nearly inescapable, preplanned raids, and the complex flesh-and-blood realities of evading or surviving them. They illuminate the remarkable lengths victims went to to protect themselves and their kin, and the limits of their ability to ward off wide-ranging physical and psychological injuries. Survivors' accounts also reveal that strikes weren't neatly time-bound events that ended when their attackers left their homes and homesteads. Families had to live with the many violations they experienced. Witnesses generated a devastating catalog of suffering that included lives lost, displacement from communities, livelihoods destroyed, bodies and spirits broken, and faith in the nation shattered. Victims described their desperate search for security as they made their way through the maze of strikes' aftermaths. The story then traces their efforts to communicate the wrongs done to them and demand that federal officials honor Black people's rights as citizens by ending this violence.

The story is anchored in well-known collections—testimonies in the congressional report for the 1871–72 Klan hearings and interviews the Works Progress Administration (WPA) conducted in the 1930s with the last witnesses to slavery.[19] Both transcript collections feature African Americans' detailed but often mediated answers in response to direct questions from interviewers. Most testimonies and interviews are filled with seemingly mundane information about the speakers' lives before and after paramilitary strikes. In the case of the Klan hearings, some lawmakers who sought information about raids as part of an investigation into electoral fraud and disenfranchisement thought these insights were irrelevant, and often dismissed this information. Many historians have followed the investigators' lead: in their desire to understand the role Klan violence played in undermining Reconstruction, shaping American politics, and maintaining white supremacy, later scholars analyzing these transcripts have often rushed past or ignored much of what survivors said about what this violence did to their families. But the personal truly is political; the war on freedom changed the course of our history, and Black southerners experienced that war, first and foremost, as individuals, families, and communities.

I wanted to follow the model of oral historian and Nobel Prize winner Svetlana Alexievich, who—in her books *Voices from Chernobyl*, *Last Witnesses*, and others—orchestrated ordinary people's voices into narratives that make victims' lives, feelings, and actions understandable.[20] I tried to listen to each voice in the chorus and understand who survivors thought they were, and what they wanted listeners to know about them and what had happened.[21] I accorded victims authority over their own stories and did not presume to know more about their values and experiences than they did. Edward Crosby and other witnesses cared about losing the vote, to be sure, but they were more concerned about their families' injuries, the loss of their land and livelihood, and their growing insecurity. Voting and office-holding could empower Black men to help quell violence. But the vote wasn't a substitute for the federal government's responsibility to uphold Black citizens' rights to life, liberty, and the pursuit of happiness. Survivors themselves effectively captured more of the human turmoil of life in the postbellum South than historians have acknowledged or communicated to the public.[22]

The frequency with which victims identified kin—wives, husbands, offspring, and parents—and invoked all the progress they had made since emancipation inspired me to learn as much as I could about witnesses' families and households as well as their livelihoods. My search through census records revealed the names of spouses and children previously undocumented in histories that focus solely on the mostly male witnesses, and I discovered voter records, marriage licenses, Freedman's Bank account records, and homesteading claims and certificates that further enrich our knowledge.[23] Evidence of lives built and freedom celebrated—marriages, births, purchases, participation in the nation's civic responsibilities—comes into view from these sources. This detective work helped me see how Klan attacks undid many African Americans' achievements, families, and lives.

Reconstruction is one of the most significant eras in American history. But Black people's experiences in this era are among the most misunderstood and misrepresented aspects of this story. Targeted African Americans' accounts of the *other* war, the one white southern conservatives waged on Black families, create a portrait of what Black southerners did with freedom and the price right-wing whites made them pay for their success. Survivors' searing recollections of the war *after* the Civil War bring to light the ways that Reconstruction did not fail but was violently overthrown.

Survivors' unflinching attention to the detail of their lived experiences of Reconstruction's overthrow makes for hard reading. Indeed, some readers might ask: Why this story right now? In a climate in which we're bombarded with police killings of unarmed Black people, vigilante attacks, mass shootings, and Black people's premature death from racism, I understand the impulse to turn away.[24] But listening—really listening—to survivors of racist violence in the past holds lessons for our current moment.

During the Civil War and Reconstruction, Black people and their allies snatched freedom from Confederates and tried to build a morally right and fair world in the wake of slavery. Some Confederates lowered their weapons against the U.S. Army but set their sights on Black southerners trying to be free, equal, and secure. This history might seem unbelievable but for a crucial fact: survivors of the war on Black people's freedom resisted their violent subjection *by testifying about it*. Facing the horrifying prospect that the world would not know what white men did to them, that there might not be eventual redress, and that free Black futures might thus be foreclosed, targeted people stepped forward, at great risk to themselves and their families, and created a register of the plundering of their freedom. Survivors' decisions to testify were informed by their individual and collective sense of self-love, self-respect, and what Toni Morrison called "self-regard."[25] In naming their attackers, detailing their injuries, saying the names of their slain kin, crying out for justice, and keeping the record alive, survivors and their descendants said Black people's lives, freedoms, and futures mattered. Testifying about the war on freedom was survivors' defense against its erasure.

Many white Americans at the time betrayed survivors by vilifying them, discrediting their accounts, turning away, and then trying their best to bury their indictment. For more than a century and a half, targeted people's testimonies about what white men literally did—not to the nation, not to Reconstruction, not to electoral politics, but to Black people's *families, bodies, psyches, institutions, communities*—have been moving through the circulatory system of the nation's institutional, legal, and cultural networks. These stories have been searching for adequate witnesses—people and institutions who would truly hear them.[26] The testimonies constituted a moral charge to build a more just world. If we say we believe in overcoming prejudice, that Black Lives Matter, then we should listen to these survivors. Their stories deserve our attention and introspection because we live in the future shaped by the nation's failure to listen to them.[27]

Understanding the war white southerners waged on Black Reconstruction from targeted people's perspectives helps us think critically about the sesquicentennial of that war, which is largely going unmarked, as well as this current moment, and how we reached it. Racism-based violence jeopardized Black people's lives and undermined American democracy during Reconstruction, and the nation's failure to confront it is why the struggle continues 150 years later. In 2010, the artist Kara Walker produced a controversial black-and-white drawing titled "The moral arc of history ideally bends towards justice but just as soon as not curves back around toward barbarism, sadism, and unrestrained chaos." The artwork depicts scenes that evoke Black Reconstruction, the Civil Rights Movement, and the election of Barack Obama but also illustrates the "moral arc of history" curving away from justice through the war on Reconstruction, the rise of lynching during Jim Crow, and the white backlash of police and vigilante killings and rising anti-Black extremism. Without a fuller understanding of the legacy of racist injustice, we live today in the space that drawing imagines, where present and past are chaotically and violently fused.

That is why this book does not shy away from the horrors Black survivors put into words. To do so would dishonor them and undermine the moral force of their indictment of the nation's betrayal. Silencing their stories makes it harder to see how this violence is reproduced today. Censoring this history would also excuse ignoring the devastating realities of this current moment, which include efforts to trivialize and suppress the teaching of it.

Instead, *I Saw Death Coming* seeks to honor African American survivors of racist violence by holding space to adequately witness what *they* said happened to them: what they wanted known about what they did with freedom, what they believed they lost to violence, how they attended to their lives in its wake, how they cared for each other, how they survived, and how they and their people carried this history. Survivors of Reconstruction violence bore witness. They testified because they wanted justice even if they didn't live to see it.

We must explore the violence they detailed because the forces driving it persist. Their stories might inspire us to assume greater responsibility for confronting racist violence and building a better future. That is what survivors wanted for themselves and their descendants, and what Americans who claim to believe in liberty owe them today.

Chapter 1

We Had to Pick Ourselves Up

A be and Eliza Lyon were lined up on the starting blocks of freedom when slavery was abolished. Having dreamed about this moment for most of their remembered lives, they ran at full speed to fulfill their dreams of family reintegration, self-determination, and prosperity. By 1870, the Alabama couple had accomplished a great deal. Abe was thirty years old, and Eliza was thirty-five. They formalized their union by getting legally married and set up their home in Choctaw County, near Butler. Abe was working as a blacksmith from his own shop, which allowed him to leave the labor camp and strike out on his own.* Francis S. Lyon, the man who had held Abe in bondage, described Abe as "a very stout, strong, athletic man, a very powerful man, a fine mechanic; a man of some temper and considerable will," although Francis had no personal truck with him.[1] Eliza left her job in domestic service with the Lyon family and was keeping her own house, occasionally doing some work on the labor camp for extra money. Their children William, Ella, and Annie were enrolled in the local

---

* The word "plantation" reflects the enslaving class's romanticized views of slavery. "Labor camp" or "forced labor camp" more accurately describes the living conditions enslavers forced upon the men, women, and children they held in bondage.

school; an older daughter was attending school in Demopolis, where Eliza grew up. Through their combined industry, the Lyons had saved six hundred dollars, and they planned to move to Demopolis, buy property, and build a home of their own.[2]

Alongside Abe and Eliza, and Edward Crosby, were several million families making the transition to life in the postwar South and establishing themselves in their new legal status and home communities. Some of those people, like Andrew and Frankie Cathcart, were further along in that transition. Andrew had toiled to purchase his release from bondage around 1850, for $350. Then he spent the next few years working, possibly buying Frankie's freedom, before spending $190 on a ninety-acre tract of land that he called his "little plantation," in York, South Carolina. Andrew and Frankie devoted themselves to making a living, including hiring additional laborers to build their wealth so they could buy their children out of slavery. Sometime after the couple secured their children's release, Andrew bought a neighboring tract and a few extra units, which brought his land total up to 188 acres.

Andrew worked on the farm, assisted by his children and grandchildren. Frankie kept house, guided her children in their parenting, and overindulged her grandkids. At ages seventy-seven and sixty, Andrew and Frankie had accumulated $850 in real estate and $150 in savings.[3] Their youngest offspring stayed close. One of their daughters lived next door in the schoolhouse, which Andrew paid to have built for neighborhood children.

The Browns of White County, Georgia, like Edward Crosby's family, were not as prosperous as the Lyons and Cathcarts. Joseph Brown dug gold at a local mine; he told the 1870 census taker he was about forty-five years old. His wife, Mary, aged twenty-four, officially kept house, but she also spent time at the mine, balancing her responsibilities at home tending to their sons, ten-year-old Thomas and five-year-old James.

Like many families after the war, Joseph and Mary found or built lodgings and added a garden plot for sustenance. They did not report having personal or real estate assets when census enumerators came through, but like Eliza and Abe Lyon, the Browns were planning for something better. In their immediate neighborhood were kin including Mary's mother, forty-eight-year-old Caroline Benson, and a male relative named Jeremiah, who was eighty. Even in his advanced age, Jeremiah continued working as a farm laborer and had $150 in personal assets in 1870. Caroline kept house while looking after two boys, Alford and Joseph.[4]

Following these and other families—examining the texture of their day-to-day efforts to pick themselves up from slavery, reassemble their families, and establish their communities—illuminates what newly freed people prioritized and the immense challenges they overcame. To African Americans, freedom at the end of the Civil War wasn't simply about being released from bondage, being paid for their labor, or even legal equality. It also involved federal certification of Black people's entitlement to access all the privileges of American freedom these three families achieved, and ones they had not yet dreamed of. Liberation meant the right to marry, have independent family homes, chart a family's course, secure dignified work and reap the rewards of one's labor, acquire land, open a business or work from home, accumulate wealth in property, and attend school—all enshrined in law and respected everywhere. Freedom also included the right to vote *and* serve in elected office, and religious liberty to practice their faith how and where they wanted, including in their own churches. But legal freedom on its own was not enough. A complete reconstruction of American society was needed—a truth revealed precisely by the ferocious, purposeful reaction to it, in villainous white resistance to emancipation and in white southerners' efforts to undermine African Americans' progress.

Previously free and newly free Black people and their white progressive allies were America's freedom fighters. They embarked on a venture to secure African Americans' right to citizenship and, through that, all the protections enslavers had denied and were still trying to deny them. That undertaking marked the beginning of what W. E. B. Du Bois called "Black Reconstruction." Pressed by African Americans' demands for full freedom and equality, Radical Republicans sought to reform the United States into a more egalitarian, multiracial democracy. Their work was so revolutionary that the historian Eric Foner calls Reconstruction the nation's "Second Founding."[5]

Far removed from the centers of political power, African Americans like the Crosbys, Lyons, Cathcarts, and Browns faced the race into freedom with many expectations. As Black Reconstruction activists in their own way, these families understood freedom's mission. Today, there's an impulse to equate freedom with release from bondage and legal equality. But newly emancipated people's visions of what freedom meant were much more expansive. Emancipation created a constellation of new possibilities for African Americans, and they quickly pulled the levers of power to make their new world a reality. The only way to fully appreciate what Confederates tried to destroy is to understand what newly freed people accomplished. Following families on that journey from enslavement to self-determination and liberation shows their voracious thirst for freedom, and how their abundant affection for their people and their aspirations for the future informed their audacious fight for a freedom as *they* defined it.

———

Slavery was not a natural condition; it had to be created. Its architecture in the United States was not only a legal system of lifelong, hereditary, race-based bondage, but also a set of social relations that reinforced where all groups stood with respect to each other. Wealthy aristocrats, slavery's designers, were meticulous in exercising their license to dominate enslaved people's lives from cradle to grave. In doing so, they deputized other whites of all classes to help surveil all Black people and police their movements, to prevent the enslaved from rebelling and liberating themselves. Slavery's creators made up the ideology of white people's supposed inherent superiority and Black people's supposed inferiority to justify this inhumane system.

The enslaved learned in their day-to-day realities that they had no rights white people were bound to respect—not to legal freedom, not to family, not even to life. They knew from lived experience that slavery wasn't just about stolen labor. It was abject social isolation, being cast out of the human order and its protections. First-person accounts from nineteenth-century freedom narratives confirm what should come as no surprise: slavery influenced bondpeople's basic views about themselves, as they grappled with their status as human chattel in a slaveholding society.

Lessons about what being enslaved meant were forged when young children were socialized to differentiate who they were in the loving eyes of their kin versus the ravenous eyes of the law.[6] The luckiest children grew up with all their immediate kin in one place. The family would have loved on children and allowed them to enjoy, as much as possible, the bliss of their ignorance of their bonded status. But with each year, the texture of family relations changed as children aged and parents braced for them to be snatched from the protective fold of their cabins and community in slave quarters: youths might be pulled into the Big House, reassigned to a neighboring labor camp, put on an auction block, or given as gifts. These were transformative moments when the full weight of their circumstances became clear. And children's worldviews changed as they learned they did not belong to themselves or their parents, as they thought; they "belonged" to their "master" or "mistress," as their property for life.

For Frederick Douglass, that moment came when, hiding in a closet, he witnessed the vicious whipping of his beloved Aunt Hester. It "struck me with an awful force," he wrote; it was at this point that he crossed through "the blood-stained gate, the entrance through the hell of slavery."[7] Douglass now knew what *could* happen to him because he was enslaved, and this horrified him.[8] The "terrible spectacle" of Hester's whipping served as Douglass's primal scene, resonating strongly throughout his life.

Enslaved people could and *did* live, work, and care for each other despite bondage. But unless they were able to purchase their freedom or have someone do it for them, and barring escape, lifelong slavery meant there was no way out. Freedom to most was a distant, illusory idea. But although slavery severely restricted many Black people's agency, it never completely extinguished the enslaved's desire to be free. People resisted their enslavement by asserting as many degrees of power over their lives as possible; these daily forms of resistance had their limits and did not bring down the whole system on their own, but that does not mean they weren't meaningful. Enslaved people might learn to read, insist on the right to name their child, sneak off to a hush harbor to practice their religious faith, or fight back when an enslaver tried to punish them. Other, underappreciated examples of enslaved people's assertion of their agency were their tenderness for their people, their infinite hope, and all the time and energy they took to imagine freedom and look for any chance to seize it.

That love and hope is how thousands freed themselves before the Civil War and how several hundred thousand did it during the conflict. When news of the war began, enslaved people looked for opportunities amid the chaos it caused on farms and labor camps. Self-emancipation still might require persistence: a Kentucky man ran away several times only to be dragged back.[†] On his last try, the man got free. He joined the tens of thousands of self-emancipated men who sought out U.S. Army camps and enlisted.[9] An enslaved Texan recalled spending the first year of the war wanting to escape, but fear of what slave patrollers might do to him persuaded him to stay put. One night, a group of ten bondmen fled the labor camp where they were all held. The young man waited to hear news of patrols catching them. And when he didn't, he said, he made up his mind to go, even though he was "half scared to death." "I sure had the eyes open and the ears forward, watching for the patrollers," he said. The Texan walked the roads at night, stepping off "at the sight of anything," and he traveled through the woods during the day. He had one perilously close encounter with patrollers searching the woods. "That sure looked like the end," he said. But he kept his composure and avoided detection. It took the young man two days to reach the U.S. Army camp, where he had a reunion with the ten men who had inspired his escape. All of them joined the army.[10]

Some people sat tight, waiting until their enslavers released them. One North Carolina woman recalled hearing stories of "fights and freedom."

[†] Self-emancipation involved an enslaved person's decision to free herself or himself from bondage. Self-emancipation could take the form of purchasing one's release, like Andrew Cathcart did, or escaping.

Enslaved people traveling between farms and labor camps carried news of the war's developments. One day the young woman heard "something that sounded like thunder"—explosions marking the U.S. Army's arrival in their community. That evening their enslaver said, "You are free. You are no longer my slaves. The Yankees will soon be here."[11]

At the war's end, some bondpeople learned of their freedom via U.S. Army soldiers stationed in their communities. Others received word through their social networks. In many instances, enslavers called the people they held in bondage to a meeting and informed them of their release. North Carolina freedman Robert Falls recalled his enslaver telling them, "I hates to do it, but I must. You all ain't my niggers no more. You is free. Just as free as I am." In a ploy to guilt some of them to remain and establish a new free labor agreement, the white man said, "Here I have raised you all to work for me, and now you are going to leave me. I am an old man, and can't get along without you. I don't know what I am going to do." The North Carolinian attributed his enslaver's demise to slavery's end. "It killed him. He was dead in less than ten months."[12]

Universal emancipation upended enslaved people's assumptions about the world, the nation, and their place in both.[13] They initially assumed freedom would mean everything slavery did not, ranging from access to the material resources produced by their labor to acceptance into the body politic. But hanging around the edges of African Americans' hope for freedom was their shrewd understanding of how difficult it would be. They knew that, as Tennesseean Samuel Childress put it, the white South's wealth had been "acquired mainly by our labor."[14] They had survived what Florida freedwoman Hannah Tutson called the "red times" of slavery—when the terror of death stalked bondpeople's every move—and the reprisal attacks that followed every attempt to escape unspeakable physical, psychological, and soul-killing violence.[15]

Black southerners who survived the Civil War had to make their way through the dying season of disease and hunger that followed. The war produced what one historian calls the "largest biological crisis" of the nineteenth century, claiming the lives of 250,000 freed people between 1862 and

1870.[16] This catastrophe was a rolling disaster of massive epidemics, contaminated waterways, and hunger, caused by droughts, troop movements slashing through the countryside, and the fact that most agricultural land was used to produce commodities instead of food.[17]

Nowhere was this calamity more evident than in communities with large numbers of newly freed people. The Emancipation Proclamation—which declared "forever free" all people held in bondage in parts of the South where Confederates were still in open rebellion against the U.S. government—went into effect New Year's Day of 1863. Confederates, however, did not recognize Abraham Lincoln as their president, so they ignored his proclamation and refused to release the people they held in bondage. Unless the U.S. Army made it to their region and defeated Confederate forces, enslavers carried on as usual. But enslaved people saw themselves as loyal citizens of the United States, and they *did* recognize Lincoln as their president. They acted accordingly and began trying to escape forced labor camps as soon as they could. Many were apprehended and dragged back. And escapees who were successful still had nothing but their freedom until they could acquire gainful work, which was difficult to secure amid the ongoing war and enslavers' fury. One man recalled, "it took a mighty long time to get things going a-smooth."[18]

That the Thirteenth Amendment's proponents did not anticipate the hardships of emancipation and enslavers' resistance is a testament to two dark truths of the era. First, most white moderates and progressives in the North and West who agreed to slavery's abolition did not do it out of the goodness of their hearts. If that had been the case, they could have abolished slavery any time before the war. Most white northerners and westerners who supported the United States in the war only accepted emancipation to try to quickly end the bloody conflict. Evidence of this truth lies in the fact that the Thirteenth Amendment barely met the threshold for ratification, even with Confederates out of government. Second, although many whites on both sides of the conflict held on to their hard feelings, a desire to move on from the conflict gradually took hold across the North and West.[19] White abolitionists and some white moderate and progressive veterans stood fast in their rejection of reconciliation without Confederate repentance. As long as most ex-Confederates brazenly defended secession and actively resisted emancipation and Reconstruction, the discord between the groups remained bitter. But white abolitionists and white U.S. Army veterans who enthusiastically endorsed emancipation were outnumbered by a larger faction of white moderates and conservatives who increasingly sought common ground with former Confederates. Early reunion enthusiasts from the North and West often seemed to see their opponents in the South as justice-loving citizens who truly believed in the "more perfect union" the founders had created in 1787 and in liberty and justice for all. This was a projection of their own desire to bring the calamitous war to an end and put the whole bloody affair behind them and to ignore white southerners' unjust treatment of Black people.

Extremists' resistance to emancipation revealed their true colors, though. After the U.S. Army and the Thirteenth Amendment broke slavery's last chain, Confederates reluctantly released the people they held captive. Many enslavers expressed their fury by quickly evicting the newly freed—without clothing, shelter, food, or access to medical care. Retired U.S. general Carl Schurz, whom President Andrew Johnson sent in 1865 to investigate the "condition of the South," reported, using army intelligence he gained from officials stationed in Mississippi, that enslavers had joined forces "to refuse labor, food or drink, in all cases, to those who have been soldiers, as well as to those who have belonged to plantations within the State; in the latter case, often ordering them back peremptorily to their 'masters.'"[20]

Decades later, in an interview with WPA personnel, a man named Tom Holland would describe the "hard struggle" after being released from captivity, an experience that resonated across ex-slaves' recollections of the time.[21] Tom likened the end of bondage to a birth, with himself as a newborn, lacking education, security, or protection. He thought the slaveholding elite and federal officials overseeing emancipation should "have given us something when we were freed." Instead, most white people turned their former slaves out "slam loose, to graze or starve," he said, without any warning or time to prepare. One formerly enslaved woman recalled, "The worst bother

Negroes had in them days was finding a place to live. Houses had to be built for them and they did not have any money to build them with."[22] Another woman remembered, "None of us had no where else to go and besides nobody wanted to go no where else, so every one of Master Joe's Negroes stayed right on with him that next year."[23] "When they turned me loose I was naked, barefoot, and didn't have nothing to start out on," one woman informed her interviewers. Because of that, she said, "we had to kinda pick ourselves up."[24]

The wartime context and the unfolding ecological disaster exacerbated the "struggle" Tom Holland described.[25] Hunger is a refrain in freed people's testimonies about their enslavement. "They didn't half feed us either. They fed animals better," Robert Falls of North Carolina recalled. "We would take anything we could lay our hands on, when we was hungry."[26] Small rations of poor-quality food had reduced enslavers' costs before the war, but they made enslaved people more susceptible to disease and premature death during the war and the first months and years of freedom. The war disrupted supply chains, cutting off access to food and medicine and thereby worsening the crisis. Droughts caused famine; armies tore through farmlands and forests. The fighting also damaged landscapes and filled towns with smoke pollution that compromised people's health. Outbreaks tore through communities. Many southern states and institutions withheld access to care, reserving it for poor whites who were also suffering.

Without having their basic needs met, thousands of Black people fell ill and died. White Americans' response to freed people's skyrocketing mortality rate was divided. Some didn't care and speculated Black people would die out. Others, ignoring white people's responsibility for former bondpeople's immiseration, worried enslavers had been right—that Black people couldn't exist without white people "caring" for them.[27]

Being turned out "slam loose," as Tom Holland described, meant being without shelter, food, or clothing amid these larger postwar environmental forces. To avoid this fate, Tom's family remained with their former mistress—until she married a man who brought in his own laborers to work the farm and abruptly evicted the Hollands. After they found a home and secured new employment, the family worked for between twenty and thirty cents a day.[28]

Despite all these hardships, when freed people were later interviewed about slavery and emancipation they were adamant in preferring the striving of freedom to returning to bondage. Struggling to start over completely from scratch was better than living under white people's control.[29] Robert Falls said, "I would die fighting rather than be a slave again. I want no man's yoke on my shoulders."[30]

One way newly freed people picked themselves up and avoided slavery's yoke was by taking advantage of U.S. general William Tecumseh Sherman's Special Field Order Number 15. The order, issued in January 1865, set aside for the exclusive settlement of Black families some 400,000 acres the U.S. Army had confiscated from Confederates, along the eastern seaboard from Charleston through Savannah to St. Augustine. U.S. officials were to distribute the land to Black families in forty-acre parcels. They honored the request Black Georgia clergy (led by Baptist minister Garrison Frazier) had made at a meeting with Sherman and Secretary of War Edwin Stanton to discuss Black people's transition from slavery: Frazier had said newly freed people needed government officials to place them on land and enable them to earn a living and save "until we can buy it and make it our own."[31] To aid their relocation and their work on the land, officials threw in some of the Army's surplus mules. Thousands of people rushed to the region, where they worked; built homesteads; acquired property in the form of horses, cattle, and furniture; tilled the soil; and opened schools and churches.

In March 1865, Congress authorized the establishment of the Bureau of Refugees, Freedmen, and Abandoned Lands, which provided some aid to newly freed people and impoverished white southerners displaced by the war.[32] Most agents working for the Freedmen's Bureau, as it became known, were white military personnel; how they operated in the field reflected the spectrum of white attitudes toward Black people and emancipation—from progressives who distributed resources generously, to conservatives who were often embittered and withholding. Although never adequately funded or staffed, the bureau established hospitals to treat the suffering and provided medical assistance. It distributed millions of rations (although never enough to meet the need) and opened more than a thousand schools. Agents negotiated contracts between freed people and their former enslavers. The bureau formed courts to ensure the freed had some rights. And it had been charged with distributing the lands Confederates abandoned or the U.S. Army seized. Not all newly freed people had access to the aid the bureau distributed. But they grasped freedom's promise with both hands, determined to work hard and diligently to secure their future.

By the summer, Andrew Johnson—a political and social conservative, opposed to any federal assistance to freed people—had ordered that all confiscated land be returned to Confederates who swore loyalty to the United States and promised to respect the Constitution. Outraged families on South Carolina's Edisto Island registered their protest with the Freedmen's Bureau. This "is not the condition of freemen," the petitioners wrote of the decision to allow Confederates to return to the island. They knew the former enslavers were sure to evict them if they refused to submit to working and living conditions that were close to slavery. "We have not been treacherous," the petitioners insisted, citing Black people's loyalty to the U.S. cause in the war and their entitlement to the homesteads and community they had built for themselves. The South Carolinians said they were praying for God's help and, more immediately, for bureau officials' "*influence and assistance.*" But they received nothing more than platitudes.[33] The families had to accept Confederates' terms or leave behind everything they had built.

Tennessean Samuel Childress echoed Tom Holland and the Edisto petitioners in insisting that freed Americans deserved more, especially because they were experiencing the lashing wrath of their enslavers. White vengeance in the South and white apathy in the White House were rendering Black southerners unhoused and hungry, even though through their stolen labor, as Childress put it, they had earned nearly "all this property" in the region. African Americans literally helped build "the South." But every day they encountered members of the slaveholding apparatus, from the wealthy plantocracy to poorer whites, who all made clear they would do everything they could to keep Black people as close to bondage as possible. Childress was one of many who described enslavers as African Americans' "worst enemy," whose hands were bloody and "whose cruelties cry to heaven for vengeance."[34] A Freedmen's Bureau agent reported civil authorities in Mobile were openly hostile to freed people, arresting and falsely imprisoning them, while "gangs of idle rebel soldiers and other dissolute rowdies insult, rob, and assault" the formerly enslaved with impunity.[35]

African Americans like Childress and the Edisto petitioners (and white Americans aiding the transition from slavery to freedom) spoke less of personal vengeance than they did of the need for justice. A Black chorus demanding just treatment after slavery rang out from Boston to Charleston to San Francisco. White chorists—ranging from abolitionists to U.S. Army veterans who called for honoring both the terms of the peace and the promises of 1776—were more muted, but were audible, nonetheless.

Black Reconstruction activists and their allies started trying to build a more just world. They knew an expansive vision of freedom was essential for ensuring Black people were socially and legally secure.[36] These freedom fighters sought to reset the balance centuries after chattel slavery turned African-descended people's worlds upside down. They also battled a stinging reality in the former slaveholding states, where, as Samuel Childress wrote, it "was regarded as a greater crime to be [B]lack [and free] than be a rebel."[37]

This knowledge, plus devotion to their people's collective advancement, fueled their pioneering work. The need for radical societal changes to give emancipation meaning was evident all around them. The Edisto Island petitioners had an acute understanding of the legal plight freed people found themselves in. "There is no right secured to us," they wrote. "There is no law likely to be made which our hands can reach. The state will make laws that we shall not be able to hold land even if we pay for it." They were, they lamented, "landless, homeless. Voteless."[38]

While enslavers continued releasing people from captivity, they also busily implemented barriers to freedom, to sustain the condition the Black South Carolinians anticipated in their petition. In late 1865, Mississippi and South Carolina passed two of the region's first Black Codes. Other states followed. Much like the Slave Codes that preceded them, the Black Codes severely limited Black people's liberty by imposing restrictions on their employment, property ownership, independence, family rights, and movement. Extremists used the laws not only to continue stealing Black people's labor, but also to perpetuate the violent domination and alienation, the denial of human rights, that had endured under slavery. The Black Codes' passage symbolized extremists' determination to retain control over Black people's lives.

African Americans across the country and white moderates and progressives in the North and West saw the Black Codes for what they were. They knew they needed a bulwark against the worst of Confederates' resistance to Black people's right to be free, secure, and equal. They appealed to federal officials for relief. Andrew Johnson and conservative members of Congress brushed off their complaints. Progressives in Congress—commonly called the "Radical Republicans" for their audacious devotion to expanding democracy and ensuring equality—responded with the Civil Rights bill of 1866, granting citizenship to anyone born in the United States, including African Americans. It was the first major piece of Reconstruction since the Thirteenth Amendment. An Ohio congressman, in a speech delivered to Congress in support of the bill, said, "[E]very citizen . . . has the absolute right to live, the right of personal security, personal liberty, and the right to acquire and enjoy property. These are the rights of citizenship. As necessary incidents of these rights are others, as the right to make and enforce contracts, to purchase, hold, and enjoy property, and to share the benefits of laws for the security of person and property."[39] But President Johnson vetoed the civil rights bill, basing his objections on the misleading claim that the legislation gave Black people "safeguards" whites did not enjoy.

Not all the rights detailed in the 1866 bill were literally inscribed in the U.S. Constitution for white people. But they were assumed, by virtue of whites' citizenship. Individual states secured these liberties for white citizens, but only a handful of states recognized Black people as citizens and accorded them these rights and protections. Whites did not need those safeguards, the bill's supporters insisted, because no one was trying to deny their liberties, as the Black Codes explicitly aimed to. White opposition to the civil rights bill wasn't limited to the South. Conservative white northerners and westerners feared a federal civil rights bill would prevent them from continuing to restrict the liberties of Black people in their regions. Supporters of the bill replied that its protections would secure *all* Americans' civil rights, including those of Black Americans. Congress overrode the president's veto and the Civil Rights Act became law.

Black southerners striding into freedom had not waited for permission to exercise these rights; they were availing themselves of them in everyday life, which is why Confederates took preventative steps to restrict them. The act simply affirmed freed people's *right* to have and exercise all the benefits of citizenship.

With their rights reinforced, freed Americans continued assuming responsibility for their well-being and remade their worlds. From reconstituting families separated by living apart or ravaged by the domestic slave trade or sexual violence, to working out new labor arrangements, all evidence points toward most Black southerners facing emancipation with hearts full of love for their people and hope for the possibilities of the future. They were eager to chart their destinies with a fully loaded capacity for self-determination.[40] Their insightful understandings of what they needed to be successful is how families like the Lyons and Cathcarts made such significant strides in so short a time, and why the Browns and Crosbys were on their way.

Freedmen's Bureau agents and U.S. policymakers routinely remarked on freedom-making families' comportment and progress. Newly freed people had acted as though they had the right to fair wages, to labor autonomy, and to be treated with dignity. And when Confederates denied them these rights, African Americans demanded federal recognition. When they received that declaration through the Civil Rights Act, they continued racing in the direction of their dreams, simultaneously working, acquiring land, building homes and businesses, farming, and establishing families.

Not everyone saw hardworking and diligent people striving to make freedom real. A Freedmen's Bureau agent claimed in a report to General

Schurz that when he visited Vicksburg in 1865 he saw "[a] great many Colored people . . . As a rule, they are hungry, naked, foot-sore, and . . . friendless."[41] The agent was one of many whites who fabricated a concern about Black people becoming "dependent" on federal assistance. He refused to acknowledge that the suffering and death he saw in some communities was caused by former enslavers' actions—evicting freed people, retaliating against those who had served in the war or who demonstrated too great a thirst for freedom—and by federal officials' failure to adequately plan for emancipation and compensate for those actions.

Another agent, however, dismissed white hand-wringing about whether Black people would work without slavery as "nonsense." They "do now and always have done, all the physical labor of the South," the agent said, and would continue doing so "if treated as they should be," with fair handling in the courts when their rights were violated.[42] "They do not refuse work," another agent wrote, "on the contrary, they labor for the small pittance and plainest food." According to this agent, if able-bodied people were struggling, it was largely because they "are too often driven off and deprived of the small compensation they labored for."[43] Another agent described the newly freed as "orderly, quiet, industrious, with an earnest desire to learn and fit themselves to their new status."[44]

In addition to hard struggle, some people's recollections of their transition from slavery to freedom to WPA interviewers in the 1930s were filled with sorrow for those who did not live to see freedom, for those among the "many thousands gone," as well as for more immediate losses. The Thirteenth Amendment ordered that bondpeople be released but did not detail the conditions of freedom, like the custody of children, leaving some newly freed families in crisis. One woman shared with interviewers her memories of being taken from her mother, who she said had been the last adult slave to leave the labor camp where they had been held. All the other freed adults had decamped quickly and escaped successfully, some apparently without their children, whom their enslavers had refused to release from bondage; they were retaining the children to place them in "apprenticeships." Any freedom this mother would have personally enjoyed by departing with the adults would have been dulled without her children, and she had refused to leave any of them. The night of a storm, the mother saw their chance. She gathered the children, and they opened the door to their cabin and ran to leave the plantation. But before the family could escape, their enslavers surrounded them. Seizing the young ones, they ordered the mother to leave, without her children, threatening that they would kill her if she stayed. "We never saw her again," the elderly woman said.[45]

Despite the struggle and misery over losses from bondage and the war, former slaves remembered there were good times, too. Georgia Telfair told WPA interviewers she was six when freedom came. She recalled her family choosing a spot that was "way off in the woods." Telfair's father cut down trees and built a log cabin. He added ovens for baking, and a chimney of sticks and red mud, with iron bars across the top from which to hang pots. The Telfairs enjoyed great, comforting meals of roasted potatoes with home-made butter from two cows Georgia remembered fondly. She said her family was never without meat because her mother kept chickens and turkeys, and the family raised hogs. The Telfairs always kept a garden full of "beans, corn, onions, peas and taters." There was "no one beating us at raising lots of greens," Georgia said, "especially turnips and collard greens." Each year the family saved up "heaps of dry peas and beans, and dried lots of peaches and apples to cook in the winter." When the winter wind howled, her mother made dried fruit puffs "that sure hit the spot."[46]

––––––––

As Georgia Telfair's remembrances make clear, what made the struggles families endured after the war manageable was the presence of their people. Enslaved people had lived with the reality of their families enjoying no legal recognition or protection. The law had said they belonged to the whites holding them in bondage, but bondpeople had their own terms of belonging, and that was to each other, until the law or the auction block pulled them apart. And even then, historical records are full of accounts of freed Americans risking life and liberty to be reunited with their kin. Families were the incubators of Black selfhood, the space where people learned they were not who or what white society said they were.[47] Those affective bonds that had guided them through slavery were now at the heart of their efforts to reconstruct their families and fortify their freedom.

Newly freed people made efforts to reunite families that had been pulled apart by sales, migrations, the war, and enslavers' resistance to freedom.[48] People departing their enslavers' places left details about their destinations in case any kin came looking for them. Family members with resources hired agents to recover kin from great distances.[49]

Black people took to the nation's roads, walking to locate their kin; they boarded trains and ships, traveling east and west and north and south, searching desperately, trying to "find their people."[50] Mary Armstrong's mother had been sold away from her to Texas. When her enslaver released her from bondage in 1863, she shot out for Texas, going from U.S. federal refugee camp to refugee camp searching for her mother—and ultimately found her.[51]

Enslavers bayed in protest at seeing freed people traveling, not toiling away. But according to Freedmen's Bureau agent John De Forest, "every mother's son among them seemed to be in search of his mother; every mother in search of her children."[52] That tireless search is how mothers like Mary Stowers found their beloved offspring. In 1846, Mary and her two-year-old daughter were sold away from her son, Willis Green, who was only four years old. Willis survived military service in the war and moved to Evansville, Kentucky. Unbeknownst to him, Mary had started searching for him as soon as she could. Willis was in town one day and heard from acquaintances that a woman claiming to be his mother was looking for him. He had presumed Mary was dead—either from the violence of slavery or the war and its aftermath. But he followed the lead and met the woman, who wept at the sight of him. Willis had been so young (and likely traumatized by his mother's departure) that he didn't remember what Mary looked like. He doubted her claims and asked for proof: could she explain how he had lost a finger on his right hand in childhood? Mary answered that their enslaver had cut off his finger "while chopping a trough." Satisfied, he accepted Mary as his mother, and presumably they reforged their connections to one another.[53]

Others sent letters to people and institutions where they thought their folk could be. In 1873, George Perry started searching for his wife, Vina Johnson, from whom he had been separated in 1830. In the interim, she had remarried and been widowed; he had emigrated to Canada and built a life there. But George never forgot about Vina. He wrote to her enslavers, inquiring about her. Discovering she was alive, George contacted Vina, who agreed to see him. The local paper reported that Vina was "all anxiety and in a fever of excitement." The couple had "a joyous" reunion and were last known preparing for their remarriage ceremony.[54]

Families even placed "Information Wanted" ads in sympathetic newspapers to find their people. In 1877, the *Southwestern Christian Advocate* reported the reunion of Charity Thompson of Hawkins, Texas, with her family. According to the newspaper, Charity had written an ad hoping to find her kin, from whom she had been separated for decades. Someone was reading the column to a Houston congregation, and a Mrs. Dibble gasped and cried out, "That's my sister! I have not seen her in thirty-three years." The sisters reunited, and Charity learned that her mother was alive, too, and longing to see her.[55]

But George and Vina, Willis and Mary, and Charity and her sister were among the minority who found their kin. Most never located their people. The domestic slave trade and westward expansion scattered families across great distances and for long amounts of time. Families did not always have accurate information about their loved ones' whereabouts. In some cases, they could not travel to find kin, or their people had died. Then there was the question of names: some individuals and families chose names that maintained ties to their enslavers to sustain kinship networks or so their kin could find them. But others longed to sever all ties and adopted new surnames to reconstruct their identities as free people. Still others changed names to shield themselves from people seeking to harm them. The decision involved a variety of factors, but whatever the reason for a name selection or a change, it could cloak their identities from their people trying to locate them.

Some families knew where their people were but could not reach them, because enslavers refused to release people from bondage or, after the war, vengefully erected barriers to families' reunion efforts. Not everyone was like Vina's enslavers, who shared what details they had about her life and whereabouts; others, stonehearted, refused to take or pass on any information. Enslavers' vindictiveness did not end there. One Freedmen's Bureau agent reported that local patrols with "Negro hounds" kept guard over the main thoroughfares and "lawless robbers" crisscrossed the countryside attacking Black men going to claim their wives or children from the whites still holding them in bondage under armed guards.[56] In many cases, these family-seeking men and women were attacked by idle veterans, planters, and overseers. Some survived enslavement and the war only to die trying to reunite with their people.

Among those who were able to reconnect, legalizing intimate unions through formal marriage was a prime concern for families like Abe and Eliza Lyon's.[57] Though barred from the legal recognition free people could access, couples in bondage had sweet-hearted, lived together, and married during slavery, bestowing a legitimacy upon their pairings that came organically, from within the Black community.[58] But state recognition secured families' coveted legal and societal protections.[59] The desire to be together and have their union and citizenship rights recognized is likely why Greene County, Georgia, residents Abram Colby and Miss Anna Walker went before authorities in July 1866, as the certificate in the historical records illustrates.[60] Relief agencies such as the Freedmen's Bureau and benevolent and mutual aid associations typically offered financial assistance, land, and housing to families who worked and established traditional units with a male head of household.[61] Policymakers set these requirements believing they should impose on freed people the lifestyle seen as best suited for their self-sufficiency, to ward off any dependency on the state for care and assistance.[62]

Families complied in part because this was compatible with *their own* visions of freedom.[63] Many freed people desperately wanted family protection and saw marriage as their way to achieve it. This might have been the case for Abram and Anna. Formal marriage allowed individuals to choose their partners and escape unions forced upon them by their enslavers. Families also thought marriage might provide some legal recourse to help curb white men's sexual predation on Black girls and women. Marriage came with legal obligations for the care of children and for fidelity, all of which some families coming out of slavery valued.

Not every African American was invested in legal recognition. There was, however, a logic to freed people's rejection of formalized unions. Some people chose not to couple. Others ran their own cost-benefit analysis and were not interested in legalizing any of their entanglements. Some older couples preferred informal marriages. They believed their unions were sufficient and did not need state recognition. Other couples liked the flexibility of informal marriages, which allowed them to leave unions as they pleased, without having to go the extra mile of severing official marital bonds.[64] Widows of veterans could not claim their husbands' pensions if they remarried. Family reconstruction involved an interplay of factors guided by the complicated realities of enslavement and freed people's wide-ranging understandings of personal and familial freedom.

Another immediate concern of many reconstructed families was determining how they would make a living. The nation's embrace of free labor had been driven by the belief that citizens had a right not just to freedom but also to rise—economically, socially, politically—using America's abundant opportunities to do so. Reconstruction's transformation of the political economy finally recognized Black people's right to join the rising tide of American prosperity.

Freed people grasped this baton in their sprint to liberty. The responsibility of providing economic security for freed families was claimed primarily by men, who helmed their households.[65] Men with carpentry skills, like Floridian Henry Reed, earned their livings by building homes and barns as well as furniture and wagons.[66] They also took their skills on the road, traveling to businesses to craft furnishings and housewares.[67] Blacksmiths like Abe Lyon worked in shops bending iron to their wills and fitting their neighbors' homes with metal gates, racks, and grates for baking and grilling food.[68] Rock mason Patrick W. Tanner worked in brickyards; men like him might use their skills and access to invaluable building tools to enrich their homes and those of people in their community.[69] Some men worked for shares, tending to livestock and growing corn and wheat.[70] Or they gave their employer every third bag of cotton and every third bushel of corn they produced.[71] Still others, like North Carolinian Essic Harris, worked on the railroad.[72] Those scratching out a subsistence living owned barnyard fowl and individual dairy cows. The eggs, milk, butter, cream, and meat enriched their diets.

More enterprising men participated in the market economy. Pinkney Dodd of South Carolina and Scipio Eager of Georgia rented horse farms and bred horses and mules.[73] Pack animals shortened travel time and gave families more time for work or play, so breeding them could bring entrepreneurial success. The Lyons possessed a horde of hogs; that substantial investment indicates they were producing cured meats and breeding specifically for the market. For market-oriented men, spending time traveling to and from town to buy and sell goods—or to have their corn ground, cotton ginned, and wheat threshed—would have been a regular part of their lives. When these men came home at the end of the day, they also completed their share of work around the farms where they lived, or in their own gardens or on their own patches of land. Wherever they worked, deep affection for their kin fueled men's drive to provide for them.

Providing for the family was not only the business of men, however. Women's work, inside and outside their homes, was crucial to families' well-being. Black women who worked from home faced endless daily tasks that sustained their families. Lucky ones had children and extended family to help. Some women led households as sole providers, for a variety of reasons, including the death or sale of spouses during slavery or the war, failure to marry after emancipation, or a disabled spouse. Although many women worked in domestic and agricultural service, others ran boardinghouses or sold foodstuffs they prepared.[74] Women's devotion to the care of their husbands, kids, and parents was the wellspring of their productivity.

Many of the men who acquired property and ascended to office could not have done so without enterprising and supportive working women at their sides. A man in Lowndes County, Mississippi, rented a double cabin and was wealthy enough to hire his own hands as he built a life with his wife.[75] Eliza Lyon's occupation was listed in the 1870 census as "keeping house." Her husband, Abe, earned enough as a blacksmith with his own shop to enable Eliza to participate in the region-wide exodus of married women from jobs requiring them to tend to white people's homes or work the crops on white farms and plantations. But this did not mean she and other married women were closed off from the labor force. To supplement their family's incomes—and shorten the time it would take to fulfill their dreams of freedom—many women worked for others in shifts, traveling to their employers' and clients' residences, farms, and businesses by day, and then returning home to their families at night. Eliza worked occasional shifts for her former master, and Mary Brown worked in the gold mine near her home in White County, Georgia.[76]

Living or working from their own homes instead of from their employers' residences or businesses could empower girls and women and give them a degree of protection. Work, like Hannah Tutson's taking in and washing the soiled laundry of her customers, enabled numerous women to be financially independent and seeded entrepreneurship. It also gave them more privacy and bodily integrity, because they were less vulnerable to sexual predation or physical attacks than those workers who lived with their white employers.[77]

With more space and time to grow their own food, families increased the size of provisional gardens they had kept under slavery.[78] Cultivating fruits and vegetables for themselves gave families like Joseph and Mary Brown's greater control over their food intake and could start the process of reversing the nutritional deficiencies so common in enslaved people's diets, which were often restricted to cheap starches and cuts of meat. Lush gardens, like the one Georgia Telfair remembered, included good eats like beans, tomatoes, peppers, onions, peas, potatoes, and yams, as well as varieties of hearty greens. Small fields held squash, peanuts, and okra. When South Carolinian Wallace Fowler wasn't working for others, he was tending to his prized watermelon patch. Families set traps for possum, squirrels, and rabbits to enrich their diets. People with small rifles and more mobility hunted for larger wild game, like deer, boar, and turkeys; those with access to waterways fished.[79] Enterprising people bartered and peddled their surplus to their neighbors or merchants, enhancing their earnings.

When they worked for themselves, families interspersed subsistence goods with market ones. One freedman in Limestone, South Carolina, tended fields of sorghum grass, which he took to a mill to be ground and whose boiled juice his customers transformed into molasses to sweeten food or make drinks. He also cultivated patches of potatoes and cabbages.[80] Alfred Wright, who lived not far away in Union County, grew peanuts.[81]

Ambitious families were equally enterprising in their cultivation choices. Families like Andrew and Frankie Cathcart's, who toiled on large farms, grew cash crops specific to their region, like cotton, corn, sugar, potatoes, or tobacco. Simon and Mary Elder became prosperous wheat producers in Clarke County, Georgia. Simon and Mary were fifty-six years old and thirty-three years old, respectively. Mary described herself and Simon as "two quiet, hard-working people, doing well," on their own with no children. The couple reported that their combined industry one season produced a five-hundred-pound bag of wheat, which they sold for twenty-five cents a pound, about $2,370, the relative labor earnings and income of which amounts to several hundred thousand dollars today. The Elders also had enough expendable income to pay taxes and hire laborers to help them cultivate their crop and thresh their wheat.[82]

To make ends meet, families blended work for themselves and for others. Tensions flared daily, as former enslavers and their allies met former slaves on the new terrain of freedom.[83] A complicated interplay of factors and evaluations informed where and for whom some families decided to work. Men who had been free before the war, like Andrew Cathcart, generally continued working their own land. Skilled laborers like Abe Lyon didn't miss a beat in the transition from slavery; they worked for their enslaver one day and hung a shingle the next. Unskilled laborers—especially those with few resources, like Mary and Joseph Brown—didn't have many options, until they saved enough money to strike out on their own. Most prospective employers, who were desperate for laborers, were former enslavers or had been clawing their way to slaveholder status before the war interrupted their efforts. Slavery was brutal and repressive wherever it existed, but enslavers' level of individual cruelty varied; freed people could gauge this and collect as much information on potential employers as possible. Edward Crosby and his wife chose to remain on the land of their former enslavers, likely thinking their circumstances were tolerable and they'd take their chances with the devil they knew. The Crosbys also might not have had the resources to relocate or the desire to leave their social networks. Besides, with few options short of leaving the South completely, most freed people were likely going to be working for *someone* who had held people in bondage, or had wanted to.

But staying put also meant creating new terms of engagement with these people. According to one Freedmen's Bureau agent, problems generally arose when white men could not "throw aside the dogma" of mastery and accept the "unpalatable truth" of slavery's end and Black people being able to reap the rewards of free labor.[84] Whites sabotaged the transition to free labor whenever they could with the hope of "embarrassing" the United States and compelling Congress to "revive slavery," the agent observed.[85]

In the new contract and sharecropping systems that emerged, the planter class found their opening to deny families economic freedom and sovereignty. Employers and laborers wrestled over the terms of the work people performed. Enslavers-turned-employers who had their finances disrupted by the war rarely had cash on hand, so they agreed to pay laborers like Edward Crosby's family in shares of the crop. Some attracted workers by offering large parcels of land, only to reduce the promised acreage within a year, using the threat of violence to force families to accept the new terms or move with nothing to show for it.

The former enslaving class tried to limit the amount of time families spent tending to their own crops or gardens, constraining their economic possibilities. Enslavers went to extreme lengths to restrict freed people's leisure time and their right, as one woman put it, "to 'joy" their freedom, including by playing, dancing, and drinking in their *own* time.[86] Planters tried to shut down venues and business establishments that catered to Black people looking to have a good time.[87] Enslavers resisted the end of the corporal punishments that were the linchpin to slavery.

Workers fought back—and some won. They insisted on raising food and tending to livestock for their families' consumption and for sale in the market economy. Families defended themselves and their people against physical discipline. They protected their time, including to play. They refused to sign contracts unless they got the conditions they wanted. Working people withheld their labor at critical times to gain better concessions, or they left in protest before the terms of agreements or contracts were met.[88] Worker wins fueled advancement toward fulfilling their dreams of economic freedom.

Skilled workers such as seamstresses, tailors, and shoemakers, along with nurses, midwives, doctors, and dentists, could reap the benefits of their skills and mobility while earning more money.[89] Prosperity like this was not in the cards for everyone. Many of those who were turned out "slam loose" endured homelessness and hunger. After slavery, "We all stayed and it sure was tough times," one woman said. She remembered in her interview with WPA personnel in the 1930s that there were periods when "we had almost nothing to eat."[90] The extent of people's social and economic struggles and successes was influenced by where they lived. Residents of Alabama, Georgia, Florida, Mississippi, and South Carolina were scattered across the rural landscape. They often lived miles outside of small towns like York, South Carolina, and Stevenson, Alabama, and bustling new metropolises, like Atlanta, Georgia, and Columbus, Mississippi. Proximity to local markets might grant families access to more resources and more financial stability. Regional institutions like banks, legislatures, and judicial circuits, and national and international market forces that had governed many southerners' experiences in slavery, continued to trouble their lives in freedom.[91] In any case, the families named here were reaching the other side of the "hard struggle."

By 1867, after President Johnson had reversed Congress's decision to redistribute Confederates' confiscated and abandoned lands among freed people, it had become clear that not all of federal policymakers' promises would come to fruition.[92] Even with these setbacks, land-hungry families soldiered on. Like so many, Abe and Eliza Lyon dreamed of having a small farm with enough land for them to feed and support their family and sell their surplus hogs and other goods in local markets.[93] Some families purchased land individually; others did so cooperatively, joining forces with kin to buy land off which they could live. The Cathcarts were already there; the Lyons were on their way, saving as much money as possible; and the Browns and the Crosbys were hoping to get there.

Additional signs of Black families' progress toward landownership can be observed in the tens of thousands of people who opened accounts in the Freedman's Savings and Trust Company, which was incorporated in 1865.[94] Floridian Robert Meacham joined many men who deposited money. Before the bank collapsed under the weight of fraud and the 1873 economic crash, some account holders pooled their resources, using their saved funds to buy land auctioned off by federal officials, create their own Black settlements, and support home- and community-building projects.

Samuel and Hannah Tutson were among the several thousand African Americans who saved enough and were able to take advantage of the Southern Homestead Act, which Congress passed in June 1866.[95] The legislation opened to settlement 46 million acres of land, from which officials and white civilian settlers had displaced Native Americans. Progressive lawmakers granted freed African Americans priority access to settlement until January 1867.

The Tutsons saved their earnings from their homestead and Hannah's domestic work, and acquired a 160-acre tract of land. One challenge for aspiring homesteaders was the need to have access to an outpost of the Freedmen's Bureau, which administered the program, to acquire such a certificate. These posts were spread far and wide, which meant that even if some families possessed the money to homestead, if they were living in remote locations and did not have the time or means to travel vast distances, then they could not participate in the boom. Samuel and Hannah were fortunate: the Gainesville, Florida, post was only about fifteen miles away from their home community.

Prospective landowners frequently encountered additional problems. Areas open for Black people to purchase land under the Southern Homestead Act were not always suited for cultivating cash crops. Newly freed people needed cash on hand to acquire resources to farm, including seeds, tools, and cattle. If enslavers in their communities denied them work or would not pay in cash, then this dimmed their prospects of settling in the Homestead areas. One formerly enslaved woman recalled that it took families two to three years to save enough money to buy land.[96] Families inadvertently found themselves in floodplains or in areas so arid or filled with rocks that little would grow; they might have barely enough to feed themselves, let alone a surplus to sell at market.[97] But this wasn't the case for Hannah and Samuel Tutson's 160 acres, on which they grew cotton and grazed livestock.

Land-hungry families encountered whites who refused to sell or lease land to them. Landless whites in their communities were vehemently opposed to African Americans obtaining land before they did. Property-owning whites tried to stop Black people from buying land, especially if they wanted more than the bare minimum for subsistence farming. Black mechanics, one Vicksburg bureau agent reported, "who have made several thousand dollars during the last two years, find it impossible to buy even land enough to put up a house," yet white men could purchase any amount of land they wanted. As the agent noted, whites knew that if they could deny Black people property or land ownership, then these freed people would be bound to return to the former slave labor camps and work for wages that barely supported themselves and their families. These whites reasoned that "this kind of slavery will be better than none at all," the agent observed.[98]

White opposition to Black landownership was so intense that, as one freed woman recalled, if Black landowners "didn't watch their steps mighty careful, the white folks would find a way" to snatch the land.[99] Hannah and Samuel Tutson had barely gotten on their homestead before their white neighbors started menacing them. "In the red times," Hannah said, she had seen and experienced too many beatings and whippings to count. After her family acquired their homestead, she didn't care what white people might try to do to her in freedom "if only I can save my land."[100]

Families sometimes tried to limit their contact with whites by relocating or separating their homes from their workplaces. Renters might find themselves living on former labor camps, but they tried to make home as far from the Big House and the old slave quarters as possible, moving the cabins they had occupied during slavery to different areas to gain a degree of privacy. Samuel and Hannah Tutson represented those who struck out completely on their own, carving small farms out of undeveloped areas. People who could not afford a lot of land independently often found themselves in autonomous Black settlements, adjacent to towns and cities, where ten to twenty families lived close together for support and protection.[101] Some settlements were so small, and their existence was so short, that local authorities did not think they merited recognition on county or state maps. But most families lived relatively near whites of all backgrounds.

With jobs and places to live, more families turned to homemaking and building social and political environs that allowed them to protect their interests.[102] Homes and communities that surrounded them constituted one of the first lines of defense in African Americans' fight for liberation. Living independently from whites in these spaces, families like Abe and Eliza Lyon's could try to heal the wounds of slavery and the war. Mary and Joseph Brown's family could love on and support each other and develop the resolve necessary to fight any new incarnations of white supremacy.

Some freedom-making families repurposed the housing structures they had occupied during slavery. Many of these were single-family-size log cabins and wood-framed shotgun homes that were at least a story and a half high. Ground floors were made of planks of wood set up on blocks that lifted two feet above ground.[103] Subfloors provided storage space. First and main floors usually included rooms for sleeping, and a kitchen. Upper half-stories provided space for storing goods and, sometimes, extra sleeping space. Families who could do so lived in housing akin to contemporary two-family duplexes, which supported multigenerational needs and could accommodate kin displaced by evictions, floods, or fires.[104] Families fenced off their dwellings to demonstrate ownership and provide a degree of protection. They also acquired dogs, for hunting and another layer of protection against intruders.

Families outfitted their homes in ways that suited their new earnings and individual styles and comfort needs. James Alston of Alabama enhanced his house with weatherboarding.[105] Upgrades also included better beds—with moss-filled mattresses instead of meager straw ones—and finer furniture, as well as what Georgia resident Columbus Jeter called the "little things," housewares meant more to elicit pride and emotional satisfaction than to serve a function. Living independently and having expendable income, families like fellow Georgians Anderson and Lucy Ferrell filled closets and trunks with treasured family keepsakes and the clothes they wanted to wear to express their individuality.[106] Families stocked their kitchens with dishes and pots and skillets they made or purchased. All the details were emblematic of how much freedom transformed their lives.

Once residents were settled in and had established themselves and their families, they turned to remaking the world beyond their individual yards. The tenderness that grew inside homes radiated outward. Black people's "picking themselves up" from slavery required an ethic of community that literary scholar Farah Jasmine Griffin describes as "a radical spiritual survival, in a place set on destroying our souls."[107] Saving each other from what the writer Kiese Laymon calls "the worst of white folks" fueled Black people's steadfast commitment to communal care.[108] The first step of building a more just world was residents' clear-eyed understanding of the hostility surrounding them, and that surviving and thriving in the face of it required cooperative work. Solidarity saw these future-oriented communities come together to engage in public acts of radical safekeeping to nourish individual development and to serve as a bulwark against the hostile white world.[109] Black radical care wasn't just a thought. It was a liberatory practice evident in Black people's day-to-day actions to collectively resist their oppression.

This ethos of love and care as a means of collective liberation yielded numerous social, economic, and cultural institutions. This included churches like Robert Meacham's in Monticello, Florida, and Henry Giles's in Nixburg, Alabama. Census assessors reported that Robert had amassed one thousand dollars in real estate, much of it likely tied to his church. Henry's community invested four to five hundred dollars of their earnings into their church.[110]

Most churches were humbler than Robert's and Henry's. Georgia Telfair said hers "wasn't much of a church for looks," because it was constructed from poles, with a roof of pine limbs and brushes. But her family went every Sunday, and, she said, "there was some sure good meeting" there. And "lots of souls found the way to their heavenly home right there."[111]

Whether they were grand edifices like Robert Meacham's or little brush arbor shelters like Georgia's, new churches provided religious instruction and were the nuclei of Black institution-building. Black churches sustained schools for neighborhood children, advanced economic enterprise, and served as a springboard for political activism. Black people's adherence to communal care also drove the opening of orphanages to meet the community's social and emotional needs and general stores to meet a community's economic and commercial requirements; African Americans built and maintained many such institutions themselves.[112] Social services also included non-church schools, like the one Edward Crosby and his wife were planning to start for children near Aberdeen, or the one where Columbus Jeter and his wife, Aury, taught in Douglas County, Georgia.[113]

Individual families belonged to these communities, and the communities belonged to them. Communities would envelop individual members in their embrace in times of celebration and need. This communal ethic was essential to African Americans remaking themselves into a new people. It also saw communities convened to provide aid and sanctuary for families in crisis, treat their injuries, and right an upside-down world into a just one.[114]

While adults like Robert Meacham, Edward Crosby, and the Jeters were working to acquire land and suitable employment and tend to their communities' educational and religious needs, their children's worlds transformed.[115] Freed parents traveled to find children whom slaveholders had sold away or had kidnapped after the war. Parents insisted on their right to full custody of their offspring, including their instruction. Taking hold of their parental roles was a touchstone of adults' freedom.

By 1870, Black southern youths like Mary and Joseph Brown's two boys and Eliza and Abe Lyon's two girls and boy faced other joys and challenges. Former slaves told WPA interviewers in the 1930s that freedom had brought youths the chance to be children. They could spend time with family and pursue leisure activities like playing with marbles or homemade dolls, jumping rope, and play-acting.[116]

Some children attended school in their communities for at least part of the year. Georgia Telfair began school at the age of eight. Her parents sent her off to class with her blueback speller, the elementary spelling book of the day, in one hand, and her dinner bucket in the other. She remembered wearing a homespun dress with a bonnet to match.[117]

Census records and WPA interviews show that not all children had the chance of receiving formal education, however. Most spent some, if not all, of their time working on a farm, alongside older kin. Children remained out of school either because their families desperately needed their labor, or because missionary organizations, the Freedmen's Bureau, or other entities had not established schools in their neighborhoods, as they had in Georgia's community.[118]

Some whites refused to relinquish their hold on Black children, instead insisting on keeping the children on their properties to serve what were called "apprenticeships" or declining to release youths into their parents' or kin's custody.[119] Robert Falls's mother had been sold away; he said his enslaver "fooled [my brother and me] to believe we was duty-bound to stay with him until we was twenty-one." Robert and his brother were likely detained in a dreaded forced apprenticeship. The enslaving class passed new laws giving them the right to exploit the labor of youths old enough to work. White advocates of apprenticeships insisted they could provide better "care" and "instruction" for underage freed youths than their parents could. Under many laws, freed youths could be seized and detained without parental permission and over parents' determined opposition. The Falls boys got free because his brother, whom Robert described as "stubborn," refused and escaped. He eventually returned for Robert and took him to work on the railroad, work Robert said he could not stand. Robert managed to locate his mother and traveled by foot to where she lived; she then took him to work with her.[120]

Parents and guardians negotiated and closely monitored children's apprenticeship arrangements that were mandated by Black Codes and later by Freedmen's Bureau officials. But they also seized parental authority to keep their children from working with anyone other than themselves, when they could. These new paternal rights allowed Doc Rountree, of Florida, to determine the circumstances under which his children would work. When the man who had held the family in bondage expressed a desire to have Rountree's children "to go and work with him for their victuals and clothes," Doc declined, saying, "I did not want them to go."[121] If the children needed those things, Doc and his wife, Ellen, were prepared to provide them.

Changes also occurred within family units and communities that reveal African American men's growing social and political power, another critical component of freedom. Freedmen's newly recognized status as heads of households shifted the balance of power in some families from women to men.[122] Abe Lyon and Andrew Cathcart were among many men who embraced these privileges by negotiating labor contracts and apprenticeships as well as working their own land or that of another for profit.

Freedom included Black people's right to own and display possessions, including weapons. They could now partake in customary rights of hunting and fishing, and of self-defense. Men acquired or maintained personal pistols and rifles they had from the war to protect their families. They organized for community defense.

This coincided with men's political ascendancy as voters and office-holders, transforming not just their families but the communities and even states in which they lived. To protect everything they had built and hoped to build, newly freed men longed to vote and run for office.[123] They knew that they were in the best position to implement radical changes, creating an American society that included Black people enjoying the protections of citizenship, social equality, and a more democratic political process. A complex interplay of social and political factors informed how African Americans ranked their priorities. Many Black veterans, and men like Andrew Cathcart who had been free before the war, insisted on political power right after the war ended. Freed men like Abram Colby, or Samuel Nuckles of Union County, South Carolina, hoped they might help their people achieve their dreams for freedom by one day serving in the state legislature. But for men like Abe Lyon, more urgent freedoms beckoned. Abe could prioritize fighting for authority in governance through the vote or officeholding after he and Eliza secured and developed their own homestead, he opened his blacksmith shop, and his children began school. Until 1867, the franchise was not yet a reality, but it was in the crowded constellation of African Americans' visions for liberation.

———————

Within years of the Civil War's end, newly freed and enfranchised people like Abe and Eliza Lyon, Mary and Joseph Brown, and Andrew and Frankie Cathcart created the types of lives that most African Americans had dreamed of having during their enslavement. They formalized social units and established gender roles and conventions that fit their visions for having their freedom recognized and their rights as citizens respected. With a composite of work arrangements, they earned money to acquire property and personal goods. Many African Americans had, in fact, made great strides.

Even with this progress, most people still struggled, alongside their white counterparts, to gain their financial footing and to create new lives for themselves. The Civil War had devastated the South's infrastructure, and freedom's implications remained inchoate. Nonetheless, families such as the Lyons, Browns, and Cathcarts were poised to transcend slavery. They could feel pride in their accomplishments, even if they still had dreams of enjoying better lives.

In her poem "The Deliverance," abolitionist and activist Frances Ellen Watkins Harper captures this storied but challenging moment of jubilee and African Americans' fight to make freedom real.[124]

> *But we soon got used to freedom,*
> *Though the way at first was rough;*
> *But we weathered through the tempest*
> *For slavery made us tough.*
> *. . .*
> *If freedom seem'd a little rough*
> *I'd weather through the gale*

From outward appearances, at least, these families had weathered the storm. They seem to have been living dignified lives, uninterrupted, handling their own affairs. For people who had started a new world from scratch and who aspired to liberation, no achievement was small; each step toward their post-emancipation dreams meant everything.

At the same time, white southerners' belief in their right to use extreme violence on African Americans flowed naturally from slavery to freedom like the current of the Mississippi, unyielding in its drive south to the Gulf. In picking themselves up, these African Americans defied racist arguments about their supposed inherent inferiority and lies about their dependence. Having lived through the darkest days of slavery, newly freed people thought they had seen the worst of white folks.[125] Their continued success in reconstructing American freedom and democracy was endangered by the racialized hate hovering over their lives.

Ex-Confederates desired to continue hoarding the nation's abundant opportunities, and they recognized the threat posed by independent Black families; autonomous Black homes, institutions, and communities; and the prospect of Black voters and officeholders. Liberated Black families would produce a polity with a wider, more inclusive dream of American freedom, and Black people would fight to establish laws that might make that dream a reality. With the Thirteenth Amendment, white southerners could not sustain slavery, but they could sustain its legacy, which is why they mobilized.

Sometimes, white loathing only lingered at the edges of social life, in the exchange of looks between one man who had hitched his future to perpetual slavery and another man who bet on emancipation. But white rage boiled as poor, landless whites seethed watching Black families transcend the hard struggle—wives like Eliza Lyon retreating from fields; children like her William, Ella, and Annie attending school; people enjoying leisure time and building thriving institutions like Robert Meacham's church; men acquiring land like Samuel Tutson did; men like Abe Lyon starting businesses; men running for office like Abram Colby. Other times that rage crashed through the center of daily life, when whites—possessed by a desire to maintain their power—forgot themselves and the expectations of the new order and presumed the right to continue violently attacking Black people as they had done under slavery.[126]

When outraged and jealous whites strove to undermine Black people's self-determination and their sense of security, they intentionally targeted these people's homes, and the places and spheres surrounding them. The very spaces African Americans created to serve as the foundation for their liberation became the primary theaters in the war against their freedom.[127]

Chapter 2

The Devil Was Turned Loose

The thunder of hooves broke the silence of the night, jarring Caroline Benson awake in White County, Georgia, and alerting her that white men were coming and that she and her family were in imminent danger. For one man, of Spartanburg County, South Carolina, it was the barking of his dogs; for another man in the same locale, it was the sound of white men's bodies crashing into his door. For others, it was the whoop of the rebel yell, high-pitched hoots of whistles or bugles, or screams coming from neighbors' yards. What these families heard was a shadow army of white men in their communities: it sounded like death was coming. After the invaders left, there was a return to an eerie silence, broken only by the cries of the dying or the pained wails of their surviving kin.[1]

Like Edward Crosby—who saw white men on horseback descending on his home in the dark of night—James Alston, of York, South Carolina, saw death coming for him in the form of disguised white men with guns in their hands. Another man saw a notice nailed to a post, threatening to slit his throat if he crossed a bridge to visit his property in Tuskegee, Alabama. Still another looked outside and saw his yard, in Chatham County, North Carolina, full of armed white men. A Florida couple's young children sat watching from the woods as white men whipped and assaulted both their parents. A father also watched, in stunned silence, as a gang beat and repeatedly stabbed his son, in Limestone County, Alabama. A wife watched, too, as her husband lay dying on the family's cabin floor near Glenn Springs, South Carolina. The things targeted people saw when they thought death was coming for them stuck with them for the rest of their lives.[2]

Southerners who dealt with or witnessed these white men conducting paramilitary strikes in the middle of the night called them "night riders" and "midnight assassins." Targeted people also used the term "Ku-Klux" as a shorthand for the Klan and other vigilante squads.[3] When Black families were awakened in the middle of the night, when death was in their yards or at their doorsteps, they understood the white men outside their homes were part of a larger enterprise intent on denying Black people their freedom. These groups of men included enslavers, Confederate soldiers, and other whites who rejected a post–Civil War world in which Black Americans could be free and coexist peacefully with whites under the auspices of the federal government.

To revamp the U.S. Constitution and create a society in which Black and white Americans enjoyed the same rights and privileges was, to racist night riders, a "radical" change, an undemocratic seizure of white conservatives' power, and therefore void. They did not even try to create a well of goodwill after having taken the country through a bloody war. They did not bother with a façade of interest in an equal coexistence with Black people. Although the Confederate army surrendered the battlefield to U.S. forces, these vigilantes made clear that the southern white man's war for domination over Black people was still on. Having failed in their fight to leave the United States, insurrectionists sought instead to remake the republic in their image.[4]

Their most significant tactic was violence. Some of this was reflexive outbursts. But the war on Black people's freedom during Reconstruction could not be sustained by rage alone; it required organization and extensive planning.

In much of the American imagination, "visits" like the ones Edward Crosby, Caroline Benson, and James Alston experienced were spontaneous reprisals—or even harmless antics. This misconception arose because Confederates and white conservative apologists deliberately crafted a mythology about Reconstruction violence, then kept that myth alive over the century and a half since. One component of this tale was to deny that any atrocities took place during "visits." Another was for perpetrators and bystanders to downplay the acts of savagery—as one resentful Freedmen's Bureau agent did when he described an attempted killing as a "rough frolic."[5] Dismissing white southerners' murderous assaults on Black people as random, or merely as the result of Confederates' understandable hurt feelings at defeat, perpetrators and their defenders legitimized a war on freedom and normalized atrocities. White disbelief encouraged what became the genocidal-like nature of Reconstruction violence.

The concept of genocide—from the Greek *genos* (race or tribe) and the Latin *-cide* (killing)—was coined in 1944 and first recognized as a crime under international law in 1946. The Nazis and their collaborators' systematic and state-planned extermination of Jews and other marginalized people during the Holocaust exemplified the United Nations' legal definition of genocide. The enthusiasm and scale of the Nazis' efforts shocked the world and inspired global campaigns to try to prevent such crimes from happening again. Today, the following acts fall under the United Nations' rubric of genocidal violence: "killing members of the group," "causing serious bodily or mental harm to members of the group," "deliberately inflicting on the group conditions of life calculated to bring about its physical destruction in whole or in part," and "forcibly transferring children of the group to another group." This violence may occur in the context of an "armed conflict, international or non-international, but also in the context of a peaceful situation."[6] The UN's definition requires both evidence of intent—verifiable proof of deliberate targeting that can stand up in an international court of law—and action to bring about the destruction.[7]

The association of Reconstruction violence with genocide may seem hyperbolic and contrary to the stories we've been told again and again about Reconstruction's supposed "failure." Confederate extremists did not kill all African Americans. And there is no evidence that Americans pursuing the

Confederate cause and their supporters organized to plan genocide. But racially conservative white southerners' *intentions* should not outweigh the effect of their *actions* on Black people's *lives*.

The anthropologist Nancy Scheper-Hughes and other conflict experts have argued that the UN's rubric enables us to *see* patterns of "hitherto unrecognized" violence. Historical patterns of deliberate targeting may not meet today's legal bar of prosecution by an international court or geopolitical bar for international military intervention. But as Scheper-Hughes has explained, the usefulness of the UN's rubric "lies in sensitizing people to genocidal-like practices and sentiments that are enacted daily by ordinary citizens as if they were the most normal and expected behaviors."[8]

What cannot be doubted is the centuries-long record of inhumane treatment the United States has tolerated against Black people. Confederates' determination to halt the reconstruction of American freedom after the Civil War is part of that record. They only reluctantly accepted the abolition of slavery as the price of defeat on the battlefield. White conservatives vehemently opposed the expansion of American democracy through universal male suffrage. They were extremely hostile to the recognition of Black citizenship and its constituent elements—that Black people had the right to any of the liberties, freedoms, and protections detailed in the U.S. Constitution, the Civil Rights Act of 1866, and the Reconstruction Amendments. In short, Confederates refused to recognize African Americans had the basic human rights of citizenship, what the philosopher Hannah Arendt later called "the right to have rights."[9] Extremists demonstrated that refusal by killing thousands of Black people who assumed they had those rights and resisted white people's efforts to deny them. With a limited infrastructure for reporting and keeping track of killings, and perpetrators and their allies' defiance of any efforts to conduct an accounting, it is impossible to know how many Black people white southerners killed. In Texas alone, former Secretary of War Edwin Stanton said in November 1868, there were too many to count.[10] White southerners did not seek to completely exterminate all African Americans, but the successive violence they used, rejecting *newly freed people's* right to any rights, was genocidal-like in nature.[11]

Examining the evolution of this relentless campaign of violence brings the shadow army that waged war on American freedom and democracy more fully into view. From reprisal attacks on newly freed people trying to leave bondage, to the white southern backlash against Black men gaining the vote, emancipation resistance was purposeful and took many forms. Contrary to popular myths about this violence being impulsive and spontaneous, it was intentional. No tactic in the white southern war on freedom was more calculated and staged than the phenomenon of night riding. Looking at raiders' general operations, their motivations and planning, before closing in on the moments of attack to highlight their strategies for catching their targets, explodes assumptions about Reconstruction's supposed "failure." Black Reconstruction didn't "fail," as so many are taught. White southerners overthrew it, and the rest of the nation let them.

———

The real business of waging war on Black people's freedom didn't happen on a battlefield, in the White House, or in the chambers of Congress. Rather than only attacking Army posts, or fighting the politicians who made freedom and civil and political rights for Black people possible, extremist whites were calculating. The work of overthrowing Black Reconstruction happened on the ground in the former slaveholding states as white conservatives got busy establishing institutions and policies that would sustain Black people's subjugation.

There does not appear to be evidence that Confederates coordinated across a state or even the former slaveholding region. That is why it is best to think of white extremists' actions as akin to what Scheper-Hughes has called a "small war"—wars that aren't formally declared and don't involve official military engagements.[12] Unlike a "big war," whose military engagements are official and unmistakable, individual assaults in a "small" one may seem so inconsequential that they become normalized. But the cumulative effect of incessant attacks makes the scale of violence and suffering more visible.[13]

Postbellum attacks were less a new development than they were an extension of wartime reprisal violence. During the war, especially after the Emancipation Proclamation, white southerners had used shocking amounts of force to try to stem the tide of Black people escaping slavery; enslavers had ramped up the slave patrol systems and organized militias to halt Black people's flight to freedom. They also attacked refugee camps, dragged self-emancipated people back to slavery, or massacred them.[14]

Whether Confederates accepted it or not, legal freedom was on the move. In December 1863, Abraham Lincoln had announced his plan for reconstructing Confederate states. The policy declared that once 10 percent of (white male) voters in any Confederate state pledged to respect the Constitution and agreed to abolish slavery, their states would be readmitted to the Union and regain their representation in Congress. In 1864, Arkansas, Louisiana, and Tennessee had agreed. All three states rewrote their constitutions to ban slavery. The U.S. Senate had passed a resolution for a constitutional amendment to abolish slavery in August 1864, and the House had followed in January 1865. By December 1865, enough states had ratified the Thirteenth Amendment that it became the official law of the land.

Confederates claimed they accepted federal authority and respected the U.S. Constitution. This appeased war-weary white northerners and westerners who grasped at any signs the conflict was truly over. But not everyone took Confederates at their word. General Carl Schurz had written of the "general spirit of violence" that pervaded the South.[15] A writer in the *New York Tribune* characterized Confederates as "lip loyal": they said one thing but did another.[16]

Both of these white men's observations were astute: white southerners who remained committed to *Dis*union would not be so easily dissuaded of their right to hold Black people in bondage.[17] Even while the states were ratifying the Thirteenth Amendment, the Confederates General Schurz called "the incorrigibles" were already refusing to recognize federal and state policies and laws abolishing slavery. Emancipation resistance is why the U.S. Army was still fighting its way across the Lone Star State to end slavery in Texas two years after the Emancipation Proclamation and two months after General Robert E. Lee and the Army of Northern Virginia had surrendered at the Appomattox courthouse.

In reaction to emancipation, a shadow army of enslavers and defeated soldiers mobilized with a wave of maimings and killings to try to stem the tide or to punish freed people. Retaliatory attacks occurred across the entire South over the duration of Reconstruction. But the violence from 1865 through 1867 was not spontaneous. It was purposeful, literally part of an emerging freedom-denying operation.

One place where it was clear that "peace" after war is a social construct, and where extremists were actively engaged in emancipation reprisal, was Alabama. In the summer of 1865, Freedmen's Bureau agents and Army personnel stationed in central and southwestern counties of the state sent federal officials reports on the atrocities they were witnessing. A Mobile agent for several Alabama counties reported "gangs of idle rebel soldiers and other dissolute rowdies" were attacking "helpless" and "unoffending" freedmen with impunity. Their activity was fueled, the agent said, by "incendiary and lying reports in the papers, and false representations" that Black people were "going to rise" up against white people, a charge the agent dismissed as "utterly without foundation."[18] Whites alleged that Black people were instigating the violence, but as General Schurz reported to the U.S. Senate, these accusations were consistently "found unwarranted by fact."[19] The truth of the matter, Captain W. A. Poillon reported, was that a "reign of terror exists" and "the life of the freedmen is at the mercy of any [white] villain whose hatred or caprice incites to murder."[20]

The rumors and fictitious newspaper reports accusing African Americans of planning to revolt against white people merit consideration. They recognize, albeit indirectly, slavery's wickedness—specifically, that Black people might have had just cause to avenge their enslavement. But there is no evidence freed people were seeking vengeance or plotting a rebellion. If anything, most Black people were desperate to get away from the people who had held them in bondage and to limit as much contact with routed whites as possible. Black people could and did defend themselves against enslavers still trying to deny them their rights in violation of the U.S. Constitution.

Extremists' unfounded claims that Black southerners were scheming to attack white people were an integral component of an audacious propaganda campaign. Confederates making or publishing these allegations chose one technique that civil and human rights lawyer Kenneth Marcus observed was favored by perpetrators of genocidal violence in Nazi Germany, Bosnia, and Rwanda: instigate violence by accusing "one's enemies of conducting, plotting, or desiring to commit precisely the same transgressions one plans to commit against them."[21] That mendacity, which Marcus has called "accusation in a mirror," seems easy enough to refute. But those similar claims during the Reconstruction era drew on white Americans' preexisting narratives about Black people's hatred for—and desire to harm—innocent white people. Any actual incidents, when examined without right-wing distortions, generally reveal themselves to be enslaved people's uprisings or other efforts to escape slavery or defend themselves against enslavers' cruelty—and negate those preexisting narratives. Black people were not attacking white people randomly; they were defending themselves against white people's collective aggression.

Nevertheless, U.S. Army officials, members of Congress, and the executive branch, concerned about the possibility of Black vengeance, took these claims seriously. Officials investigated and *disproved* them. But disinformation like this is such a historically proven mechanism for inciting mass murder that observers of present-day conflicts around the globe see such accusations as a harbinger of genocidal violence. No matter how baseless, the shadow army's accusations rallied white troops by demonizing Black people to justify retaliation and then "cast aggression as self-defense."[22] White southerners who were irrationally "afraid" of freed people or "worried" about Black competition for jobs and rights received the message: get the Black people before they get you. Investigators' reports of white southerners' ongoing and intensifying attacks on African Americans indicate the troops understood the assignment.

One July 1865 report of Alabama "murders and barbarities" included multiple hangings, incidents of Black people being chained to trees and set on fire, and countless disappearances as incidents of white reprisal spread. "Murder with his ghastly train stalks . . . and revels in undisputed carnage," the reporting agent wrote; the bodies of lynching victims were often left hanging.[23] In one case, a man at Magnolia Bluff was ordered out of his home and a gang's five attack dogs were set upon him, leaving him nearly dead at the time of the report. A preacher at Bladen Springs reported Choctaw County's main roads stank with the decomposing bodies of people likely trying to escape continuing enslavement. Murderous attacks on Black people who were leaving or had left bondage were not random; they were calculated to punish those who dared to be free.[24]

Vigilantes targeted Black Alabamans attempting to flee by waterways, where they had no means of escape. Many were shot aboard boats. Others were taken off vessels and killed, and their bodies were thrown in the Alabama and Bigbee Rivers. Two white men, one report reads, took a woman off a steamer and threw her into the river, along with the coop and chickens she was traveling with, telling her to "go to the damned Yankees." She drowned. Conditions were so bad, the agent concluded, that "to leave is death; to remain is to suffer" under the threat of it.[25]

A surgeon at the Montgomery post hospital reported not only killings but also the mutilations he treated. One set of cases involved a white overseer who happened upon a party of two men and three women camped near a main road. The overseer scalped one woman, killing her; he also cut the ears off two women and a man, and severed another man's chin. Their supposed "offenses" may have involved an attempted escape, or simply a failure to return to the plantation on time. In such cases, it was not unheard of for assailants to keep the severed body parts as trophies. Maiming was a special kind of evil: even if victims lived, and not all did, they would do so with horrifying permanent injuries, physical reminders of the price they had paid for trying to be free.[26]

Army personnel in Alabama tried to bring some torturers and killers to justice, to little avail. A Selma provost marshal saw numerous cases involving whites killing Black people trying to leave plantations for town or trying to return for their people after they had been driven off. The officer attempted to arrest suspects, but they escaped. Even when some killers were charged, their peers often served as judges and jurors, disallowing Black people's testimonies in court, which enabled any white person who attacked or killed Black people to act with impunity. Black life at Selma, the officer concluded, was "insecure."[27] Outside this and other cities, in the isolated rural areas where most African Americans lived, conditions were abysmal.

The greater Vicksburg area had also descended into disorder. Agents reported Black Mississippians were "in a much worse state than ever." White extremists there were somewhat restrained by the Freedmen's Bureau's presence and willingness to arrest and punish offenders. One agent confessed, however, there was "no such thing as civil protection" and nothing to be done for those living twenty or thirty miles away, forcing people to submit or to crowd into cities or areas near army posts where, he said, "they can be protected."[28]

As the killing spread across the region, white conservatives from around the country joined forces in dismissing reports of atrocities committed in Alabama, Mississippi, and elsewhere—no matter the source. As historian William Blair has shown, they refused to give credence to reports from not only Black observers but also white ones, including U.S. Army personnel, senators and congressmen, and members of the executive branch like Secretary of War Edwin Stanton.[29]

If white conservatives could not completely disprove lawlessness in the South, one strategy in their propaganda campaign was to prevaricate and downplay reports of white people's attacks on Black people. There was nothing new or different about this violence that merited any federal attention, conservatives insisted; it was a "normal" feature of the white southern "culture" that had sustained an enslaver–enslaved social order. But Confederate defeat on the battlefield and emancipation had changed everything, and both enslavers and newly freed people knew it. Under slavery, white southerners had been incentivized to preserve the financial value residing in enslaved Black people; now, because emancipation had altered this calculus, when Black people resisted, whites exacted vengeance by killing and maiming them.[30]

Some white conservatives also excused the killings as the result of Confederates' wounded egos or the slavocracy's "nervous anxiety to hastily repair broken fortunes" from the war and slavery's destruction.[31] But they were wrong, according to Schurz. The white South needed laborers. And although many former enslavers remained steadfast in their refusal to even try free labor, slavery "in the old form" was not all Confederates wanted; their actions revealed malice. Fueled by what General Schurz described as slaveholding and non-slaveholding whites' "bitter and vindictive feeling" since "the Negro has ceased to be property," white vengeance escalated.[32]

Denying atrocities in one breath and exonerating the killers in another was a strategy that worked. It effectively inspired more white southerners to wage war against freedom. In many ways, bureau agents' reports from Alabama and Mississippi were a preview of the South's downward spiral of reprisal violence and Confederates' fervor to torture, maim, and massacre Black people.[33] News of the violence and its capacity to blunt freedom spread too quickly—to too many extremist whites in too many different parts of the South—to be contained. Copycat violence sprang up across the region as Confederates took new steps to reinstate the social order they had enjoyed during slavery.

While the Civil Rights Act of 1866 had positively affirmed Black people's rights—to make contracts and acquire land, to custody of their children— massacres that same year show the passage of new civil rights legislation did nothing to discourage white violence. On May 1, in Memphis, a white police officer moved to arrest a Black veteran, and the soldiers' friends tried to prevent the police from jailing him. This was one of several confrontations between soldiers and the city's white police force. The situation quickly escalated when an unknown person opened fire. A white mob, including police and firefighters, swept in, attacking Black veterans, civilians, and even white northerners working as missionaries and teachers. The hordes killed forty-six African Americans and raped five Black women. Whites targeted Black people's homes, businesses, churches, and schools for destruction with surgical precision. A congressional delegation went to Memphis to investigate what had happened, but no criminal proceedings were held. The event seemed to mark an inflection point for extremists' understanding of how the nation would respond: they could rampage, rape, and massacre Black people with impunity.[34]

White New Orleanians heard the message. On July 30, 1866, Black and white delegates convened in New Orleans to rewrite Louisiana's state constitution after the Pelican State refused to recognize Black men's right to vote in its amended 1864 constitution and passed freedom-constricting Black Codes. Black delegates, some of them U.S. Army veterans, staged a protest demonstration, and a white mob, including law enforcement, attacked. The mob opened fire. Delegates defended themselves. When the mob ran out of ammunition, they obtained reinforcements and extended their assault to the nearby neighborhood. They injured dozens and killed more than two hundred people, most of them Black veterans.

Despite the violence, many white progressive officials initially believed the Civil Rights Act's guarantee of legal freedom was enough. But white northerners and westerners didn't know enslavers' depravity as intimately as Black people did. Or they knew and did not care. Meanwhile, a lifetime of servitude had taught emancipated people that legal abolition alone would not be enough to break enslavers' determination to control their lives. Emancipation reprisal and the Black Codes inspired more Black people to push progressives and moderates in Congress to take a firmer hand in reconstructing American freedom in the South. In June 1866, Congress passed resolutions for a new constitutional amendment to make the protections and safeguards of the civil rights bill permanent.

The Fourteenth Amendment slowly made its way through the states. Many former Confederate states refused to ratify it. In March 1867, progressives in Congress responded to white southern belligerence by passing three Reconstruction Acts, which outlined the terms of Confederate states' readmission to the Union. Congress divided the South into five military districts and appointed military governors. The first act required that all males, except Confederate leaders, be permitted to participate in constitutional conventions to form new state governments and write new state constitutions; that meant Black males had to be included, too. The new constitutions then had to be approved by a majority of voters in the state. And lastly, to return to the Union fold and regain their sovereignty, the states had to ratify the Fourteenth Amendment—which they did, albeit reluctantly.

Henry Louis Gates Jr. has called the summer of 1867 the "first Freedom Summer."[35] Like the 1964 Mississippi Freedom Summer Project, which organized a massive voter education and registration drive, the Reconstruction Act's enfranchisement of Black men saw a wave of Black voters at the polls. With their states under military authority, Black men in the South voted in huge numbers. Some Confederates, in protest, abstained from voting. Hardliners' absence gave Black men a numerical edge in writing more progressive state constitutions and electing officials who would help reconstruct Black Americans' freedom. The new forward-looking constitutions that Black officeholders helped write included taxpayer-funded, integrated public school systems, land reform, debt relief, integrated jury service, and guaranteed access to public accommodations. With access came Black people's right to be "treated as one of the public" in inns, leisure spaces and entertainment venues, public transit, and drinking and dining establishments.[36]

For white extremists, seeing Black men like Edward Crosby and Abe Lyon enthusiastically voting and serving in office, transforming their states and localities, was the final straw. What had been a calculated campaign of emancipation violence started to include organized election violence. Politically radicalized whites launched a torrent of successive attacks in 1867, striking Black voters and officeholders with tactical precision, taking perverse pleasure in attacking those without as much power as they had. Some belligerents used their paramilitary training from the Civil War or local militias. Purposeful in their mission not to be caught or captured, most conducted their operations far away from Army outposts.[37]

Reprisal violence continued. But elections were a new battlefront. When Confederates saw that Andrew Johnson's administration was not going to drop a punishing hammer on them for secession and the considerable loss of life and treasure from the Civil War, they went about resurrecting as much of the old racial and economic order as possible. Black people using their individual and collective political power to elevate themselves and fulfill their visions of freedom were not part of this new structure. Hard-liners saw Black freedom-making through voting and officeholding as a threat and worked to rip it out by the roots.

Soldiers in the expanding shadow army attacked and assassinated Black voters and their white allies before or during elections, using the same tactics as enslavers had during the initial waves of emancipation reprisal. They expelled Black residents from towns or neighborhoods Confederates were determined to control, despite not constituting the majority of the population. Secret white terror groups sometimes formed in direct response to Black political organizing around groups such as the Union League. The Union League had formed in northern states to support the U.S. cause during the war.[38] It shifted south during Reconstruction to foster newly enfranchised African Americans' support for Republican candidates. Klan attacks forced Union League clubs to meet in secret, and even prompted campaigns of armed self-defense. Direct attacks on members and their families, however, expedited the Union League's decline in the South.

Leading up to the first local elections following the Reconstruction Acts' passage, attacks increased. As right-wing whites honed their skills and moved into position to steal the 1868 election, raids' deadliness increased as well. William Blair describes the waves of assassinations as "the killings fields of 1868."[39] One place this happened was Louisiana, shortly after citizens ratified the new constitution, which enabled Black men there to vote and run for office. A congressional investigation into a massacre revealed white extremists killed or wounded more than two thousand Louisiana Republican voters, politicians, and their families in the weeks leading up to the 1868 presidential election. "Midnight raids, secret murders and open riots" kept the people "in constant terror" until progressive candidates ceded political power. White rampages and massacres were the norm in and around New Orleans, filling the region "with scenes of blood," the congressional investigation revealed, with Klan threats posted across the city, warning Black men to avoid the polls or pay the ultimate price.[40] Black people resisted, and many were killed for it.

Confederates in Louisiana's St. Landry Parish responded to Republican electoral wins with violence. They spent the summer of 1868 terrorizing Black families outside of Opelousas, slaughtering an untold number of men, women, and children with impunity. By fall, right-wing whites were flush from their bloody achievements and ready to steal the election.

White conservatives got their opening for their next strike at a Republican rally six miles away in Washington, Louisiana. Extremists began menacing Unionist Republicans in the open. When a small band of Black men prepared to rescue a Republican being attacked, right-wingers spread unfounded rumors that the Black band was preparing a rebellion; this lie instigated a gathering white mob. Twenty-nine Black men were snatched and almost all of them were executed. For the next two weeks, vigilantes tore through neighborhoods and communities, hunting down and assassinating Black people. Some reports estimate more than 250 fatalities, with approximately another hundred people seriously wounded with life-altering injuries; most of the victims were African American. A white conservative paper reported "the [white] people were generally well satisfied with the result" of what came to be called the Opelousas riot.[41]

As satisfied as the Pelican State's shadow army was, belligerents weren't done. A subsequent congressional investigation revealed Confederates had marched some Republican voters to the polls and forced them to cast ballots for conservative whites running on the Democratic ticket.[42] White southerners had already drawn plenty of blood since the war ended, but they were only just getting started.

The violence extremists unleashed on Black voters and officeholders in 1867–68 motivated progressives in Congress to pass resolutions for a third constitutional amendment. The Fifteenth Amendment declared the right to vote could not be denied by any state based on "race, color, or previous condition of servitude." It enfranchised Black men outside the South as well. Edward Crosby was among the several million Black southern men eager to vote.[43] Once these men began voting, they did not stop of their own volition.[44]

New voters recognized that political power to enact their visions of American freedom did not stop at the ballot box; it was maximized in elected and appointed office. This inspired men to run and their supporters to help them win. Newly enfranchised Americans' impact on the political landscape was immediate and significant. Hiram Revels was lifted to the U.S. Senate representing Mississippi, becoming the first African American to serve in Congress. Richard Harvey Cain, Joseph H. Rainey, Jefferson F. Long, and Robert Smalls were among those who joined the U.S. House from Black-majority communities in Georgia and South Carolina.[45]

African Americans had their sights set on freedom-making and helping chart the nation's destiny through officeholding closer to home, too. Abram Colby joined the Georgia state house. Black Mississippians elevated Robert Gleed, a resident of Columbus, Mississippi, to the state senate to represent the eighteenth district.[46] Samuel Nuckles of Union County joined the South Carolina legislature. Charles Pearce, of Tallahassee, was elected to the Florida senate.[47] Jonathan C. Gibbs, resident of Jackson County, Florida, became a secretary of state.[48] In doing this work, these men hoped to make their dreams of living in an interracial democracy real by working in concert with their fellow citizens to fashion the nation's new governments.

Progressives in Congress believed constitutional protection would shield Black voters and officeholders so they could reconstruct freedom in the South. The Fifteenth Amendment, which was ratified in February 1870, prohibited *states* from passing laws denying men the vote. Its framers assumed citizens would fall in line and respect the Constitution. But the amendment said nothing about private individuals attacking and killing voters or driving out officeholders. Extremists used that to their advantage while the amendment was making its way through the states.

————

Black men's insistence on voting and officeholding elicited another strategy from the shadow army. Hard-liners did not only attack Black voters and officeholders at the polls or political meetings. They preferred ambushing the men and their families in their homes. These paramilitary strikes—like the white men's "visit" with Edward Crosby after he tried to vote—represented a new front in the war on freedom. Extremists' attacks on Black people in their homes, and on their community institutions, conveyed white southerners' rejection of Black people's right to have rights: not just their legal equality, the vote, or their service in elected office, but life, security, family, home, property, education, religion, and community—all the freedoms formerly enslaved people cherished and had achieved.

Reprisal and election violence continued. But political factions, criminal gangs, and aggrieved clans and neighbors converged to form an alliance of white extremists who replicated earlier strategies to purge African Americans from their communities or render them powerless.[49] Examining night riders' motivations, outlining the structure of this violence from a distance, and then moving in closer to first-person accounts of the tight spaces of attacks clarifies what targeted families were up against.

Former slave Isaac Stier described Mississippi's reign of terror to WPA interviewers as a time when "the devil sure was turned loose."[50] Raids like the ones Stier remembered carried a larger societal and cultural message: Black families did not have a right to any of the rights provided in the Constitution, including the newly established ones. Once combatants declared that families were outside the boundaries of the Constitution's protection, these assailants determined that whites could do anything to Black people they wanted.[51] Targeted people's humanity only registered in culprits' minds so they could exploit it.

Although political factors inspired night riding's rise, white people observing election violence were impressed by the coordinated nature of extremists' actions and the effectiveness of their attacks. More white men would replicate these strategies and expand their activities to wage war against Black people who defied white supremacy through non-electoral means, including financial success and personal dignity. But limiting Black men's authority in southern and national governance and stopping Black people from exercising any of the new rights they acquired remained a priority. If belligerents could not subjugate their targets, killing them was the next logical step. Indeed, for some extremists, wanton slaughter of Black people was the primary objective.

While night riding is presumed to have occurred outside the bounds of law, it was a critical part of entrenching the white supremacist reality that marred the transition from slavery to freedom. The historian Laura Edwards writes that, "clutching at the remnants of what they had, these men refused to enter into the new legal order, unwilling to accept Black men as equals in law."[52] Extremists capitalized on white moderates' anxiety and ambivalence about freedom and exploited the gaps between strongholds of federal power and the isolated terrains where most Black southerners lived. Fissures between the letter and fact of the law were also ripe for abuse. Legally, the civil rights legislation and constitutional amendments treated African Americans as equal players, but federal lawmakers enacted policies without acknowledging southern white men's ability to maintain legal authority over Black people through their domination of local legal systems.[53] White attackers used violence, taking advantage of the legal confusion of the time, to construct a postwar order that served their interests. Still dominated by the enslaving elite, the legal system was happy to help extremists complete their mission. Confederates' lawlessness was, as W. E. B. Du Bois reported, initially "spasmodic and episodic." But it was becoming more organized.[54]

In the wave of strikes washing over southern states, the white fraternity of private vigilantism converged with the more organized agents of state coercive force. Civil authorities, one Freedmen's Bureau agent wrote as early as 1865, "are not willing to grant the freedmen the rights to which their freedom entitles them," which regularly required military intervention.[55] U.S. officials observed that the administration of law was "a farce" in Alabama, where the administrators "themselves [were] desperadoes and engaged in the perpetration of the very crime they are sent forth to prohibit or punish."[56] Confederates in Mississippi could "not be entrusted" with any matters pertaining to Black people, another bureau agent reported, until they had demonstrated their acceptance of Black people's legal status as free.[57] Even with civil rights legislation, the amendments, and new state constitutions, the postwar state was in flux, with some government opera-tives working part-time and officers being deputized temporarily, blurring lines between formal state authority and vigilantism. Many law enforcement officers and policymakers embraced the Confederate cause and colluded with extremists, creating mayhem and a culture of impunity for more atroc-ities to occur.

African Americans' bravery in reporting attacks they experienced or observed—to law enforcement, elected officials, Freedmen's Bureau agents—and in testifying before Congress is why we know so much more about the details of night riding than we do about earlier reprisal killings and the assassinations of voters and officials. The report from the congres-sional investigation into night riding, and WPA interviews with former slaves who lived through Reconstruction, reveal how calculated the shadow army's strategies were, as well as their numerous motivations and methods.

Night-riding attacks were often triggered by hard-liners' desire to stop Black people who were advancing too quickly or who threatened white domination. They attacked one man because he voted the Radical ticket in the Upcountry region of South Carolina and because they knew he had a pistol. Samuel and Hannah Tutson were struck because they refused to vacate their Florida homestead, despite being menaced for months. "All the time I was planting my crop they worried me," Hannah said.[58] Black people who refused to stand by while whites burned their churches or schools were terrorized by armed squads, as were people who insisted on receiving their contracted share of a crop. This white rage seems sponta-neous, but it was fueled by and occurred within the context of an ongoing larger, calculated freedom-denying operation.

That campaign is why whites organized raids rather than only attack these Black people directly in interpersonal encounters. Night riders were purposeful about their operations, particularly when and where they struck. Whether the hit was indiscriminate or targeted at a specific family, it required careful assessments about where it was politically and legally safe to conduct raids and for how long. Extremists were less likely to stage raids in any one area for long, which made it harder for African Americans to mount communal defenses or for military officials to send troops. Vigilantes did not bother areas where the planter class tolerated no interference with their labor force. In these areas, the slavocracy's use of reprisal killings had its intended effect of curbing Black people's aspirations for civil and political rights or driving them away from the community. White men also avoided bastions of state control where governments maintained a monopoly on violence, as North Carolina and Texas did by mobilizing state militias in some areas. For a time at least, the shadow army also avoided certain strongholds where Black men were well armed and had shown an impressive ability to defend themselves.[59] Yet even within a limited space to operate, right-wingers committed extensive atrocities.

In hot spots, if white elites and elected officials were not actively participating in the violence themselves, they were rarely willing to take the action needed to stop it. When targeted people protested or asked for relief, most local white power brokers fabricated claims of their helplessness against the will of vengeful extremists or of those who were "afraid" that Black people were conspiring to stage insurrections. Political elites occasionally intervened in individual cases of Black people they knew. Georgia governor Joseph E. Brown, for example, put up a reward to find the assassins who had killed a Black man who had personal ties to his family.[60] But many white elites and officeholders had turned deaf ears and blind eyes to the slaughter, as one does when one agrees with or does not care about the means of the violence and the sought-after end.

Authorities' failure to intervene invited more whites to make their fantasies of racial domination a reality. Genocidal violence, journalist Philip Gourevitch writes in his book on Hutu extremists' campaign to destroy the Tutsi people in Rwanda from April to July 1994, "is an exercise in community building."[61] Similarly, terrorizing Black people was a socializing tool for white southerners. Strikes fostered greater cohesion among the planter class, yeoman farmers, and landless whites who wanted to halt the reconstruction of American freedom. Class had kept white southerners deeply divided before and during the war.[62] Historically, the slavocracy relied on non-slaveholding whites to help monitor and control enslaved people's behavior, but enslavers brooked no interference with the people they held in bondage. Poor and landless whites who composed the slave patrols knew to tread carefully abusing enslaved people they apprehended off farms and labor camps lest they provoke enslavers' wrath. But after the Civil War, many white southerners joined forces across class lines in their commitment to preserve their social and political supremacy and to make Black people understand that their emancipation would not be the same thing as white freedom. Enslavers and overseers struck first with menacing reprisal violence. Middle-class whites and landless whites joined the war to stop Black men from voting and running for office. Extremists' ability to get away with attacks clarified the power that whites enjoyed to seize and possess Black people in every way possible. It spurred more and more whites to muster into service to carve a path of destruction and death through Black people's newly built worlds.

Hard-liners in the fight against Black people's freedom came from all ranks of white southern society. Their army was composed of former Confederate soldiers and men who had dodged formal service, as well as members of paramilitary gangs. These men and their kin were united in their opposition to Black people advancing beyond slavery.[63]

Familiarity with raids was widespread enough that more whites started using the threat of calling in a strike to exert power over their Black neighbors, tenants, or employees. Even white children—learning from their parents to exercise their postwar superiority—got in on the game of terrorizing Black people. Mississippi legislator Robert Gleed reported, "there was not a child of eight years that would not threaten us in the streets, and all over this county, with [these] midnight assassins."[64]

An attack on elders Wallace and Charlotte Fowler of Glenn Springs, South Carolina, shows how more whites were joining the fight against any Black people who dared challenge white people for any reason. Sometime in the spring of 1871, Wallace fussed at a white boy destroying his watermelon patch. Wallace used the prized patch to make his living. He told the white boy to stop and did not think any more of it. Unbeknownst to Wallace, the boy did. He must have told his father, who rallied a pack of men to punish Wallace for his temerity.[65] When the raiders came for him, he was tending to a grandchild while Charlotte was ill with fever. Wallace opened the door to their home and the men opened fire, shooting him in the head and killing him.[66]

Night-riding strikes intensified as more whites across the South saw the effectiveness of paramilitary violence for transforming or maintaining the balance of political power and for robbing and terrorizing Black people as well. This is why there was so much diversity in the motivations behind attacks, why attacks occurred over so wide a terrain, and why some victims were at a loss searching for a precipitating incident before strikes occurred. Although attacks were planned, determining specific reasons behind each of the multitude of them is impossible. But the circumstances of strikes and night riders' statements to their targets clarify the freedom-denying intentions behind their actions.

Some extremists struck to assert a claim to ongoing mastery over Black people's lives and the fruits of their labor. During the 1870–71 growing season, Warren Jones, a Georgia sharecropper, produced thirty bags of cotton. When Warren, who was thirty-nine years old, went to claim his share, the white planter refused to pay. Warren persisted, indicating that to support his family he would have to seek work elsewhere. The white planter threatened to sic the Klan on Warren's family if he tried to leave.[67] Warren might find new employment, but not before he could relocate his family to a secure place. In the end, the planter did not give Warren a chance to leave. In March 1871, he sent Klansmen to Warren's home, where they performed a masked display of their power to come for Warren, hoping to cow him into submission. The men did not physically harm Warren or his family, but they made clear their ability to do so.

Joining white men lashing out at freedom were those who conducted raids with specific political objectives.[68] These night riders, driven by strategic aims, struck out with calculated killings of voters, assassinations of political leaders, and reprisals and insurgent attacks directed at Freedmen's Bureau agents or army personnel at their outposts across the South. Attacks on public figures were intended to terrorize everyone in the community.

White southerners did not escape belligerents' politically motivated hits. Whites who supported the U.S. cause in the Civil War were raided, too. So were poor whites scraping by, who knew that if they interfered, or resisted their own oppression, the plantocracy and their lackeys were ready to treat them the same way they did Black people. And most self-preserving whites were determined to avoid that fate at all costs, even if it meant joining, endorsing, or simply ignoring the extremists' cause.

Vigilantes conducting raids capitalized on gaps of federal oversight and a dwindling military presence, especially in states that had returned to the Union fold. As federal officials and the U.S. citizenry came to believe that the fire-eaters advocating disunion and war had been neutralized, they lowered troop levels in the South; they did not realize that, for many white southerners, ending the military conflict was not the same thing as surrendering the Confederate cause. The retreating armies paved the way for those who rejected emancipation and Reconstruction to recreate as much of the prewar world as possible. When and where the Army withdrew, the night riding and midnight assassinations advanced.

For landless whites, emancipation and citizenship rights for Black people were their worst nightmares come to life. They had to compete with a suddenly huge population of free Black people, and despite believing they were racially superior, some found themselves outworked by people like Warren Jones capitalizing on their entrance into the free labor force. They also encountered people they had known as bondmen and bondwomen who now had surpassed them economically or were well on their way to doing so. Freed children, like Abe and Eliza Lyon's, were receiving educations; freedwomen, like Hannah Tutson, were working from home and running their own laundry businesses. Mary Brown only worked at the gold mine when she needed to. Men, like Abram Colby, were serving in office. Poor and working-class whites were outraged by this scale of Black achievement in such a short time while they were still scraping by. Samuel Simmons, of Beech Springs Township, South Carolina, experienced the fury of working-class whites enraged that his landlord had replaced all the white tenants on his property with Black ones. The landlord could charge them more rent and extract cheaper labor from them than he could whites—but the outraged and suddenly homeless white men did not attack the white planter.[69] They punched out and down, forming a paramilitary gang to conduct raids on the Black tenants.

Strikes gave white men, even those who never had held people in bondage, a chance to personally experience the power of dominating Black people. In the group of seven Ku Klux who attacked Henry Latham's family in York, South Carolina, five of the gang were given the chance to hit him six or seven times each.[70] In October 1870, men in Limestone Springs, South Carolina, took turns whipping Clem Bowden; he later said of the attack, "my wounds had become such a misery to me" that he lost control of his senses. One of the men even took a piece of Clem's left ear as a trophy.[71] The whippings and the cutting might have been a way to reenact slavery or give those aspiring slaveholders the opportunity to act out their sick fantasies.

Although white men were the primary actors, night riding gave middling and poor white women opportunities to dominate Black people, too.[72] In May 1869, Diana Williams, who lived three miles outside of Rogersville, Alabama, got into a dispute with a white woman who accused Williams of stealing some soap she had left at the spring they both used for washing. Diana rejected the accusation, and the woman got offended, saying she "would not let any nigger bitch sass her." Brandishing a gun, the white woman said that if Diana did not shut up, she would shoot her. When Diana refused to be cowed and attended to her business, the woman promised to have her whipped.[73] The white woman knew if she attacked Diana, the Black woman would defend herself. Instead of risking a beating, she solicited her male kin's help putting Diana in her place and preserving the racial balance of power.

Five white men soon visited Diana's home. Terrified, Diana sought sanctuary in her home's loft but two of the invaders followed her up. One of the brutes struck Diana with a gun on the side of her head, "knocking me senseless," she said. When she regained consciousness, they ordered her downstairs. One man put his gun to her breast and told her that if she did not comply, they would kill her. She followed them out four or five hundred yards from the house and listened as they debated what to do to her. The white woman's husband tried to get Diana to follow them even farther out, but, possibly fearing they would rape and kill her for talking back to his wife, she refused. He ordered his subordinates to pick her up and carry her away. "Then," Diana said, "all of them struck me with sticks and took hold of me and carried me out of the gate."

Once her attackers got her outside the gate, they beat Diana over the head and back with sticks until she collapsed. It was only then that they stopped and told her to get back inside her home. The vigilantes' parting shot was to tell Diana, "If you ever say anything about the Ku-Klux being here, we will kill you."[74]

Night riders offered various, often blame-shifting or ridiculous "explanations" for ambushing their targets. The white men's justifications show that while raids began in direct relation to elections, they soon spread to quotidian disputes, like Diana Williams's with the white woman, or Wallace Fowler's over his prized watermelons. Elsewhere, a white man tortured and interrogated a paraplegic man, asking him about his alleged role burning white people's homes and "ravishing" white women.[75] In another case, vigilantes confronted a man because, they claimed, they had overheard him making boastful statements damning white terror. Other people received "visits" because they dared to generate serious profit independent of whites, or to fight and work in the U.S. Army. Whatever reasons terrorists offered— including no reason at all—attacking Black people centered around white rage over freedom and white people's insistence on domination.

Another case in point is the attack on the Nichols family. Night riders surrounded the family's home in Jackson County, Florida, and called on Matt, the patriarch, to go outside. He appeared, as did his son, Matt Jr. The assailants were preparing to carry the father and son away towards the nearby woods when Matt's wife, Maria, charged out of the house, verbally and physically trying to stop the white men from completing their mission. Rather than leave Maria alone or order her back inside, the men forced the entire family about a mile into the woods, where they killed them. The men slit all their throats but seemed to take their rage out on Maria in particular:

her throat was cut from ear to ear, and her hair was torn out by the roots. Though many details surrounding the attack are unknown, the white men's vengeful fury and lack of mercy are clear from reports the Nicholses' horrified neighbors made to authorities.[76]

Gangs of white bandits also frequently targeted prosperous Black people. Attackers might strike shortly after their marks completed major transactions or received substantial payments, as in the case of one Alabama man who, hours earlier, had purchased an expensive wagon and other goods at the local store. Assailants destroyed precious equipment their targets needed to earn a living; in Winston County, Mississippi, whites attacked a teacher and shoemaker, destroying his tools and undermining his livelihood.[77] One man earned extra money playing a fiddle, a fact he said his South Carolina attackers were well aware of when they broke his instrument "all to pieces and smashed it up."[78] Other tactics included driving sharecroppers off the land just before or after the harvest to reap the full crop, as well as basic looting, robbing families and individuals of their earnings and cherished possessions.

As the May 28, 1870 attack on the Ferrell family in Troup County, Georgia, shows, perpetrators were opportunistic but nonetheless strategic. Anderson, the patriarch, was forty-five years old. His wife, Lucy, was thirty-two years old. The Ferrell's barking dog, Flora, woke Lucy from a deep sleep in her bed. Next came an anguished yelp from Flora, and then silence. Sensing danger, Lucy sprang from her bed to look outside and saw white men surrounding her family's home. The men had killed the dog.

Lucy woke Anderson. Talking to the men through the closed door, the terrified couple listened as they demanded entry, claiming they were searching for an escaped prisoner and had a right to enter the family's home to check for him. Anderson recognized the ruse and refused. But Lucy, worrying this might make things worse, signaled to her husband to open the door. Within seconds, the group of white men burst in and held the couple and their children captive.

The family stood aside as the gang rummaged through their belongings, stealing their possessions. As the men talked and moved about, Anderson and Lucy realized they knew these men. Anderson called one attacker by name, which escalated an already intense situation. When Anderson refused to surrender a knife the men discovered on him and to open a locked trunk storing precious belongings, one raider leveled his gun and fired at him, grazing him in the head. Anderson fled. The men gave chase, but finally gave up and departed.[79]

Night riders' decisions to invade occupied homes like Anderson and Lucy Ferrell's—rather than burgle them while the families were absent—reveal that thievery was only a secondary priority. First and foremost, white men marked Black people, not their property. Whites staging raids were seeking violent confrontations in which they hoped to assert their dominance.[80]

Extremists' attacks were intended to overwhelm targets with paramilitary force so they could upend the worlds in which targets like the Ferrells lived, and to inflict extreme pain. To do this, perpetrators needed to seize Black people violently, to take complete possession over them, and to grant them few, if any, means of escape. Such overpowering attacks enabled vigilantes to both violate their targets' physical bodies and breach the lives these African Americans built after slavery.[81]

Men like those targeting the Ferrells were among the vigilantes and paramilitary groups who chose to strike under the cloak of darkness. Beyond concealing culprits' identity, nocturnal raids were more likely to catch victims off guard. The practice allowed extremists to attack their targets at their most vulnerable—in their homes, likely asleep and defenseless—and hold families hostage there. Along with the polling place, the Black family home was a specific front of the white war on freedom.[82] After all, as Laura Edwards has argued, Black homes provided the "legal basis for African Americans' independence."[83] Violating families there was an act of aggression intended to undermine their sovereignty and disturb social bonds, to, as one anthropologist who studies attacks on families during violent conflict put it, "reorganize life through death."[84]

Numerous observers likened extremists' behavior toward Black people to that of wartime combatants. William Coleman described death squads he saw invading his community near Louisville, Mississippi, as coming "riding up in great droves like they were going to the army to fight."[85] "They came charging up like a party of cavalry," Caroline Benson said of white Georgians who attacked her family in the middle of the night.[86] White men carried guns and other lethal weapons, as well as the accoutrements of slave punishments, such as shackles, whips, and clubs. Enterprising raiders attacking Black people even turned their victims' own farm tools and household items into weapons against them.

A successful siege required planning, as revealed in perpetrators' careful surveillance of their marks. Unbeknownst to families, raiders stalked people they targeted. Just before they struck, some lay in wait, surrounding homes, standing in the darkness while targets finished their daily activities and went to bed thinking they were secure.

In the tight space of a night-riding strike, most families or individuals had no place to run. If the targets' homes were large enough, their armed attackers crowded inside.[87] If they weren't, the men forced targets outside into their yards, where they had more room to whip, rape, maim, and beat, like Diana Williams's attackers. If the invaders worried about interference, either from family members or neighbors, then they dragged or forcibly marched their captives into the wooded areas adjacent to their homes like they did the Nichols family.

The attack on Essic and Ann Harris's family shows the often precise nature of strikes. Theirs started on a normal winter day in Chatham County, North Carolina, just outside a hamlet called Beven. Essic worked a full day on the railroad, "cutting new ground" before going home to Ann, four of their six children, and his nephew, who was helping him work on the farm. The family tended to daily chores, enjoyed dinner, and went to bed.

Shortly after that, as though the Harrises were being watched, a knock on the door woke Ann. "There's somebody at the door," she said, shaking Essic awake. As he jumped up, both of their doors burst open. Armed white men barged inside the eighteen-by-twenty-foot home and demanded Essic's gun and gunpowder. Being outnumbered and outgunned, and not wanting to endanger his family, Essic handed over his weapons. Satisfied, the attackers left.[88]

Whether it was for hunting or personal protection, being armed was a newly acquired right for Black people like Essic. In the war against Reconstruction—intended to overturn the freedoms the Civil War had unlocked—Black men's right to bear arms was not one that belligerent white men were going to respect.[89] They often surveilled Black men's purchases of weapons and ammunition. Vigilantes tore through communities disarming families like the Harrises. Extremists knew that, if given the opportunity to defend themselves and protect their interests, Black people would fight back. To achieve their goals, night riders needed to deny their targets the means to do so by denying their access to guns at the point of sale or seizing them after they were acquired. With Essic disarmed, it was easier to strike him again, which is what the white men later did.

Essic had worked another hard day and returned home to Ann and the children. After the day was done, the couple was sitting up. Ann was tending to homemaking duties, and Essic was sitting by the fire. When she saw Essic nodding off, Ann encouraged him to go to bed, and she joined him shortly thereafter.

The family's dog woke Ann, who again woke Essic. He peeked out the window and discovered his yard full of armed white men. Essic extinguished the fire and grabbed the new gun he had acquired, possibly unbeknownst to the men.

Just then, the white men broke through one of the windows and started firing inside. Essic later recalled, "I don't reckon there was five minutes' time when they were not shooting," during a strike that lasted more than an hour.[90]

Essic clambered to safety, away from the windows and into a corner, but he had been struck several times by flying debris. Ann got between the bed ticking and the mat of the couple's bed. The children scrambled under the bed and "got in a pile, right on top of one another, like a parcel of pigs," Essic recounted. All of them remained quiet, except the family's newborn, who, according to Essic, "cried a while, and then it didn't cry at all. The others did not make any fuss at all," while shots "were flying all over where they were."[91]

As some men were firing and proclaiming their victory, thinking they had killed Essic, others were trying to enter the house. Essic had propped several bushels of corn behind the door, so when the terrorists charged it, it refused to go all the way down. This antagonized his attackers but delayed their entry.

Conveying the pandemonium of the raid, Essic explained, "I never had time to see what my family were doing . . . I thought they were all dead." This fear inspired Essic to act. "I felt it to be life and death anyhow," Essic said. "I thought my wife and children were all dead. I did not expect anything else" while "[gun]shot just rained [down] like rain."[92]

Essic was wounded in several places, including his arm, which he could hardly use. He aimed his gun and fired at one of the invaders, striking him in the chest. Capitalizing on his attackers' stunned silence, Essic ordered his nephew to get his five-shooter, trying to scare the men away. They heard his command and debated setting his house ablaze to force the family outside.

"They had been there so long my fear was over," Essic later said. "I had no fear at all by that time—not a bit." Undaunted, and believing he had nothing to lose but his life, Essic reloaded his gun with what he said was "an uncommon load . . . a dangerous load" and fired again, an act that drove the gang away.[93] The white men had planned two raids, but they had underestimated Essic's resourcefulness and composure.

The element of surprise gave home invaders the advantage. Most captives who reported attacks had no indication that extremists were coming for them. Augustus Blair said the attack on his family in Limestone County, Alabama, was unexpected. "I had no dream of being pestered by anybody," he said. "I stood in such a way I didn't think anybody had anything against me. They had been at my house once before, but didn't interfere with me, and I had been resting safe" since moving there in 1867.[94] "I never had a falling out with a white man in my life," Essic Harris told investigators after he reported having his home shot up with his family in it.[95]

In the minds of Black southerners who were attacked, they were conducting the daily business of life in the postwar period and working toward liberation. Nothing prepared them for what happened. With deep histories in their communities and extensive social networks, most victims saw themselves as upstanding citizens and even esteemed community members. As long as they did their work, minded their business, and tended to their families, Black people told themselves, everything would be fine. Augustus Blair said that although he had seen whites run his Black neighbors away, "I didn't think anybody would ever interfere with me."[96] For a time, this type of rationalizing allowed people like Augustus to believe they would not become victims. Augustus's and Essic's assessments of their standing in their communities were not incorrect so much as they were out of step with the emerging war on Black people's right to be free, equal, and secure. Their only offense was maximizing their freedom. But as the attacks continued, people living in night-riding zones felt an incredible sense of insecurity as they realized everyone was vulnerable.

Most raiders adopted a stealth approach. The Ferrells were one of many families who woke up to white men surrounding their homes; some families weren't aroused from slumber until the men had barged through their doors. John and Mary Thommason discovered they were under attack when bullets pierced the walls of the room where they slept in their York County, South Carolina, home.[97] A veteran living on his farm in New Market, Alabama, was only alerted to white men's presence when he heard the rallying whistles from a distance. Soon they surrounded his home, and there was an armed man at every window ordering him to go out or they would shoot inside. He went outside; when he did, one of the gang seized him and walked him to the road. The men grabbed hickory sticks and branches and whaled on him. The Black man's supposed transgression was being among a band who had performed music for a white couple. "The laws of the country didn't allow Black and white to mix together [socially]," the men told him. The pack ordered the Alabaman to run and shot at him as he fled.[98]

In waging their attacks, home invaders used both sound and its absence to their advantage. Unleashing the rebel yell evoked the fighting of the war, revealing how these white men saw themselves and expected to be seen by their targets. One man of Yorkville, South Carolina, was awakened by what he said was "a monstrous noise outside the house" made by white men who were knocking and hollering.[99] In other cases, though, attackers preferred silence, as with the killing of the Ferrells' pet Flora, to stop them from alerting their owners to impending dangers. To muffle the sound of their arrival and get closer to their prey undetected, some men tied their horses up hundreds of yards away and approached people's homes on foot. This was how a gang of fifteen got to one family in Pickens County, Alabama, in May 1870. "The whole host of them run against the door and just mashed the door, and throwed it across the house, and then commenced shooting at me," the patriarch said. They fired at him nine times.[100]

Silent attackers got the jump on Patrick and Missouri Tanner's family, too. On a late June night in 1871, Missouri and her daughter, Adriana, were sitting up chatting in their home, just outside of Spartanburg, South Carolina. All the other family members, including the patriarch, Patrick, and Adriana's husband, William Moss, had gone to bed. When someone knocked on the door, Adriana, without getting up, invited them to come inside, thinking it was kin or one of their neighbors. It was only when the door burst open that she discovered "they were not the right kind of folks; they were Ku-Klux." The men wore masks with "horns on their heads and tassels on."[101] By the time families like the Tanners understood what was happening, there was no way to escape.

Stealth approaches enabled vigilantes to grab William Henderson, who was taken from his home, bound, and nearly drowned in a Colbert County, Alabama, creek near the Tennessee River. Disentangling himself from the rope constraining him, hiding beneath the surface until the men left, and swimming 900 yards covertly to shore is what saved William's life. With his body wracked by cramps, William crawled out of the river.[102] Attacks like this left little doubt some whites intended to kill Black people, and often in ways that intensified the victims' suffering.

In another example of how purposeful raiders were, many attempted to cloak their identities. Some adopted the use of tar-blackened faces. Others wore masks, like the vigilantes attacking the Tanners did. One Jackson County, Georgia, witness described his attackers as white men dressed in black with "oil cloths, breeches, coats, caps, and veils over their faces."[103] Whatever night riders' agendas, or however they looked or sounded when they arrived, what resonated most with their targets was what the men did. They counted upon their impressive numbers to discourage resistance. Most families knew there were too many men for them to take out without risking greater injury, a calculation invaders made when planning raids.

Even when vigilantes arrived, some targets reported not immediately knowing their intentions, revealing another layer of the psychological terror families felt. One man, targeted in Huntsville, Alabama, in November 1868, said that when vigilantes first approached, he "didn't know [they were] going to murder" him. The men chased him into a crater and threw boulders down on him. He grabbed one of his attackers, dragging the armed white man into the hole. The bloodied man seized his assailant's gun and held the man at bay until Army personnel came and the invaders dispersed—but not before taking back the gun, depriving the victim of the ability to protect himself if the men came again.[104]

Assailants strove to dominate their prisoners, taking away their choices and limiting their options of survival.[105] Trapping families in their homes increased the chances victims would be physically and psychologically wounded multiple times. The Harris family's attackers had to shoot their way in during the second raid because they could not gain entry, but force was not always required. Once attackers gained access, they subjected their prey to games of horror. Invaders insisted on compliance with every single one of their commands. But victims' acquiescence rarely satisfied the gangs. This was made clear by invaders' endless, twisted demands—that targets confess their sins, or show their captors proper respect and appreciation for any relief given, as though vigilantes needed to create willing victims. When they came for him at his home near the Tyger River in South Carolina, a gang of fifteen men tried to force Elias Thomson to pray to God for mercy or absolution. Elias refused: he was, as he said, "not much for prayer." Elias could have also declined on the grounds that the physical act of praying—getting down on his knees, bowing his head—would have taken his attention off the men and rendered his wife, Maydeen, their children, and him even more powerless to protect themselves.[106] Elias's ability to retain his composure probably saved this family.

Another strategy for enacting racial hierarchy was vigilante bands' common use of sexual and gendered violence.[107] Today, rape as a weapon, and not a by-product, of war, is established fact. But the fact and legal recognition of rape as a war crime in the U.S. has an older history. The Lieber Code of 1863, which was written during the Civil War and codified how U.S. Army soldiers should conduct themselves, had three articles pertaining to rape. The rape of enslaved girls and women was a common feature of slavery because U.S. laws failed to recognize rape as a crime against Black girls and women. The Lieber Code acknowledged Black girls and women as victims of rape for the first time.[108] The U.S.'s explicit prohibition of soldiers from committing sex crimes and the military courts' prosecution of more than four hundred cases indicates how widespread martial rape was during the Civil War.[109] Racism-based sexual violence before and during the Civil War gives context for understanding extremists' use of it in their war on freedom.

In April 1871, a pack of white men invaded Frances Gilmore's home in the Locksville district of Chatham County, North Carolina. In a savage attack, they whipped Frances, set fire to her pubic hair, and cut her genitals. It took Frances three weeks to recover enough to travel to report the assault to a U.S. commissioner.[110] Essic Harris also reported that night riders had raped numerous women and girls in his neighborhood. Harriet Hernandez said extremists running wild in Cherokee County, South Carolina, "did [Black women] scandalous."[111] Vigilantes' games were such that one man said hearing stories of families held hostage in Hancock County, Georgia, was common. The man also detailed the strike on his family, when he said white men "played the mischief there," including "molesting" his wife and "badly treat[ing]" his daughter.[112]

White men who fought this war through girls' and women's bodies shredded the social tissue of Black communities, which was their intent. Rape during raids could break the bodies and spirits of its immediate victims. It also broadcast the sexual violability of Black women and girls in the white war on Black freedom, which could undermine family and communal unity.[113] Any children born of these rapes could wreak further havoc in the lives of victims and their people. One philosopher who examined patterns of martial rape in the 1992–95 Bosnia-Herzegovina conflict argues that whether rape as a weapon of war occurs in the context of a formally declared war or not, it can serve as a "bonding agent" among soldiers during conflict.[114] Extremists celebrated sexually dominating their targets—Black girls and women and their kin.

Henry Hamlin's account of a strike on a group of railroad workers in Trinity, Alabama, further illustrates vigilantes' freakish perversions. The workers finished their shifts and retired to their worksite cots and beds at the day's end. Ku Klux snatched the Black men and carried them to where the attackers had stashed their horses, tied them together—harking back to the coffles of slave trading and transporting—and marched them across the railroad. The gang took them to one of their other targets' homes, but Henry escaped through the window and the white men followed. They caught him wearing only his underwear and tied him to the group. Others took three hundred dollars of the family's money from the man's petrified wife.

The vigilantes led the coffle away. Then, Henry said, "they just rode over us, galloped over us, and made us run, and kept riding over us [with their horses]." The attackers interrogated Henry and the others about alleged involvement in the Union League; Henry refused to answer. As the attack continued, "we would fall down," Henry said, "and they would ride plum over us."[115] They hollered, "Get up, God damn you!" and threatened to "blow your God damn brains out!" if the prisoners did not obey.

The men kept driving their captives on by foot. As they approached the graveyard, and Henry and the others realized their attackers were going to kill them, they cried out in protest. "O Lord, I am going to die," Henry thought, "I can't do no more; I am overpowered; I have to go."[116] Desperate to escape, Henry fled and survived.

Vigilantes were capable of strikes at any time of year, a demonstration of the sheer size of the army amassed against Reconstruction and of its soldiers' commitment to the cause. Wiley Hargrove, of Pickens County, Alabama, said that four men came on one of the coldest nights of November 1870; and "they took me out and whipped me, and my wife, too."[117] Year-round night riding suggests how much traction the war on freedom gained with so many white southerners in such a short period of time. Although the members of the planter class who refused to release the people they held in bondage (and attacked those who fled) were early to the front lines, they were joined by defeated veterans and landless whites. These white reactionaries didn't come for African American families "by ones," as Sterling Brown's 1932 poem "Old Lem" explained, nor did they "come by twos" either. They came instead "by tens." And sometimes by hundreds. Confederates were not engaging in spontaneous attacks. They were purposeful and considered.

———————

Survivors like Ann and Essic Harris and Henry Hamlin shared their stories with friends, relatives, patrons, and associates. Even when victims did not speak out, neighbors who witnessed assaults on families did, using the same antebellum social networks that had enabled Black people to coordinate the movements of freedom seekers, spread news of rebellion or the war, and disseminate information about loved ones.[118] Witnesses to these stories of attacks told other people when they encountered them in social spaces like church, and they wrote letters and relayed information when they traveled to conduct business or visit kin. Once stories of night riding entered the local communication network, news spread quickly and far, beyond the epicenters of attacks to the hinterlands of neighboring communities. This might have been why Essic was armed, and why he acquired new weapons after the first strike.

People encountering these storytelling chains sometimes dismissed accounts of white men invading Black people's homes, especially if they lived in remote places or if the wave of strikes had just reached (or not yet landed in) their communities.[119] For many, it seemed unthinkable, especially if African Americans were not instigating violence—and no reliable news reports said otherwise. Confederates had initiated surrender to end the war, after all. They might have been frustrated with the consequences of Reconstruction, Black folks reasoned, but if they were truly upset, they could take it to the president and lawmakers. Encounters with slaveholders and overseers during slavery would have familiarized them with the one-on-one exchanges with aggrieved white folks, as would disputes involving freed people and their white employers and neighbors. But as night riding spread from one enclave to the next—and grew from efforts to suppress Black voters into a campaign to dominate Black people in all areas of life—the communication shifted from sharing the news to conveying the undisputed danger.

Even as the tenor of reports changed, some people misinterpreted the situation and assumed they were in no danger.[120] Once people accepted the veracity of the stories they heard, they shifted to rationalizing attacks. They persuaded themselves *they* would not become victims, assuring themselves night riders only hit people who deserved it. By the time people reasoned they needed to take precautions, it was too late.

Once more than one strike occurred or when victims started to include people with high standing or those whose activities should not have offended whites, fear circulated and intensified. Residents worried constantly about being attacked. A Georgian man fled his home at night after a white band in Pike County asked about him and his whereabouts. One night, he unknowingly passed his pursuers on the road as he was returning home from preaching. By the time the men returned for the Georgian two days later, he had fled his community for Griffin.[121] Unhappy that they could not get their target, the terrorists shifted their attention to another man, whom they killed. No family was safe when night riders came to town.

As Black southerners understood that what they had initially believed to be isolated, sporadic attacks were actually part of a region-wide war against them, they were filled with dread.[122] With the devil turned loose, in Isaac Stier's words, no Black people were secure in any of the expanding fronts of the war on their freedom. And the culprits might be anyone. People in night-riding zones were consumed by a fearsome question: would they survive if death tried to come for them?

Chapter 3

I Didn't Know How Soon They Might Come to Send Me Up

Night-riding strikes are often envisioned as attacks on individuals, mostly men: voters like Edward Crosby, politicians running for or serving in office, or landholders like Samuel Tutson. But to pierce freedom's heart, extremists needed to do more than deny men like Edward the vote and Samuel his land; they needed to attack the institutions at the very center of freedom—the home and family—splintering the sense of sanctuary a home provided from the harsh world. More significantly, this also meant vigilantes were more likely to catch their targets with their kin.

Being attacked and held hostage as an individual was disturbing enough. Having one's loved ones held captive, too, was harrowing. The more people vigilantes imprisoned in their games of horror, the greater the chaos, the more unpredictable the variables, the greater the possibility for harm, and the greater the likelihood targeted people would be killed. They needed to strategize to avoid attacks and survive them if they couldn't. Perhaps some people, knowing they might be targeted, romanticized standing their ground—acquiring weapons and envisioning themselves as heroes or heroines capable of violently and easily dispensing with their attackers. If so, those fantasies likely dissipated when raids actually began and the white men's deadly intentions were made clear.

The way some newspapers reported "visits" and the ways some historians have written about them may leave the false impression that they were preventable. But that's only because we haven't respected survivors' testimonies of how inconceivable and torturous raids were. For people looking at attacks with what one scholar calls "arrogant eyes"—ones that organize the world and everything in it with reference to their own judgments about their power—driving off attackers, fleeing, or avoiding a raid altogether seems easy.[1] This is unfortunate; people who themselves have never considered the structure of violent coercion often mistakenly believe African Americans were either completely passive during strikes or possessed superhero strength to dispose of extremists. The prevalence of false assumptions is evident in popular appraisals of white paramilitary assaults—the idea that if Black people hadn't done anything to provoke white people, they would not have had to worry about attacks, or the idea that a gun was the best defense against white violence. The implied verdict is that if Black people hadn't been so arrogant, had behaved, and had fought hard enough, they could have protected themselves from this violence. These misconceptions also feed an insistence on only centering armed Black men who fought off their attackers, celebrating them as self-determining agents in any histories of white extremist violence. The implicit argument is that armed self-defense is the only response to white violence worthy of understanding. Such actions were courageous, to be sure, but they were probably not the most common reaction to white aggression. Meanwhile, victim-blaming judgments and arrogant presumptions of what it was like for Black families to be held hostage by white men during Reconstruction downplay how extremely dangerous these raids were and dismiss what *survivors* themselves thought it took to live.

Targeted people's testimonies illuminate the complex flesh-and-blood realities of surviving the war on freedom. The accounts survivors actually gave of strikes—from their descriptions of strikes' inconceivability to their endeavors to cheat death during them—challenge popular misconceptions about how much resistance was possible. Victims' descriptions of extreme fear, panic, compliance, appeasing their attackers, of sleeping outside to avoid being captured, and of armed self-defense: these provide a counter-narrative to stories told about Reconstruction.

––––––––

Samuel and Hannah Tutson's homestead was seven miles outside of Waldo, Florida. They worked the land, and Hannah also earned money as a washer-woman, allowing them to maintain their home and 160 acres. Furious at their achievements, their white neighbors tried to force them to vacate their homestead and return to the forced labor camp, but the couple refused to leave. They had passed through bondage, secured their freedom, and acquired the farm fair and square; they were not about to let others' resentment stand in their way. Hannah couldn't imagine anything worse than slavery. But that was before night riders came for her family.

When the white men with blackened faces crashed through the Tutsons' cabin door in May 1871, the couple was not alone. Samuel was fifty-three or fifty-four. Hannah was forty-two or forty-three. With them were the family's three youngest children: a daughter who was about ten years old; S. L., the five-year-old son sleeping in bed; and the ten-month-old baby girl, Mary, cradled in Hannah's arms.[2] But neither Hannah and Samuel nor the children expected to be attacked and they were not prepared to defend themselves.

Night riders' very arrival communicated in the starkest of terms Black families' vulnerability to being seized, emotionally degraded, and physically harmed. Or killed. The amygdala, the brain's threat detector, activates targeted people's stress response. The prefrontal cortex or frontal lobe of the brain acts as a kind of "watchtower," collecting information about what is happening and calculating a response that can turn on a dime. The amyg-dala and the prefrontal cortex function in synthesis to preserve life.[3]

Of course, even the body's hard-wired defense system could not make it easy to preserve life during one of these strikes. They were inconceivable, chaotic incidents in a war waged on unsuspecting civilians. Night riders planned raids to create chaotic circumstances in which they could completely dominate or execute captives. Home invaders prioritized suppressing and offsetting their captives' resistance and minimizing their own risk of injury or death. They did this by limiting means of escape, communicating their deadly intentions, and exploiting their targets' desire to live. Members of the shadow army did not hesitate to kill their captives, however, especially those who resisted; Freedmen's Bureau reports from 1865 to 1868 indicate dozens of fatalities across different southern locales each year, and the consensus among historians is that these statistics represent a mere fraction of the total number of victims.[4]

The physical and mental powers needed to evade or survive home invasions were labyrinthine. The circumstances of blitz attacks, and the responses to them, were as diverse as the individual perpetrators and victims. Captives may have experienced the air contracting as the worlds they inhabited flattened; they found themselves suspended in the in-between space of a strike, where time and place ceased to exist, and they were consciously aware of the nearness and possibility of death.[5] Each person inside homes under attack faced literally existential questions of how to survive. Individuals understood that any decision could be a matter of life or death for them—or their loved ones. Examining victims' descriptions of attacks frame by frame explodes presumptions about the uniformity of responses and what it took to survive being held hostage by gangs of armed white men.

Individuals in the grip of a strike would experience the classic fight-or-flight stress response. Night riders intuitively anticipated these reactions and hindered both options. Surviving a strike or part of a strike then required the victims to modify their reactions to their attackers' behavior from one moment to the next. When the amygdala releases stress hormones, shifting the body into alert mode, the rush of cortisol and adrenaline sometimes fuels the strength and courage an individual needs to fight or flee; in other cases, the hormonal response undermines the ability to think and act rationally. If this causes the victim to behave bizarrely or unpredictably, it can make them even more vulnerable to harm.[6]

The most effective strikes were ones in which night riders completely overwhelmed their targets by seizing them and depriving them of any means of escape. The very real possibility of being killed in a raid was clear, as the attack on a twenty-five-year-old man named Jasper Carter shows. In May 1871, a posse abducted Jasper from his home in Haralson County, Georgia, and took him on a murderous spree. He wanted to escape but could not, because, he said, "I was overpowered and had no chance to get away."[7] Being surrounded by twenty-six men, Jasper understood there was little chance he could escape without being shot down. And Jasper wanted to live. So along he went with the men as they tortured and killed members of Jasper's community. Compliance with white men's orders was a common split-second self-preservation strategy. It was how Jasper and so many others survived.

Compliance might preserve life, but it did not always guarantee protection from injury. Night riders also used implied and stated threats of killing their targets to coerce them into submission so they could assault and whip them. When a gang struck William Hampton Mitchell's place in the spring of 1871, they found three generations of his family living in their home in the Lawrenceville district of Gwinnett County, Georgia. The eleven men hitched their horses a hundred yards away from the house and walked up, yelling, "Open the door!" Hamp, as the forty-seven-year-old man was called, moved to comply, but before he could, they pushed the door down, barging into his home.

The night riders asked if Hamp had a gun; he admitted he did and that it was loaded. As his family was outnumbered, Hamp knew he could not start firing without risking his people's lives or his own. The Mitchells all remained calm. They did not want to do anything to antagonize the men. The family likely communicated with their eyes while monitoring all the white men and following their orders. The raiders used the family's compliance to their advantage. They disarmed Hamp, and several men took his son-in-law outside and whipped him. Other men in the gang pistol-whipped Hamp's wife, Susan, bashing her on the head. Another stepped up, thrashing Hamp with a hickory branch. Then another called his father-in-law outside and whipped him in different stages.[8]

Hamp and his people initially did not believe the men would physically hurt them, based on their compliance with every request in the early part of the raid. "But they did it, though," he later said with disgust. While some of the men were whipping other members of the family, two men stood by the door and "kept punching me with a pistol about on the forehead and head," Hamp said, "till they made the blood come."[9] Finally the men left, but not before breaking Hamp's gun and ordering the family to stay inside for three hours on threat of putting forty bullets in them.[10] The Mitchells complied, which spared their lives.[11]

The Tutsons found themselves similarly trapped and overpowered, stunned by the men's entry into their home. Neither Hannah nor Samuel had a place to hide or time to think. Their attackers moved on both adults so fast that the couple could not communicate and strategize, much less fight off the men inside their small home. Confronted with the impossible, the Tutsons would have felt time stopping. Each individual in the family became hyper-focused, evaluating what was unfolding before their eyes and considering the actions they needed to take to live in that moment, the next moment, and the one after that.

While Samuel and Hannah were coming to terms with the reality that there was little chance to get away without endangering each other or their children, the attackers easily seized both adults. They grabbed Samuel, marched him outside, stripped him, and tied him to a tree before taking turns whipping, pistol-whipping, choking, and stomping on him. Two men went for Hannah, snatching Mary from her clutching arms and throwing the child across the room. With the child stunned into silence or screaming in pain, the duo choked Hannah into submission before marching her outside a quarter mile from her home, stripping her, and tying her to a pine tree.[12] It was Hannah's worst nightmares realized.

When people lacked prior knowledge about attacks, or believed they had done nothing to provoke a raid, they were unaware death might be coming for them and unready to defend themselves. The family of Mr. and Mrs. Jerry Garrison of Cherokee County, Georgia, in October 1868, also had no warning. "We did not know we had an enemy in the world," Leanna Garrison said. "We had very nice neighbors there." Her family assumed they were in good standing within their community.[13] No one in the family was primed to deal with the pandemonium that unfolded.

The couple's adult son, Samuel, had come to visit Leanna, who had been ill. The family—which included Jerry, Leanna, who was about "fifty odd years" old, Samuel, who was twenty-seven years old, a daughter, and two other sons—had just finished dinner and were catching up when the shots tore through the walls of their home. Samuel was struck in the shoulder and his brother in the hip. Jerry stepped outside to talk the gang down, but they shot and killed him before he could.[14] All the rest of the family could do was try to escape the hail of bullets.

In other cases, white men harassed families for days or weeks before striking them. This is what happened to the Tutsons, and to Doc Rountree, the homesteader who lived with his wife, Ellen, and ten children in Live Oak, Suwannee County, Florida.[15] A white landholder wanted Doc, who was thirty-seven years old, to abandon his homestead and to seek work and shelter elsewhere. He was denying the Rountrees their right to purchase land, to work their own land and no one else's, and to reap the rewards of their labor. Doc and Ellen had already refused the white man's insistence they apprentice their children to him. Doc stood fast even in the face of repeated harassment, as was his right as a free man, a father with parental rights, and a landowner.

Sometime in fall 1868, Doc, Ellen, and the children were in their home at around nine or ten at night when a small gang stormed inside. There were too many white men for Doc and Ellen to fight off. They were singularly focused on avoiding death and knew resisting would get them killed. Doc said their attackers "flung" the family out into their yard, where they whipped Doc, Ellen, three of their sons, and one of the daughters.[16] As the gang assaulted the family, they asked Doc, "Didn't you know that we don't allow damned niggers to live on land of their own?" Man to man and in a fair fight, Doc could perhaps have fended this landholder off. Bringing a raiding party and overpowering Doc *with* Ellen and the children present gave the white man the unfair advantage.

The mayhem typical of strikes gave some individuals the chance to escape. After watching in horror as the men dragged off Samuel and Hannah Tutson, their ten-year-old daughter gathered her little brother and the baby and fled to a nearby field. The Tutson girl took refuge near a log heap and hid there, plying the baby with gooseberries to prevent her from crying, which might have led the men to them.[17]

Some targets had the luxury of enough time and quick thinking to conceal themselves inside their homes. Targets hid to avoid being seized or killed. They also hoped that in their absence night riders would not harm their kin. This wasn't an illogical calculation. It worked for many families—but not all.

When a gang came to Columbus Jeter's home in Douglas County, Georgia, in April 1871, to punish him and his wife, Aury, for running a school, Columbus had an employee who was boarding with them answer the door. This gave Columbus time to climb up the chimney, wearing only his shirt and underwear. Columbus hid there while the fiends interrogated his kin about his whereabouts. The white men probably had the family under surveillance and knew Columbus was home, which is why they refused to leave without him and assaulted his people. The Jeters would not reveal Columbus's location.[18]

For many captives, attacks themselves were unbelievable, which made it harder to cope with the fact that they were happening, much less how to live through them. Some became disoriented by the unreality of it all. The disorder of strikes caused some targets to miscalculate the situation, exposing themselves or their loved ones to even greater harm. These were likely the forces at play when night riders attacked Henry Reed's family, in Marianna, Florida, in October 1869. "Nobody had anything against me," Henry, who was thirty-five years old at the time of the "visit," said, explaining the unexpected nature of the raid and his family's inability to strategize. "There was nothing against me on account of my behavior or character," Henry insisted. The men tried to lure him outside with an obvious ruse but even amid the shock, Henry and his wife remained calm.[19]

Henry's teenage son panicked. Thinking the only way he could live was if he escaped, the boy jumped from one of their home's windows. The white men shot at him, which left both Henry and his wife thinking their much-loved boy was dead. The raiders ordered Henry to go with them, and when Henry hesitated one of the men said, "[C]ome out of that house, God damn you . . . [or] I will get [more men to] tear your house down, and blow your God damned brains out!" Henry felt powerless. "I did not know what to do," he recalled.

Mrs. Reed was hysterical, crying, "[M]y son is dead, and they want to kill my husband." Believing this was true and that he might be next, Henry escaped by climbing out another window and seeking shelter with his former employer; there he met up with his son, alive, but wounded by a bullet that had grazed his ear. When Henry returned home, he found Mrs. Reed alive but distraught, he said, walking "about the house moaning for her son that she thought they had killed."[20]

It was not just the unpredictable essence of the strikes that made them frightening affairs; white men's deadly intentions and need to assert a godlike authority over their targets heightened the alarm already-terrified people felt. Strikes' deadly nature forced the families the white men seized to desperately act out a range of survival responses that is wider than usually considered. Galloping fear stopped some individuals from making rash decisions. But it paralyzed some targets, rendering them incapable of defending themselves or even fleeing.[21] Maria Carter's husband, Jasper, became mute when a gang came for him, suggesting fear paralyzed his vocal cords.[22] As Henry Reed's son's escape out the window shows, people panicked, misreading the situation and acting in manners that increased their vulnerability.[23]

Being restrained or injured during any part of a raid narrowed captives' range of responses. Vigilantes struck the Walton County, Georgia, home of Charles and Caroline Smith twice in 1871. Charles and Caroline were ages thirty-nine and thirty-five, respectively. In the March raid, the invaders hit, and Charles fled the scene, followed by a round of gunfire. The October gang struck so fast and in such great numbers the family could not fight or flee even if they wanted to. A terrified Caroline heard them in the yard and woke Charles. "I had not got awake good then when I heard her hollering, 'Ku-Klux! Ku-Klux!'" Charles said. Charles ran to the door to see what was happening and before he could do anything, he said, "they gathered me up."

The men, a posse of between twenty-five and thirty, took Charles out into the yard naked from the waist down, stripped his shirt off him, and beat him with rocks, hickory sticks, and pistols. "Eight men struck me eight licks apiece . . . on my bare back," he said. By the time they finished, Charles was in crippling pain; they ordered him back inside his home, and he obeyed to avoid being killed.[24]

Body injuries like Charles's demanded attention and could consume all a victim's physical and mental energy.[25] Resisting an assault while the body is overcome by pain and focused on avoiding further injury or death is virtually impossible: fighting back requires, as one scholar writes, "a wider vision of the world." People in agony are rendered "incapable of such a view" because they are hobbled by and trapped inside their bodies' pain.[26] Targeted people suffering any of these debilitating injuries during raids had a difficult time using their bodies to run or fight back. It was only when their pain subsided, and they regained their ability to see the world beyond it, that they could act.

While Charles was trapped in his pain, there was nothing he could do to protect Caroline and their five children. The men ordered Caroline outside. She complied to avoid being killed. The men made her kneel on the ground. "They stripped her stark naked," Charles later said. "They whipped her and raised welts and knots." From her body's injuries, Charles estimated Caroline was struck twelve times with the whip and in the beating, suffered about fifty blows. "She was hurt pretty bad," he said.[27]

The brutes made Charles's younger sister, Sarah Ann, get down on the road, like they did Caroline. They "stripped her stark naked as she came into the world," Charles said.[28] Then the night riders struck Sarah Ann about forty times with hickory sticks and beat her with their pistols, fists, and the stag handle of a whip.[29]

Caroline's mother remained in bed, terrified the vigilantes would go in on her, too. This did not stop her from crying out to her family and perhaps begging the men to stop hurting them. One of the fiends stormed in to where Caroline's mother was lying and told her to "shut up her mouth and put her head under the cover, or they would give her a little."[30] She complied, to spare her life. During assaults like this, family members were incapable of protecting themselves or their loved ones, unless they submitted, and sometimes even when they did.

Targeted people's sense of their own personal survival or the collective survival of their kin informed the decisions they made during strikes. This, plus the attacking white men's caprice, is why captives' responses were so diverse. The Smiths wanted to protect each other, but as Charles's inescapable pain shows, that was not always possible. Some reacted in measured, calculated ways like Caroline's mother did. Some responses preserved life, and others increased the possibility of injury or death. Attacks forced family members to make a range of impossible decisions in often short periods of time.

Twenty-six men struck the Haralson County, Georgia, home of newly-weds John and Tilda Walthall in May 1871. John heard them approaching, snuck outside, and crawled under the house, unbeknownst to the sleeping Tilda. Believing John was inside, the men started searching the house.

They jerked Tilda, who was twenty-one years old, out of bed and attacked her. They threw her to the floor, kicking and stomping on her. Then they beat Tilda over the head with their guns and pistols, trying to get her to tell her husband's location.[31] Some men circled around the home, near the garden. They pulled off a plank and discovered John lying there. They snatched John up, made him and Tilda hug, and beat the couple as they clung to each other. Then, the brutes dragged John farther away from the house, pulled his clothes off, and beat him with sticks before finally shooting him. John Walthall succumbed to his injuries the following evening.[32]

Present at the assault on the Walthalls was abductee Jasper Carter, along with another kidnapped Black man, Charles Little, who were unwilling spectators to this terror spree. After the men killed John, they took Jasper a few yards from the house, stretched him on the ground, and whipped him, administering about 150 licks. "There are welts on my back now, if I make no mistake, as big as your finger, and as black as a man's hat," Jasper said.[33]

Jasper's explanation for why he did not run—he was overpowered and had no chance of running *and* living—put targeted people's split-second reasoning in life-threatening situations in stark relief. Having been seized, having entered the space of death and watched the abandon with which night riders first beat the Walthalls and then shot John, Jasper calculated the odds and concluded his best chance of surviving the raid was to not fight back or run away.

With raids lasting anywhere from minutes to several hours, targets' sense of their free will and how to survive ran the gamut, swinging around as though it was on a pivot, ranging from total submission (like Jasper Carter's) to self-preserving resistance (like the Tutson girl's deliberate actions to escape with her siblings) and back, depending on what was happening to them or family members at the time. This processing, both individual and collective, occurred in flashes and shifted during the strikes as imprisoned people groped for what they understood to be logical means of survival.

———

News of deadly attacks like the one on the Walthalls circulated around neighborhoods and communities like a murmuration of starlings. These whispers, communicating vivid details of attacks, flowed out from the sites of strikes, gathering force and changing shape and meaning as more and more tellers spun the stories to accommodate their own needs and reflect their own verdicts. Survivors contributed stories of their and their people's violation, searching for adequate witnesses, people who were capable of hearing their accounts of violation and engendering an ethical response— that is, one that moves beyond empathy and helps the injured party get justice or end the violence.[34] Witnesses to fatal attacks on people they knew relayed information on their behalf. Perpetrators spread information about their deeds, too. All the particulars generated fear, and dread of death seeped into families' homes and took up residence in people's minds as whatever sense of security they might have had started to fray.

This fear inspired people living in night-riding zones to adopt new survival strategies. This included sleeping outside and away from their homes to avoid being imprisoned and killed in them; they called this practice "lying out." Charlotte Fowler said her family and neighbors near Glenn Springs, South Carolina, were "as afraid as death" of being targeted. "There is now a whole procession of people," Charlotte said, "that have left their houses."[35]

Fleeing families' destinations varied. One Alabama man said his family crawled "under the house, and down by the garden palings, and around the cribs, and in the corner of the fences; me in one place and my children in another."[36] The woods and fields near Black people's homes and villages became highly trafficked in night-riding zones, as some potential targets reacted to news of strikes by seeking refuge wherever they could. People who were more fortunate, or were not worried about being too far away from immediate family members, boarded with kin. But not everyone had that luxury, so they had to take other precautions.

Two weeks before Christmas 1870, twenty-six men came for Alfred Wright, in Pacolet, South Carolina, claiming they "came from hell for Wright." But Alfred was in the woods, "sitting looking at them like a rabbit sits in the bushes," he said. The moon was shining so brightly that if he had got too close, he would have been detected. Alfred watched as the men stormed into his house, encountering his wife and daughters. The men made a lot of noise and stole some of the family's property and harvest.[37]

One targeted Alabama man recalled being frightened and dazed by the arrival of a posse of twenty-five in his Huntsville neighborhood. "I went in the house and shut the door and there was a hail to have the door opened, and I locked it and they rode it down," he said.[38] The men were there to frighten the family, but it does not appear anyone was physically harmed on that visit. The gang continued to menace the man, however, so he asked the woman who had held him in bondage what he should do and sought any social protection she might have to offer. The white woman told him she did not know and suggested he return home or leave the community. Knowing the men were still interested in seizing him, this man was reluctant to act on either of those recommendations, but finally, at his sister's insistence, he returned home. Almost as soon as he closed the door, three shots hit it. Sometime thereafter, it started raining "about as hard as I ever heard it, and it thundered and lightened," he recalled. "I was scared and tried to get under the floor," he said. "I ran out of the chimney, and I saw all of them."[39] The white men confiscated the man's weapons and ordered him to leave the community.

When stories of raids like this one permeated communities, more and more people began to sleep outside and away from their homes, to be on the safe side, either because they had already been attacked or because they expected to be. Others did not lie out, unless or until they knew they or their family had been targeted. In November 1869, night riders in Madison County, Alabama, came several times for one man, including once when they disarmed him. He began sleeping outside his home, but as he later explained, one night he was awakened by the anxious cries of the women in his family during a strike in his absence. The man did not rush into the house to their defense. He confessed, "I was standing out two hours and a half before they left there."[40] Knowing he was the men's target, he thought that if he went inside they would kill him.

One man began sleeping outside and away from his home when assailants near Glenn Springs, South Carolina, killed a community elder in May 1871. "I laid out in the woods for months like I was a dromedary or a hog or cow, afraid to go into the house," he said. "I didn't know how soon they might come to send me up." Unable to live with that uncertainty, the man joined the band of folks hiding and sleeping in the woods.[41]

Lying out was one widely adopted strategy for avoiding death or life-altering violence in most communities with active night-riding threats. But it was not a universal tactic. The practice varied significantly from community to community and from family to family. Families in night-riding zones ran their own individual cost-benefit analysis about lying out. And because conditions in the war on freedom were dynamic, individuals' and families' calculations changed from one day and from one minute to the next. In some cases, by the time it seemed reasonable for a given family to run, it was too late, because the men had already arrived.

Lying out helped families avoid being trapped with Ku Klux in an enclosed space. But the strategy had other benefits as well. Individuals could lie out without the hassle and cost of moving their families, and without completely abandoning their crops or property.

Whites launched their attack on people near Haralson County, Georgia, in 1871, whipping and stabbing residents there. Families in Jasper Carter's neighborhood knew of attacks but prayed for the best, believing that since no one had died, they could sit tight. That changed when they heard about the brutality unleashed on John Walthall, which kindled the kind of fear Jasper said left half of the people feeling afraid to stay inside their homes at night for fear the same thing might happen to them. "I have not stayed in my house one night, as I ought to, since corn planting, more than I am here now," Jasper said, after seeing what the white men who kidnapped him did to John Walthall and others on their spree. "I go on and do my work in the day-time, and on Sunday I knock about," Jasper said. "If I get a chance to get home and set something to eat before dark, I do it. If not, I go into the woods without it and go to sleep."[42]

When night riders began terrorizing White Plains township, one South Carolinian did not pack up. Instead, he tried to spend as much time as possible inside and with his people, and only headed outside to the field near his house at sundown.[43] The man dealt with his normal business during the day—working, attending church, and spending time with family. But when night fell, he headed outdoors or to hiding places nearby, including under wagons and in stables.

Others sought shelter near fences or in crawl spaces underneath their homes. Rather than stay within earshot or viewing distance of their homes, still others went farther away, depending on where they lived and the location of shelters. During peaks of violence, there could be small societies hiding out as families tried to dodge raids.

One man from Glenn Springs, South Carolina, who started lying out in May 1871, described the circumstances surrounding his decision to lie out and the accommodations he chose. White men raided the man's home while he, his wife, and their children were in bed. The man obeyed the night riders' orders to go outside. The lead raider grabbed the man and put a quilt over his head, then ordered the other attackers, "Shoot him, God dam him; shoot him." When the others hesitated, the quilt they used to hood the man slipped. "I thought to myself if I have to die might as well die running," he later said.

One of the attackers shot at the man, but this did not stop him. "I run as fast as I could," he said. Another raider gave chase on horseback and fired four shots. One ball clipped the man in the head, but he said, "I got away." Encountering a steep bluff, where he knew the horse and rider could not maneuver, the man kept running until he thought he was safe, lying out for the rest of the night, and listening when raiders killed his neighbor.[44]

After that dreadful night, the man said, "I am afraid to stay in my house."[45] To avoid recapture, he roamed from one place to another at night. Sometimes he went "out in the old fields, and on rainy nights, I get under any wagon shelters or barns, or something on the plantation."[46]

People with advance notice, like the Glenn Springs man, had time to prepare and pack things to make their stay better. Those trekking to the woods carried bedding and tarps to keep themselves warm because they could not start fires, especially close to their homes, without being detected. Families also packed food for men and women lying out in case hunger struck before they returned home the next day.[47]

When inclement weather rolled in, people who were lying out found improvised solutions. In the spring of 1871, William Coleman, of Winston County, Mississippi, typically slept in the woods near his home when danger felt close; on rainy nights, though, he took shelter in his horse's stable, right under the trough. Major storms also tended to discourage raiders from staging attacks in the first place. Still, with night riding a year-round problem, dangerous exposure to the elements was not unheard of. Many suffered frostbite while lying out. The fact that people were willing to take such risks suggests how desperate they were to avoid being trapped in their homes when night riders descended.[48]

People lying out might do so for weeks or months at a time. Men and older boys likely to be targeted were the primary candidates for extended sleeping away. Abraham Brumfield of York, South Carolina, spent four weeks outdoors, he said, "to keep out of the way of the Ku-Klux—every night raiding and shooting dogs, and nobody else couldn't rest hardly."[49]

As head of households, charters of their families' future progress, and participants in electoral politics as voters and candidates, men were more likely to be targeted. Men were also apt to be physically stronger and get the best of the family's food, which could make them healthier and hardy enough to withstand the physical travails of exposure to the elements. Lying out also put some men in a strategic position to see or hear the raiders coming and possibly defend their homes and families from within the woods. For others, it was a way of hopefully drawing violence away from their people.

Although men and boys were the first to go, lying out often turned into a family affair. "The women would be so excited when their husbands left," Reverend Elias Hill, of Clay Hill, South Carolina, said, "that they would go too, with the children." He described a neighbor who was joined by his wife "and little babe in the rain every night until late spring."[50]

The composition of the family could also determine who did and did not lie out. Families with young children and kin with disabilities had different considerations than those without them. After a spring 1871 raid, one man spent a good "part of the time in the woods" near his home near Cowpens, South Carolina. On rainy nights when he "thought no person could stand it to travel," he went home. But the rest of the time, he stayed in the woods: he did not know for sure if or when death might come for him, so he had to prepare for any eventuality.[51] His wife wanted to be by his side for comfort or protection, but she remained at home. "I was afraid about it," the woman said, "but being my little children were there, I couldn't take them [out], and I had to bear it."[52] The couple made the calculated choice that lying out could endanger the health of their seven-month-old baby and a sickly young daughter. Avoiding death from exposure was the only reason they could tolerate the separation.

The case of Charley and Harriet Hernandez reveals how lying out could spare some family members while leaving others in danger. Charley left home in the fall of 1870 because white men kept threatening him for trying to vote; according to Harriet, the persecutors said that "if they saw him anywhere about they would shoot him down at first sight." Charley had "not laid in the house ten nights since," Harriet said. "That is what they all have to do—men and women both." Women left home because the white men, in Harriet's words, "took out the spite on the women when they couldn't get at the [men]."[53] Harriet was one of those women. So was her daughter, Lucy. When night riders could not locate Charley, they snatched the mother and daughter out of their home and carried them away toward a fence. There, the men threw them down on the ground about twenty yards apart from each other and sexually assaulted them.[54]

Families in night-riding zones faced impossible life-or-death decisions. Fearing they might be attacked, the Hernandezes reasoned Charley's lying out would save his life. At the time, they could not have anticipated the different ways white men waging war on freedom would think of to hurt them. Charley lived, but Harriet and Lucy endured the full wrath of the men's vengeance.

———

Survivors' accounts reveal that people vigilantes imprisoned experienced both the presence and absence of opportunities to exercise free will, even within the space of a single attack. In each attack, everyone actively assessed what was happening to their family and them, and their odds of surviving different scenarios. The duration of strikes also saw some targets' responses evolve. Armed self-defense was one response. But so was trying to appease or negotiate with their assailants, or running away.

Black people who were armed could and did strike back.[55] The forming of Black militia companies and of Union Leagues, and other acts of self-defense, show some African Americans were well armed in the larger paramilitary warfare of the post-emancipation world and gave as good as they got. Sustained night riding was less common in these communities.

Attacks on Lewis and Sally Jackson show that, for targeted people, power did not only or always rest in brandishing guns, as many assume, but rather in keenly assessing the situation. That meant having not just functioning weapons but also the advantage of prior experience, to see past the natural stress response and accurately perceive the evolving circumstances of attacks. And it meant making on-the-spot decisions to increase their odds of living.

Night riders came three times for Lewis Jackson, a veteran who had served in the Fortieth U.S. Tennessee Colored Infantry Regiment. The first time, a group of up to one hundred staged a blitz raid, snatching Lewis from his Stevenson, Alabama, home in broad daylight, in a roundup of suspects who were sought for allegedly having shot into a white person's home. Lewis's lack of preparedness enabled the men to capture him. Lewis ran the numbers and knew that if he tried to fight off his attackers, they would kill him.

The second time, three men came and ordered Lewis outside. When he refused, they threatened to come in on him. "If you come into my house you will not go out," he told the trio. Lewis even shot at the retreating men to communicate he was primed to fight.[56]

Lewis's shooting at the men likely prompted the third "visit." By this time, Lewis knew he might be attacked and had more time to prepare to defend himself, advantages born only of the terror of the first two. When the white men came again, Lewis had locked his gate, so they could not get close to his home on horseback without him knowing. At some point, he had burrowed a hole in the wall of his home, through which he could see and possibly shoot at intruders. Lewis was armed with his pistol "all loaded six times," he said. As he was preparing to shoot, however, his wife, Sally, said, "Don't shoot them; they are too many; they'll overpower you and kill you." Lewis listened, which probably saved their lives.[57]

While the assailants were trying to break through the gate, Sally—whom Lewis described as being "pretty brave" throughout the raid—yelled that she was going to town to see how many men were away from their houses, so she could report them. Lewis used this opportunity to escape. "You never saw any one in your life go for it like I did," he said.[58]

Three visits elicited three different responses. Lewis and Sally calculated the risks of death and surviving in each one and acted accordingly. Their bets paid off. The Jacksons' contrasting reactions to different styles of attack reveal both the realities of what African Americans often faced amid violent raids and the logics behind some of their responses. Like Lewis and Sally, many captives had a sense of their power during strikes, but the varied ways they acted illustrate the calculations Black people made in their fight to live.

The calculations also show African Americans' expertise appeasing and negotiating their way around violently capricious white people to optimize survival. Anderson and Lucy Ferrell calmly allowed vigilantes to search their home for an escaped prisoner they knew they were not harboring. A fifty-three-year-old Walton County, Georgia, man named Reuben Sheets invited five Ku Klux targeting his family in March 1871 to sit at his table, where they presumed to counsel him on his behavior and test his defiance of white power. When the men asked Reuben if he was afraid of them, Reuben said he was—because they were aiming their pistols at him. But with his family to think of, Reuben remained calm, and eventually the men left without injuring any of them.[59] In May 1871, Elias Thomson refused his attackers' order for him to pray, but he tried to keep things light in his exchange with the men who came for him, by laughing with them, keeping their attention on him and not his family. Elias thought playing along might persuade the white men that he and his family did not represent a threat to their interests, and that they would leave his home without hurting them. It wasn't enough. Suddenly, the men started whaling on him with a whip. These families calculated the risks and made what turned out to be an informed and accurate assessment of what they needed to do to escape death.[60]

That reasoning was on display when Joseph Nelson refused to appease his attackers in 1869. When the gang came to his barn and tried to lure him out to discuss what he described as "some kind of fuss," Joseph, who was about twenty years old, declined. "If anybody can kill me any quicker than I can kill him," Joseph told the men, "just let him do it." He boasted his father's double-barrel shotgun was as good as any weapon they had. Joseph made clear he had the gun and knew how to use it. "I will not be stopped by anybody," he said. On another occasion, Joseph and a group of men were leaving to go to Jacksonville, Florida, and had made it about fifteen miles from Marianna when armed white men overtook them and asked where they were going. Joseph told them it was "none of their business." The men kept harassing Joseph's crew and he eventually conceded he was going to Jacksonville but affirmed his comings and goings were no one's business but his own.[61]

Charles Hendricks did not just refuse, he fought back. "They had their pistols in their hands," he said of the posse invading his home near Pinckneyville, Georgia, in December 1870. Charles, who was forty-two years old, and lived with his wife, Martha, who was twenty-eight years old, grabbed at their weapons and tried to take them. "I tussled with them until I got to the door," he said, "and then I broke and ran, and they shot me."[62]

When fifteen to twenty men came for Willis Johnson—who had refused to leave his Newberry County, South Carolina, home in June 1871—they first tried to ram his door, then got an ax to chop it down. Once they entered and ordered him to strike up a light, Willis obeyed the command but then, with his pistol, shot one of the men in the center of his back. As the Ku Klux scrambled, Willis shot again until they were out of his home. After that he ran.[63]

The fall 1868 raid on Columbus and Aury Jeter's family is an example of an evolving array of responses. Columbus and Aury were ages thirty-eight and thirty-two, respectively. Columbus hid when the men came to retaliate against the family's success and to dissuade them from opening a school. The Jeters ignored their attackers' threats and commands to reveal Columbus's hiding place in the chimney. He would have stayed concealed, but when one of the men got physical with Aury, her piercing cries were such that Columbus tried to sneak a peek to check on her.[64]

"Fire up the chimney!" one man yelled when he saw Columbus. Columbus hollered for the men to stop, thinking they would kill him if they lit a fire or started shooting. He said he thought surrendering "would be better than to allow them to kill my wife and children."[65] Columbus's employer, who was in the gang terrorizing the family, wanted to punish Aury for lying about Columbus's whereabouts. He charged at Aury, calling her a "damned bitch." When Columbus moved to intervene, the white men tried to cut him with a knife. "If you cut me with that knife," Columbus told the man, "I will hit you with this stick." The man lowered the knife but still threatened to kill Columbus.[66]

The attackers dragged Columbus outside while he begged, "Master, don't kill me," hoping to calm the men and escape death with submissive behavior. They blindfolded Columbus with an apron and took him to a tree, where they tried to tie him up, but he escaped only to be shot as he fled. Columbus was able to run far enough away to avoid being shot at close range, which saved his life.[67] During the raid, Columbus remained acutely alert to the presence and absence of opportunities to submit, resist, and escape.

As strikes commenced in their neighborhoods and villages and then became widespread, people had to calculate what they might do if those they knew were in danger. Would they organize in advance and coordinate a defense? Would they betray people or be betrayed? Would they listen to raids and to their neighbors' pleas for assistance, and do nothing to avoid their own victimization? Maximizing their survival meant strategizing.

Lewis Jackson's Black neighbors heard white men at his home but did not go to offer him and Sally assistance fighting off their attackers. They had good reason to stay put and secure their own homes. When Lewis fled, night riders menaced his neighbors, including a man named Sir Daniel, whom they went looking for. Sir refused to open his door to the white men. For some, the threat of deadly violence was too high to intervene—too high to provide shelter for or acknowledge any association with someone who was targeted.

Night riders' arrivals saw some targets betray other people in their households. James Hicks hid in his home's loft when a mob of one hundred and fifty came for him in Caledonia, Mississippi. He allowed a man he boarded named Edmund Gray to interact with the men while he hid. "I was scared . . . mighty bad," Edmund said of being awoken by the attack and forced to face the men, who started destroying the property trying to get at James.[68] The men began with the fence, before proceeding to cut down a corner of the house.[69] This was a final straw for Edmund. The men gained entry and Edmund climbed up the loft to get James, enabling the attackers to carry him and his wife away and whip them.[70] When confronted with the real possibility of physical injury, or worse, death, Edmund made the only decision he believed he could to protect himself: give up James.

Some targeted people tried to scare off their attackers. Vigilantes came for one man in York, South Carolina, just before the 1868 election. The men claimed to be there looking for a boy. The man knew it was a ruse and was determined to fight back. "I told them if they didn't leave my door, I would give them a load of shot," he said. Believing the Black man would make good on his threat, the men left, only to return. "They shot all in my house and knocked down my door, and aimed to come in," the man said, "and I knocked them down as they came."[71] This man's calculation and his luck paid off.

To completely fight off gangs, most families needed to mobilize the same way their attackers did and to have the type of weaponry that could kill men at a distance and hold several rounds. Some had pistols for personal protection, but these were rarely a match against a heavily armed posse of night riders, and most gun owners knew this. Targeted people may have been able to fire off a shot or two. If they were lucky, they could strike one of their assailants and scare off the rest, like Willis Johnson had. If they were not, they were easily overpowered or slaughtered. Men who had the greater firepower of shotguns and double-barrel guns could level the playing field. Many long-gun users had to prepare each load individually, determining the amount of shot based on the size of the target, and doing all this while under attack, which could leave them exposed.

When vigilantes invaded Avery, a twenty-acre Black hamlet just east of Stevenson, Alabama, Sir Daniel said, "we never saw any peace at all. They would not let us be for a space of three weeks without coming to see us." Sir said the Ku Klux came via train; they all got out, barging into Black people's stores and groceries and stealing goods like coal oil. He said, "They were going to burn that little town of Avery." According to Sir, "I couldn't tell how often [vigilantes terrorized the community]; it was so often, and they had got so bold, I couldn't keep count."[72] Sir recounted the story of a Black man named Miles Pryor who returned fire and almost died when the white men retaliated but managed to escape.

Armed self-defense did not assure survival; in attacks, like the July 18, 1871, one on Robin and Betsy Westbrook, in Marengo County, Alabama, it increased the likelihood of death. Night riders came for Robin, but he refused to open the door. "I will hurt some of you before I get through," Robin told the brutes attacking his family. One of the men struck him over the head with his double-barreled shotgun. Robin grabbed his weapon, and when his attackers saw, "the whole crowd came in and commenced shooting at him."

Robin was in the corner where Betsy was, and when the attackers began shooting, Betsy's adult son, Tiller, tried to escape.[73] "This little low man catched me by the hand and went to lead me out of the door," Tiller said. "I caught on the door facing and jerked loose from him and jumped out over another man standing at the door."

As Tiller jumped, the man struck him in the back of the head with his gun. Tiller ran, and his attacker had fired two loads from the shotgun by the time Tiller had run about fifteen steps. "I kept running," Tiller said, "and went away from there." Tiller returned the next morning and discovered his stepfather, Robin, was dead.[74]

Alfred Richardson of Clarke County, Georgia, was more fortunate than Robin Westbrook. Alfred was elected to the legislature in 1868. When Alfred learned some white men planned to come "break [him] up" to arrest his political activism, he prepared for a raid. Alfred later said that by the time the men arrived, he had barricaded the door to his home and stashed weapons in his garret. As the vigilantes chopped down the door, Alfred went upstairs, where his pregnant wife, Fannie, and three preteen daughters were hiding; he said he "thought I would stand at the [top] of the stair-steps and shoot [the raiders] as they came up." But the posse burst through the door firing, which overwhelmed Alfred. He hid in his garret. When Fannie cried out for help, the men shot at her "some twelve or fifteen times." Alfred fired on the men, killing one, which forced them to retreat. Both Alfred and Fannie sustained injuries in the shooting, but they survived.[75]

Alfred's experience of feeling overpowered by the scale of the raid on his family and having to recalculate how to survive it was shared by many targeted people. Anderson Ferrell had two weapons but determined it was not wise to use them with so many men crowded into his home. Mitchell Reed, who was twenty-two years old, was "sort of expecting" the Jackson County, Georgia, vigilantes to come for him, because "he had heard they put out threats," but he took no preparations to defend himself, which made it easy for them to get the better of him when they struck and whipped him in April 1871.[76]

Men like Robin Westbrook and Alfred Richardson had to face attackers on their own. But some communities rallied to defend themselves collectively. In 1871, George Fleimster organized a group of men in Morgan County, Georgia, with what he said was "all the arms we could get" to guard the jail and protect another Black man who was accused of sexual assault. The Black men stood sentry over the jail until white merchants refused to supply them the gunpowder and shot they needed to defend the accused man and themselves from any whites coming to the jail to lynch him. "They would not let us have the first bit in the world," George said.

During the standoff, George, who was twenty-seven years old, informed the mayor "they were sure to kill that man . . . They did not put him back in jail for anything else but to kill him." The mayor told George not to worry, and that the Black men needed to withdraw from the jail. But George countered, "Somebody ought to do it; it is your business to have somebody guard it; you are the mayor of the town."[77]

The authorities' failure to protect the accused Black man left his defenders "demoralized and dropped down," George said. This and their inability to acquire additional guns and ammunition made them withdraw from their posts, and shortly thereafter the jailor opened the door for white men to storm the jail for the man. "They shot the man's guts out," George said, "They shot him twice in the head." The vigilantes beat the man's uncle nearly to death and attacked others in the community. Whites raised the stakes, targeting George for subverting their authority, which he said made him realize "it will not do for me to stay in my house, for they will kill more if they kill him."[78] George left his home community in September 1871.

White southerners' decision to make Black people's homes a primary theater of the shadow war was a brutally effective way of achieving their objective: to deny Black people any freedom beyond their release from bondage. Planned attacks on their homes forced victims to think and act quickly. Targeted people did everything possible to elude capture and to avoid being killed. But what captives perceived as possible during largely inescapable attacks was not neatly ordered or static. Survivors' testimonies reveal that living through raids required an agency that shifted, rotated, and spun from one person to the next and from one moment of a strike to the next. In highly coordinated strikes, families the night riders "visited" had fewer options of escape and drew on a wider range of survival strategies than assumed today. That so many lived to tell their stories is a testament to how shrewd their many calculations for surviving raids were.

Chapter 4

They Deviled Us a While

I f you want to kill me, kill me," Adaline Fullerlove told the extremists surrounding her home. Night riders ambushed the family in Choctaw County, Alabama, on an April night in 1871. The family's patriarch, Robert—who was targeted for his insistence on voting for the Radical ticket—was making his way home from Mobile, where he had been conducting business. Inside the family home were Adaline, the couple's sons, Taylor and Alexander, and their daughter-in-law. The white men fired fifteen shots inside and set the house ablaze, hoping to draw the Fullerloves out.[1]

Robert later reported that, as the flames leapt higher and higher, threatening to consume the house and her family with it, Adaline "begged and begged them and made all the apologies she could in the world not to burn her and her children in the house alive." The men were not persuaded by Adaline's pleas. According to Robert, they "cursed and rebuked her for everything." Adaline then hollered for her neighbors, hoping to alert them of her plight and persuade them to help, but initially, nobody came.

Desperate, as her house burned and she and her children risked injury or death, Adaline yelled at the men to go ahead and kill her, then snatched a bucket of water to battle the fire. At some point, in an act of radical communal care, a neighbor finally called out to see if the family needed assistance, which prompted the vigilantes to disperse and allowed Adaline to put out the blaze.

The entire family survived the hit, but although Adaline's heroic action saved their home, the structure sustained significant damage. The Fullerloves spent the next several months living in fear of being attacked again.

Vigilante raids like the one Robert and Adaline's family endured interrupted the normal occurrences of daily life. For most families, it was an ordinary night until a strike revealed it wasn't, and their homes became the latest theater in white hard-liners' war against freedom. Examining couples', parents', and siblings' actions during moments of attack reveals some of the extraordinary lengths targeted people went to to protect each other and to mitigate the strikes' harm. Protection was no easy undertaking amid the harrowing violence of family captivity, especially when attacks were sustained over long periods of time.[2] Rendering their captives helpless to protect loved ones was part of the sick gratification extremists gained during attacks. One of the Fullerloves' sons was shot during the earliest part of the strike, which left him incapable of helping to fight off their attackers (if the family had weapons), or of running (if they had been able to). The fire intensified the horror the family felt: Adaline was so desperate to extinguish it that she was willing to expose herself to a murderer's bullet.

Bold actions such as Adaline's were critical to family survival. They were not always on display, though, nor could they be, in the mayhem of attacks. In that span of time, in some instances, an individual's focus on preserving his or her own life, and no one else's, rose to the surface. In others, the survival of the collective—family, neighborhood—remained the priority. But not every captive had the same capacity for courageous action as Adaline and her neighbors displayed. When extremists came for them and theirs, families relied on their kin or themselves to survive. Affective bonds, physical and psychological ability, and neighborly relations could be critical in determining who survived and how.

Black people's familial bonds were crucial to surviving the harsh world. They also informed how victims of raids experienced the horror of attacks.[3] Moving from looking at the gamut of reactions of targeted people to the rise of paramilitary strikes to the more granular details of how families tried to keep each other safe, and how belligerents' violence disturbed Black family dynamics—forcing captive husbands and wives, parents and children, and especially vulnerable people to make decisions that could mean life or death for themselves and the people they loved—enhances understandings of how agonizing strikes were and their capacity to undo victims.

Familial and communal care was a defining feature of Black people's ties to their literal and fictive kin. Black people went to remarkable lengths for their kin.[4] Enduring coupling, doting parents' eternal, unconditional love for their offspring, and children's belief in their parents' astonishing, heroic powers exemplify some of the ways Black people tried to protect each other—against all the odds. Black people's ethic of care radiated outward to the community. Communities watched over each other's well-being. They showed each other grace. They went to desperate lengths to protect each other from harm.

Black people's communal ethic of care had been the driving force behind their fight for freedom during the Civil War. That ethos fueled the journey from enslavement to liberation, as seen in the fight to reassemble families and the demand for family legal protections. That animating principle of community care was why one of the first things freed communities did was create schools, like the one Columbus and Aury Jeter opened. It inspired the building of little hush harbor churches, like the one Georgia Telfair so vividly remembered as being "not much for looks" but saving so many souls. It was why Black men who went to the polls or to the legislature knew their votes and work in office didn't belong to them as individuals—they belonged to their communities. African Americans' testimonies abound with expressions of Black people's devotion to each other before, during, and after strikes.

———

Hours before a raiding party descended on them in December 1870, good-natured sparks flew between Smith and Caroline Watley, of Coosa County, Alabama. Caroline had asked her husband to purchase her some shoes while he was out. At the store, Smith bought the shoes and other things, but had a troubling exchange with whites interrogating him about all the money he was spending. Smith had money for shoes, was purchasing a mule for $150, and was even making inquiries about buying a wagon.

Smith was concerned enough to share the details of the exchange with Caroline when he returned home. He asked her why some people with whom they had had cordial relations suddenly seemed hostile. Caroline did not know, but she told Smith he and their son should lie out.

Not enjoying the prospect of sleeping outdoors in the cold (and perhaps the prospect of being away from Caroline), Smith demurred, saying he did not want to go. "There's some rascally trick after you by the white folks," Caroline pressed. Hoping to lighten the discussion and perhaps secure the promise of a night of loving, Smith joked "just for devilment." "You have got a good pair of shoes and don't want me to sleep with you tonight," he teased.[5] Caroline would not be moved but Smith insisted on not lying out. When the white men came, Smith was tucked into bed next to Caroline.

The couple collaborated to survive the strike. "Here is the Ku-Klux," Caroline cried, as vigilantes shot the family's dogs. "Hush, he'll kill you," Smith said. Caroline got up and put on her clothes and walked across the house. Seeing her husband remain frozen in place in their bed, Caroline took him by the hand and pulled him out.[6]

When Smith got up and looked outside, he saw there were twelve white men. "I can't whip all these men," he reasoned. Caroline agreed, telling her husband not to open the door or go out.

Fearing the posse might start shooting if he did not open the door, Smith moved to open it, which sparked an argument between the couple. "She hung to me," Smith said of Caroline's resistance, "and I threw her away and opened the door."[7]

The gang seized Smith and took him outside, where, he said, "they made me strip my shirt . . . then they set in and whipped me, all six at once." As some of the raiders whipped Smith, Caroline fled the house.

The men had abducted Smith's brother-in-law, Jesse Watson, and some of them stripped Jesse to whip him.[8] Smith was disoriented by the whipping and panicked about not knowing Caroline's whereabouts, and if the attackers had gotten to her, too. "There was so many around me," Smith said, "I couldn't find her." With the intervention of a neighbor, Smith got free; he eventually found Caroline out by the horses, not dead or injured as he feared, but collecting details about their attackers and any items they were carrying so she could identify them.[9]

Other households, faced with the existential dilemma of surviving strikes, struggled to coordinate their responses. On October 17, 1868, night riders struck Thomas Allen's two-family home in Jasper County, Georgia, which Thomas shared with his sister and their respective spouses. The white men asked for a light, claiming they had been hunting and their dogs had treed something near Allen's home and they needed assistance. Thomas doubted their claims and refused to open his door or even make up a light. But against Thomas's wishes, his brother-in-law, Emanuel, did.[10]

When he unlatched the door, the white men began shooting, striking Emanuel, who cried out and fell. Hearing his sister's piercing screams, Thomas crossed over into her living space and struck up some light to assess the damage. Emanuel had taken "four or five number one buck-shot in his breast. He seemed to be dying very fast."[11]

Thomas wanted to run to get a doctor who might save Emanuel and provide some protection. Wearing only his shirt and underwear, Thomas asked his wife to give him his shoes and clothes. She refused, saying the men would kill him if he went outside. A doctor might save Emanuel's life, but the men firing into their home would probably kill Thomas if he tried to leave for help. Thomas was willing to take the risk. Mrs. Allen was not. She might have suspected Emanuel couldn't be saved, and she was not going to lose her husband, too. Thomas could not leave to get help without proper clothing, and Mrs. Allen was determined he would not have it. Her refusal saved Thomas's life, but it could not spare her brother, who died from his injuries.[12]

Couples' coordination was another vital survival strategy. Abraham Brumfield was already awake and on the lookout when barking dogs woke his wife, Emeline, from her sleep. Emeline sought Abraham in the dark of their home; when she found him, they discussed how they might survive the coming raid. Abraham went to the lower end of the house and Emeline to the chimney so they could both look outside. Emeline saw people running through the woods, coming directly toward them. She said, "Ku-Klux! Ku-Klux!"

Abraham saw a throng of white men, wearing disguises, descending on his home with guns in their hands. He shot out of the house and found a hiding place near a fence that was twenty yards from his door, far enough away to go undetected but close enough to monitor the situation. As the men crowded into the Brumfields' home where Emeline remained, Abraham waited.

The pack barged in and called for Abraham, claiming they had traveled from North Carolina to York, South Carolina, to punish him for engaging in "big talk" about what he might do with his civil and political rights to make the most of his freedom. Emeline told the white men her husband was not home, and they started threatening her, accusing her of lying. "If I am a God damned liar," Emeline charged back, "you may come in here and get him." Unable to locate Abraham, the men threatened to blow Emeline's "God-damned brains out" if she did not tell them where he was. "Then you will have to shoot me tonight," Emeline said, standing firm in her determination to shield her husband.[13]

Emeline's defiance and their inability to locate Abraham prompted the men to search the yard. Abraham moved to the cover of a pine bush, watching and remaining calm as they came within ten steps of him, close enough for him to hear them discuss their plans to go home.[14]

Abraham's decision to run and hide in the face of certain physical danger (if not death) was a calculated choice. Emeline's stand was a risky gamble that paid off. The Brumfields' quick, coordinated thinking helped them both survive the raid.

Harriet Postle went to bed with her husband, Isaac, beside her in their home four miles outside of Rock Hill, South Carolina. But when Harriet woke up to noise of white men coming for her family, she was alone. The men crammed inside the couple's home, interrogated Harriet about Isaac's whereabouts, and called her a "damned lying bitch" when she said she did not know where he was. Somehow amid the chaos, Harriet recognized a loose plank leading to their subfloor and suspected Isaac had crawled down there. Harriet moved her chair directly over it, taking the men's physical and verbal abuse, while trying to keep herself, her children, and Isaac all safe until they left.[15]

John Lewis was asleep when night riders came for him at his home near Spartanburg in June 1871. His wife, Adeline, alerted him to their arrival. John peeped out of the security hole bored in the wall near his bed and saw the men and heard them order him outside. Either trying to determine a way out, or sensing the futility of flight, John stalled, which prompted one of the terrorists to call Adeline by name and order her to open the door. She followed the man's command, likely fearing what might happen to her family or her if she refused. She de-escalated the situation and John went outside, as ordered. He had done nothing to justify being whipped, he told the raiding party. But outnumbered, John could not fight off the men. Several of the night riders gave him about twenty-five lashes each before leaving.[16]

As couples and families tried desperately to protect each other, sometimes gender roles and conventions appear to have been turned on their head. Most men tried to protect their wives and their children unless they were incapacitated or overwhelmed by strikes. In other cases, women like Emeline Brumfield shielded their male partners, offering them cover when they hid or fled.

Although extremists could come specifically for women, men were often night riders' primary targets, so women's protective stances toward their husbands, fathers, and sons show role reversals. Women's protection of the men and boys in their lives put them at risk of being brutalized, as did being alone to face vigilantes on their own.

Mary Brown wasn't alone, but as the primary target of raiders, she experienced their full wrath. In May 1871, white men claimed a white woman had accused Mary of planning to go to Atlanta to report the killing of a man in the community. Mary said she told them, "She told you more than I know, then."[17] Mary had heard a neighbor had been killed, but she said she did not know who was involved and had no reason to report anything.

A gang of thirty to forty men invaded the Browns' home in White County, Georgia. The raiders quickly seized Mary's husband, Joe, dragged him outside, and beat him, using fifteen- to twenty-foot-long sticks. "They wore out a long fishing pole on him," Mary's mother, Caroline Benson, said. "They had him down, and put a chain on his neck and dragged him about a great deal."[18] Bound and beaten, Joseph was in no position to help Mary and Caroline.

Mary initially panicked over the horror of being seized. But she said she "got over my scare," thinking she'd be fine and wouldn't be harmed: she knew she had hurt no one and had committed no crime. That was before the men tore off Mary's clothes. "They did not pull them off," Caroline said, "but just jibbeted them off, like paper."[19] The attackers "made all the women show their nakedness," Joseph later recalled. "They made them lie down, and they jabbed them with sticks."[20]

The men saved their worst for Mary, whom they whipped savagely. Not finished, the brutes threw a chain around her neck and choked her until she passed out. One of her attackers even said, "I would rather kill her right now." But the others seemed to accept her denials of being an informant, and relented.[21]

Couples tried to defend each other when they could. But targeted people did not necessarily have every avenue open to them to cheat death, nor free will over the entire duration of the strike. That was the case for Abe and Eliza Lyon, the couple who had sprinted to freedom in the little Choctaw County, Alabama, village of DeSotoville. On June 6, 1871, Abe had spent the day in his cherished blacksmithing shop and Eliza had finished her home-making tasks. The children had completed their chores and lessons, with time for play after. They were all in bed at their home at eleven P.M. when someone knocked on their door and asked if Abe was home. The family had never heard any threats and "were not thinking about such a thing," Eliza later said. Abe answered that he was home and got up from the bed to open the door. But something—perhaps the sight or sound of the visitors and his awareness of the threat they posed, or just a feeling, his skin tightening and puckering with goose bumps—so terrified Abe that he did not move.[22]

Human bodies and minds are wired to sustain themselves, and when under attack focus solely on survival and avoiding injury.[23] When the mind detects threats to life, like Abe experienced, it triggers preprogrammed escape plans by secreting stress chemicals to propel the body into action, specifically to survive by running, hiding, or fighting.[24] But as Abe considered a possible exit strategy and the implications for Eliza and their three children, he might have felt heavy, as though he were in a nightmare from which he would soon awaken. However this wasn't a dream, and that horrified him. Eliza, who remained calm, said Abe "looked like he was in a perfect scare," suggesting his body's defense circuitry had shut down and that he was paralyzed by fear. Abe remained in that state, forcing Eliza to act in hopes of guiding her husband to safety and protecting their children.[25]

As their understanding of the situation became clearer, the fear that had struck Abe also befell Eliza. "Don't go out Abe," she said, "it sounds like more voices than one." Perhaps propelled by a burst of adrenaline, Abe looked out the window to confirm her suspicions. As he did, their attackers ordered him to come outside. Abe returned to the trancelike state and did not move.

Seeing Abe's paralysis, Eliza sprang into action. She jumped up and shut the door, pushing her husband away and then ordering him out the other door. Abe followed Eliza's commands, moving across the house in the dark, but when he discovered the bottom door bolted, he panicked.

He "was so scared," Eliza recalled. He "wheeled around in the room in his scare," not knowing what to do. Abe's panic was contagious. "I was scared too," Eliza said, but she remained composed enough to unlock the door.[26]

Eliza's hope that her husband would regain control of his senses was soon dashed; Abe remained in his perfect scare, standing as though his feet were bolted to the floor. Eliza ran behind Abe, intending to push him outside, but just then, the invaders burst through the door and threw a rope over his head.

According to Eliza, the men "drew his arms down to him and picked him up deliberately and toted him out."[27] Abe begged, "Lord have mercy on me." After that, Abe gave up fighting and allowed the men to carry him away.

Eliza yelled to her neighbors or any passersby for help. The Lyon family was not living very near anyone, but they were close enough for neighbors to hear loud hollering. Still, no one came. Eliza would later make a point of this in her testimony about these events; the breach of the communal code of Black survival stayed with her, and perhaps she recognized strikes' capacity to alienate targeted families from their communities.

To silence Eliza's screams, the attackers put guns to each side of her head, one in her face, and another on her chest. "They told me if I didn't hush hollering they would blow a hole right through me," she said. Afraid, but not paralyzed by fear, Eliza knocked away one gun with her hand. The men, while angry at her resistance, held fire, but Eliza said they told her "they would finish with me directly."[28]

The night riders carried Abe away from his home and up a hill nearby. Eliza did not follow, but she paced along their porch trying to see what was happening and determine her next move. Before she could act, she saw the flash and heard the blast of a double-barrel shotgun. Then, one of the men shouted an order for the rest of the gang to fire, and they did.[29]

After the terrorists killed Abe, Eliza spotted them returning to her house. "I knew they were going to kill me, as they told they would," she said. Eliza ran inside to get her three children so they could leave together. But as she did, she saw there were seventy-five men back in her yard. "I could see their faces," Eliza said, "they were standing so close to me."[30]

As the extremists got in position around the house, Eliza went to gather her children to flee, but she discovered fourteen-year-old William had already run. Moving with twelve-year-old Ella and eight-year-old Annie by her side, Eliza snuck out back and traversed a field neighboring her home. They stopped at a thicket of woods about a quarter of a mile away to monitor the men's activities and take stock. She could go no farther without knowing William's whereabouts, but staying rendered her girls and her vulnerable to discovery.

Eliza watched from the woods as the white men made up a light and began searching and ransacking her home. "They tore up everything," she said. Wearing only their night clothes, Eliza and the girls moved farther into the woods as the night riders "shot off all the pistols in the house." The crowd shot the family's dog and stood outside firing off their weapons. "It sounded like there was over a hundred shots at once," Eliza said.[31]

Eliza had done what she could to protect Abe. Some targeted people were lost to physical pain they endured, but others, like Abe, were lost to the absolute horror of strikes.

Wiley Strong, who was tucked in bed next to his wife, must have heard the night riders' arrival, because he snatched his gun and slipped out of the house, without notifying his sleeping wife. Wiley stayed close enough to monitor the men's actions. The vigilantes called for Wiley by name, but he said, "I didn't know them, and they didn't know me," so he did not present himself.

The band entered Wiley's home and began interrogating Mrs. Strong. Wiley watched and listened from outside as the raiders stood in his doorway interrogating his wife, demanding she reveal his whereabouts—which, of course, she did not know.[32] The invaders tried to force Mrs. Strong out of the house, but she refused, terrified of what they might do to her. They responded, "Come out, or we will burn the house down around you." "You will have to burn it down," Mrs. Strong shot back, "for I will not come out." It was only when one of the brutes moved to strike Mrs. Strong with a piece of iron that Wiley came out of hiding and entered his home's rear door with his gun.[33]

Wiley said the men ordered him back outside, threatening to "shoot me all to pieces" if he resisted. "I went out there," Wiley said, "fearing they would kill me." One of the men got a piece of a board about three feet long, four inches wide, and a half inch thick, and beat Wiley with it until the assailant was tired. With the other two men pointing their pistols at him, Wiley could not fight back or run without being shot. Meanwhile, Mrs. Strong watched in a state of fear, unable to protect her husband without endangering herself.

———

Because night riders attacked families in their homes at night, Black children both witnessed attacks on their adult kin and endured a fair share of the same violence meted out to grown-ups. And just as strikes upset gender dynamics between husbands and wives, so too could they distress and invert parent–child roles, especially as white men routinely treated youths like cannon fodder in the war against freedom. Attacks involving children forced adults to weigh any decision they made during the strike against their offspring's needs and behaviors. Children of all ages saw their parents' vulnerability and powerlessness. Fright could immobilize parents whose children were being victimized. With children involved, whether they were young or adults, the havoc of strikes was even more disorientating and devastating.

Jackson Surratt woke up when he heard someone trying to break down the door of his home in Cherokee County, South Carolina, in May 1871. Jackson opened it and found a gang of white men accusing him of voting the Radical ticket. They blindfolded Jackson and escorted him from his home. The night riders gave him fourteen licks each before releasing him.

The next time terrorists struck the Surratts' home, they inquired about his son. Jackson acknowledged he "was scared" but opened the door to the men, fearing the consequences would be deadly if he refused. According to Jackson, as one group seized and blindfolded him before carrying him from the house, another group ran inside. One man grabbed a rope and jerked Jackson's daughter; his wife, Jane; and her son all out of their beds, along with a seven-month-old baby. Before Jackson knew it, he said, "they were bringing them all out."

One member of the posse ordered another to make a light as they forced the Surratts outside and about seventy yards from their home. They ordered Jackson to lower the fence and made him and Jane jump two logs together before forcing them to lie down as they cut switches for whipping them. "They had us nearly naked," Jackson said, underscoring everyone's vulnerability to sexual assault.[34]

As the men whipped Jane's son, Jackson recalled thinking, "I believe if I lie here they will put me and all my folks through so I can't do any good." There was one man in his community with the power to save his family—the man who had held him in bondage. Jackson told himself, "[I]f my old

Master is for me, he will strike for me tonight and save me, and I must do my best [to survive]."

Jackson rose up and ran about fifty yards before stumbling. He got up again, "and took right through the woods, and ran until I run over a log." Looking back, he discovered his attackers had not followed. He stopped for a moment, before fear that they would catch him made him run again, toward the swamp. This was the last he saw of the gang.[35]

In the meantime, Jackson had left Jane and their children to face the attackers.[36] "They deviled us a while," he later said. As the men were whipping Jane and the children, they asked her whether she worked; it was less a question than an accusation. Among Black people's freedoms guaranteed by the Civil Rights Act of 1866 and the Fourteenth Amendment was the right to decide for themselves when, where, and how much they worked. Some Black women had withdrawn from both domestic service and farm work to tend their homesteads for their own families. Freedom-denying whites resented their choices and lashed out.

"I did [work] as far as I was able," Jane answered, defending herself. "I was not able to do hard work." Finding her explanation unacceptable, her attackers just whipped her, lashing her about forty times. "They whipped me from my ankles clear up to . . . above my waist."[37] The men whipped the remaining family members together, with switches and sticks Jane said were thicker than her thumb.[38] They whipped her son "miserably bad" and unleashed their fury on her little girl, too.[39] Like any parent, Jackson and Jane had probably envisioned themselves as their children's providers and protectors, but raids could be so harrowing they threw parents' protective roles into disorder.

The raid on Augustus Blair's family near Fort Hamilton Hill in Alabama's Limestone County illustrates some parents' powerlessness when it came to protecting their older children from harm. Eighteen-year-old William Blair, Augustus's only son, whom the family called Billy, attended a social event where he clashed with three young white men in 1868. One of the men pulled a knife and tried to slit Billy's throat. Billy surrendered, throwing up his hands; other Black people attending the gathering intervened to prevent him from being killed and escorted the Blair boy home to his family. As they were all dispersing, the young white men warned Billy they would have him Ku Kluxed.[40]

Shortly thereafter, the white youths either went themselves or rallied their older kin and made good on their threat. It was a "mighty cold" December night, Augustus recalled: he kept the fire going while he was "abed and asleep with all my family." Around eleven P.M., the pack came.[41]

The night riders barged into the room that held Billy and his older sisters, Civil War widows Eliza Jane and Charlotte, and seized him. They took Billy outside, with two of the men holding back Billy's head and another two pistol-whipping him in the face.

The invaders moved fast. Augustus snatched his boots and followed them a quarter of a mile, up a hill, and to a clearing as they dragged Billy, punching and stabbing him all the while. Augustus said he "crept right around behind the patch of briars and laid there," about twenty yards away, reasoning, "if they killed him I wanted to find him."[42]

Either Augustus did not have a weapon, or he felt it would be futile to try to fight so many men. Brandishing a weapon could even antagonize the men and provoke them into taking Billy's life and his own. So Augustus made a harrowing decision: unable to protect his son, he chose to stay and bear witness. Augustus watched as they stripped Billy naked and continued attacking him with a knife. He was close enough to see the blows and to hear the interaction between Billy and his attackers. Billy cried out about the pain the assailants were causing him, but they denied his complaints about his injuries. "I feel the blood running down my pants," Billy said. One of the men replied: "You will have no use for blood no how, mighty soon." The men took Billy down to the ground and beat him on his head. Augustus said Billy "never hollered but once," but he could hear his son's death rattle as some of the white men choked him and others cut him with the knife as they held him there.[43]

It was cold and dark that December night in Alabama, so Billy Blair's attackers, expecting to be in the clearing for some time, struck up a fire. The light allowed them to see the damage they had inflicted on Billy, and the gang's leader told them they had done enough. He reminded his boys they needed to "spare life."

"You feel here and see how you like these gashes," one of the men taunted Billy. "Do you reckon they will do you?" Another man ordered Billy to stand up. Augustus said his boy "was so weak that when he went to get up he was staggering, and one of them catched him by the shoulders and held him, and just then one hauled off and struck at him." Billy staggered—from blood loss, Augustus thought, because "the road was bloody all the way up the hill."

The men jumped and stomped on Billy, shot off their pistols in the air, then got on their horses and rode away.[44] Only when he confirmed the coast was clear did Augustus go to his boy and carry him home. It is possible he experienced paralytic fright, akin to Abe Lyon, and could not stop the armed men from attacking his child. Whatever the reason, Augustus could not fulfill his obligation to protect his child without putting himself in danger.

Parents faced impossible situations during strikes and clearly did what they thought was in their best interests and that of their children, regardless of the children's ages. But, as the whipping of the Surratts' children and the attack on Billy Blair show, parents could not protect their children from harm in a raid, especially if they were outgunned and outmanned.

————

Children living in night-riding zones typically faced and witnessed direct physical violence during strikes in which the adults in their lives were the primary targets. Adults' incapacity often saw children step forward either to save a parent, or themselves, when they could. On October 29, 1869, a gang of sixty-five white men surrounded the home of Abram Colby. Colby was in the process of being harassed and expelled from the Georgia legislature, but he insisted on still exercising his right to vote and encouraging other Black men to do the same, a move that angered whites in Greene County. The raiders broke down the door of Colby's home and dragged him outside, where they whipped him.

Abram's mother; his wife, Anna; and their young daughter, Amanda, tried to protect him. The men ordered them to stop and, recognizing the risk to their own lives, Anna and her mother-in-law followed their commands. Amanda did not. When Amanda kept begging the men not to hurt her father or carry him away, one of them leveled his gun at the girl to subdue her. It was only then the petrified child stood down.

Abram survived the assault but, in his opinion, his little girl did not. Although the men did not kill Amanda outright, Abram believed the trauma of the raid, seeing him dragged away, and having a gun drawn on her had contributed to her premature death shortly thereafter. "She never got over it," he said.[45]

Children like Amanda Colby were some of a freed community's most vulnerable members. From the ravages of losing their parents to witnessing violent strikes or enduring them personally, children are always sucked into conflict, whether the nature of the fighting is between formal armies or citizen militias. Young people become collateral victims or, sometimes, prime targets in campaigns of genocidal violence. In conflict, differences like age can matter little to perpetrators, unless or until it serves their agendas.

In night-riding zones, captives were often familiar with the people assaulting them, and children could use their knowledge of their attackers' identities to try to shield themselves from harm. When whites struck William Henderson's home in northwest Alabama, they found him with his wife and his twelve-year-old son, Mack. The boy tried to escape when the night riders came in, but one caught Mack and shoved him back inside. Mack recognized his attacker and said, "Mr. Holesapple, you let me alone."[46] During the attack on Columbus and Aury Jeter's family in response to their efforts to start a school, one of the invaders seized the couple's twelve-year-old daughter, Emily, jerking her out of bed. She knew her attacker and called him by his name. The white man answered, assuring Emily he would not hurt her.[47]

Physical assaults children endured during strikes could also take on a sexual dimension, especially because so many were roused from bed in a state of undress. Four youths were present during the strike on Mary and Joseph Brown's family: Joseph and Mary's boys Thomas and James, and two girls. The boys did not go outside when the Ku Klux came, perhaps because they were terrified and hiding, or because the band did not call for them. The girls did, which put them in harm's way.

The attackers made the girls lie down with and alongside the women and expose themselves. "They jabbed them with a stick, and went to playing with their backsides with a piece of fishing poles," Joseph said of the sexual mischief the men made with the children.[48] Because they were bound and being beaten themselves, none of the adults present was in any position to intervene.

Night riders frequently communicated a willingness to maim or kill every one of the people they imprisoned, and they often exercised extended periods of complete control over their hostages and demanded compliance with every request. The presence of children during strikes worked for and against attackers. Vigilantes could use parents' love for and desire to protect their offspring to get them to obey their commands. But children, especially the young ones, were also unpredictable, and parents' efforts to attend to them distracted them from following night riders' orders. The very nature of raids increased the likelihood youths would be exposed to violence.

Blitz attacks often found families in their beds, with the youngest children sleeping next to their targeted parents. Adults, including able-bodied men who were sometimes in the best position to fight back, were immobilized physically during the early phases of strikes, which made it difficult to protect their children from harm. Jackson and Jane Surratt's seven-month-old was in the bed with Jane when the men snatched her out. Jane was forced to lay the infant down and the baby lay there screaming, which threw both parents into a panic. "I was powerfully uneasy about my baby, and could not keep still for it," Jackson said.

Night riders tried to maintain complete control over their captives. A hysterical baby, whose parents might be tempted to comfort or protect it, threatened their power, a fact Jackson understood. He knew the fiends attacking them might react by silencing his child, which could leave it injured or dead. Jackson could not comfort the infant without drawing a response from their attackers. Recognizing their father's impotence, and wanting to help, the couple's other young children were able to calm the baby down without further antagonizing the raiders.[49]

Although neither Jane nor Jackson mentioned their infant being whipped, Harriet Hernandez, one of the Surratts' neighbors, who was also attacked by night riders on a separate occasion, said "even the [youngest] child in the family, they took it out of bed and whipped it." "They told them if they did that they would remember it," Harriet said.[50] The men whipping these young victims wanted to impart life-shaping lessons about Black children's vulnerable position in the world.

Youths were just as terrified as their parents were; however, some, like Amanda Colby, might have lacked the full mental capacity to understand what was happening. Some kids cried uncontrollably, which could intensify the situation by drawing the men's attention, possibly forcing parents to choose between complying with night riders' commands and protecting their children. Parents had reason for concern.

The terror of children's situations—and their parents' inability to make the night riders leave—found youths asserting their own agency and taking action to intervene when their parents were under attack. This included running out of the house, like Eliza and Abe Lyon's son, William, did, or begging night riders to spare their parents, as Amanda Colby did, despite repeated warnings to stop. Another family's boy scrambled under the bed but was dragged out by his heels.[51] Children could not always accurately gauge the behavior of their attackers, and their naturally lower impulse control sometimes led to their victimization.

Some parents allowed themselves to be beaten and carried off, to keep their attackers' attention on them and not their children. Martin Anthony's adolescent daughter, Mary, ran under the bed when they came for him in August 1869. Vigilantes did not harm Mary Anthony because she remained in her hiding place. Instead, the teen watched and listened as their attackers beat Martin and carried him from their home. Martin was afraid they would shoot him and knew any move he made could draw Mary out and expose her to the men.[52] So he did not fight back, to protect his child.

Parents did ignore white men's commands that endangered their offspring. When men came looking for Lewis Jackson at Sir Daniel's home in 1869, he and his wife were tending to their two-day-old child. Sir's newborn's presence in his home guided his refusal to leave it when vigilantes ordered him to, as well as his threat, after some discussion with his wife, that they would have to come take Sir at their own risk.[53] The band left the family alone, but Sir Daniel fled for his safety.

Sometimes parents found themselves powerless in the face of a greater number of men or a fear of personal annihilation if they intervened. Try as they might, there was nothing some of them could do to spare their children. This was the case for Augustus and Letty Mills, whose four children were with them in their Walton County, Georgia, home when the white men came in March 1871. There was Isaiah (six years old), Jesse (three), Emma (two), and Mary, the infant, whom Letty was nursing.[54] Residing with the family was sixteen-year-old Tobey, whom they boarded and employed. When the night riders arrived, rather than answer the door himself, Augustus told Tobey to do it. The teen was no match for the gang shoving their way inside, which roused Augustus, Letty, and the three kids from bed.

The vigilantes made their prisoners get down on their knees. Letty said they made Augustus "stretch out on the floor and gave him a good beating." One attacker went around to each of them, striking them on the head with a pistol. Letty said her little girl began to cry, and a man went to her and said "if she did not hush he would mash her."[55] The men kept striking the adults and youths, too many times to count. "I never paid any attention to the number of licks," Augustus recalled. "As quick as one would get done beating another would fall in and beat us."[56]

Night riding put young children in the immediate presence of the death of their caregivers. Charlotte and Wallace Fowler's young grandson followed Wallace out of the bed and out the door when he went to check the noise night riders made on the night of May 1, 1871. "You know," Charlotte Fowler later said, "in the night it is hard to direct a child." The little boy watched

Wallace get shot in the head. Terrified, he flew into the house, crying out to Charlotte that the Ku Klux had "killed grandpappy!"[57]

Abram Colby's statement that his daughter, Amanda, "never got over" the raid is revealing of the ways night riding wounded children directly and indirectly. Abram did not explain what he observed of his daughter's emotional grief, but her symptoms likely included sleeplessness, a nervous stomach, night terrors, or an intense (though rational) fear of whites or of nightfall. Night riders continued terrorizing her family, trying to dissuade her father from serving in office or encouraging other Black men to do so, which only prolonged the girl's distress, and likely facilitated her death.

Black youths like Amanda Colby were exposed to the same violence as the adults in their lives, even though young ones experienced it differently because of their increased vulnerability.[58] Children who survived night-riding strikes were the last firsthand witnesses to the horrors that occurred.[59]

———

Targeted people escaped and defended themselves if they could. Like youths, and like people experiencing paralytic fright, physically vulnerable, differently abled, and emotionally sensitive people could not always protect themselves or their kin to the same degree as their able-bodied counterparts. Physical abilities and physical and mental health informed freed Americans' experiences of the world.[60] Some of these men, women, and children experienced emancipation differently from their able-bodied peers, who could do the physical work needed to earn their own livings. During strikes, escape or resistance could be impossible for someone missing a limb from an accident, or suffering from a degenerative condition. Vigilantes took advantage of their conditions and used captives' disabled bodies to hurt them physically or psychologically. Taking care of them during a strike could expose their caregivers to harm.

Wiley Hargrove was one of those differently abled people targeted. Wiley and his wife, aged forty-two and forty, were living in Pickens County, Alabama, he said, "on a piece of land I bought and paid for." At some point in his life, one of Wiley's legs had been amputated from the thigh down. He used a walking staff to get around. On the day of the November 1870 election, Wiley walked to the polls to cast his ballot.[61]

Wiley's disability did not interfere with his ability to manage his land or to vote for the candidate he thought might best ensure his freedom, but it did hinder his ability to fight off the men who came for him. The white men barged into Wiley's home on a wintry November night after the election. They snatched the couple from bed, dragged them out of their home, and carried them about a quarter of a mile, where four more men waited. The men "talked outlandish, like those out-country people," Wiley recalled, adding, "they came from betwixt the moon and the seven stars," as though they were ghostly beings from the afterlife. "You damned old crippled son of a bitch," one of his attackers said, likely in response to his protests, "you could walk four miles to vote against me." According to Wiley, the men stripped the couple, stretched them "out on the cold, icy frost," and whipped them. Mrs. Hargrove could not fight off all the men herself, and she could not flee without risking greater injury or possibly death, or without leaving Wiley behind, something she did not do. Wiley's capacity to fight was severely limited. Wiley and his wife endured a savage whipping and beating and had to make their way home afterward.

Reverend Elias Hill was another disabled target. "I had often laid awake listening for such persons, for they had been all through the neighborhood, and disturbed all men and many women," he said of the men terrorizing his community in Clay Hill, South Carolina.[62] Elias and his brother lived next door to each other, and on the night of May 1, 1871, invaders struck his brother's home first.

"They attacked his wife," Elias recalled, "and I heard her screaming and mourning." Awakened by his sister-in-law's cries, Elias could not understand what the Ku Klux were saying because of the distance and the "outlandish and unnatural tone" of the attackers' speech. Then Elias heard them "have her" in the yard, he said: they were sexually assaulting her. His sister-in-law was crying and "the Ku-Klux were whipping her to make her tell where I lived." Understanding the only way she might end the men's assault on her was to reveal Elias's whereabouts, Mrs. Hill signaled where Elias's home was located.[63]

Unlike other targeted people, Elias could not flee or otherwise defend himself. "I was disabled from walking when I was seven years of age," Elias later told his interviewers.[64] When Elias's father bought his mother out of slavery, he said, the contract "compelled" the buyer to assume responsibility for Elias's care. The planter class established a cruel practice of casting out bondpeople with severe physical or mental disabilities whose labor they could not steal. Disposing of disabled bondpeople deprived them of community and means of support, which could result in them being sent to state-funded poorhouses or insane asylums. Seeing this practice as enslavers shirking their duty of care for the people they held in bondage, states passed laws compelling the buyer to assume complete responsibility for the person's care so they would not become burdens of the state. Seeing Elias and his mother as property, and not as kin, the contract did not assume or care that Elias's father would surely provide for his well-being; it compelled him to do so as the buyer.[65]

As he got older, Elias's range of mobility was further constrained when his arms started drawing in and causing him great pain, which a doctor ascribed to rheumatism. He described his legs as being "so short—all my limbs drawn up and withered away in pain," which suggests Elias may have suffered from polio.[66]

Elias could not run or even move to hide when he heard the six men coming for him. The raiders found Elias in his bed, hoisted him up, and carried him outside into the yard between the brothers' homes. They placed him on the ground beside another boy they had captured, then interrogated and beat them for their supposed role in a string of fires, and for allegedly ordering Black men to assault white men. Elias denied starting the fires: after all, his disability made their accusations "unreasonable."[67]

The men used Elias's body against him. The gang dragged Elias by his shriveled legs toward the fence line farther away from the homes and left him there, "knowing I could not walk or crawl" to get back. Elias lay there, he said, "chilled with the cold, lying in the yard at that time of night, for it was near [one] o'clock, and they had talked and beaten me and so on until half an hour had passed since they first approached." After ransacking the house, the vigilantes returned to taunt Elias, asking him if he was afraid.[68]

The men attacking Elias did not limit their assaults to verbal taunts. "One caught me by the leg and hurt me," Elias said. When he moaned in pain, one man ordered him to hush, then grabbed his horsewhip and struck Elias about eight times on the hip bone. "It was the only place he could hit my body, my legs are so short," Elias said, "all my limbs drawn up and withered away with pain."

It was only the orders of another man that made Elias's assailant stop. One of the sadists used a strap and collared Elias, planning to drag him to the Catawba River and drown him. But they changed their minds and continued interrogating him.

Finally, the men went and ordered Elias's sister-in-law to come pick him up and carry him inside. As Mrs. Hill followed their commands, they struck her with the strap, herding her along as though she were a piece of livestock, until she laid Elias on the bed. Elias survived, but his physical powerlessness during the strike magnified his sense of horror.[69]

———

Captives' sickness also shaped how targets experienced "visits." Poor nutrition during slavery slowed some Black people's growth and increased their susceptibility to various diseases. With emancipation, people gained more control over their diets, but some of them faced a new challenge: securing enough food. Poor diets brought on by displacement, crop failure, or crop destruction by vigilantes or white neighbors would have rendered them undernourished, less healthy, and more susceptible to illness.

Numerous survivors said they or people they knew were sick when they were attacked. They rarely named their ailments, either because they did not know or did not think it was relevant. When night riders ordered Augustus Mills to get up, he initially declined, explaining he "had been chilling," likely meaning he had a fever. The men, however, did not care. "Get up," they commanded. "We will cure you of chills; you never will have any more," one of them said. Augustus complied, to avoid physical injury or death.[70]

Feverish conditions like Mills's would have weakened people and made it difficult for them to run or fight back. Research on how people act under the threat of death suggests some targets' minds and bodies ignored their illnesses and physical weaknesses to increase their chances for surviving raids. Even if targets could run, their illnesses slowed them down. What is more, surviving a strike might have expended what little mental and physical reserves they had left. Raids and their aftermaths prolonged or exacerbated people's illnesses.

Other temporary conditions that would have shaped the experience of a night-riding "visit" were being in the final stages of pregnancy, having just given birth, or recovering from miscarriages. Numerous male survivors identified pregnancy as a cause of their wives' additional physical vulnerability during attacks. Missouri Tanner had reached the end of her pregnancy within a month of her family being attacked in June 1871 and was confined to bed.[71] The record does not reveal whether the pregnancy ended with a live, healthy birth, but Patrick Tanner's description of his wife's vulnerability shows even if vigilantes did not physically harm pregnant or confined women, the extreme fear their arrival presented was likely damaging.

Women, like Missouri Tanner, who were either in the last stages of their pregnancies or had just given birth, almost certainly lacked the same range of physical mobility as they might have had during their first or second trimesters or several days or weeks after they delivered.[72] Maria Carter was lying in after delivering her baby, which spared her from being whipped along with her husband in April 1871. Instead, one of the men jabbed her on the head with a gun. She said, "I heard the trigger pop. It scared me and I throwed my hands up," to push the gun away. The man put it back again, but Maria kept resisting.[73]

James Alston's wife was "in the family way, soon to be delivered," he said. She probably couldn't have run from the men who targeted her family if she had wanted to. She did not get the chance, because she was in bed asleep with James when the bullets tore through her bedroom wall and one struck her in the heel of her foot on a night in June 1870.[74]

Pregnancies with complications or difficult deliveries exacerbated women's and their unborn or newly born children's vulnerabilities to the forces of raids. A night-riding strike destroyed the kind of secure and healthy conditions desired for expectant and postpartum mothers' well-being. The women's ages and health during their pregnancies—and whether or not they had already delivered children—were also factors that could have made surviving a raid easier or more difficult.

When night riders came to Sir Daniel's place, he said, his wife was "greatly excited" by the men's arrival, because she feared for their two-day-old baby's safety and because she was physically vulnerable and perhaps unable to run or help her husband defend their home and little one. Mrs. Daniel asked her husband, "[W]hat are you going to do?" and he responded, "I don't know what to do." Any decision they made could result in them and their baby being harmed. She begged Sir not to obey the men's orders, crying, "For Lord's sake don't go out, or I'll die."[75] Mrs. Daniel assessed the situation and understood she could not fight the white men off, nor could she live in a world and raise their baby if her husband went outside and the men killed him.

Targets of night riding were all vulnerable to harm, but people bore the burden in different ways. Sex, age, health, and physical and mental vulnerability shaped both how targets experienced violence and what culprits did.[76] In the immediate aftermath of raids, attacked people began the process of trying to account for what had happened to them and to heal their physical and psychological injuries.

In orchestrating harrowing raids, night riders forced people they held captive to literally fight for their lives. White men's decision to strike *families* multiplied the disorder and further complicated targeted people's endless calculations to survive. Any decision an individual made—to protect themselves or a loved one—in mayhem involving torture, rape, whipping, and killing had a ripple effect with literal flesh-and-blood consequences for everyone. The sheer terror some captives felt drained them of any semblance of free will, which is exactly what their attackers intended. These diabolical choices night riders forced on households strained familial bonds, which added to the many physical and psychological harms victims endured.

Strikes were unbelievable: victims' minds struggled to make sense of what was happening. The events undid many individuals and families. And survivors faced no end of existential questions: Would they live through a raid? How could this have happened? Were they safe? If so, for how long? What could they do to prevent further attacks? Would they stay in their home and community, or would they need to leave? And what would become of them and their families in the aftermath?

Chapter 5

I Don't Ever Expect in This Life to Get Over It

As night riders beat Andrew Cathcart, he pleaded for deliverance: "O Lord, have mercy upon me! Lord, have mercy on my soul!" He later said, "I expected that to be my last word."[1] Vigilantes suspended the people they attacked between life and death. An invasion's end was the only thing that broke the spell and released captives from this suspended state.[2]

Andrew survived. But attacks in white men's war on freedom occurred with the disruptive force of personal hurricanes. They were studded with details—not just life-altering physical injuries but deep psychological wounds, disrupted family dynamics, soul-killing individual and communal betrayals—loaded to raise the risk of long-term suffering. Andrew captured this truth when he said, "I do not believe I will ever be over it." Sixty-seven years later, Isaac Stier, a formerly enslaved man interviewed by the WPA, used the word "disastered" to describe what he observed white men do to families.[3] Disasters are extraordinary—in the words of one sociologist, "*un*manageable, *un*expected, *un*fortunate, *un*planned, *un* events in the extreme."[4] Scientific knowledge of trauma did not yet exist. But survivors didn't need it. Isaac's use of disaster as a verb, the catalog of fatal and life-altering injuries, and survivors' intuition that they would "never get over it" illustrate Black people's clear-eyed understanding of the totalizing nature of attacks. Fresh off the heels of a raid, survivors exiting that in-between space found themselves living in the wake of the disaster Stier described.[5] One Clay Hill, South Carolina, woman—whom three raiders sexually assaulted—said that, after the men left, "I had no sense for a long time. I laid there, I don't know how long."[6] Most of the newly released experienced a moment of euphoric relief as they understood they had lived.[7] But how they survived the *un*thinkable, and why, remained initially *un*knowable. Figuring that out would be part of the many hard tomorrows ahead of them. What victims endured during strikes reverberated throughout their lives.

Clem and Minerva Bowden had to make their way home after night riders abducted them on a wintry night in the Upcountry region of South Carolina and viciously assaulted them in October 1870. "When we got home," Clem said, "we could not kindle up a fire to warm ourselves by, if our children had not been there to kindle it for us." Minerva was whipped "until she was helpless," so grievously injured that "she could not get up the next morning."[8] Clem added, "I was severely hurt. I don't ever expect in this life to get over it."[9]

For people like Cathcart and the Bowdens, injuries from attacks on their families, the loss of kin, and the destruction of home, community, and even way of life left them stupefied. The world untouched by assaults kept spinning, though, which meant survivors could not afford to stand still. The inevitable realities of life and devotion to their people pulled former captives back into the world and forward in time. Survivors came to understand rather quickly that surviving strikes was not the same thing as being out of danger or emerging unscathed.

Statements like Andrew Cathcart's, and Clem Bowden's concern about "never getting over" what had happened, were not just turns of phrase. The similar language reveals the shared nature of survivors' understanding of their experiences, and of their shared need to communicate a dark, often ignored, truth: night-riding strikes were not neatly contained events that ended when white men left families' homes and homesteads. Survivors were unmistakably clear about how these raids leached into the marrow of victims' lives.[10] That's because they endured or observed wide-ranging physical and psychological injuries they recognized as having the power to undo individuals, families, and communities long after their attackers left. Indeed, that was the shadow army's goal.

Bound forever to what happened, targeted people had to live in the years that followed with the many violations—compromised health, loss of ability and of livelihood, moral injuries—they experienced during their attacks. Strikes turned victims into philosophers. Nothing—neither slavery nor the Civil War—had equipped most targeted people to deal with what happened. Survivors keenly assessed and ruminated on the afterlife of strikes. When targeted people conveyed their doubts of ever "being over" disastrous attacks, they were living through and anticipating their own and other people's unmaking. These appraisals point to personal nadirs, to victims having to figure out how to live with what had died in them during the raids.

But not everyone shrank into themselves from horrors they had experienced. In their centuries-long enslavement, African Americans forged what one historian describes as a "codex of survival," including a "soft blueprint of hope" for transformative change that had sustained them through emancipation. Charting survivors' progress shows how that codex guided them through the aftermath of calamity as they assessed their injuries and began their initial efforts to remake themselves by seeking medical treatment, and justice.[11]

The very existence of Andrew's and Clem's accounts also points to traces of that blueprint of love and hope. Love for themselves and affection for their people—the kind of self-regard and devotion that inspires someone to fight even when they are terrified, and that curls around those who are suffering and lifts them up. And the kind of hope that grows, for the religious, from appreciation of the Lord's mercy, and for nonbelievers, from having been spared. Hope for life on the other side of a strike and beyond all facets of white supremacy. Hope that people who heard their stories would try to help make things right. And with the transformative potential of love and hope, a glimmering belief in the possibility of justice.

————

Because some targeted people's lives remained in imminent danger, and the full scope of their tragedies were still unfolding before their eyes, some of them passed through these processes of exiting the in-between space of an attack slower than others. Strikes, despite the white men's departure, did not have neat and clear endings. Hannah Tutson and Eliza Lyon were among the many who did not have the luxury of being in a dazed state for long, with life-and-death matters commanding their attention and requiring action. And yet some, like Abram Colby's daughter, Amanda, remained stuck, hovering in stunned disbelief, devastated and unable to cope. Still others lived through the fallout as strikes' aftereffects ate away at them.[12] Whatever physical or psychic wounds survivors carried with them, they had to have support systems—people to cling to who understood the wickedness that had given rise to this violence and were willing to make the world good and kind again—to help them progress through the maze of disaster.

White men had invaded Hannah Tutson's Florida home, dragging her husband and her out to separate locations and sending their three little ones to the woods to hide. She had lived through being beaten and repeatedly sexually assaulted by the deputy sheriff. The white man had poured liquor over her in one of many acts of debasement, including making her pray for her life during his assault.

It was still dark when the men finally left Hannah alone. But their departure did not end her ordeal. At first, the silence surrounding her led Hannah to believe she was her family's only survivor. Her body had sustained serious physical injuries, including a likely prolapsed uterus. Hannah could not rest, much less seek treatment, however, until she found Samuel and the children.[13]

Love and desperation pulled Hannah out of the stupor of the raid and back into the realities of its afterlife. Hannah walked, with her ripped dress barely covering her bloody body, back to her home; her house had been torn down. Samuel and the children were nowhere to be seen or heard. Hannah could not bear to face the men again on her own, so she sought help.

Calling out that there had been "murder," Hannah walked on to ask at her neighbors' if any of her kin had come to them or if they would help with the search. All declined and turned her away. It is possible they did not want to invite whatever hell had befallen the battered, barely clothed woman on their doorsteps into their lives. The neighbors urged her to search for her family instead. Their refusal to help illustrates the ways strikes could sabotage the ethics of community.

Hannah turned back toward her family's land, eventually finding Samuel, whom the men had whipped, still tied to a tree. Hannah and Samuel spent the last hours of that night in stunned disbelief, distressed by their children's absence. It was not until well after the sun rose that their daughter saw it was safe to lead her siblings home. Only then did Hannah know they had all survived the raid, and that she could begin to get the care she needed and the family could begin to reassemble their lives.

Individuals and families attacked by the shadow army had a range of primary concerns as they made their way through the initial warren of strikes' aftermaths and began to reckon with what happened. First, the attack itself had to have truly ended. For Hannah and Samuel, that didn't happen when the men left them alone but when their children returned home safe and as unharmed as possible, given the circumstances. Then, the aftershocks had to abate enough for victims to process. When they stepped into the limbo of a strike's aftermath, survivors felt a profound appreciation for having lived. They mentally and physically mapped the world decimated by the attacks and the new one left in its place. It was only then that the Tutsons found family and friends who gathered them in the communal embrace and provided some of the care they needed to move forward.

Eliza Lyon had watched from a distance as white men killed her husband, Abe, after grabbing him while he was paralyzed by fright. She spent the night in the woods, in her bedclothes, hiding with her girls by her side, wondering what had happened to her son, William, who had disappeared during the raid. After their attackers finally left and she saw she could return without harm, Eliza went to survey the damage and confirm the gruesome details of her husband's death.[14] She was horrified by what she saw; a coroner later reported that Abe's murderers had inflicted more than thirty bullet wounds and an attempted decapitation. Eliza sifted through the wreckage of her ransacked home, looking to salvage what she could, and went searching for William, finding the terrified boy safe, if not sound, at a neighbor's home.[15]

Families like Hannah's and Eliza's then turned to practical matters. They had to figure out their next moves. For Hannah and Samuel this meant seeking treatment for their injuries, finding shelter, and contacting kin to help rebuild their home. For Eliza, this meant burying Abe. Because her attackers had threatened her life, Eliza joined other families in dispensing with customary funerary practices.[16] With raids still occurring, it was not safe for survivors to wait for kin to travel, then hold a traditional funeral and meal to honor the dead and comfort the living. These families relied on people in their community spheres, like Eliza did; other people targeted by the men contributed to the initial inquest and helped her with Abe's burial. Even as they buried their dead, targeted families had to determine whether the attacks they had endured were one-time events or if they were liable to be struck again, and if so, when, and what precautions they could take, if any. Lack of security denied those living in night-riding zones the time and space they needed to fully process what happened and begin to grieve their losses.

Survivors' priorities—escaping, avoiding more violence, identifying secure spaces—often vied with one another. Like Eliza and her girls, and the Tutsons' children, many hid until the coast was clear. Augustus Blair's wife spent the night in a cotton patch in the freezing cold, believing she was more secure there than moving about and risking detection or returning to her family. When the sun rose, she could see the men were gone, and it was safe for her to return home. Sir Daniel's neighbor Lewis Jackson departed Stevenson, Alabama, by train shortly after the attack on his family ended; his wife, Sally, and the rest of the family remained behind.

In the case of George Houston, of Sumter County, Alabama, his people, including his brother and four community members, formed a ring of protection as he hid in Sucarnoochee swamp. The men stood sentry throughout the night, waiting for the sun to rise so they could arrange a convoy to transport him. George was injured, with open, bleeding wounds, but he recognized it was too dangerous for him to run or get help.

"I laid all night in the rain," George said. Although he was exposed to the elements, the August weather in 1869 helped him fare better than victims who were attacked during the winter months. After George spent the night bleeding in the rain, his people transported him to Bennett's Station, seven miles from the county's courthouse, where he boarded a train. "I never stopped until I got there," he later said. "I have not been there since."[17]

————————

Like Hannah Tutson and George Houston, survivors were often injured in a variety of ways. Clem Bowden's wounds were too severe for him to get to authorities on his own. Clem's wife, Minerva, and older daughter had deeper and stronger ties to the white elite than he did, so they traveled to Spartanburg to report the attack, hoping to set the wheels of justice in motion. The Bowden women appeared in court and testified under oath, which seems to have prompted some judicial action on their behalf. Clem could not bear witness himself, he later said, because "I was then almost passing away."[18]

"I have never been right in my head again," Letty Mills said, recalling the beating she received when men assaulted her family, including her four children.[19] Andrew Cathcart's injuries left him physically lame and unable to work his fields for more than short stints—a devastating loss for a man who had bought himself and his loved ones out of slavery, and who had acquired what he described as his "little plantation."

Children and adolescents would never again be kids in the same way after their families were attacked. They had to deal with a host of physical injuries that required attention. After one of the men attacking the Tutsons snatched their youngest child from Hannah's arms and flung the infant across their home, the baby had a difficult time walking: when she put pressure on one of her legs, she screamed in pain, Hannah said. Henry Reed's teenage son survived a blast of gunfire as he leapt through a window to escape, but his ear was grazed, leaving him injured and permanently scarred. "She has not been able to do much since," Jane Surratt said of her daughter's injuries from the whipping and beating she received during the attack. "I don't believe she will ever get over it," Jane added, echoing other survivors.[20]

Injured survivors needed urgent medical care. After Billy Blair's attackers finally left him, his distraught father, Augustus, did not have the luxury of worrying about being attacked again. He was in the fight of his life to save his boy. Augustus carried a profusely bleeding Billy home, then sent the family's young boarder to locate Dr. Frank Blair. But the doctor would not come. Desperate, Augustus sent for Frank's father, Dr. John Blair. (The Blairs had likely held Augustus's family in bondage, and they retained the name to signal their past and present association.) John Blair came and surveyed Billy's wounds. "I don't think I can do him any good," the doctor conceded.[21]

A shocked and anguished Augustus pushed back, asking, "Are you going off without trying to do him any good, doctor?" Chagrined, Dr. Blair asked the family if they had any tallow and castile soap. They did, and the doctor spent the next two hours making a poultice and a salve, and dressing Billy's wounds.

"You couldn't touch him anywhere," Augustus said, "from his shoulders down to the tips of his toes. There was no place in his legs or feet that you could touch him."[22] Billy was "cut to pieces." "The calves of his legs were split up and cut across," Augustus said, "and his thighs were split open and cut across, and his knee looked like they had tried to take the cap off of his knee, and all his hands and arms were cut and slit up too." Even the bottoms of his feet were split open.[23] When Billy was stable enough to travel, Augustus hired a wagon to take them to Huntsville. Augustus's beloved son died about a year later, having never recovered from his injuries.

Whipping was a common feature of attacks. "My fingers on this arm will never get right in the world," one South Carolina man explained. "My fingers have no feeling."[24] "I couldn't bear any clothes around me," he said of his other injuries.[25] The whipping left him "so crippled up," he was stooping low.

Survivors made clear that the physical dimensions of the attacks they had endured had not ended when the white men left their homes. Hannah Tutson said of her lasting injuries, "Sometimes now I can hardly walk." Vigilantes firing into James Alston's home had struck him. The ball, which remained lodged in his back, "injures me a good deal, I think it will be for life," he said. James's wife, who was seven months pregnant at the time of the raid, was also shot in the heel of her foot. She "has been injured a good deal," he said.[26] The extent of targeted people's injuries also seemed to reveal themselves more over the course of the days following an attack. "They disabled me so I could not feed myself for two days," one South Carolina man said.[27]

Wounded people often turned to trusted healers for initial medical care.[28] Using saltwater to treat people who had been whipped or beaten was a skill that kin and community members acquired during slavery.[29] Next came a deeper cleansing with a gentle oil-based soap. Healers then applied tallow, a rendered form of animal fat used as a salve, to limit scarring and blistering.

Some survivors turned to doctors instead of healers, and patients occasionally learned just how close they had come to death.[30] A doctor revealed to one Alabama man that, had the bullet in his neck struck less than an inch in a different direction, it would have hit a vein and killed him.[31] The treatment victims described receiving from doctors ranged from good to negligent, as they sought the removal of bullets or fragments, or attention for brain injuries. One Alabama man was treated for being kicked in the head by an attacker wearing a boot spur that cracked his skull. "I laid six months with it before I got well," the man said.[32]

As desperate as survivors often were, seeking medical treatment from doctors came with many challenges. Medical science in the Civil War era predated the germ theory of disease and antibiotics. Most doctors lacked knowledge of sterile techniques and antisepsis practices. So even if survivors with infected wounds found doctors, the doctors might not have been able to help them.

Doctors were not always in geographic proximity to injured victims to provide them with the timely treatment they needed, or they were away or otherwise unavailable. After being attacked, Columbus Jeter immediately tried three times to contact a nearby doctor but received no answer. He passed out and was rescued by a Samaritan who took him home and brought a doctor to treat him.[33]

Victims needed to have money on hand or demonstrate means of paying, because doctors refused treatment without payment or an in-kind services or goods agreement in advance.[34] One doctor initially attended Columbus, but because he had no cash to pay the physician, he had to seek further care elsewhere. The new doctor removed four pieces of shot from his body, and Columbus paid him using five bushels of corn.[35]

Henry Lowther's case shows another troubling aspect of strikes and survivors' pursuit of care from medical professionals. Henry, who was forty-one years old, was snatched from a jail in Wilkinson County, Georgia, and kidnapped and castrated in August 1871. Afterward, his attackers laid him down and told him, "as soon as you can get to a doctor, go to one." Believing Henry would survive but remaining determined to drive him from the community, his kidnappers said, "as soon as you are able to leave, do it, or we will kill you next time."

Naked and bleeding profusely, Henry hoped to make it the two and a quarter miles to the nearest doctor he knew. He went to one of the guards who had held him in the jail before he was snatched, and asked for help, specifically that he go and retrieve his clothes for him. The man refused.

"You must," Henry countered, "I am naked and nearly frozen to death." The man took some pity on him and helped Henry dress so he could continue what would become an odyssey for aid.[36]

"I could hardly walk then," Henry said. He asked the jailer's son for assistance, and he, too, declined.[37] Henry staggered throughout the town, begging for help. He went to a store and saw a few white men he knew. They asked Henry what he wanted. "Help," he replied. The men were not persuaded and offered no assistance.

Henry pressed on. At one point, he stopped by the side of a house to keep from passing out. Henry stayed there for a few minutes, then pushed the final quarter mile to the doctor's house and called for him. But the doctor did not answer.

"The next thing I knew," Henry said, "I was lying on the sidewalk in the street—seemed to have just waked up out of a sleep."[38] Thirst gripped him. "I had to go about a quarter of a mile to get some water," he said.[39] As Henry continued staggering throughout the area, he started having problems breathing, but the water gave him some relief.

In what would be the last fifty yards of Henry's plight, he found the house of a Black woman and asked her to go get his wife. Henry's son happened to be nearby, possibly searching for him, and he went looking for the same doctor Henry had visited for treatment. This time, the doctor answered. In a brutal irony, the reason the doctor had been absent before, Henry said, "was that he was off on this raid."[40] This realization compounded the moral injuries Henry suffered.

Even when they received proper treatment, the injured still had to recover enough to resume their daily activities. People who were whipped often experienced intense fevers while their bodies worked to fight off infection. Those with gunshot wounds and concussions needed to rest and heal. Survivors who had sustained emotional injuries needed peace and quiet. For many targeted people, the story of what had happened to them would be forever inscribed on their bodies and minds.

————

Research has revealed that the mind's response to threats to life can cause long-lasting damage; as neuropsychiatrist Bessel van der Kolk famously put it, "the body keeps the score" of what has happened to it.[41] Targeted families had lived through the horrors of slavery, the Civil War, and the murderous wave of reprisals that immediately followed emancipation.

Night-riding strikes following so quickly afterward had the power to compound traumatic injuries, trapping some victims in existential crisis.[42]

The accumulation of Black people's traumatic injuries could make strikes all the more soul-crushing. Moral injuries from being attacked could damage victims' psyches. Raids could hollow victims out, imperiling a person's capacity for joy, compromising their ability to love, undermining their talents. The constellation of betrayal from raids' many horrors could dismantle survivors' sense of self and their assumptions about the world and their place in it. Spiritual distress isolated survivors from kin and community, and reduced their capacity to live fully in the world.[43]

Survivors of night-riding attacks described their feelings in ways that register high on the Impact of Events Scale, a tool medical professionals use today to measure suffering from a traumatic event, evaluating the frequency of distressing feelings over a set period of time.[44] The scale is designed to allow patients to communicate their psychological pain even if they don't have the precise medical vocabulary to do so. Although people targeted by Klan attacks didn't have today's lexicon of trauma or the benefit of psychotherapy, their descriptions of their distress weeks, months, and years afterward illuminate their profound suffering.

A survivor's state of physiological and psychological hyperarousal, which allowed them to cope during an attack, did not always abate in its aftermath. "If I hear a stick crack I am watching to see them come and take me," one South Carolina survivor said. At those moments, he might have been mentally transported to the raid he had experienced. He could have felt chest pains or a sense of impending doom. He might have even tried to reorganize his life to avoid situations where he felt this way.[45]

Targeted people had problems sleeping because they could not stop their minds from processing attacks. They anticipated being struck again, either literally by vigilantes, or figuratively by flashbacks and other symptoms of their minds' inability to reconcile what had happened to them. Jane Surratt could not sleep well in her home after being whipped alongside her young children. Knowing she and her husband, Jackson, could not protect them there would have intensified Jane's distress and inability to rest. After the family moved to Spartanburg, Jane reported, "I have slept the best that I have rested in two months since I have been here in town."[46] An Alabama survivor experienced similar anguish. "After they whipped me," he said, "I never rested [soundly] another night until I got plumb out of the State."[47] Living in constant fear of another raid made it difficult for victims to get physical and emotional relief, which could precipitate other psychological problems.

Three weeks after the raid in which she was tied to a tree and then whipped and sexually assaulted, Hannah Tutson was experiencing psychological distress. Even though she had washed and washed, she still smelled the liquor her assailant had poured over her as he violated her. Intrusive memories such as these could roil Hannah's emotions, triggering flashbacks and sending her heart racing.

Many victims described being more sensitive to noises at night and to unexpected events than they had been before. After he saw armed white men on horseback bearing down on his family's home, Edward Crosby said, there were nights when "I didn't sleep more than an hour, and if there had been a stick [that] cracked very light, I would have sprung up in the bed."[48] Many remained on edge, anticipating another attack. "They are all scared," another South Carolina survivor said, discussing his family and people in his community. But having been struck once, he knew the difference between fearing something could very well happen and having it occur. "I have been stung once, and even a burnt child fears the fire," he said.[49] He and other survivors understood that their fear was rational, given what had happened to them—and might yet again, with perpetrators and their allies running free.

Survivors' sense of hyperawareness also indicated injury. The gang who attacked one South Carolina man said they would not "bother" him again, but their initial strike represented a shocking violation. Despite the men's promise, the victim remained troubled about his family's security and his ability to protect them. "Of course, I looked for men in that house ever since. I am watching about."[50] Simultaneously remembering what had happened while always girding for what might happen made it difficult for survivors to be mentally present, a point reflected in Edward Crosby's statement about not knowing "what to be" at times after white men had targeted him.

"I was living under fears of being attacked again," an Alabama survivor said. He felt this way despite being well known and generally liked by people in his community. "To tell the truth, I am not over it yet," the man said of the strike, during which he had been shot. "I cannot rest satisfied, because I know how this ball felt in my neck," he added. The man's statement indicates the ways physical injuries were linked to emotional suffering. When asked if he still felt fear of being attacked again, despite no immediate threat, he answered, "[A] little doubt still seems to arise; I can't help it to save my life; it will come up sometimes."[51]

Witnesses also shared stories of people they believed had died due to the horrors they experienced.[52] Speaking of his daughter, Amanda, Abram Colby said night riders had "frightened her to death": "She never got over it until she died."[53] The fright the Colby girl endured from the man leveling his shotgun at her could have initiated her withdrawal from the world. Doctors in twenty-first-century conflict zones report instances of resignation syndrome, a disorder in which young victims give up on life.[54] Such a condition could explain what Abram observed in his daughter before she died.

Children's sense of safety generally starts forming in relation to their parents or adult guardians, unless these caregivers are emotionally distant or abusive. Caretakers are a child's primary source of comfort in moments of injury or crisis. During the raid, Amanda could not turn to Abram, whom the men had carried away, nor to her mother, Anna, who was trying to keep herself and the rest of the family secure. After the original strike, night riders continued terrorizing the family, crowding around their home and sometimes firing inside. Abram spent considerable time lying out at night and returning home as needed to avoid being captured. Tending to the family's needs in Abram's absence probably consumed Anna's time and energy. Under these circumstances, there was little, if anything, a family could do to avoid violence once vigilantes arrived. Continued harassment could have deprived Amanda of time she needed to recover, which might have contributed to the girl's undoing.

Children were not alone in being shaken to the core. When the Thommasons of York County, South Carolina, were attacked, white men firing into the family's home sent shot within three inches of Mary Thommason's head. Mary lived through the strike, but her husband, John, said, "they scared her so, she died."[55] When the fight-or-flight response is activated by a terrifying event—like being under fire and having a bullet come as close as the one that nearly hit Mary—a targeted person can experience massive amounts of stress hormones overloading critical organs and causing them to fail.[56] If too much adrenaline floods the heart, the victim can die immediately; if it spikes the liver or kidneys, then the decline occurs at a slower but steady pace, which could explain Mary's demise and John's attributing it to the strike.

Survivors were certain in their understanding that, even if a person did not succumb, living after a strike was not the same thing as being able to heal from it. "I have never got over it yet," Abram Colby said. "They broke something inside of me, and the doctor has been attending to me for more than a year."[57] He reported having a hard time getting up each day. Abram's injuries from his kidnapping were physical, but his statements indicate psychological wounds over the repeated raids and his daughter's death, which was followed by that of his wife, Anna, shortly thereafter.

Abram and other survivors discussed their grief, but it is not hard to imagine the other emotions roiling them.[58] Abram never used the word "guilt," but his political activism plus survivor's remorse, combined with a sense of his own helplessness to protect his daughter from harm, might have troubled him. Indeed, he said Amanda's death was "the part that grieves me the most of all."[59] Abram wept openly when he gave his testimony.[60]

Beyond their descriptions of psychological distress, it is not always clear what survivors observed in their loved ones or themselves that led them to believe they would never be the same—"never getting over it." But many accounts detailing the anguish shine some light into the dark void of the historical record. "They took me off in such excitement," one Alabama man said, "I did not hardly have my mind for two or three weeks." The man suffered significant blows to the head in his assault. "I hardly knew anything," he said of his injuries. The attack and not being able to identify the culprits, he said, were enough to "disturb a man's mind."[61]

Post-strike distress changed Harriet Hernandez's life, too. "I am afraid to go back home," she said. "I have got the trembles." The head trauma Harriet experienced could also have led to recurring memory loss and other symptoms, including headaches, vision loss, and sensitivity to light and sound. Fear of being attacked again added to her misery. She was not returning home, she said, "not unless I see that I can have peace."[62]

Mental and emotional descents could take some victims to and past the edges of madness. Having a gun drawn on her could very well have pushed Abram Colby's daughter into psychosis or a trancelike state. Abram never described Amanda's symptoms, so we simply don't know what happened. But survivors' refusal to eat or inability to control their emotions might have been among the behaviors witnesses observed in their loved ones but did not name in historical records.

Targets of night riders might have experienced shame for a variety of reasons—from how they behaved during a strike to who they had become in its wake, especially in the judgments of kin and people in their community. Many "visited" families carried the social stigma of having been attacked in the first place. Families were further stigmatized once knowledge of the many ways white men had violated them became public.[63] Some neighbors acted like Hannah Tutson's, who turned her away without offering any help, and kept their distance. They treated survivors as though association would mark them, too—as though the violation were contagious. But with many culprits still at large, it was justifiable to fear being attacked for having too close an alliance with victims.

Parents' helplessness and men's inability to protect their families from harm might have resulted in these adults harboring feelings of contrition.[64] Failing to fulfill an expected role could leave survivors feeling disgraced, as though they were somehow accomplices to perpetrators; this in turn could have engendered a sense of utter failure. Some men fled at the sight of night riders; one South Carolina man only returned to face the gang at his wife's urging. Shame from her condemnation of his abandonment could have informed his decision to go back into his home to face the men. Jackson Surratt escaped, but his wife, Jane, and their very young children were whipped in his absence. Some male survivors like Jackson or Augustus Blair could have judged their own actions—or been judged by their loved ones or communities—as failing to fulfill their responsibilities as defenders and protectors. This could result in men burning with self-condemnation of their perceived inadequacy, sinking into an abyss of self-hating despair or lashing out at themselves or others.

Though survivors of raids did not have the language of trauma familiar to people today, they understood and tried to communicate that they and their loved ones were writhing underneath the weight of what they perceived to be violations of moral codes.[65] Through the abject nature of the violence, perpetrators intended to demonstrate all the ways free Black people had no place or protection in postwar southern society. Survivors observed their new circumstances and theorized their own psychological trauma and the corrosion of community.[66] Their articulation of the strikes' impacts—Abram Colby's wide-ranging grief, Harriet Hernandez's hyper-vigilance and anxiety—point to the multilayered nature of the injuries victims endured.

Slavery had exposed Black southerners to barbarous violence, the physical and psychological pain of which it is impossible to quantify. Slavery was abolished, but in the context of a bloody war. Black people were at the center of that conflict and experienced their share of its many catastrophic effects. New psychological injuries from night-riding strikes could bleed into older ones endured during their enslavement or the war, but the traces of the earlier ones remained. Accumulated trauma had the power to break victims' spirits.[67] These victims who lost loved ones, parts of their hearts, and their memories of the way things had been and would never be again fell apart gradually, bit by bit, day by day. Betrayals by neighbors who failed to help Abe and Eliza Lyon and Hannah Tutson in their time of need added to targeted people's suffering and illuminate the unraveling of threads binding the social fabric.[68] Survivors understood that, as far as their attackers were concerned, their lives had no value. Community betrayal compounded their vulnerability, adding to their feelings of alienation.[69]

This is probably why, when Alfred Wright was asked why he feared to return to his home in upstate South Carolina, he answered, "I am afraid of my being destroyed, just in the way they aimed to do it, and I heard them say they would do it."[70] Alfred's use of the word "destroyed" conveys his understanding of how little his life mattered to whites who hated him and what his freedom represented. In the things night riders said and did to targets like Alfred, their belief that Black people had no rights that whites were bound to respect—including, in some cases, the right to life after slavery—was evident. Survivors often experienced the horror of learning their persecutors were white people they knew, even people they thought they had positive relationships with. They lived through the savagery of strikes only to endure the knowledge that their white neighbors were active participants in the attacks or would sit passively and offer them no assistance in their search for amends and answers.

———

One thing survivors like Alfred Wright, Hannah Tutson, and Henry Lowther faced as they grappled with their physical, psychological, and psychic injuries was understanding what had happened. This was a difficult task because, to many, the white war on Black freedom was incomprehensible. For victims, this meant recalling the series of events leading up to and continuing during raids, to understand what had happened to them and why, so they could move forward and possibly take action to bring their attackers to justice. Hannah kept going over the fights she and Samuel had had with the neighbors trying to make them abandon their homestead. Eliza Lyon did the same over Abe's encounters with any hostile whites in his blacksmith shop.

As victims moved throughout the world after attacks, recalling what had happened was a process that was easier for some than for others.[71] People who experience traumatic injury may have difficulty recalling what happened to them, for fear they might lose themselves emotionally in the process. Rather than risk psychic collapse, they often suppress memories of attacks.[72]

Between the effects of stress hormones and the bedlam of attacks, developing a comprehensive understanding of what transpired in a strike could be difficult. People who had endured attacks together interrogated one another, as if trying to assemble mental puzzles. Samuel Tutson likely asked Hannah specifics not only about what had happened when the deputy sheriff led her away, but also about the men's initial arrival and what had happened when they stormed into the home. This questioning was consistent for individuals as well as for families, friends, and co-workers who were attacked together. Survivors pieced together the events and who was involved by relying on people who were in the immediate space of a raid, neighbors or employers who may have watched or listened from the periphery, and secondary and tertiary witnesses who might have learned about the strikes from the perpetrators themselves. Essic Harris collected information from his white neighbors who had observed the gang firing into his North Carolina home with his wife, Ann, and children inside.[73]

Many witnesses never gained complete memories of the raids they endured. Some, like Henry Lowther, might have found themselves playing a constant loop, mentally reenacting the events of a strike. The rush of adrenaline amid emotionally and physically traumatic events transformed what victims saw, felt, and heard, shaping what they remembered or forgot about their attacks.

Gunshot and stab wounds as well as whippings and beatings often led people to lose consciousness.[74] Harriet Hernandez was struck so hard in the head during the physical and sexual assault she experienced, she said, that she "saw stars."[75] Mary Brown's attackers choked her with a rope until she passed out. Henry Lowther passed out from blood loss and dehydration. Blacking out or experiencing blinding pain from head injuries could cause gaps in survivors' memories. These injuries also created conditions for victims to suffer from physical or psychological shock during or immediately following an attack. These varied symptoms would have included dizziness, rapid pulse and breathing, enlarged pupils, skin that became clammy or ashen, and confusion.

Shock also shaped what these victims did or did not remember about their attacks. Some survivors' memories lacked specific details, like the order of events and the number of their attackers, which perplexed authorities.[76] Targeted people's answers to investigators' questions about the number and identity of attackers were imprecise, reflecting the chaos of strikes. "I was so frightened I don't know [how many of them there were]," Jane Surratt said. "But I think there was six or seven . . . I was so frightened that I don't remember."[77] One Mississippi man felt the same fear and experienced the same lack of comprehensive recall as Jane. "I didn't know how many men there were," he said, "they frightened me so when they came that I couldn't tell anything about it."[78] Clem Bowden also admitted, "I was almost deranged, and did not know myself."[79] If Clem barely knew himself amid the pain he endured during the strike, he likely missed some details of his assault or that of his wife, Minerva. The imprecision and gaps in survivors' knowledge and memories created opportunities for people to question the veracity of their accounts.

Investigators and inquiring minds demanded knowledge of how many times victims had been struck by the sticks, whips, belts, and knives night riders used. "I never paid any attention to the number of licks they gave," Letty Mills said, when asked about the men beating on her young children and her. "As quick as one would get done beating another would fall in and beat us," she explained.[80] When it came to the number of stripes they received, if victims could not recall precisely, they relied on counts or assessments taken by loved ones and by healers and doctors who treated them.

If families were going to make sense of what had happened to them and obtain a degree of personal or legal justice, then they needed not just memories but convincing legal evidence to substantiate their claims of criminal behavior. Caroline Watley knew this, which is why when the white men were attacking her husband, Smith, she snuck out back to collect information about them from their horses, which were stashed nearby.

Enslaved and free Black people faced restrictions on their ability to participate formally in the southern legal system, especially as witnesses against white defendants, but they were hardly ignorant of the rules of legal proceedings and criminal investigations.[81] Black southerners' lives and freedom were tied so inextricably to the law, they had to be what one historian calls "savvy legal operators."[82] They gleaned their legal educations through a variety of means. Antebellum legal proceedings were local affairs; hearings and trials were often conducted in homes, yards, or community meeting places. This open legal culture granted Black people access to knowledge of how the law worked.[83] The knowledge was, as Laura Edwards explains, "so widely diffused that southerners knew exactly what to do when they encountered a suspicious event."[84] Smith Watley knew to swear out a warrant on his attackers, whom he easily identified, having known them for twenty years.[85] Robert Fullerlove's family knew to leave their home standing with fifteen shots and charred wood, as evidence of what had transpired.[86] African Americans, then, "had intimate knowledge of the legal system: they knew not only the process but also understood the underlying logic."[87]

Survivors used this insight to assemble the kind of information that would be useful for acting after a strike. The need to know who had attacked them, the details of what their attackers had done, and why drove victims' search for answers. If they felt safe enough to do so, families investigated attacks themselves and collected testimonies from witnesses. In time, they started the process of accounting for what had happened and contacting authorities. Eliza Lyon could see for herself that night riders had shot and nearly decapitated her husband, Abe, but it was the coroner who ultimately explained how many times he had been shot.

Survivors did their best to identify disguised or masked attackers during strikes. Andrew Cathcart monitored the shape of his attackers' heads and bodies, the sounds of their voices, and their clothes, including the design of their coat pockets and pants. Andrew's daughters identified one invader from the scar left by a boil.[88]

Knowing culprits' identities could also be useful during an attack. Mack Henderson's command to his attacker to let him alone had startled the man, who had kept the boy from following his stepfather outside with the band kidnapping him.[89] Calling one of her family's captors by name, Columbus and Aury Jeter's daughter, Emily, had elicited a verbal promise to not harm her, a promise the man had kept.[90] These revealing details about their attackers' identities was crucial in families' search for answers.

Some families knew their attackers, but for people who did not, identifying them was a priority. If they could determine the identity of one invader, knowing the men's social networks, they could probably pinpoint others, too. Willis Johnson lay out for the rest of the night after the strike on his family. The next morning, he returned to his home in Newberry County, South Carolina, to reconstruct the raid. He tracked the men by their horses and footprints through his oat patch.[91]

Other survivors could get a fix on some of their attackers because the men, to better see their prey, had made members of their raiding party or members of the families they were assaulting strike up light. But this did not stop survivors from investigating after the fact, too. Thomas Allen was one of many who conducted crime-scene investigations. As soon as there was enough light to see, Thomas went outside and counted 180 shot marks in his house, including on the bedstead where his wife and child had been sleeping. "They will be there until judgment, or until the house shall rot down," Allen swore. The Allens' damaged home would serve as evidence of the strike and stand as a monument to the betrayal of their freedom.[92] Augustus Mills saw his family's attackers' horses because the white Georgians struck so close to dawn. "I went to track the horses," Augustus said, "and we tracked Felker's mare right to the stable door."[93] Successful tracking was often dependent upon experience and conditions like light, weather, and terrain. "I saw the tracks where they came there," one Spartanburg County, South Carolina, man said of raiders who whipped him in March 1871.[94] Another South Carolinian discovered the band attacking him, in a separate March 1871 raid, had ridden their horses to an area about 150 yards from his home, where they had hitched them before walking in on foot.[95] Still another, after being stripped and whipped by vigilantes on a rainy April night in 1871, said, "I could judge from the horse tracks that there were more than two horses there. Some were horses and some mules." Knowing which white men had horses versus those who traveled with mules, which men were related or associated together, could help this survivor identify the culprits.[96]

Having been viciously whipped and choked to the point of passing out, Mary Brown did not know how many times she and her family members had been hit. She did know, however, that she had been struck "with hickory switches . . . as large as my thumb, and all the cane part they wore out." Mary saw the sticks during the attack, she explained, adding that her people found them the next morning. The "ends of the switches were all frazzled," Mary said.[97]

These inquiries appear to have been communal and family affairs. Smith Watley explained that, having been able to identify one night rider whose mask slipped, he and a group of men followed the horse tracks raiders had left in his yard, hoping to identify the rest.[98] Robert Fullerlove did the same thing after returning home and learning men had set his house on fire with his family inside it. Robert and his sons, Taylor and Alexander, both of whom had been injured in the raid, tracked the pack's horses out west, "the way they always come," Robert said.[99]

Alfred Wright and his son and daughter tracked their attackers, too. "I saw my pindars [peanuts] were gone. I knew that the pindars were taken and I was the only one in the settlement . . . who had any quantity of pindars, and the hulls were all along the road, without any kernels, but of course there had been something in them or the hulls would not have been there."[100] Alfred and his family followed the trails of the discarded hulls the thieves had stolen and eaten on their departure, which he said led "plumb up" to an attacker's house.[101]

Henry Lowther could not investigate the crime scenes of his attack and its aftermath himself. He asked his son to visit the doctor's house to see if there was a "large pool of blood there," as Henry was sure there would be, from his attempt to get treated. Some locals deterred the young Lowther from getting close enough to the doctor's property to see anything. Concerned Black women in the community visited Henry and informed him "that the blood was there all over town; at the doctor's gate, and everywhere else." The amount of blood they described seeing did not surprise Henry. "It was running a stream all the time I was trying to find the doctor," he said. "I thought I would bleed to death."[102] The blood trail could substantiate Henry's claims of what the white men had done to him, and of his journey for assistance.

Survivors' and their allies' collection and presentation of evidence reflected their need to understand what had happened. Communal investigations, like the Black women's intelligence about the bloodstained trail Henry had left, represented the ethos of care and responsibility for one of their own. A community's post-strike embrace might have lessened victims' feelings of isolation. Investigations also indicate targeted people's initial confidence in their ability to activate their newly acquired right to eventually summon the law on their behalf. All of this contributed to African Americans' sense of themselves beyond their victimization and their desire to reclaim their power and to position themselves to rejoin the race for life and liberation.

If men like Alfred Wright and Henry Lowther had any doubts about the difference freedom made or about their place in the nation, entering the matrix of a night-riding raid and having their lives turned upside down and inside out provided striking clarity about their abjection. Families knew the people in their communities—neighbors, patrons, and civil authorities who watched them be brutalized or offered no assistance—could not necessarily be trusted to help them get justice or even protect their lives. With raids still occurring, victims lived with the mental anguish and the dread of being raided again. For many, with no security where they were, the only solution left was to take flight.

Chapter 6

They Never Intended to Do Me Justice

Eliza Lyon found herself in a race to reach the Tombigbee River. She had watched from a distance as night riders killed her husband, Abe. Sometime after meeting with the coroner, she quickly buried Abe's body and sold anything left of value to support herself and her four children.

Authorities convened a grand jury, but something must have spooked Eliza. Terrified the pack might return for her and her children, she grabbed what she could carry and left DeSotoville, Alabama, making a beeline for the waterway. The family's homeplace, Choctaw County, was in Alabama near the border with Mississippi. When Eliza and the children left their hamlet, they had fourteen miles to cover before they would reach a crossing at Tompkinsville and find a ferryman willing to carry them across to where they hoped they would be secure.

As they traveled through what had been their small farming community, they would have passed farms with rows and rows of recently planted cotton and corn, with tall green trees of the wilderness in the background. Eliza did not say whether she and the children traveled by foot, astride horses and mules, or in a wagon. Or whether they took the main roads through town or walked paths in the uncultivated wooded areas. She also did not mention whether or not she and the children were alone or if they had assistance. What she did say was that she could not stay in DeSotoville.

Abe's killers had other plans. Members of the same gang had set Mrs. Robert Fullerlove's home on fire with her and her family inside of it, and had torched two churches and schools, triggering the grand jury. Either monitoring the Lyons, or perhaps hearing community gossip about their plans, a pack of ten set off in pursuit when they discovered Eliza and her children had fled. The criminals worried she might report their murderous deeds to outside authorities.

At some point in Eliza and the children's journey, they might have realized they were being chased. The family picked up their pace. Unencumbered by young children and personal belongings, the white men threatened to overtake the family, until, around ten o'clock in the morning, the sky opened up with a storm. The family's trackers slowed, perhaps pausing to take shelter. But Eliza and the children kept racing toward the river, where they crossed to Tompkinsville.[1]

Eliza fled because she knew she and her family were no longer secure where they lived. But for those who survived harrowing night-riding attacks, "safety," even in a new location, was a relative concept. In the poem "Home," Warsan Shire writes of displacement by violence; the narrator notes that geographically and socially established people do not abandon the comfort and safety of their homes and all of their property for no reason. "No one leaves home, unless home is the mouth of a shark" or "the barrel of a gun."[2] Frantic escapes may be triggered by paramilitary violence upending a community, or by being marked as undesirables who must be cast out or slaughtered. People do not leave home, Shire's poem explains, "unless home chases you," breathing in your ear that any place else is safer than where you thought you belonged.[3]

For Eliza and the children, home had been the space that sustained them in their journey to freedom. Now, it was the cursed community where Abe's killers could leverage their deeds into wealth and power. Down, but not defeated, Eliza wanted to live, and she knew Abe would have wanted that for her and the children. So, she fled the place her family had called home, rushing into the void of uncertainty; any place was more secure than her bullet-riddled house in a town where white men were able to claim Abe the way they had. With the wickedness of white supremacy further revealed, and victims' trust in their communities broken by night riders' actions, people like Eliza responded to the collective message that their lives did not matter. Hope for a future, and for another place they might call home, pulled Eliza and other targeted families forward through the maze of strikes' aftermaths.

Survivors' desperate search for long-term security after they were attacked was often the next step on their journey through the labyrinth of disaster. Many victims made frantic escapes like that of Eliza and the children. A number of families made short-term decisions for *individuals* to leave immediately after they were attacked. Absconding saved lives and gave survivors a chance to report the violence to local and state authorities who might end it. But dislocation also deprived family members of the social and economic support they needed after a strike. Displacement put families in financial free fall. If the violence in their communities did not abate and authorities' apathy forced them to lower their expectations for judicial redress, cast-out people had to accept the loss of everything they had achieved and make long-term relocation plans for *entire families*.

––––––––

If night riders' objectives were to drive some Black families out of their homes and off their land, they might give targets leave-or-die ultimatums. "They told me that they were coming again in six weeks," said Daniel Lane, after a pack of men pistol-whipped him. "Now, if a man is warned of danger and he stays and is caught again, it's his own fault."[4] Daniel was not a foolish man; he recognized the threat to his life and departed Morgan County, Georgia, with the quickness.

Doc Rountree's attackers had insisted he leave the community. When Doc rejected the idea that he should forsake home as well as the land and property he had acquired, his attackers' leader was furious. A defiant Black man who owned his land and was determined to protect his family's freedom threatened his former enslavers' view of the world and could not be allowed to remain. Doc said the white man told him that if the Rountrees did not leave, "He would kill every one of us."[5]

Like Daniel Lane, Doc and Ellen Rountree were not foolish. Their attackers did not give them the luxury of six weeks to be gone. The couple decided their lives were more valuable than their property; they left as soon as they could. Doc, Ellen, and four of their children were still wounded from the savage beatings and whippings they had endured. Doc said, "I could not walk far." But the family knew they could not stay in the vicinity of their home or in town without being attacked again. They left their little farm in Suwannee County, Florida, and headed to the nearby woods, thinking they might be able to find a place to camp, rest, catch their breaths, and decide what to do next.

Rest did not come easily to any of the Rountrees. The leave-or-die command denied them the opportunity to gather their belongings or seek treatment for their injuries. Hiding in the woods, they were exposed to all the elements. Throughout the night, Doc heard the night riders invading other people's homes. "They scared me so, I got almost right well," he said. The closeness of rural communities meant outcast families like the Rountrees probably couldn't seek shelter with relatives or friends without drawing the white men to them, too. Doc, Ellen, and the children left, looking for a place more secure than Live Oak.[6]

Cast out—chased by the barrels of guns, the ends of whips, the fires leaping from homes into the night sky, and the thunder of vigilantes' horses' hooves coming for them—survivors like the Rountrees flocked to local thoroughfares, byways, railways, and waterways, trying to escape the shadow army. Some escaping parties hid in the outskirts of wooded trails, fearing their hunters would catch them. Taking pathways they or their loved ones could have traversed during the antebellum years—as people fleeing the daily grind of bondage, the threat of sale, or a punishment—survivors also probably hid in caves or swamps.

Most outcasts were bolting from isolated rural hamlets and moving toward centers of government or military authority, where they thought they might receive the protections under the law now enshrined in the Constitution. The Rountrees made their way to Jacksonville. Clem Bowden relocated his family from their home just north of Limestone Springs, South Carolina, to the fringes of Spartanburg, where he rented a place and established a yearlong work contract. The Bowdens had not slept under the same roof for nearly a year after their first raid. "They were alarmed," Clem said of his family, "and afraid to stay where I am."[7]

Clem's family was suffering from the first strike, in which he and his wife, Minerva, were beaten, when a white man visited while Clem was away. The white man told Minerva he was Ku Klux and there to "persecute" the new Black residents of the area. "It scared my folks almost to death," Clem said of the prospect of enduring another raid.[8]

"I had a place where I could have a tater patch and things for the children," Clem said, but "they have been scared for their lives." His family's fear prompted Clem to move them to Spartanburg proper, where he hoped they could rest and begin to recover. When investigators pressed him about why he had abandoned the new place for yet another one, Clem confirmed that his children, who ranged from preteens to young adults, would not sleep there because they were terrified of "being destroyed." It was only when Clem moved them to the center of town, where it might be harder for assailants to get at them without witnesses and law enforcement possibly intervening, that his family could rest easily.[9]

Strikes were atrocities unto themselves, but what many victims encountered in the immediate aftermath revealed how the nightmare that began when invaders arrived continued long after they left. Survivors' understanding of their abjection and resulting lack of security sparked their flights from home, stretching out the upheaval vigilantes brought. White neighbors, doctors, and law enforcement officials who provided little to no help revealed themselves, at best, as passive witnesses to survivors' suffering or, at worst, accomplices or actual perpetrators, rendering night-riding victims' worlds even less secure than they had previously imagined. "Nobody there seemed to have no use for us—[we had] no old friends," one South Carolina man explained of the lack of patrons, particularly white people who might intervene on targeted people's behalf or offer protection.[10] The refusal of whites in their communities to assist them accentuated the depth and breadth of the marks outcast families bore.

Unless they received leave-or-die threats like the Rountrees did, however, many families stayed and tried to get a degree of justice. But to do this, survivors had to identify and communicate with adequate witnesses who might help them. Essic Harris reported the raid on his family, and his shooting of one of the night riders, to a U.S. commissioner who investigated violence in and around Chatham County, North Carolina, in May 1870.

Earlier that year, progressive lawmakers in Congress had stepped up their efforts to halt the white armies waging war on American democracy and Black southerners' freedom, passing the first of the Enforcement Acts to help bolster the Fourteenth Amendment and the Civil Rights Act of 1866. This legislation made interfering with voting a federal offense, required federal oversight for voter registration and elections, and authorized the president to send in military forces when terrorist groups interfered with the democratic process. U.S. commissioners were appointed to inquire about acts of violence and lawlessness. If targeted people got no recourse via local authorities, then they could report to members of U.S. circuit courts, who might have authority to issue warrants and facilitate trials.[11] President Ulysses S. Grant, who had been sworn into office on March 4, 1869, beefed up the Army's presence in some affected areas, but there were significant gaps in its protective coverage.[12]

The commissioner arrested some of Essic's attackers, but they and their accomplices alibied each other. A white posse harassed Essic, ordering him to drop the case against his attackers or pay the ultimate price.[13]

When Augustus Blair got to Huntsville with his son, Billy—who had sustained extensive injuries from being repeatedly stabbed and beaten by his assailants—Gus filed a formal complaint. Authorities arrested eleven white men and held a grand jury inquest into the vicious assault. It was during this time that Billy died of his injuries. Then, as was common in cases such as this, most of the culprits ran off; Augustus said only three showed up to the U.S. court.[14] This, combined with reports of how the legal and judicial systems were handling such cases, would not have bolstered Augustus's belief that Billy's killers would be punished.

Survivors reporting attacks to local authorities must have felt that their social position was high enough—and the savagery visited upon them great enough—that they were in a good position to get justice. News of the raid on Thomas Allen's family—in which vigilantes killed his brother-in-law and almost their entire family—was shocking and circulated quickly throughout the Jasper County, Georgia, community. Authorities convened a formal inquest, concluding that at least three guns had been fired, one loaded with slugs, one with buckshot, and one with small shot. Investigators also found the shot lodged in the bedstead where the family had been sleeping.[15]

During much of the military occupation of the former Confederate states, Army and Freedmen's Bureau personnel had turned civil and criminal cases over to local authorities. Some bureau agents could have directed survivors like Augustus Blair and Thomas Allen to magistrates to report violence. However, as the military presence shrank and the bureau collapsed thanks to chronic underfunding, some survivors had nowhere to turn but local policymakers and law enforcement. In hard-liner strongholds, victims of raids were less likely to get fair hearings, if any hearings at all. Judges and juries were often vigilante sympathizers, if not perpetrators or abettors themselves.

As violence continued and culprits managed to evade capture, prosecution, and conviction, some victims increasingly recognized the futility of pursuing criminal or civil cases locally. They calculated the risks and determined that seeking legal and judicial assistance at the state and federal levels was safer. Others simply surrendered and never reported attacks to law enforcement.

"I never made any complaint at all because I saw it was not necessary," Robert Fullerlove said. Everyone in his Tompkinsville, Alabama, community knew that white men had shot into his home and set it on fire, with his family inside of it. It was part of a larger spree, in which night riders killed

Abe Lyon and torched two churches and schools. The killing and burnings prompted a grand jury.

Because the system seemed to be moving in the direction of something akin to justice, the white men who had attacked Robert's family continued threatening his life, making it unsafe for his wife, Adaline, and their children to stay in or near their home at night.[16] Robert understood he had not done anything wrong by voting for Radical candidates or accumulating the wealth he had. However, he appreciated the dangerous times in which he lived and understood that being in the right was not as important as being alive and protecting his family. Appreciating the absurdity of the situation in Tompkinsville, Robert asked investigators, "What is the use of a man trying to live in this world in that condition?"

Three hundred miles to the east, in Walton County, Georgia, another man's response to investigators captured precisely how ineffectual he thought they were. "What?!! Get justice from the Ku-Klux in that country!?!" he asked. "I was done satisfied that we never could get justice from the Ku-Klux there; they would have killed us before we could get it."[17] Cheating death, as survivors like this man knew, meant forgoing seeking justice.

Beyond a general sense that pursuing justice through formal means was futile, survivors who tried to file complaints were often thwarted along the way. One man filed a complaint in Colbert County, Alabama—after he was attacked following a dispute with his landlord—that made it to trial by a U.S. commissioner. But supporting witnesses failed to appear because they were afraid of retribution.[18]

Anderson Ferrell tried in vain to gain restitution after men invaded his home, robbed his family of their belongings, and killed his dog. He reported the violence to his employer and patron, a white man named Judge Ferrell, who was probably the man who had held Anderson in bondage. The raid occurred on the judge's land, so Anderson thought he might get justice for the injuries he had sustained.

However, after spending six months attempting to have the pack prosecuted and recoup damages for lost work and stolen property, Anderson said, "I saw they never intended to do me justice." If Anderson's patron was not complicit in the raid, then he seemed to object to having the culprits Anderson identified prosecuted. Without the judge's support, Anderson and his family had little chance of seeing the brutes who had terrorized them punished.

Judge Ferrell and other leading white men wanted Anderson and his assailants to settle out of court. The perpetrators promised to pay restitution but never followed through, so Anderson let his case stay within the courts. "So far as pay was concerned," Anderson said, "I wanted the law to take its course." Anderson professed his "love" for the judge's family, but also felt he'd been betrayed: "They went back on me."[19]

A disgusted Anderson packed his family up and relocated to Atlanta. The last Anderson knew, the men who had invaded his home were awaiting trial. Whatever hope Anderson may have had about getting justice and maybe returning home dissipated when he realized no such relief was forthcoming, especially not from people who had enabled night riding by failing to help punish it. White men's dogged pursuit of Anderson and others underscores the danger of trying to bring offenders to justice in a war against Black freedom.

Distrust of the local legal system and fear of retribution or death unnerved survivors. "Times are very dangerous," one South Carolina man said. "We did not know what minute they would come on us and kill us." Vigilantes were still running loose, "riding from one place to another all the time."[20] Alfred Wright, who had identified his attackers by their trail of discarded peanut shells, declined to press charges when asked to by investigators. "I had to save my life in this place," Alfred said. "I was scared at the same time, like all the balance."[21]

Survivors' fear of reprisal and suspicion that criminal charges might not yield convictions were well founded. Federal prosecutors brought charges of voter intimidation and suppression in a circuit court against a group of South Carolina white men for Klan attacks in the 1870 election. Concerns about whether the federal government could assert its authority and prosecute white South Carolinians who were accused of interfering with elections and terrorizing African Americans dogged prosecutions: some sympathetic Washington policymakers wanted to intervene, but they ran up against a legal culture that still favored states when it came to prosecuting crimes against civilians within their borders. For survivors living in bastions of extremism—and until Reconstruction's massive expansion of federal power reached the criminal justice system—this custom put a finger on the scale favoring vigilantes.[22] Of those indicted, few were found guilty. Convicted white men served little to no time, paid minor fines, fled to evade justice, or were later pardoned.

Although fear and white apathy discouraged victims from having criminal charges filed or bringing civil lawsuits, there were additional factors at play hindering their efforts. Finding funds to retain and pay an attorney after losing property, cash, or employment could be difficult. Additionally, survivors needed to find lawyers who were allies and not culprits themselves; who would not take their money and run or throw their cases; and who were unafraid of being victimized themselves and would not betray them. Even if they had trustworthy attorneys, they were not confident that offenders or witnesses who could substantiate their claims would appear in court. They had little confidence that all-white or mostly white juries in the same communities where night riding occurred would convict white vigilantes, even with sufficient evidence of their criminal deeds.

Facing either indifferent or ineffectual officials at the local and state level as well as challenges bringing criminal or civil suits, many terrorized people held out hope for federal intervention, at least for a time. After witnessing an impressive show of federal force during the Civil War and Republicans' aggressive expansion of federal power during Radical Reconstruction, some targeted people thought federal officials could stop paramilitary strikes as well.

But overall, optimism could be hard to come by. One man who lived outside of DeSotoville, the Lyons' Alabama hamlet, said night riding was ruining the region for Black people. "I don't reckon there is a colored man in ten miles around me who has got any heart to work," he said. He insisted he had as good of a crop as other Black folks he knew, but he could not make anything of it. "I have no heart to work all day, and then think at night I will be killed," he said.[23] A South Carolina man—who described himself as being "a poor old critter, trying to live right and do what is right, as near as I can"—said that to be "cut up without having done nothing, for I have done no harm," was too much.[24]

———

Amid ongoing attacks and authorities' failure to bring perpetrators to justice, cast-out people had to accept their plight, escape, and secure new locations quickly. They based their relocation decisions on several factors: where violence was and was not occurring, where they had people, and if they had enough cash on hand to start anew. Fortunate ones, including those who did not receive leave-or-die commands, might be able to reside with kin in the community or a neighboring one. Other refugees from night riding were systematic in the decisions they made to leave the places they had called home, and about where and how far away to go, especially if they hoped to get justice or return. Wherever they relocated, displaced people needed employment and money for food and shelter, or to hire a lawyer or move their kin, which likely informed their selection of their ultimate destinations. The first to go also struggled with being separated from their kin, their homesteads, and businesses. Surveillance of victims' comings and goings, as well as continued raids or threats thereof, made it difficult for families to remain connected and for outcast individuals to attend to their affairs. Many families could only watch as the lives they had built unraveled.

Since family patriarchs were often vigilantes' primary targets, they might decamp immediately to avoid being killed and secure protection for their families by reporting the violence to authorities. Clem Bowden left his family, walking as far as he could. He took his steers with him to protect his investment, and to use them to work and earn money on his fifty-six-mile journey away from home. At least nineteen hours by foot, the trek probably took him a few days. When Clem left, he, like other refugees who hadn't received ultimatums, probably initially thought he would be able to return home; that was not to be. "I have not been on the other side of the Pacolet River since," he later said.[25]

Doc and Ellen Rountree made their way out of what had been their home community traveling on foot and in various stages of injury, which slowed progress to their destination. Torn, bloody clothes from their whippings and beatings, or hastily packed bundles full of personal belongings, betrayed survivors like the Rountrees as refugees to anyone they encountered. Some people threaded their way to sanctuary with mules and wagons—slow means of transport, on difficult roads. Luckier families who had enough cash and access to faster transportation could board ships or trains to reach their destinations, like one man did after spending a night bleeding as he hid from his attackers in Alabama's Sucarnoochee swamp.

For a few targeted people, the Army's arrival in or near their hometowns—in response to Congress's and the Grant administration's growing concerns about reports of atrocities—provided relief from violence and allowed families to return home. After being dragged out into the yard, beaten, and choked until she lost consciousness, Mary Brown was displaced from her White County, Georgia, home for about nine weeks. "I did not see the inside of my house," she said. "I did not get a chance to make any crop."[26] Mary went back and was less afraid because soldiers were camped about a half mile from her house.[27]

Mary's husband, Joseph, echoed her feelings about greater confidence accompanying the troops' arrival. "I was afeared to go back; I stayed ten miles from home," Joseph said, "until the troops came for me and fetched me home." Joseph said he knew people who had "been away from home—all summer, afeared to go home."[28] The Browns had to start over from scratch, but as long as the troops were there, they could do it from home. That said, newly deployed troops' imprint was too small to shield all families. People in communities outside their protective shield were on their own.

Sometimes survivors' attackers and accomplices pursued them to their new locations. As soon as Henry Lowther was well enough to travel, after Wilkinson County whites castrated him, he hurried to Macon to file a report with a magistrate. He tried to stay in touch with home. "I wrote a letter back to my wife," Henry said, "and the Ku-Klux got hold of the letter and read it and found out where I was. Five of them came up there and stayed a week, hunting for me; and I left there."[29] The men who had castrated Henry and then chased him from one community to the next would not let him return home.

As Eliza Lyon's escape and Henry's story illustrate, some night riders and their abettors surveilled families after raids. They were monitoring efforts to report violence to federal officials. Culprits were also looking to finish what they started, whether that was to strike someone who had evaded attack, to further harm the family unit, or to ensure entire families vacated land that whites wanted to claim. They ordered men to decamp and then kept eyes on them to see if they complied.

Unhappy facing the prospects of separation from their people, community, and business affairs, some marked men, like Georgia state legislator Abram Colby, tried to remain. Abram recalled, "They got after me, and swore they would kill me if I stayed there."[30] His Black friends were afraid that if he stayed in Greene County after his initial kidnapping and beating, whites would make good on their threats. They encouraged Abram to leave, even though they continued supporting his fight to stay in office, expecting their friend could return for good one day.

Abram had initially decided to serve out his term in office and be with his family and manage his affairs. For a year he traveled back and forth from Atlanta. Then Abram stopped, he said, "because they Ku-Klux my house every time I go home." One time, he discovered their tracks all around his house, evidence of nighttime surveillance that had taken place unbeknownst to the family. "Any day that I am home," he said, "I may expect the Ku-Klux at my house." Abram remained away from his home for all of 1871. Anytime Abram tried to visit his family and sleep in his bed, he had to be on alert for the men's arrival. If he thought they might come or heard them coming, he went to stay in the woods.[31] On one occasion, just before the election, after returning home from church, Abram found his dogs agitated. One of Abram's sons opened the door to greet him and "just as he did so a bullet came through the door and went into the ceiling," he said.

Abram seized his guns and went upstairs, thinking, "I could shoot through the window." His attackers anticipated his response. "They just peppered all that side of the house with shot and bullets," he said.[32] Abram had already been lying out, but this was no way to live. He knew he could not remain there in peace, so he left.

Abram's reluctance to leave is understandable. Flight severed relocated men's direct ties to their spouses and children for weeks and months at a time, an even greater burden so soon after the tragedies these families experienced during strikes. "As for my wife and children," one man said, "I do not know how they are getting on; I cannot tell anything about it."[33] A great number of displaced men were in a similar, agonizing condition.

Thomas Allen left his family in Jasper County, Georgia, to report the violence to his U.S. senator, who Thomas hoped would use his influence to stop the attacks. Instead, Senator Joshua Hill told Thomas, "You are a good fellow, but you are going among mighty bad men if you go back there; it is hard." But "if I was you," the senator told Thomas, "I would go back." Thomas had barely survived the raid on his home. He had watched his brother-in-law die from the countless bullets white men had fired. With continuing threats to Thomas's life, returning home without protection or the state's commitment to enforce the laws that would punish vigilantes was a hard sell. It took months for things to calm down enough for Thomas to simply visit. The anguish of his displacement is painfully obvious. "I am going back home," Thomas swore, "my family is there, and all that I have in the world is there; I have done nothing wrong, and I am going back there."[34]

Cast-out men, like Thomas, left behind crops and paying jobs, with their business affairs unsettled. Some managed to sneak back into their communities to check on kin or property but their pursuers menaced them. Smith Watley—having survived an attack alongside his wife, Caroline—then ignored his landlord's command that he stay put, complete his work, and relocate only at the end of his current contract. Fearful of another attack and well outside the U.S. Army's zone of security, Smith had to calculate the risks of heeding the white man's advice or doing what he felt was necessary to survive. Smith said he reasoned, "they can't do me any harm if I leave now."

The next day, he took his mule and fled to Montgomery, leaving Caroline and the rest of the family behind, presumably to follow once he could support them.

"I left all my property," Smith said of his prior life in Coosa County, Alabama. "It is all there now." Smith tried to give it a go from a distance, having his landlord manage his affairs at home. He gave the man "eleven hundred pounds of lint cotton for twenty-eight acres." The man plowed a few days and charged Smith forty dollars for the work.[35] (The landlord had also followed Smith to Montgomery to claim the mule, perhaps as compensation for unfinished work.) Smith realized remaining unemployed and away from home while his landlord extorted him was unsustainable. He snuck back to work his land and see Caroline and the children whenever he could. As soon as his attackers learned of his presence, though, he set off to avoid being struck again.[36]

Vigilantes' ongoing monitoring further jeopardized family bonds and undermined displaced men's efforts to reunite with their loved ones, or even escort them to safety. Raiders' and their allies' ability to monitor the mail, like they did with Henry Lowther, reveals how wide the net of white southerners' complicity in the war against freedom was.

Surveillance is why some outcast patriarchs had to rely on letters and storytelling chains to get secondhand news from home. Henry Giles was the deacon of a Nixburg church that was burned by disguised gunmen in reaction to the central Alabama congregation's status as a Radical stronghold.[37] "I made my wife and children lay down in the back of the orchard to hide themselves," Henry said. White men had warned him that vigilantes "were coming that night," which allowed him to take precautions.[38]

Henry fled with only the clothes on his back. "I had to leave my business all undone, and run away to make my escape," he said, underscoring the danger he faced and his sense of helplessness.[39] "I couldn't go back there to see how it was."

While he was away, he began to suspect his family might be keeping the full truth of their situation from him.[40] Henry remained in constant communication with his wife, either through written correspondence or sending word through kin. In each exchange, Henry tried to collect information to ascertain when he could return home. But Mrs. Giles remained stingy with details, as though she was "afraid to send me any word," he said.[41] Henry's wife probably did not want to say anything to provoke him to return prematurely, before things had settled down.

In time, Henry learned why it was not safe for him to return. Whites in the community had taken advantage of his absence to continue menacing his family and help themselves to their property. "They just took everything," Henry said. "They took a cow and calf from me, and my corn and my meat I had there," he said. Instead of stealing in the thick of night, the brazen plunderers came in the light of day. "They had no fear," Henry said, "because they had run me off and they took it as they pleased."

With Henry gone, Mrs. Giles was unable to protect their property against packs of white men. By remaining on their homestead, Mrs. Giles was making a stand for her family's right to retain their home and property. But she also wanted to live. So whenever armed squads came, Henry said, his wife "had just to hide the children out, and do about some way or another to keep them from perishing."[42] Whites even took the church papers out of the trunk Henry had there, and "all the wine, and all the bottles, and the tumblers, and everything."[43] The rest of their things were "all scattered from east to west," he said. Other people Henry encountered told him he should not return home "because death would be my portion."[44] "I couldn't go back and fix up nothing," he said. What happened to the Gileses shows how firm a grip strikes' tentacles had on families weeks and months after "visits." Displacement hamstrung men's ability to financially support their families. Many reported falling behind on their crops. They also possessed livestock that needed tending. Their wives and young children struggled to manage everything alone, and it was unlikely that kin left behind could fend off menacing men stealing their property or destroying their crops. Mary Elder, who was whipped with her husband, Simon, in November 1869, was so "anxious to get away" that they abandoned some of their wheat.[45] Friends and family, to whom people like Mary and Simon might have turned for assistance, were often facing their own struggles for survival and were therefore unreliable. This is one reason why displaced men prioritized returning home and reuniting with their people.

Separation could be intolerable for family members who remained behind. Charles Little's wife refused to be left behind in Haralson County, Georgia. When Charles was leaving for Atlanta, Mrs. Little informed him, "[If] you are going to leave home, I will leave the house." She was pregnant, and she made clear she was not going to be separated from Charles or stand sentry over their homestead alone.[46] Mrs. Little took a stand. She and Charles left for Atlanta together.

Jack Johnson's wife remained home, overseeing their family's affairs, after he fled their Laurens County, South Carolina, community. A white man named Mr. Reizer and a gang came to take Jack's trunk of tools, and while they were there, told Mrs. Johnson "she had better hunt a home some other place."[47] Jack believed the pack did not physically assault his wife because she was well respected and "brought up well by her masters," he said. But Mrs. Johnson's situation in their community was increasingly precarious. Whites there began shunning her, refusing to speak to her and telling her "she had better go away." The lower edge of Laurens County, where the Johnsons had made their home, "was a bad place for Negroes," Jack said. Columbia, which was seventy or so miles southeast, was safer.[48]

Mrs. Johnson's continued presence was a form of resistance and protection of their property. Jack was gone, but the couple presumed his absence was only for a short time. She remained to maintain their family affairs until he returned. As long as Mrs. Johnson stayed in place, Jack and their family had a home to which he could return. By driving her and the rest of their family out with the threat of harm, local whites sent a message: the place the Johnsons had called home would not let them stay. When Jack spoke with investigators, he was still displaced from his community and his wife was still standing her ground. The record doesn't show whether whites succeeded in driving her out or Jack was ever able to return home.

———

Attacks, surveillance, and widespread white collusion and silence about strikes increasingly persuaded more families to leave their communities for good. Their former homes carried only the promise of further injury. Authorities would not stop the killings or do anything to bring attackers to justice. As survivors realized how insecure they and their families were in their hometowns, they often had to start making long-term plans to relocate and start anew.

The family of James Alston, a state legislator of Macon County, Alabama, survived the raid in which a mob stood outside his gate and released a barrage of bullets into the home: 265 pieces of shot lodged into the siding, and sixty passed through the window. Another five were lodged into the headboard of the bed where James and his wife slept. Two narrowly missed his head and burst through his pillow; and except for the fortunate placement of a foot roll, four more bullets would have ripped his feet apart.

James was hit in the hip and back. His pregnant wife was shot and one of his children was shot, too. With the ball still lodged in her foot, Mrs. Alston was unable to walk.[49] "I had to leave there to keep from being shot," James said, "and to keep my wife from being shot," again.[50] White men had threatened James before, including attempts to bribe him to leave office, but he had refused to leave. Now, having come so close to being killed, James knew he could not stay and live.

Simon Elder fled his Clarke County, Georgia, homestead right after his captors left. "I kept traveling from one place to another all that night," he said. Simon made his way to his landlord's home, hoping to get shelter and assistance, only to discover that the couple's son might have participated in the strike on his wife, Mary, and him.[51] That personal betrayal persuaded Simon to leave. He remained in the community for two more nights, ensuring Mary was as safe as she could be and handling whatever he could on such short notice. Simon hired a wagon to take him to Madison depot, where he caught a train that carried him roughly sixty miles to Decatur. Mary joined Simon in the city later. "I have lived there ever since," Simon said.[52]

Once the outcasts decided to leave, they often realized that getting out and making it to a new permanent residence was not always easy. Lack of funds or support systems in distant areas slowed down victims' decisions to decamp. In addition to physical injuries and transporting all their belongings, families faced obstacles like rising waters along waterways they would normally cross with ease. Others may have had unpaid debts; landlords and store merchants had an economic incentive to keep debtors in town to collect what they were owed. For many families, it was harder to stay than to leave (or, leaving was hard, staying was impossible).

During and after Reconstruction, tens of thousands of African Americans abandoned the South's rural, underdeveloped villages for its towns and cities. Some were seeking opportunity. But as extremists attacked people in their communities, more were fleeing violence and dispossession. One survivor told WPA interviewers that a strike had been the catalyst for his family's flight. He recalled his family walked nearly fifty miles from Columbus, Georgia, to Eufaula, Alabama, where, he said, they thought "it was safe to be."[53] Flight from night-riding zones was one of several massive migrations of Black southerners in the late nineteenth century.

When survivors resolved that they could no longer remain in their hometowns safely, they began their flight, often moving within a five- to fifty-mile radius of their homes. Others who did not yet have the wherewithal for a bigger move headed instead to the closest town or county seat; there, they might stay with kin, or at least be close enough to visit their families or try to manage their financial affairs, including tending to their crops and raising enough money for an eventual move.

As they left the places they had called home, there were probably instances when cast-out people saw each other traveling in opposite directions, as some newly targeted people escaped while others like Smith Watley snuck home to check on their property or escort their families out to safety. Eliza Lyons' group might have encountered other Choctaw County escapees in makeshift camps in the woods or open clearings as families settled down for the night. Refugees from white terror encountering each other exchanged information or offered directions, food, or medical treatment for those who were wounded. Other victims who were hiding out in the woods might have been the ones who alerted Eliza's party to the fact that Abe's killers were gaining on them.

Augustus Mills's separation from his family was short-term. Gus left for Atlanta hours after he, his wife, Letty, and their four children were beaten. Letty and the children moved out of the house for their safety around the same time, but they did not arrive in the city until about four weeks after Gus did. They waited in Walton County, Georgia, until Gus secured housing and started scratching out a new existence for them in the place they hoped would be their new home.[54]

Within days of being shot, Columbus Jeter fled Douglas County, Georgia, bound for Atlanta. He tried to get help moving Aury, Emily, and the rest of the family but no one would provide it. Columbus did not say whether it was because people in his community did not want to be labeled accomplices and then be victimized themselves, or because they were so busy handling their own affairs or plotting their own escapes. But the lack of outreach and refusal of requests for assistance both expose the limits of community in a war on freedom and illustrate night-riding strikes' corrosive effects on communities. Columbus handled a few of his business affairs and then walked roughly twenty-two miles to the city.[55] Aury left Emily and her sibling in the care of a family friend to join Columbus in Atlanta. The Jeters planned to obtain sufficient work, secure housing, and then send for their children.

Fear and a sense of moral injury kept many survivors away from their homes for good. Anderson Ferrell left Troup County, Georgia, but reported that his white acquaintances tried to get him to return, perhaps to testify against his attackers or resolve any unpaid debts he might have had. Anderson would not be bothered. "I could not succeed when I was there," he said, "and I shall not pay out the little I have made to go there for foolishness."[56] Troup County was done with Anderson, and he was done with it.

Mississippi state senator Robert Gleed saw entire families on the move in his community near the Louisiana border. For several months, families in the northern and eastern sections of Monroe County, on the eastern side of Mississippi near the border with Lowndes County, experienced what Robert described as "a disturbance." Assailants, he said "were raiding about there every night pretty nearly" for almost two months. Moving in squads of fifty to sixty men, they whipped and threatened some Black people. But gangs also kidnapped and disappeared others. "They have never been heard of since," Robert said, leaving their families to presume they were dead.

"They could not be protected," Robert said of Black people in Monroe County.[57] The slaughter prompted discussion and plans of flight. "It was difficult," Robert explained, "to get the people to remain at home at all; they were leaving home altogether, and squads moving off to Louisiana." Whole families "moved from the neighborhood on the east side of the river and went away from there on account of the murdering of several parties there."[58] The more families fled, the more emboldened their attackers might become, rendering any families that remained even more vulnerable.

Other night-riding survivors moved west or north. Reverend Elias Hill was among those who sought to go farther. "Reading history," Elias said, and assessing what he described as the "present aspect of affairs" in the South led him to conclude it was not possible for Black folks to "live in this country peaceably, and educate and elevate their children to that degree that they desire." This deduction prompted Elias and seventy to eighty South Carolinians to investigate relocating to Liberia via the American Colonization Society.[59]

Families in Elias's area had organized a system to alert each other when night riders crossed the creek into their Clay Hill community. Whites had promised to lend their support, but when a gang came for Elias—using his disabled body against him, and torturing and sexually assaulting his sister-in-law—the neighbor they asked for help refused to come. They learned one white man had said Black people should just get used to this. Recognizing they could not count on their white neighbors for assistance, several families decided it was time to leave the United States altogether. When Elias's white neighbors got wind of his efforts to make travel arrangements, they posted a notice in the newspaper identifying him as one of the leaders of the emigration scheme, which again brought vigilantes to his and his brother's homes.[60]

African Americans "leave the country in many instances because they are outraged," Reverend Henry McNeal Turner, who had also been elected to the Georgia legislature, said of the insecurity that night riding caused in Black people's lives. They only go "because their lives are threatened," he explained. "They run to the cities as an asylum." Freedom-seeking African Americans worked in rural communities for an entire year, and then received nothing because of violence. If they challenged the oppression whites expected them to endure and insisted on exercising their rights as citizens, then they faced violent attacks.[61]

"If I could have stayed at home," Thomas Allen said, "I would not have been here [in Atlanta]." Thomas fled with his crops in the ground. "I never got anything for them," he said. "My wife had no education, and when I came away everything went wrong."[62] For Thomas, living on land he owned, rented, or cropped was the best way for his family to thrive. Thomas had made a life in Jasper County, Georgia, and had been driven away from it after night riders shot up his home and killed his brother-in-law. Thomas was separated from his family, and his wife's lack of education, and her mourning her brother's killing, made it harder for her to manage their affairs in his absence. Thomas was not alone in straining under the weight of his family's plight. "There are thousands in my condition," he said.

Emanuel Fortune—the father of future activist and newspaper man T. Thomas Fortune, who established the Afro-American League in 1887 and founded and edited the New York *Age*—assessed conditions in Jackson County, Florida, trying to illuminate attacked people's plight there. "There got to be such a state of lawlessness and outrage," he said, "that I expected that my life was in danger at all times, and I left on that account."[63] Someone told Emanuel that because he was a political leader and "very obnoxious," he could go missing one day and no one would know where he was or what had happened to him.[64]

"I think there are persons living here today [in Jacksonville]," Emanuel explained, "who had to flee from Columbia County, and also from other counties . . . They talk with me and tell me of their difficulties," he said.[65] Survivors' discussion of other neighbors and kin who fled underscore the ways storytelling chains spread information about night riding and responses to it. From these exchanges, Emanuel would have known the white men swearing to disappear him could make good on their threat. Timothy Fortune was old enough during the attacks on his family for them to have left a deep impression of the injustice at the heart of the war on his family's and his people's freedom. It is likely they inspired him to become one of the very first anti-lynching crusaders.

When investigators asked Robert Fullerlove if he would go back home, he answered, "I can't," stressing that his displacement was not a matter of choice. As for what he would do with his land, Robert responded, "I will do something with it; I don't know what."[66] Robert appreciated the dangers he faced returning home and his property's value to his family's future well-being if he didn't return home. He and his wife, Adaline, were thinking about leaving. "All the people in the neighborhood are fixing to go," Robert said, "there is no peace in the neighborhood. Not a bit." Black people "can't stay in peace."

Insecurity in the places they called home tormented survivors. Most people did not want to go back home, South Carolina state legislator Samuel Nuckles said, "unless something is done" to protect them. He was one of many refugees who expressed a passionate affinity for their home communities. "I don't know any other place I would rather live," he said. But "it has become so I can't live there, and it seems I am hardly living here [in Columbia, South Carolina, the state capital, to where he fled]—merely providing."[67]

Perilous conditions in his home community are why he declared, "I am a refugee from Union County."[68] Samuel had been returning home after a legislative session in Columbia when two of his sons had met him along the way and told him to stop. White men had raided the family's home and threatened to kill Samuel if he returned.[69] Samuel ignored the threats and went home anyway, but he left when he realized how ready his pursuers were to make good on their promises. "I cannot go back there," he said.

When he departed, he was accompanied by three of his sons, who had also been targeted.[70]

Home would not let these families stay. It was now the shell of their burnt-out cabins or bullet-ridden houses. It was the place where the families had to sleep outside to avoid being violated again. Home was the place where their attackers were still roaming freely, either prowling around under the cloak of night or strutting proudly, boasting of their power, in the light of day.

———

Flight marked the beginning of families' social and economic descents, erasing many of the post-emancipation gains they had made. Families lost many if not all of the possessions they could not carry when they escaped or relocated. They also lost their livelihood and wealth that could have put them on the path to multigenerational prosperity. Compounded traumatic injury and the loss of security, bodily and familial integrity, home, and community intensified victims' suffering. Outcast families struggled in the days ahead, and many of them would never be the same.

Had targeted people been able to leave on their own terms—on their own schedules and having settled their affairs—relocating might have been better. Clem Bowden said he had "fifteen or twenty acres of corn and cotton" ready to go when he fled, not knowing when, or if, he'd be able to harvest it. Leaving as they did, chased as they were by both Ku Klux and an understanding no one was coming to save them, horrified most survivors.

As they gained a better appreciation for the ways displacement separated them from their kin and stripped them of their wealth, survivors recognized strikes' impacts did not end when white men stopped attacking them. The effects continued long afterward. They compromised families' stability. "I am suffering," James Alston said. "I have been in this place [in Montgomery] sixteen months, not allowed to go to my own property [in Tuskegee]. My horses, one of them, is killed; taken away from me and the buggy cut up; my house and lot is there, and I am not allowed to go near the county."[71] James's account illustrates the economic contrails flowing outward from attacks. The vapors of insecurity lingered over displaced people's lives for years to come.

Some dispossession by night riding was swift and immediate. It included families losing everything, including what they called the "little things," from clothing and mementos to work tools. Families that lost foodstuffs like cured meats, molasses, rice, or wheat were deprived not only of sustenance but also possible earnings from selling their surplus in the marketplace.

When white South Carolinians fired on the home of Andrew Cathcart's daughter while she was in bed, she managed to escape the shooting. With Miss Cathcart gone, her attackers were free to pillage. "They got all her things out of the chest and threw them on the floor and tramped over them," Andrew said, "and took two or three pieces of clothing, some silver thimbles, and several other things . . . They took a jug of vinegar and burst it among them. They destroyed a heap of things."[72] The frame structure of the schoolhouse, where Miss Cathcart lived, was also destroyed, a loss of forty to fifty dollars.

More significant losses included the wrecking of houses, which often led to homelessness and ruination. Vigilantes demolished Samuel and Hannah Tutson's Florida home by pulling down the structure as well as their fences, which allowed the cattle to come in and consume or trample their unharvested crops.[73] Wiley Hargrove said that when white Mississippians struck his Pickens County home, "they tore down everything they could—a bucket of water, and dishes, and everything over the floor, just as though I had been a dog."[74] When Doc and Ellen Rountree's family fled Live Oak, Florida, they abandoned all their property. Doc went from homesteading to being a dispossessed and poorly paid farm laborer, which was exactly what night riders striking his family wanted.[75]

For many attacked people, dispossession was a slow-moving disaster. Men who were temporarily or permanently displaced left behind their families as well as their crops. In some instances, kin could handle the harvest or negotiate sales of property. "My crop is there," one man explained of his life in Choctaw County, Alabama, outside the village of DeSotoville, "and I have some hands there going on with a brother of mine."[76] He had the kind of assistance that might slow the steep economic decline most displaced people experienced. For a time at least, this man was one of many who held out hope they could return home for good, or at least be able to settle their affairs.

But as days turned into weeks, which turned into months, many of the displaced realized there was no going back and no recovering their accumulated losses. Warren Jones explained the troubles many Georgia refugees had once they relocated to Atlanta. "When I came here, I did not have a cent in the world," Warren said.[77] For the thirty bags of cotton he had picked, averaging 501 pounds each, Warren and his people should have received fourteen cents a pound. At the end of the season, there were 15,030 pounds of cotton worth $2,104.20, of which Warren said he was owed half. His relative labor earnings would have come to roughly $179,000 in today's dollars.[78]

Without that income, Warren had to rely on any cash he had on hand. Securing a new place to stay would have burned through any financial reserves men like Warren had, so he would have needed to acquire work quickly. All families were in a more financially vulnerable position than they had been before a strike. A man's skills, his physical ability after a raid, the availability of laborers to help him rebuild, and the labor scene in his new town all informed the intricate interplay of families' recovery efforts. Warren wasn't physically injured, but his family was clearly suffering in Atlanta.

The gang's continued pursuit of Clem Bowden made it too dangerous for him to harvest his corn and cotton or gather the family's belongings. His young son, however, was able to travel undetected, and without harassment, back and forth between their homeplace and their new residence in the center of Spartanburg, which helped save some of their crop. "Some was destroyed," Clem said, "and some was taken out of the field afterward," by either the men pursuing him or opportunists.[79] The Bowdens were able to recover a small amount of money to live on in their new location.

Sir Daniel reported the kinds of problems families faced settling their affairs on the run. "I had a good deal of property," Sir said, "and all of that was destroyed." After swearing to kill white men demanding entry to his home, Sir said, he knew he "had to get right away from there at once." As he was in the process of leaving Stevenson, Alabama, Sir faced white men claiming his property and livestock and demanding money with menacing intent. Continued threats to his life prompted Sir to decamp. This left Mrs. Daniel, who had their newborn to care for, to tend to their property and settle the family's remaining affairs, with the help of his sister. At home, Sir knew with precise detail how much livestock he had and the status of his crops, but staying on top of his family's livelihood from a distance was impossible. "I lost it," Sir said of his property and his newly acquired wealth.[80]

Those who built their lives on horses, mules, cows, and steers lost it all to theft, slaughter, or abandonment. These families were deprived of the livestock's market value as well as means of labor, given their reliance upon oxen to plow fields and mules and horses to dray. When another survivor escaped his Huntsville, Alabama, neighborhood, he had to abandon his hogs. In his absence, they were "destroyed and killed up," he said. "I didn't save nothing except what I could haul away." The Alabaman admitted he was somewhat comforted by the fact that "at least the storekeepers didn't lose nothing; I had to pay them after I came here." But "they took my horse and everything," he said.[81] The man got out and might have been able to demonstrate his creditworthiness to shopkeepers in his new home community, which could have allowed him to acquire what was necessary to take care of his family as he tried to rebuild.

On top of the death of his beloved son, Billy, Augustus Blair's financial losses were extensive. "I had a good deal of property down there [in Limestone County, Alabama]," Augustus said. He reported he had thirty head of hogs and four bales of ginned cotton. Augustus got a man to help collect his cotton and sell it, but the Blairs still lost about five hundred dollars, the relative labor earnings of which ranges between $83,800 and $144,000 and the relative income amounts to $185,000 in today's dollars.[82] Augustus might have been able to limit his losses had he been able to harvest the rest of his crop and settle his affairs, but his attackers told him he had better be packed up and gone in two weeks, "crop or no crop."[83]

"My wife had to sacrifice my property," George Houston said. Sumter County, Alabama, night riders struck his family and ordered him to leave within two days. George did, catching the first train available, and in the process lost two horses which he had on payment, two mules, sixty acres of land—all told, five hundred dollars.[84] George tried to get back to his home, but he said the circuit clerk wrote to him saying "it would not be safe" for him there.[85]

Robert Fullerlove owned several hundred acres of land but said, "[N]ow I never expect to set my foot on it no more." He was in the process of losing his cattle, too, including seven milk cows and more than twenty oxen.[86] He also listed corn, fodder, and hogs among his losses. The family had some of their crop in the ground when the men came, he said, but not much.[87]

White men's assault on Robert on his way to report violence was the final straw that convinced him to leave his community. This attack was especially frightening because Robert had not left his home since the raid, and he also did not know if his attackers had used his absence to strike his family again. "I have been imposed on," Robert said. "I have been pestered and sleeping out of doors instead of sleeping in the house; I have a good house, but is it any use for me to go in it, but not go to bed?"[88]

Robert did not feel safe returning home and staying. When asked where he would go, Robert responded, "I don't know where. I had a notion of going to Kansas." His neighbors were already leaving, he said, because "they can't stay in peace."[89] If Robert relocated, he might join his neighbors in getting some physical peace, but he would probably have to leave a lot of his life behind and abandon his wealth.

Not being able to settle their affairs added to families' misfortunes. Without a cent in the world, it was difficult, if not impossible, for displaced people to secure food or shelter in new locations, where they lacked patrons or people to testify to their creditworthiness. Eliza Lyon, who fled with all the belongings she and her children could carry, faced new hardships in escape. She and Abe had been saving money from their patch of land and his blacksmith shop. The couple had a teenage daughter attending school in Demopolis, Alabama, and three younger children at home. "We had some money in the house," Eliza said, "but I don't know whereabouts he put it, but we had it in a little square box." Eliza believed the family's money box "had about $600 in it," based on the last time she said she and Abe had been "looking over it," planning their financial future. Eliza had envisioned using some of the money to pay for their daughter's education, while the couple had discussed using the bulk of their reserve to move and buy or build a home in Demopolis.

The raid had arrested her plans. In addition to killing Abe, the fiends ransacking the Lyons family home must have discovered the money box. "If it was in the house, or under it," Eliza said, "they got it . . . I have never seen it."

Eliza's hardship was compounded by the fact that, in her escape, she had to abandon the family's other property, including Abe's blacksmithing business. "I left everything," Eliza said.[90] "I left my hogs down there," she said, itemizing the loss of the family's wealth, "and left a wagon we had paid $75 for, and we had a great many other little things." Even if Eliza had been bold enough to ignore the threats, she could not have run her husband's shop herself, tended to their farm, and cared for her children all at the same time.

"I am very much oppressed now," Eliza said, revealing her family's financial descent in Demopolis. "I haven't got anything; they run me off from all I had." To make matters worse, Eliza did not have a support system in her new location; she was cut off from people who knew her and might have been able to help her secure a job, lend her money or give her credit, or watch her children while she worked. Like other refugees, she needed employment, housing, and food. "I can't get any help," she said four months after the attack, suggesting any goodwill or charity she might have received wasn't enough or had run out.[91] Asked about any other property, from Abe's shop, Eliza said Abe "only had some five or six hoes, and I sold them to get some money to come up here."[92]

Columbus Jeter was injured during the strike on his family in Douglas County, Georgia. This hindered his efforts to regain his livelihood and support his kin when he moved to Atlanta. "I cannot do much work and I have not a cent," he said. Columbus left his corn in the hands of the sheriff, possibly hoping he would secure it so Columbus could sell it upon his return.

Because Columbus could not travel back home safely, he said, "My wife had to take a wagon and go for things herself; I could get no protection to come away." Columbus said a man took pity on him and gave him a bit of cash. Without it, he said, "I don't know how I would have lived."[93]

————

Families like Eliza's and Columbus's, displaced from their homes and communities, found themselves without shelter and had to quickly secure new arrangements. Housing insecurity and the slow-moving disaster of dispossession were tied to another issue: unemployment.

Augustus and Letty Mills's family experienced hard spells when Augustus fell sick after he, Letty, and the four children relocated to Atlanta, sometime after night riders beat them. When asked whether he was working, Gus answered, "all the time I was able; I have been sick some."[94] Illness or recovering from injuries slowed people's paths to even a degree of well-being after a strike.

Displaced people found themselves out of work or other means of employment. Wage laborers might see their income disrupted, especially if they needed to care for injured family members or had been injured themselves. Depending on their skill levels and the employment opportunities where they had relocated, targeted people might not skip a financial beat, if they were lucky, but it's unlikely that this was the norm.

As for land-owning or land-seeking families, attacks stripped them of independence and self-sufficiency by driving them into the wage labor force. Samuel Nuckles said he and his sons were "knocking about," working when and where they could on the railroad or draying on the street with their two mules.[95] The Nuckleses were not alone. Strikes threw many families into financial free fall. Desperate to stop their downward spiral before they reached the bottom, men took any work they could. In these situations, surviving men had to make financial and emotional adjustments to their new situations. Letting go of their dream for freedom and the promise of reaping the rewards of their hard work and sacrifices they had made would not be an easy undertaking.

Daniel Lane's family struggled in Atlanta. "When I first came here," he said, "I was not able to do anything, much. Then I knocked about," cutting wood and then working in a livery stable. Daniel earned one dollar a day, considerably less than he had made at home.[96]

Once the outcasts secured new jobs, they often had to wait to earn enough money before trying to secure better housing, rebuild, or move their families closer to them. One South Carolina survivor found new employment, but his employer did not want children on his property, so he had to pay additional rent someplace else. "We only have what the children have on their backs," the man said, "we now just lay down on the floor with no covering, no beds."[97] Providing for his and their material needs would have eaten away at the South Carolinian's earnings.

Columbus Jeter's statement about not knowing how he would have lived without a Samaritan's generosity underscores the ways families struggled. Without money or charity, obtaining shelter and providing sustenance for their families was difficult. Conditions had gotten so bad, Henry McNeal Turner said, that displaced people flocked to cities like Demopolis, Atlanta, and Jacksonville, and "preferred knocking about and catching pennies here and there rather than to work the entire year in the country and at the end of the year be turned out of their homes, with their wives and children, and have nothing."[98] His phrase "catching pennies" might mean literal panhandling, or might be a more figurative reflection of how much uprooted people's prospects had been transformed by night riding. Outcast people lost property as well as patrons who might employ them during hard times or offer them credit. In their new towns, many were isolated, islands unto themselves, and had to scratch out an entirely new living, accepting paltry wages and any other charitable donations available. Churches and relief agencies in cities like Atlanta and Columbia probably offered survivors some assistance, but there does not appear to have been the kind of documentation of these efforts that would facilitate historical analysis.

When survivors scanned the horizon of night riding's effects, they calculated the losses and saw strikes' breathtaking devastation. Many victims lost virtually everything. In their testimonies, witnesses did not always provide the dollar amount for their material losses, but from those who did we can get a sense of the relative value of their losses today.*

Measuring Worth Relative Value of Commodities, Income, or Wealth from Losses Declared in 1871 at the Klan Hearings*

Name	Stated Loss	Real Price (2020)	Labor Value— Unskilled (2020)	Labor Value— Skilled (2020)
Jones, Warren	1,052	24,100	179,000	303,000
Blair, Augustus	500	11,400	83,800	144,000
Lyon, Eliza	675	15,400	113,000	194,000
Coleman, William	473	10,800	79,200	136,000
Cathcart, Andrew	590	13,500	98,800	170,000
Taylor, George	500	11,400	83,800	144,000
Johnson, Jack	600	13,100	99,300	168,000

*Equivalent amounts in 2020, via MeasuringWorth.com

These families had "picked themselves up" after slavery. They had done what federal officials and free people insisted they do—work hard, save their money, and acquire land of their own so they could be independent and self-sufficient. Their itemizations of their losses put a dollar value on the crucial wealth the night-riding strikes robbed from African American families. Indeed, the fact that these families had achieved a degree of wealth most likely was a critical factor in their being chosen by vigilantes as targets.

---

* The loss of income, wealth, and property in the past is difficult to measure today. I used the Measuring Worth tool (https://www.measuringworth.com/index.php) to calculate the approximate relative worth of the combination of the loss of earnings, savings, and property survivors detailed. The value amounts range from five figures to seven figures. Of Measuring Worth's values for Commodities, Income or Wealth, or Project for 2020, the most recent year of calculations available. I chose the calculation for the labor value and labor earnings because I believe that approximates how targeted people understood their losses. I included the real price for transparency. It's imperfect, but it acknowledges the difficulty of measuring the historical value of losses.

For families like Robert and Adaline Fullerlove's, leaving home to avoid violence was not the same as being all right. It erased much of the economic progress they had achieved. Flight broke families' social and communal ties and their ability to receive social support. Getting help in new social environments may have been difficult, if people in a position to offer assistance or end violence did not understand or believe what survivors said had happened to them. Receiving communities might have looked upon desperate survivors as troublesome, or as deserving of what had happened to them. They might have also seen the survivors as emotional and economic burdens, which only added to the survivors' sense of moral injury.[99] As demoralized as many displaced families were, they could not go back to the barrel of the gun, the snap of the lash, or the white men promising to finish what they had started.

Not knowing what was to come and how they would cope intensified the night-riding diaspora's feelings of abjection and informed survivors' decisions to make home any place other than where they had been attacked. The changed directions of their lives, reinforced by the compounding nature of the tragedies that had befallen them, guided their need to call upon federal officials to honor the promises they had made African Americans when they extended them the full protections of citizenship.

Chapter 7

What They Did Is Hurting My Family

Once Samuel Tutson had recovered enough from being tied to a tree, viciously whipped, and abandoned until his wife, Hannah, found him, he went to report the attack on his family and the destruction of their home. Samuel consulted a white lawyer and judge for Clay County, Florida, with whom he'd had previous discussions about his neighbors' efforts to drive the Tutsons off their land. The man advised the couple to stand fast and not leave their property. Rebuild, the judge urged them; he advised Samuel to make the house sound enough to reside in and, "if anybody come there, to kill them." Samuel listened but knew this advice might expose his family to another attack.

A deputy sheriff among the pack had sexually assaulted Hannah, underscoring the futility of reporting the raid to local authorities, so the judge directed Samuel to a county magistrate thirty miles away in Whitesville, who collected the family's information, but nothing was done. They had cotton for the market and what Samuel described as "right smart corn and potatoes," and they didn't want to abandon it. "Now, I paid too much,"

Hannah said of the land they had acquired and the life they had built. "I have worked too much to lose it."[1] Samuel traveled another forty miles to Green Cove Springs, to report the crime to federal authorities with the circuit court. He was determined to find what he said was "any law" available to Black southerners.

Somewhere along the way, someone issued a directive to the local sheriff, who removed the deputy from his position and arrested the culprits. One of the men attempting to drive the Tutsons from their land paid the accused men's bonds. Then he menaced the family by having Hannah and Samuel arrested for false reporting. They were released only when a white patron paid their bond in exchange for their prized ox. The couple still needed to recover their livestock so they could use it for rebuilding and harvesting their crops.

Samuel and Hannah Tutson's ongoing insecurity and uprootedness were common for survivors of the shadow army's attacks. So were their hassle and the high costs of their back-and-forth efforts in the labyrinthine pursuit of justice. Then, the social and political winds that had allowed white southerners to attack African Americans with impunity began to shift as the federal machinery cranked to life, giving rise to another journey for the Tutsons, this time to tell the world what white men waging war on freedom had done to them, and were *still* doing.

Print media covered the South's descent into what progressive members of Congress described as a "reign of terror," but often in ways that obscured the scale of the attacks that were taking place. With headlines like OUTRAGES ON FREEDMEN—CALLS FOR TROOPS, most reporting in white centrist or progressive papers documented the brutality via telegraphic summaries: "MORE KU-KLUX MURDERS ARE REPORTED IN MURRAY COUNTY, GEORGIA."[2] Right-wing and Klan-sympathetic papers downplayed the shadow army's violence, ignoring it altogether or trivializing the barbarity by insisting extremists were just lashing out, engaging in expected and easily pardonable "ridiculous fun."[3] These reports sowed doubt, casting Black people as perpetual liars whose accounts could not be trusted. White conservative news outlets largely claimed—without any real or convincing evidence—that if violence occurred it was because Black people had acted atrociously toward white people.

To Americans consuming these telegraphic summaries of attacks from a distance, the incidents probably seemed like discrete eruptions. With skimpy reporting about who was targeted, beyond victims' race, it might have been difficult for readers to appreciate what was really happening in these disturbances and their real human costs. Coming off the heels of the Civil War, which left nearly a million dead, Americans might be forgiven for being numb to more killings. Much of the white majority seem to have been shruggingly indifferent. Among whites who had only accepted universal slave emancipation purely as a device to end the war, resentment over Black people's subsequent insistence on—and acquisition of—civil rights was high. This thinking could have led some whites to believe uppity Black people were only getting what they deserved. And even if some whites were paying close enough attention to see that this was not just one random massacre or mass killing, but many, these distant observers might absolve themselves of their duty to act: the more deaths that registered in their minds, the more impersonal they might become.

Up close, especially to African Americans, reports of outrages registered differently. The portrait of mass atrocities coalesced more quickly. To them, extremists' deliberate targeting of Black people was unmistakable, prompting calls to stop the slaughter. After experiencing the staccato barrage of 116 lynchings, massacres, and mob events in their state, from fall 1867 through spring 1871, Black Kentuckians, led by Henry Marrs and Henry Lynn, saw the pattern and drafted a memorial, reporting organized bands "mainly composed of soldiers of the late rebel armies, armed, disciplined, and disguised and bound by oath and secret obligations have, by force, terror and violence subverted all citizen society among colored people."[4] White southerners are "killing our people without provocation," they said. Echoing Samuel Tutson's experience in Florida, the petitioners asserted that Black victims of white violence had "no redress" in local and state courts, only the federal courts, which are "in many cases unable to reach them."

Members of the Black press saw the pattern of purposeful attacks and killings as well, in both the repeated mass casualty events and extremist media coverage of them. In response to vigilantes' apocryphal stories of "negro supremacy" and unruly Black people, editors at Philip Alexander Bell's *The Elevator*, in San Francisco, asked: "Pray tell us what would have become of the whole [white] families and communities who during the war were left literally at the mercy of [B]lacks?"[5] Like the Kentucky memorialists who pleaded for the "enactment of laws for the better protection of life," the *New Orleans Tribune* was among many Black papers that specifically decried the insecurity of Black people's lives. In a report on the killing of freedmen in Caddo Parish, Louisiana, the *Tribune* asked, "[W]hen shall human life be secure in Louisiana?" and "[W]hen shall justice be meted out to murderers?"[6]

Black freedom fighters for Reconstruction who had battled for African Americans' right to have rights—to freedom, family, and pay, to vote and serve in office, attend church and school, acquire land and open businesses— recognized the nature of mass killings, too. When a mob of Georgia whites killed septuagenarian state senator Joseph Adkins and the white media justified it by alleging rape, Henry McNeal Turner and James M. Simms, both of them ministers and Georgia legislators, insisted these were "base and unmitigated falsehoods." Adkins was one of many Black Georgia power brokers who had been "brutally slaughtered," the two wrote. Adkins had joined Turner and Simms in a public appeal before members of the U.S. Congress for protection or the means to better protect themselves from hostile white Georgians who had expelled Black lawmakers like Turner and Simms from office and who were attacking Black citizens. But despite "earnest entreaties" from local and state policymakers, and a petition from Black Georgians mirroring that by their Kentucky counterparts, "Congress adjourned and went to their homes, and thus have given their moral influences in favor of the assassin," Turner and Simms charged. Black people's trust in federal officials was fraying.[7]

Turner, Simms, and Adkins's personal appeal was part of a steady stream of reports to members of Congress about "southern disorders": the attacks on voters, the efforts to deny officeholders like Abram Colby and Sam

Nuckles the right to serve out their terms. Radical federal policymakers answered by calling for a comprehensive investigation. Congress and the states had ratified the Fourteenth Amendment but proceeded to act as though the due process and equal protection clauses would enforce themselves while the carnage continued.

African Americans' accounts were largely substantiated by federal officials like the Freedmen's Bureau agents who had sent reports to Secretary of War Edwin Stanton. The bureau, according to William Blair, had become "a de facto investigatory arm of the legislative branch."[8] Secretary Stanton was one of a few members of the executive branch who took bureau agents' reports of southern disorder seriously. Secretary Stanton read them and concluded civil law was "almost a dead letter" in parts of the South where vigilantes were running loose, especially in counties where law enforcement officers partook in the violence. Former Confederates and their apologists denied atrocities were taking place. Stanton countered this denial by saying that accounts of lawlessness and crime in Texas, for example, were "so far from being exaggerated do not tell the whole truth." Targeted people "have no course but to leave their homes or be murdered at the first convenient opportunity," he said. Stanton notified President Andrew Johnson in an 1868 report that the only remedy was the "firm support of the army until these outlaws are punished or dispersed."[9]

Johnson had dismissed this and other reports of atrocities and of civil authorities' collusion with extremists, even from officials in his administration and in the U.S. Army. He insisted that ex-Confederates had accepted the Reconstruction Amendments and he had opposed sending troops to stop the attacks.[10]

In 1870, hearing conflicting reports, including those from hard-liners and their allies dismissing and denying violence, the Senate asked President Grant to inquire into threats to the execution of the law. The president reported to the Select Committee of the Senate to Investigate Alleged Outrages in the Southern States that parts of the United States were in a state of lawlessness and asked for emergency powers to suppress the violence. Governors in Arkansas, North Carolina, and Tennessee deployed state militias that eventually restored a degree of order there, though too late to prevent mass atrocities. But Alabama, Florida, Georgia, Mississippi, and South Carolina were among the states who remained steadfast in their refusal, so the violence there continued.

———

Hearing reports of killings, assassinations, and other civil rights violations and local authorities' failure to bring known culprits to justice, progressives in Congress had passed the Enforcement Acts in May 1870 and April 1871 and appointed U.S. commissioners to extremist strongholds to investigate attacks and begin criminal proceedings. But few white Americans supported justice-minded progressives' efforts to hold extremists accountable. Right-wing whites' objections to these measures were swift and fierce. At every turn, Klan-sympathizing citizens and lawmakers from across the nation dismissed reports and outcry of disorder. Belligerents bemoaned the Enforcement Acts' efforts to protect life and the integrity of the democratic process. Exhibiting an indifference to the loss of Black people's lives and livelihood and Confederates' violations of the Constitution, conservatives accused congressional Republicans of overreaching their authority and illegitimately infringing on white southerners' states' rights. White conservatives and moderates in the North and West were increasingly apathetic, eager to let white southerners tackle the "problem" of Black people's insistence on being free, secure, and equal. For a time, progressives continued trying to reconstruct American freedom.

Rather than depend on the unpopular use (among white conservatives and moderates) of military authority to restore order, lawmakers designed the Enforcement Acts to lean heavily on the federal courts. But these institutions were not well suited to the task, as federal prosecutors' efforts to try white South Carolinians who attacked people like Patrick and Missouri Tanner's family proved. Federal courts soon found themselves overwhelmed by hundreds of cases. Many of the judges had been appointed by conservative presidents and likely shared their ideological opposition to using federal power specifically to check extremists waging war on Black people's freedom.[11] That didn't exactly facilitate victims' and their allies' pursuit of justice.[12]

Meanwhile, the Joint Select Committee to Inquire into the Condition of Affairs in the Late Insurrectionary States formed, intensifying the government's halting intervention.[13] Congress established this bicameral committee to conduct a forensic investigation into the contexts, causes, and consequences of racial terror and election disorder. The committee was composed of five Republicans and two Democrats from the Senate and eight Republicans and six Democrats from the House of Representatives. Almost half of the committee hailed from the former enslaving states.

Although bipartisan in theory, the committee was dogged by sectarian fights about the investigation, and its scope narrowed. Massachusetts congressman and former U.S. Army general Benjamin Butler said he wanted to "clear the skirts of the southern people" so loyal Americans could know "where the peace stands."[14] Progressives wanted to pursue the truth, formally acknowledge the atrocities, denounce the violations of human rights and the democratic process, and determine a course of action to restore the peace. Right-wingers and Confederates who had returned to power voted for the committee's formation, but not in good faith; they undermined it from the start. Hard-liners echoed the white conservative press's minimizing attacks as harmless pranks and shifted the investigation's framing from "southern disorders"—which presumed a disruption of law-abiding behavior—to the more neutral focus on the South's "affairs."[15]

Investigators fanned out from the capital, heading west and south to the states that hadn't undertaken sufficient action to attend to lawlessness—Alabama, Florida, Georgia, Mississippi, and South Carolina. They summoned and invited perpetrators and victims, soldiers and civilians, and officials to hubs and access points—places like Macon, Atlanta, Jacksonville, Montgomery, York, and Spartanburg—to establish the facts and determine possible forms of redress. Although not pursuing criminal accountability, lawmakers used juridical procedures to interview witnesses who appeared before them. Witnesses at the congressional hearings swore oaths to tell the truth, giving bureaucratic formality to the proceedings. Investigators asked narrow questions about election violence, sometimes dismissing evidence that might not stand up in a court of law or information that did not fit their agendas.

Investigators' competing agendas cast a cloud of doubt over Black people's and their allies' reports of genocidal-like violence in the South. Right-leaning lawmakers wanted to end Reconstruction and roll back all the rights African Americans had gained. That agenda informed the questions they asked witnesses at the hearing and the narrative they constructed to deny the reign of terror killings. Left-leaning lawmakers wanted to end the violence and sustain the legislative reforms of Reconstruction, including the Thirteenth, Fourteenth, and Fifteenth Amendments. That objective influenced the questions they asked and the narrative they constructed, detailing the killings and their links to the Confederate cause. Those partisan objectives and the two competing narratives lawmakers produced from their investigation made it hard for white Americans concerned about the reconstruction of democracy to see what targeted Black people knew— namely, that Confederates were violating the peace and the U.S. Constitution. The white American majority's combined inability and refusal to see the atrocities made it hard for progressive lawmakers to take more purposeful steps preventing Reconstruction's overthrow.[16]

————

Surviving the loss of kin, home, land, livelihood, and community occupied most victims. Officials summoned some Black witnesses directly, relying on targeted people's efforts to obtain justice through local magistrates. Survivors also responded to news about the hearings with a sense of duty to educate Congress and the nation about the atrocities they had endured, and they appeared at the sites to add their accounts to the record.[17] Still living in the immediate wake of strikes, they walked, and they boarded wagons, boats, or (if they had the means) trains, to have their say. Mrs. Wiley Hargrove, who had been attacked with her prosperous husband, was one of many who were too sick or frail to travel.[18] Benjamin Leonard, a disabled man from Greene County, Alabama, walked part of the thirty-six miles to

Livingston and was carried by a neighbor and fellow survivor the rest of the way to the hearings. Having already been displaced to Atlanta or Spartanburg, some only had to cross town, as Eliza Lyon did in Demopolis and Augustus Blair did in Huntsville. Others traveled dozens of miles, as Samuel and Hannah Tutson did.

When the Tutsons headed north to Jacksonville, they hoped lawmakers were summoning them in good faith. Being called on to testify might have been a validation of their membership in the American polity and formal recognition of the wrongs done to them. They had already testified in the local criminal trials for the raid, but the verdicts were pending. Having been peppered with rude, minimizing questions, Hannah didn't have much confidence in her family's attackers being convicted, and the equally pressing issue was that their white neighbors were still trying to take their land. She hoped federal officials summoning them to hear their stories might be more sympathetic and might help them keep their land and live in peace. The only way that would happen was if federal officials offered their protection and took action to enforce existing laws and bring perpetrators to justice.

But African Americans' participation in the hearings was a complex issue, a reality Samuel, Hannah, and other survivors knew. Although their civil and political rights were now enshrined in law, the implementation was still being worked out in an era of major state reformation. White resistance to equality was widespread and strong enough that there was still a chance Black people's rights would be nothing more than paper promises. The possibility of Black people who were brutalized by white men gaining justice in a system built around white male supremacy remained in the balance. Aside from their being attacked in the first place, nothing made the tenuousness of the Tutsons' rights and standing in the nation clearer than their inability to get a semblance of justice in local and state forums.

Families like Samuel and Hannah's were often socially isolated; no one, except people who had experienced similar atrocities, could truly understand what they had gone through and how they felt about it. Survivors encountered disbelief and disavowal from people who presumed they brought violence on themselves. Vigilantes inflated their activities to seem more politically significant than they were or denied them altogether, tearing the fabric of reality and raising questions about the veracity of African Americans' accounts.[19] Targeted people would have known about slanderous allegations and conservative white press reports minimizing attacks. Living in the aftermath of strikes, they were exhausted and just trying to hold on—Hannah and Samuel to their land, Mary and Joseph Brown to the hope the troops who made them feel secure would stay. A cloud of sorrow filled the air, but it was broken up by rays of hope. The doubt and denial they faced, in response to the injustice of losing their rights and their homes, steeled their resolve to subject themselves to another ordeal to set the record straight.

Witnesses arriving at the congressional hearings' sites knew lawmakers were not seeking criminal accountability, or reconciliation, or healing. These sites were not spaces where survivors would be able to give simple narratives of what had happened, without interruption or skepticism. Augustus Blair had no illusions about lawmakers bringing back his beloved boy Billy. Leanna Garrison knew they couldn't resurrect her darling husband, Jerry, whom extremists had shot dead when he stepped outside to stop the white men from shooting into their home. Hannah Tutson knew they couldn't heal the injuries from her sexual assault or stop her baby girl's pain from being thrown across a room. But she and Samuel might have hoped some federal action could help them stay in their restored home and on their land. Fellow homesteaders Doc and Ellen Rountree had already been displaced from their house, land, and community, and might have pinned their hopes on returning home. Having dealt with white people all their lives, survivors understood their audience; they would have to navigate investigators' agendas and the internecine politics of Reconstruction to have their stories heard. Clear-eyed, they hoped policymakers and fellow citizens would rebuke perpetrators and facilitate their prosecution.

But Augustus, Hannah, Doc, and Leanna understood they were appearing before federal officials to narrate their accounts and those of people who could or would not testify. They knew the obligations that came with participating in a truth-finding process.[20] All victims knew for sure was that they had pursued and achieved their visions of freedom and fulfilled their responsibilities as newly recognized citizens. They had done nothing to provoke attacks; their successful advancement in life had sparked the war on them. They spoke with one voice about what they had achieved since emancipation and what they were losing to violence.

Witnesses made their way to centers of local government—the imposing structures of state capitol buildings, courthouses, and meeting places. Some of the buildings might have been damaged in the war. Others were brand new thanks to rebuilding efforts. Their cladding ranged from simple weatherboard siding, to commanding brick, to Greek Revival finery. Many were two stories high and had common rooms with lofty ceilings, large windows, and rows and rows of benches that accommodated large crowds. Black people were usually denied access to these spaces unless they had been elected to office, were parties to civil or criminal proceedings, or they were there to service them.

Survivors entered rooms full of skeptical white strangers—members of Congress, local officials, state legislators, Freedmen's Bureau agents, law enforcement officials, night riders and their defenders, the press, and the curious public. The records indicate witnesses did not hear all the proceedings. Many of them only entered the room to give their testimonies and respond to questions. In those rooms across the South, survivors answered intimate questions about the unthinkable horrors they had endured, spelling out in graphic detail what had happened to them and people they knew. The testimonies reveal that survivors wanted to show lawmakers and their fellow citizens the sinews of violence, the human toll, in flesh and blood, from the loss of kin, life, home, livelihood, community, instead of anonymized in reports and headlines.

The Civil War and its aftermath brought the federal government's intervention into Americans' lives like never before. Black southerners felt the force of its power acutely. It had allowed the Tutsons to secure the homestead their white neighbors were trying to drive them from. It bestowed upon Edward Crosby the right to vote, and upon Abram Colby, the right to legal recognition of his union with Anna Walker and to serve as a Georgia lawmaker. It vested Lewis Jackson with Second Amendment protections and Doc and Ellen Rountree with the authority to shield their children from exploitative apprenticeships. Abe and Eliza Lyon could send their older daughter to school, and they could save six hundred dollars from his black-smithing and her domestic work to purchase land. These men and women all understood the new promises of equal protection under the law and federal intervention in response to local and state negligence. Having experienced apathy, ineptitude, and indignity in their local pursuit of justice, these targeted people sought to invoke the civil contract of Reconstruction and remind investigators of their responsibility to honor the law and the Constitution.

Charles Pearce, a state senator in Florida, informed the subcommittee in Jacksonville about Black Floridians' futile appeals to Governor Harrison Reed. The governor acknowledged Black citizens' complaints about vigilantism in Jackson County, but Pearce said Reed claimed his "arms are paralyzed; there was not power enough in the government to protect the loyal people of the counties where outrages existed."[21] Black North Carolinians appealed to Governor William Woods Holden for assistance to little avail.[22] Both state executives were sympathetic, but the challenge of governing states shattered by the war, and the extent of right-wing whites' sowing disorder, overwhelmed them; terror sprees on their turf added to state executives' already full political plates while also exposing their vulnerabilities.

Investigators pelted Black witnesses with questions about their culpability for the disorder. Why were you whipped? Had you had a quarrel with anyone? Were you involved in politics? One asked Elias Thomson, "Do you say that nobody is troubled who behaves himself?" Elias answered that was usually the case. Elias said he thought "my character would help me" avoid a visit. But it didn't.[23] Investigators asked another South Carolina witness, "Had you done anything that you know of to cause these people to come and treat you this way?"[24]

Conservative hard-liners lobbed dismissive, blame-shifting questions and comments. Survivors in turn pushed back against slanderous allegations that without slavery Black people had reverted to their "inherent" savagery and were the aggressors. "I never had a falling out with a white man in my life," Essic Harris insisted.[25] Augustus Blair said that although he had seen whites run his Black neighbors away, "I didn't think anybody would ever interfere with me," much less kill his son.[26] Charlotte Fowler said that her murdered husband, Wallace, "did no harm to anybody; he didn't believe anybody would trouble him."[27]

White terror demonstrated to targeted people that local legal and judicial venues were not well suited for reconciling their claims against whites, which was why they turned to federal officials.[28] Floridian Richard Pousser explained "there is no use" in trying to get justice because "you cannot get justice" in his town of Marianna. Victims exposed themselves to reprisal by coming forward to local authorities, only to face situations that, Richard said, "will make it appear that a colored man is a liar." Perpetrators' denials, fused with sympathizers' refusal to believe Black victims' accounts of atrocities, made some survivors afraid to have authorities file charges against their attackers. For Richard, there was no use in even bothering to get justice if the federal government was not going to honor its constitutional promises of due process and equal protection.[29] "We cannot get protection unless we have assistance from the government," he said.

"We look to the government of the United States to protect us," Larry White echoed. Black Floridians could not count on the "shallow" government of their state, Larry said, and had no confidence in its ability to fulfill its responsibility for protecting Black citizens. This was why he and so many he knew had fled their home communities.

"We are all afraid to go back," Larry explained. His cohort of petitioners told their governor that white men "were killing us like dogs," but got no relief. "It seems to me," Larry said, "if I was governor all over the State, and the people were to get wronged in the State, I would send men right there and stop it" like he knew other governors had.[30] Having already lost everything to strikes, or understanding they were on the path to ruin, survivors like Larry saw testifying at the hearings as their opportunity to relay their stories of personal disaster and compel the federal government to step in where municipalities and states had failed.

Black witnesses knew that electoral politics and their embrace of voting rights to fortify their freedom had catalyzed attacks and the resulting investigation. To have their stories recorded, survivors had to fit their testimonies into the existing language of Reconstruction—Union, loyalty, citizenship, and respect for the nation's laws. This meant witnesses needed to highlight their loyalty to the U.S. cause, their lack of culpability, and the nation's responsibility to them as law-abiding citizens. And they needed to take advantage of any opportunities to illuminate the wider truth of the war on their freedom.

With the injustice of attacks reverberating throughout their lives, this wasn't hard to do. Robert Fullerlove spent little time talking about himself as the individual target of political violence; he wanted investigators to know how it made his family insecure when white men went unpunished after torching his home, shooting his sons, and forcing his wife, Adaline, to risk being shot to extinguish the fire. The nation's political system was under attack but targeted people like Robert and Adaline bore the brunt of the violence.

Augustus and Letty Mills wanted lawmakers to know that their attackers had aimed not only to deny Black people the right to vote and serve in office, as so many assumed; they also had wanted to inflict pain in all areas of Black people's lives, a goal they had achieved by savagely beating the couple and their young children, leaving them with life-altering injuries, and displacing them from their home and community. Strikes were not simply about the force asserted, witnesses like Augustus and Letty insisted; they carried with them local and state denial of their right to be free and secure. The assault had left Augustus, Letty, and the children adrift in a roiling sea.[31]

Reverend Elias Hill had been attacked, in part, because he was a member of a group planning to emigrate to Liberia. White men in York, South Carolina, had published Elias's name in the newspaper as the person at the helm of the scheme. They had been outraged that Elias's company of emigrationists had had the temerity to thwart their subjugation, and they had targeted Elias because they believed that, as a community elder, he had the kind of social capital needed to successfully shepherd the group.[32]

Elias told lawmakers he and his people did not want to leave their community or even their homeland. But as long as night-riding strikes continued they felt they had no choice. Elias explained that his cohort of survivors hoped lawmakers would condemn the violence and convince extremists in South Carolinians to "cast off" their tolerance of white terror. However, the only way they could stay was if they could "live in peace," Elias said.[33] A more assertive intervention by federal officials was needed to make this happen, an intervention witnesses like Elias hoped to inspire.

Survivors tried to help investigators understand that strikes were not contained events that concluded neatly when the attacking faction departed. The force was reverberating through their lives, as Eliza Lyon tried to make clear when she said, "I am very much oppressed now," explaining her family's suffering after Abe's killing and their displacement. With perpetrators running free and determined to evade justice, the threat of reprisal violence was all too real. Witnesses had to share enough information to be credible and achieve their goals but limit the risks of retaliation.

Witnesses at the congressional hearings practiced self-protection whenever they could, especially given the very public nature of the proceedings. For some, this started with who answered summonses. Patriarchs, like Samuel Gaffney, outnumbered matriarchs, even though women were targeted and harmed by white men, too. Samuel had been lying out when the white men came, so his wife and children had endured the strike and therefore knew the identities of the attackers. But only Samuel appeared at the hearings. When lawmakers pressed about why he was present and his wife was not, Samuel dissembled, explaining, "I didn't think it was any use to fetch her." He also cited Mrs. Gaffney's inability to walk the distance to Spartanburg.[34] As the head of his household, the intended target, Samuel might have felt confident relaying Mrs. Gaffney's account himself. Or, he might have been trying to protect her.[35]

A sixteen-year-old boy from Jackson County, Georgia, whom attackers pistol-whipped in a raid on his family, was one of the youngest witnesses at the hearings whose age was recorded, despite adolescents' victimization and capacity to testify.[36] Lucy Hernandez—the teen who was sexually assaulted alongside her mother, Harriet—did not appear. When Spartanburg investigators interrogated Harriet about Lucy's absence, Harriet deflected, explaining that she herself needed to testify. The Hernandezes might not have wanted Lucy to be revictimized by appearing before the committee.[37]

Reprisal attacks on people who reported violence to authorities underscored the danger families like the Gaffneys and Hernandezes feared in having their matriarchs and kids testify. The ethics of community protection suggest some families concluded that, if there was going to be any punishment to be had for appearing as a witness, men and in some cases adult women would bear it. "The Black people have injured themselves very much by talking," one survivor informed lawmakers.[38]

Before he appeared at the York hearings, Andrew Cathcart had not shared his attackers' identities with many outside of his immediate circle of trust. When investigators asked him why, he answered, "Because they would have killed me." Andrew had once named names only to receive notice his attackers or their allies would seek reprisal if he did not shut up. Fearing for his life, Andrew began staying at his white patrons' homes. Andrew's white acquaintances assured him they had handled the situation by extending him their protection, and he wanted to believe them. "They told me I need not be afraid," Andrew said. But having been attacked in the first place, Andrew had no confidence in their promises.

"Mark you, I am a Negro and cannot read or write," Andrew said, "but I know some things." One of those things he knew was the importance of revealing his attackers' identities before the committee, and not relying solely on white South Carolinians' promises to defend him.[39] Andrew looked instead to federal officials for relief.

Patrick Tanner did not share Andrew's faith. He resisted identifying his attackers because if he did, he said, "this man may injure me worse than before." Investigators were unmoved and insisted he name the men who had attacked him. "The government is trying to do its best to give [targeted people] protection. It is not for the purpose of bringing trouble on you, but to stop the lawless proceedings, that we ask you this question," an investigator pressed.[40]

Patrick said the strike already had jeopardized his livelihood. "I have a large crop on hand," he explained, which he had worked "mighty hard" to care for. Sleeping outside and being distressed by what had happened to them had made it hard for the Tanners to tend to their crops. Patrick wanted federal officials' help, but said he was "afraid they will injure me hereafter if it is ever known that I have told . . . I wouldn't want it to be known that I have told you."[41] The hearings were public, and news outlets around the country were covering them. Ohio congressman and Klan sympathizer Philadelph Van Trump said, "[I]f you do tell somebody will know it."

"We should insist on having the names . . . we shall never know who did these things unless the witnesses be required to tell the names," another investigator chimed in. Van Trump tried to coax Patrick into naming the attackers by minimizing the harm the Tanners had endured and their galloping fear of being struck again, stating, "They didn't touch you that night, you say? They didn't hurt you at all."

"What they did is hurting my family," Patrick insisted, rejecting Van Trump's efforts to trivialize his family's victimization, and using the present tense to convey their ongoing suffering. The Tanners survived, Patrick conceded, but at great cost. And reprisal for naming names at the hearings was no trifling matter.[42]

While Benjamin Leonard was in Livingston, Alabama, to testify, a white man threatened him, telling him, "You had better leave here."[43] So Benjamin did, despite the great effort it had taken to get there. When investigators later asked why he had turned back toward home, to Greene County, Benjamin answered, "Because I felt uneasy."[44] He did ultimately testify, but he worried his wife, Emily, and their two sons were being targeted in his absence.

"I feel myself in great risk doing these things," John Childers told investigators in Livingston who asked him to relay stories of attacks on other people in his community. "I have no support in the state of Alabama. I am a citizen here, bred and born; and have been here for 42 years. If I report these things I can't stay at home." When examiners continued to press for night riders' names, John responded, "I am in a tight place where I am, and I wish to give you gentlemen all the satisfaction I can, but, in the same time, I must be particular in saving myself, because it is just as well to be in one gun-boat as another."[45] John wanted lawmakers to understand the threat to his life and his and his family's well-being was ongoing.

Robert Fullerlove left Tompkinsville for Livingston determined to report what had happened to his family and maybe gain some protection. This was until white men harassed him on his journey to the proceedings. "I don't go away to go back," Robert said, revealing his understanding that testifying endangered his family and him. Robert informed the committee, "[A]fter last night . . . a dozen people got that subpoena; they couldn't make it out" of town.

Robert had made it out, but at the hearings, he testified that he knew "if I go home to-night or to-morrow, or next day, when they hear I am at home," vigilantes would come for him. Robert could lie out away from his home at night, but he would not be able to handle his affairs. "I can't go to my shop," Robert said, because "some of the men will be shooting at me, killing me for what? For my rights . . . I wouldn't be a bit surprised when I hear from my family again, if the house is burned up, or the corn-crib, just on account of this subpoena."[46]

Witnesses understood investigators would not offer financial or legal relief, but they believed answering the subpoenas and telling their stories remained important for having more perpetrators arrested and prosecuted. Still, that did not erase the risks they faced.

In fact, it heightened them, advocate for victims and Mississippi state legislator Alexander K. Davis explained, as he shared with investigators the intelligence he got from people he encountered in Macon. Survivors there planned to participate in local grand jury proceedings, only to arrive and discover perpetrators on the jury. Others knew, or suspected, culprits had united to seek reprisal against people accusing them of crimes. By Alexander's account, even sympathetic white men with significant social standing feared speaking out.

Alexander explained that some targeted people did not believe federal officials would make any meaningful effort to arrest violence and protect witnesses. They knew "that their testimony before this committee will simply amount to informing the outside world as to these outrages, and that is about all." Alexander said Black Mississippians understood congressional investigators "will not lend any aid at all to bring these parties to justice, and it will only place them in the position of being more obnoxious to these men and more liable to be killed."[47] For some of Alexander's people, testifying and putting their lives in jeopardy for a box-ticking exercise was not worth the risk.

Survivors hoped federal officials would intervene by boosting federal troop levels in their communities and filing federal charges for civil rights violations when state and municipal authorities failed to prosecute extremists who targeted Black people. But finding themselves, as John Childers put it, "in one gun-boat or another," they knew they needed to prioritize their safety. For some targeted people, like the ones Alexander Davis knew, the peril of testifying was too great. Others believed "informing the outside world to these outrages" was an unmissable opportunity—especially when there was so much disinformation about strikes, and fear-based inaction only incentivized other whites to violence.

———

Patrick Tanner's discussion of the ongoing impact of the raid on his family reflects survivors' desires to show they were living honorably—demonstrating their full potential for freedom before they were attacked—and to convey the full extent of their suffering. Witnesses itemized an extensive list of woes, illuminating strikes' long, spiked tails and how they lashed survivors again and again, ensuring the arc of surviving white terror rarely bent in the direction of recovery.[48]

Patrick said his wife, Missouri, suffered profoundly from the attack. Pregnant at the time, she could have experienced derangement or simply been unable to care for herself. If Missouri had lost the child she was carrying, she might have suffered dissociation. Whatever the source of her misery, her troubles clearly distressed her husband.

Attacked people described their infirmities in great detail. "I never got over it; I don't know as I ever will," one South Carolina man said of his physical injuries.[49] George Roper was one of several witnesses at the hearings who voluntarily put their bodies into evidence, verifying their claims of physical injury and pain.[50] George, who had been struck several times by armed men, told investigators in Huntsville, "I have the pistol-ball now," pointing to the knot underneath his clothed skin. George had paid a doctor ten dollars to remove one of the balls, and he removed his coat to show investigators the scar. "You can feel the bullet here above the elbow," he said of the remaining ball.[51] Of their own initiative and at the behest of examiners, witnesses displayed fresh stripes from whippings, scars from bullet wounds and stabbings, and burns from being hanged or dragged, revealing their familiarity with cultural practices demanding the display of bodily pain.[52] Witnesses like George understood they could not simply tell investigators, so they let their bodies talk, avowing the truth of what they endured.[53]

Neither Leanna Garrison nor Charlotte Fowler had visible physical wounds, and their slain husbands had been buried. But in case investigators in Atlanta doubted her account of Jerry's killing by massive gunfire, Leanna brought the bullet-ridden coat he had been wearing to show "he was willfully murdered," she said.[54] At a hearing in Spartanburg, Charlotte Fowler stated that one of her husband's killers had dropped a chip from a fire on Wallace's chest as he lay dying after being shot in the head; when lawmakers pressed her on the point, she produced the burnt shirt Wallace had been wearing as proof.[55] Eliza Lyon did not take her husband's clothing to the hearings in Demopolis, but she did take the broken-off knife Abe's killers had used. Presenting damaged clothing or a murder weapon attested to the fatal injuries the men had sustained, while also symbolizing the widows' understanding of their duty to carry what had happened to Jerry, Wallace, and Abe with them until they obtained justice and what they hoped would be protection for themselves and their families.

Investigators at some sites had doctors on hand to see if witnesses' bodies confirmed their stories. Conservative interviewers and doctors used these examinations to try to discredit witnesses, while radical and moderate ones used them to buttress witnesses' claims. After being accosted on his way to testify, Robert Fullerlove submitted to a forensic examination.[56] Scipio Eager was another witness who put his body into evidence at the investigators' request. Night riders whipped the twenty-four-year-old man and killed his brother in April 1871. He showed the scar on his forehead "to prove for itself," he said, that he had told the truth about his attack. Scipio then displayed his back, revealing what appeared to be extensive marking, prompting one investigator to ask, "Those were all made by that whipping?" "I did not say that all were made by that whipping, but some of them were," Scipio answered, suggesting some scarring came from his enslavement and the rest were fresh from his attack.[57]

Other survivors presented evidence of injuries that might never heal. Jesse Brown, whose skull had been cracked when a night rider kicked him with a brass spur, complained, "[I]t pains me now; every time it goes to rain it bothers me a heap."[58] For people like Jesse, attacks represented multiple catastrophes.

Debility following raids was familiar to Samuel Stewart of Walton County, Georgia. When Samuel fought back, his attackers shot him at close range, hitting him in the right arm. He told investigators in Atlanta that because the local doctor had been afraid to treat him, he had lost the use of his arm. "I did not get able to work for two years," Samuel said, "and I have very little use of my arm now." When an examiner asked Samuel if he was still able to find work in his trade as a carpenter, he answered, "No, I cannot use my right hand with tools in it, and I cannot raise my hand to my head; I have not been able to put my right hand to my face since then. It feels numb now, like it is asleep."[59] Samuel's injuries probably plagued him for the rest of his life.

Injuries such as the one Samuel described interfered with survivors' ability to meet their obligations, work, or care for loved ones. Samuel had been earning two dollars a day doing carpentry work for people in the community. Without two functioning arms he was less productive; his injuries reduced him to doing odd painting jobs. He could have sold his tools to provide for his family, but his attackers had stolen nearly half his stock, more than two hundred pounds of saws, hammers, and other tools. Samuel wanted investigators to know he had gone from being able to provide for his wife and children to being, as he said, "barely able now to make a support," despite being "well known" in his community.[60]

Jack Johnson, who had fled his home in Laurens County, South Carolina, leaving his wife behind, exhibited licks from either fists or whips from one of his attackers. Jack also showed his hand, saying, "[T]his finger he broke entirely so that I cannot turn a drill in my hand."[61] "I am not well yet," Columbus Jeter said of his injuries. "I cannot do much with my left arm." He added, "You can feel the shot through my shirt. I cannot do much work and I have not a cent."[62]

Samuel Stewart's stockpile of tools was one of many examples at the hearings of the wealth African Americans accumulated once emancipation gave them more control over their lives, and of how well many did charting their families' course. Lawmakers had informed witnesses there would be no financial compensation for their losses, so survivors had no reason to misrepresent their earnings or property. Still, those who could offered census enumerators' and tax assessors' estimates of their property's value to substantiate their statements of what they owned. Despite slow economic growth and fights over wages and contracts, survivors' testimonies show some Black people's material advances after slavery and how the war on freedom erased this progress.[63]

Eliza Lyon's account of losing hundreds of dollars in the crops her family could not harvest and livestock they could not sell was just one of many Black witnesses' attempts to communicate that they had made good use of freedom's economic possibilities. Smith Watley's articulation of his success as a blacksmith and Hannah Tutson's of her earnings as a laundress showed investigators proof of their industriousness. Augustus Blair's family and others had hired laborers to increase their productive capacity and their wealth. Men like Robert Fullerlove had purchased land and planted crops to feed their families and generate profit. Collectively, witnesses made clear how they had picked themselves up from slavery.

After being attacked, many had fled their homes or were bracing to, communicating to lawmakers the realities of dispossession as a consequence of night riding. Witnesses itemized what Hannah Tutson, William Coleman, and Eliza Lyon called "all the little things"—personal property destroyed, cherished mementos stolen or abandoned—revealing how many targets had used their earnings to furnish their homes with goods and accoutrements that suited their personal tastes.

Sam Nuckles's fear of returning to his Union County community and Samuel Tutson's struggles navigating the legal and judicial system conveyed how difficult it was for families to avoid revictimization and recoup their financial losses. They wanted policymakers and their fellow Americans to know strikes had left them destitute, compounding their victimization long after their attackers had departed.

Witnesses testified to the social and political consequences of this destabilization as well. Black southerners had built new homes and communities for shelter, security, and uplift only to lose them. Andrew Cathcart's and Caroline Smith's accounts of attacks on schools and Warren Jones's and Henry Giles's stories about churches being destroyed showed the committee the vibrancy of African Americans' institution-building. These beacons of freedom had served their communities' needs until the white men struck. Now they were gone. Communities spent precious funds to rebuild vital institutions, if they had the means. In other communities still living under siege, there was no indication these places would ever be rebuilt, much less returned to any previous glory.

Deadly attacks on politicians and voters like Jerry Garrison struck at the heart of Black leadership in the age of freedom. Assassinations also served as deterrents to prospective voters and politicians. Men like Robert Fullerlove and Wiley Hargrove who were struck because they had voted for Radical candidates might have decided to stay away from the polls.

John Lewis remained committed to voting, despite having been whipped. "I will vote just as I did at first," John said. "They will whip me for it anyhow," he assured the committee, "but I will vote again."[64] Extreme courageousness, like John's, shows that some targeted people believed withdrawing from politics only played into perpetrators' hands. Self-determination, people like John knew, was key to Black liberation. To achieve it, Black people had to continue to fight.

Edward Crosby knew voting for his interests over his landlord's put his family and himself at great risk for injury or death. People who withdrew from the political scene would not be able to work toward creating and maintaining more democratic governments. Retreating from electoral politics to avoid being held hostage or assassinated was certainly a logical decision for individuals, especially those who had been captured or were worried about it, but John Lewis and others knew it came with communal costs. That's why they called upon federal officials to fulfill their responsibilities to protect citizens exercising their rights.

Survivors explained that white extremist violence—and not Black people's alleged indolence—compromised some targeted people's ability to meet the obligations and responsibilities of freedom. Night riding stripped families of the wealth they had accumulated after slavery. It undermined institutions that advanced communities' needs. Families and communities couldn't continue transcending their enslavement if they were constantly rebuilding what white men destroyed. Clem and Minerva Bowden wouldn't be able to pass on property and cash to their kids. Robert and Adaline Fullerlove's children and future grandchildren would not be able to inherit the wealth the couple had been accruing before the raid. Few witnesses indicated being able to provide the same quality of life for their families as they had before white men attacked them.

Families like those of Charlotte Fowler and Eliza Lyon, who lost patriarchs in attacks, experienced emotional grief as well as the decline of whatever financial security they might have enjoyed. Charlotte and Eliza lost out on the years of productive economic activity Wallace and Abe could have provided. Night riding forced widows to scrape by, working harder and possibly relying on kin to bear all the burdens resulting from having been attacked.

The killing or disabling of craftsmen and tradesmen like Samuel Stewart meant fathers could not pass on skills to their sons, which in turn hindered a family's upward social mobility. Death or disabling injuries forced families to live on less than they had before, which constrained families' wealth across several generations. Unless new opportunities or skills were acquired, the loss of the trade in the family likely contributed to socioeconomic decline.[65]

When outcast families fled their communities, they wanted lawmakers to know, they had left behind life-sustaining property. "Have you been back?" Atlanta investigators asked a woman who had fled Columbus, Georgia, in 1868. She said she had not. "I was working honorably for my living" the woman insisted, in case there was any doubt. She had been the proprietor of a boardinghouse, as well as a washerwoman and cook. "They say I shall not go back," she explained. "I have lost everything I had there." The woman had lost her home and part of her livelihood to the strike and could not tend to her unsettled affairs without exposing herself to more harm or possibly death. These new burdens increased her and other displaced people's vulnerability to the forces of the harsh world.[66]

The despair survivors exhibited at the hearings suggests night riders took away a semblance of who some of their targets had planned on being after slavery. The futures victims had envisioned when they were lined up on the starting blocks of freedom would not be as they had imagined.

———

Samuel and Hannah Tutson and other witnesses fulfilled their responsibilities to themselves and their kin—alive and dead—and their duty as citizens by testifying at the congressional hearings. They probably left the hearings with no more certainties than they had arrived with. The Tutsons testified wanting the world to know about the assaults on their lives and dignity, and that the suffering their family had experienced had not ended when their attackers left; that it had lingered, casting shadows that hovered over different areas of their lives and menaced their futures. If closure was possible, it is not clear that Hannah, Samuel, and the other witnesses had a sense of it at this time.[67]

Survivors spoke with one voice, narrating a dark history of Reconstruction and a searing indictment of the nation's failure to protect freed people and honor their rights. Andrew and Frankie Cathcart, Mary and Joseph Brown, Eliza and Abe Lyon, and others like them, the committee's report on "the Late Insurrectionary States" and supporting records show, had been agents of their own freedom. From family restoration and making an honest living, to the fight for equal rights and not only voting but also serving in office, they had picked themselves up and taken their destinies in their own hands. They did this in spite of many whites' stonehearted objections to Black freedom and self-determination, even in the face of racist violence.

Would their fellow Americans heed Black people's warning? Only some did, like an outraged woman named Faith Lichen, who wrote a letter to Frederick Douglass's newspaper, *New National Era*, in response to news reporting on the proceedings. "Turn on your persecutors," Faith urged targeted people. "Kill, burn, and destroy," she said. Faith ended her letter describing herself as "making faces at the peace" that was obviously not protecting Black people's lives, limbs, or property.[68]

Some governors organized state militias in response to reports of violence taking place at the hearings. Alabama, Virginia, and Georgia excluded Black men from joining them to help protect their own communities, which sparked protests. Some Black Georgians planned lawsuits contesting their exclusion and asserting their right to help defend their people from racist violence.[69] Others formed and maintained militia companies for their "own enjoyment and pastime," and for their own protection. White Georgians ordered these groups to disband, but Black Georgians, knowing they were within their rights, refused; in response, they were set upon by racist whites, who executed four militiamen and whipped countless others, according to one account.[70]

Hard-liner whites attacked families transcending slavery and those trying to defend them. Vigilantes plundered not simply Black people's political participation or land, but also their lives, spirits, and livelihoods.[71] Nothing but hard days filled the horizon for these families. In the stark clarity of Clem Bowden's refrain—"I don't ever expect in this life to get over it"—lies evidence of their despair, their sense of how attacks marked a sharp break from their prior transcendence of slavery, and their awareness of the hardship before them.[72]

Clem and the Tutsons joined countless others making clear the rending of African Americans' freedom and the unmaking of their families and their worlds. They appeared at the hearings to ring the alarm about extremists waging war on freedom, violating the terms of the peace.[73] They could see Reconstruction's end, and possibly their freedom, looming on the horizon. There could be pride and strength in testifying and comfort in knowing they and their families weren't alone in their suffering and grief. And yet, after saying their piece, they recognized that truth-telling proceedings on their own aren't inherently restorative.

In many ways, the hearings, and how lawmakers conducted interviews, worked as intended. The committee gathered the information it sought about southern disorders from witnesses, and it published the edited transcripts of the hearings and trial proceedings, as well as other documents, in thirteen volumes of firsthand testimony in 1872. At the time, the voluminous report constituted an institutional nod to atrocities, infused with denial of their existence, reflecting what lawmakers and their fellow Americans simultaneously knew and refused to know about the wrongs detailed at the hearings.

Partisanship informed what lawmakers took from all witnesses' testimonies, as well as what they wanted the American public to know about their findings from their investigation. Conservatives and progressives on the committee wrote separate reports. Confederates who had returned to power authored the minority report, representing the minority party in Congress—the Democrats. The minority report dismissed Black witnesses' accounts as "utterly unworthy of belief" and toyed with baseless claims about Black people menacing powerless white people. The document is foundational in developing what would become the big, apocryphal lie of the Lost Cause: that white southerners had been and were continuing to be, as the report's Democratic authors wrote, "defamed" and "put at the mercy of semi-barbarous negroes of the South, and the vilest of white people."

Right-wingers insisted—with a historical gloss familiar to anyone who has viewed D. W. Griffith's 1915 film *The Birth of a Nation*—that any violence was "the natural offspring of as corrupt and oppressive a system of local State government as ever disgraced humanity."[74] In short, Confederates had had no choice but to rise up and overthrow their Black oppressors. Extremists also took important lessons on terrorism's usefulness for clawing their way back to political power.

Moderates and progressives representing the majority party in Congress, the Republicans, who wrote the majority report, said there was a "remarkable concurrence of testimony" from targeted people, civil authorities, and federal observers that confirmed the former slaveholding states were in disorder, and that shocking violence had, they said, paralyzed the "arm of civil power" and left civil authorities "terror-struck."[75] White men were resisting the Reconstruction Amendments, "committing atrocities and crimes that richly deserve punishment."[76] Republicans found states were being "overrun by violence; midnight raids, secret murders, and open riot," which kept people, they wrote in the report, "in constant terror," as communities were filled with "scenes of blood" before elections.[77] Vigilantes had, they said, "demoralized society, and held men silent by the terror of [the Ku Klux Klan's] acts and by its powers for evil."[78] Congress had acted appropriately passing the Enforcement Acts, the majority said, addressing right-wing whites' charges of legislative overreach. The majority party said targeted people should not be left without protection. "As long as the legal and constitutional powers of government are adequate to afford it," the majority report said, Black southerners and their allies, as unoffending citizens, should have it.

The majority report noted that constitutional and legal "relief" for targeted people would "come only from a ready obedience to and support of constituted authority." It conceded that "southern communities do not seem to yield this ready obedience" to the law. That should not "deter the friends of good government in both sections from hoping and working for that end," however.[79] The Enforcement Acts had suppressed some of the violence in the Carolinas but "this should not lead to a conclusion that community would be safe if protective measures were withdrawn," the report's authors cautioned. They recommended the protective measures remain in effect "until there remains no further doubt of the actual suppression and disarming of this widespread and dangerous conspiracy." Its authors suggested district and circuit courts receive more resources to "secure speedy and certain justice to be administered, and leave no hope of impunity to criminals by the law's delay."[80]

African Americans told their stories of world-unraveling violence and asked federal officials and their fellow citizens to respect their rights. But the will to protect Black people's freedom was in diminishing supply. The question of which interpretation prevailed and whether truth or denial would succeed remained in the balance.

Chapter 8

A Revolution in Reverse

R evolutions may go backwards," observed the white abolitionist Thomas Wentworth Higginson—commander of the U.S. Army's first all-Black regiment, the First South Carolina Volunteers—in 1863.[1] But violent resistance to Radical Reconstruction shows revolutions don't just "go" in reverse on their own. Their aims get abandoned. Their achievements get rolled back, their beneficiaries recast as villains and their advocates violently vanquished. The truth of their histories gets warped in rebranding. But on the whole, Higginson's observation was right. Tracking how repeated sequences of violence, followed by a lack of accountability, contributed to ever more violence after the Klan hearings, the story of the nation's abandonment of Reconstruction comes into focus.

———

Societies experiencing atrocities struggle to put a stop to and then meaningfully address them. Perpetrators want to advance their aims to the end and propagate baseless lies to do it. Victims want violence to stop, and they want justice. A small cadre of observers believes in justice and accountability. The rest, especially those who are safe from being targeted, and atrocities' passive beneficiaries, simply want to move on and wipe the historical slate clean.

Only a sliver of the population will reckon with the truth—targeted people who have no choice, perpetrators who revel in cruelty and its spoils, and observers who believe in justice. The war after the American Civil War was no exception to this pattern. It saw the undoing of the "Second Founding," the organized abandonment of victims of white terror, and the historical erasure of both. All of this made—and makes—unearthing atrocity's truths *and* preventing more violence even harder.

Functioning legal systems struggle to handle the magnitude of mass atrocities. And most of the insurrectionary states did not have functioning legal systems, at least not ones that were willing to respect Reconstruction policies and were committed to stopping the violence and dispensing justice. Extremists across conservative white America reframed or minimized the killings, spinning improbable lies casting their resistance to emancipation as legitimate. They folded this into the Lost Cause mythology valorizing Confederates, insisting they had fought nobly for states' rights, not to preserve slavery. The white South's valiant defenders, they claimed, had been outmanned and outgunned on the battlefield and then punished by meddling, tyrannical white northerners who were now subjecting them to rule by uncivilized Black men.

White southerners who had resisted Reconstruction were at turns sensitive to charges of disloyalty and resistant to accepting Black people's right to anything other than pay for their labor, and sometimes not even that. Seeing the peace in strictly white conservative terms, they never saw their mistreatment and slaughter of Black people as a violation of the peace. To hear reactionaries tell it, progressives in Congress were using fabricated charges of racist atrocities to malign Confederates and deny them their rightful participation in the American democratic process after surrender. They played on white Americans' contrivances about emancipation and their concocted fears of equality as a zero-sum game for white people. Right-wingers' claims undercut the white public's ability to see the extent to which white southerners attacking Black people were violating the Constitution. They also pretended their interests and opposition to Radical Reconstruction were purely about protecting the separation of power between the states and the federal government. The thousands of Black people and hundreds of Unionist whites whom reactionaries had killed were not worth a mention.

Whatever else there is to say about Confederates, their gall was tenacious and irrefutable. Arrogance and impudence were a great public relations strategy that also provided tactical cover for sustaining the war on freedom. And despite the rapid extension of federal power during Reconstruction, including the federal response to political violence with the investigations and Enforcement Acts, the national legal system favored local and state control over law enforcement and criminal justice proceedings and white supremacy. Extremists had no incentive to back down. If anything, the violence with impunity rallied more to the Confederate cause. In this environment, what price, if any, would white southerners pay for waging war on Black people and their freedom?

At the congressional hearings, lawmakers and the public encountered irrefutable evidence of atrocity and southern disorder, and the social and political aims of Reconstruction were in danger. The truth of Confederates' ongoing war was established. Targeted people and their allies called upon the nation to honor the promise of freedom and equal protection. They wanted justice and needed to know if and how they could move forward.

But not enough white Americans believed Black people's and their white allies' accounts of violence or assumed a responsibility to do anything about it. Concerns raised by the Mississippi survivors that Alexander Davis had advocated for during the Klan hearings—that the world would know outrages occurred, and "that is about all"—were well founded. The outside world knew, but would it matter?

President Grant thought it did, on some occasions and for a time at least. In 1871, using his authority under the Enforcement Acts, his administration increased U.S. Army forces in some communities beset by violence. There were hundreds of arrests. But with so many perpetrators and victims, so much chaos in reuniting the country after the Civil War, so much white

American resistance to Black freedom and Reconstruction, and so little social and political will amongst the majority of white Americans to invest in the resources to secure justice for African Americans who had been targeted and had their rights violated, the war against Black freedom revealed the limits of expecting the law to address white injustice. Mass killings of Black people were like an X-ray of American freedom and democracy, exposing its internal flaws. And at every one of the exposed fractures were Black people trying to be free, secure, and equal.

With hard-liners serving as judges and jurors and favoring the despotic, antebellum status quo—and even contesting the federal government's power to conduct the trials—few terrorists were convicted, and those who were rarely served time. Nonetheless, the hearings and prosecutions, plus the Grant administration's installation of troops, had a suppressing effect, momentarily diffusing some organized attacks and killings. But diffusing the violence from the war on Black freedom wasn't the same as stopping it. Ultimately, Grant lacked the interest and political support needed to bring extremist violence to heel.

Lawmakers conducting the hearings had the power to act, especially under the Reconstruction Amendments. Beyond capturing African American survivors' stories and publishing and preserving the records of the hearings, however, they failed to meaningfully combat the violence. Congress and President Grant weren't alone in abdicating responsibility and abandoning survivors. It's fairly clear that most white Americans—from some federal officials to bystanders, to perpetrators themselves—expressed little contrition or had few moments of self-reflection about the killings and the rolling back of Black people's rights. Even fewer were willing to act, which is why the violence continued.

Abolitionists like Thomas Wentworth Higginson knew the shadow armies' attacks on African Americans were reversing the revolutionary aims of Reconstruction. So did President Grant and the progressive senators and congressmen who wrote the majority report for the Klan hearings. But they were all increasingly in the minority, as more Americans embraced what became a policy and practice of organized abandonment, strategically refusing to listen. They rendered survivors of atrocity, in novelist and human rights activist Arundhati Roy's words in 2004 about atrocities in the twenty-first century, "deliberately silenced" and "preferably unheard." Most white Americans preferred not to think about these people, so they didn't.[2] A generation of white Americans ignored—collectively refused and insulated itself and history against—the truth. Survivors' testimonies continued circulating, in search of adequate witnesses.

Meanwhile, the war after the Civil War did what its agents intended: it disenfranchised voters like Edward Crosby, drove lawmakers like Abram Colby from office, stripped people like Henry Giles's family of their property and probably their land, and left the bodies and minds of people like Hannah Tutson, Andrew Cathcart, and Harriet Hernandez with life-altering injuries. It corroded targeted people's communities by undermining residents' perception of personal safety and security, and their relationships, all of which intensified social disruption, distress, and the loss of civic trust.[3] It forced targeted people to live in fear and with impossible choices, which in turn enabled more former Confederates and both Klansmen and Klan sympathizers to regain control of local and state office.

Even after the wave of federal arrests of vigilantes repressed attacks, white supremacists across the country continued working to secure white people's dominant position in society by denigrating Reconstruction. One example of widespread white indifference to killings and opposition to Black people enjoying freedom and rights comes in the form of Democratic congressman Samuel Cox, a conservative and a member of the rabidly racist Copperhead faction. As a U.S. congressman from Ohio, Cox railed against emancipation and was a proponent of the white moral panic about "miscegenation," holding that consensual sex between white women and free Black men would be disastrous for the nation. Cox had no concern about the open secret of masters', overseers', and slave traders' sexual predation on enslaved Black girls and women. He rejected the Freedmen's Bureau because it helped formerly enslaved people who faced (in their words) the prospect of being turned out "slam loose" with no housing, food, or means of acquiring them until they found paid labor. Cox subscribed to the view that Black people would not work without the coercive violence that had powered slavery, and he insisted that any assistance fostered dependence. He said, "[I]f slavery be doomed so, alas, is the slave. No scheme . . . can save him. No Government farming system, no charitable [B]lack scheme, can wash out the color of the Negro, change his inferior nature, or save him from his inevitable fate."[4] But Congressman Cox wasn't finished.

After moving to New York and being elected to the House of Representatives again, Cox was one of many white senators and congressmen in the Forty-first Congress who treated Black lawmakers and voters to a string of disparaging remarks. And he continued his denigrating assault on Black citizens who were voting not only for their own interests but for those of all Americans. In the context of congressional debates about confronting Klan violence, Cox disingenuously insisted that white conservatives had supported Black voters. He sneered at the realities of African Americans' work to overcome their enslavement in face of the war on their efforts to do so. And he derided Black congressmen for not doing more to elevate freed people.

South Carolina congressman Joseph H. Rainey, the first African American member of the House of Representatives, used one such occasion to push back at Cox's and right-wing whites' twisted representation of what Black people wanted and were trying to do to achieve it. "We ask you, sir, to do by the Negro as you ought to do by him in justice," he said. Rainey's rebuke cited Cox's vote against each of the Reconstruction Amendments and the Enforcement bills because, as Rainey explained, Cox and men like him knew "those measures had a tendency to give to the poor Negro his just rights, and because they proposed to knock off his shackles and give him freedom of speech, freedom of action, and the opportunity of education, that he might elevate himself to the dignity of manhood."[5]

Rainey noted that Black voters, including in his home state, had not done anything to hurt white people, Democratic voters specifically. Unlike white conservatives, Rainey said, Black people had not passed any "proscriptive or disfranchising acts," not even in places where their numbers put them in the political majority. Instead, Rainey reminded the chamber,

African Americans secured "alike equal rights to all citizens, white and [B]lack, male and female as far as possible." South Carolina's liberal constitution "towers up in its majesty with provisions for equal protection of all classes and citizens," Rainey said. We have "never attempted to deprive any man in that State of the rights and immunities to which he is entitled." Rainey's articulation of the truth mattered little to Americans like Cox, who believed more in preserving the unearned privileges of whiteness than they did in liberty and justice for all.

Extremists, and their abettors in the form of people like Congressman Cox, never backed down from their belief in the justness of their cause of perpetual white supremacy and Black subjugation. They had no reason to, as they reaped the political rewards of the assassinations, the economic rewards of stolen property and land, and the social rewards of broken families, sabotaged institutions, and corroded communities. Confederates and their allies continued to resort to episodic violence, especially during the run-ups to elections or during uprisings of Black workers. One example of election violence occurred in Eutaw, Alabama, on October 25, 1870. White conservatives, including Klansmen, attacked a political rally of Black citizens on the courthouse square. They killed at least four and wounded dozens. To avoid being slaughtered, Black voters remained home on election day, November 8.[6]

Perpetrators of atrocities and their apologists were able to continue their murderous assaults on Black people because they remained free and generally avoided any meaningful punishment for their crimes. There was no formal accounting, and African Americans' deaths, upended lives, and ongoing suffering only mattered as tools right-wingers kept at the ready to exorcise African Americans from the political process and roll back their civil rights. Whenever racial conservatives could not achieve their social and political goals legitimately, they turned to violence.

President Grant and members of Congress faced increasing pressure to end Reconstruction's expansion of freedom and experiment in multiracial democracy, no matter the costs. From right-wing whites ready to reacquire the reins of southern social, civil, and political life, Grant and lawmakers heard demands to remove remaining U.S. troops from the South, as well as claims that continued military occupation threatened the fragile "peace." From white northerners and westerners who wanted to move on from the problems plaguing the still insurrectionary states, the president and Congress heard there were "more pressing issues" facing the nation (such as imperialist exploits, including stripping Native peoples of their land and sovereignty in the West). In all, even officials and citizens who expressed interest in accountability never wanted to assume responsibility for achieving it, effectively pardoning perpetrators.

It wasn't enough for extremists to attack and kill Black people without mercy, contrition, or even formal judgment; they and their white conservative allies across the country generated a new reality, using racist lies to lay the foundation for future violence and further perverting the experiment in egalitarianism and multiracial democracy. They added Reconstruction chapters to the Big Lie of the Lost Cause. The lie was not one story but a cottage industry of invention with multiple strands of fraud, fiction, falsehood, and outright disinformation, transmuting to accommodate the times and the tellers' and listeners' needs.[7]

Pulling on established threads from the minority report at the Klan hearings, right-wing whites developed the apocryphal tale of Reconstruction's "failure." In it, they portrayed all white southerners as loyal to the Confederate cause (erasing white Unionists and progressives who challenged the story they told). According to white conservatives, if anyone was being harmed or treated unjustly, it was Confederates, who were being menaced by despotic progressive white northerners' meddling. Lost Cause partisans placed the blame for Reconstruction's shortcomings—any corruption, mismanagement, and spoils—squarely on supposedly ignorant Black voters and officeholders, as if they alone were responsible, as if these political problems did not predate their enfranchisement, and as if these issues would magically disappear if Black people stopped voting and serving in office. The South's new public school systems, asylums, parks, orphanages, and homes for the elderly—behind which Black voters and officeholders were a driving force—were a favorite target of charges of "Negro misrule" and "wasteful mismanagement," even as white southerners hoarded these new public goods for themselves. The brave men of the Klan, right-wingers argued, had risen only to relieve the white South of the ruinous burden of illegitimate Radical policies and profligate spending that encouraged Black people's ambitions. Any violence white men used along the way, Lost Cause inventors and enthusiasts insisted, was a legitimate response to Black people's lechery, incompetence, and criminality.

Lost Cause enthusiasts could do this because many white moderate northerners and westerners harbored some of the same racist resentments about emancipation and citizenship and were so eager to move past the Civil War and Reconstruction that they resumed seeing Confederates as faithful Americans. Frederick Douglass had observed this as what he said was white people's tendency to "look at public questions more through the medium of feeling than of reason."[8] White moderates' and progressives' "feelings" would not have been an issue for Douglass and others, had it not been for the fact that, under whiteness as a political project, Black people's very lives—from torture to manslaughter through planned mass killings—so often hinged on white people's feelings.

White northerners and westerners *felt* Confederates were good, misunderstood people in their heart of hearts, who understandably *felt* aggrieved by losing their cause and chattel slavery, and who openly sustained the war's fighting by directing their fire primarily at Black people. By accepting the lie that no white southerners were doing anything wrong in the war after the war, and by not holding anyone who did wrong responsible, most white Americans happily and quickly exonerated their southern counterparts for the atrocities and absolved themselves of doing enough to stop or punish them. Many white people felt an imaginary return to normal, and as a result, Black people continued to be targeted and to die.

Short memories are the privilege of oppressors and their enablers. White Americans' collective embrace of the superficial patriotism of reconciliation between the white North and white West and the white South, and then the Lost Cause narrative, bred the cult of erasure of the war on freedom and the countless Black casualties. The liars and those lacking a conscience became so proficient that their deceptions lived long after they did, perverting the truth while serving future generations' objectives of hoarding privilege and freedom. Alexander Davis's cohort of survivors' concerns about their testimonies not finding adequate witnesses to right the wrongs they had endured proved prescient, as white Americans built a citadel out of a memory of postbellum reunion and reconciliation.

———————

For African Americans who sounded the alarm, particularly for survivors like Eliza Lyon, Abram Colby, and Mary and Joseph Brown, it was gutting to realize that their fellow Americans and their government could listen to their sworn testimonies and still decide they would, in the words of Hannah Arendt, describing the search for the best strategies for justice and healing after the tragedies of the Holocaust, "not punish the unforgivable and that they would then forgive and forget what they would not punish."[9] Confederates had already gotten away with instigating the Civil War. By demanding only that Confederates accept emancipation and take a loyalty oath, Andrew Johnson's Reconstruction set a low bar for readmission to the Union. African Americans were betrayed again when Johnson rescinded Sherman's Special Field Order Number 15 and effectively evicted newly freed people from their lands. Given carte blanche by the president, extremists then waged war on freedom. And now, they were about to get away with that, too. This latest betrayal compounded the sense of injustice and moral injuries survivors felt.

It's not clear that any official statement could have meaningfully compensated victims, but they didn't even get that. Survivors discovered that only among themselves and empathetic allies could they create arenas in which to share their personal truths of how the war on freedom was unmaking their worlds.[10] It is likely that they continued to tell their stories, in search of justice.

Knowing with certainty what happened to witnesses and their families after they testified is difficult. Some—including Andrew and Frankie Cathcart, Joseph and Mary Brown, Abram Colby, Eliza Lyon, and Patrick and Missouri Tanner—disappear from many federal historical records, perhaps because they died, changed their names, or relocated, leaving their independent households for someone else's. Given the insecurity most described when they appeared at the trials and hearings, extended instability and transient existence seem likely. Later witnesses would report that some people who testified at the Klan hearings were slaughtered when they returned home.[11] When witnesses from 1870–71 do appear in federal or state census enumerations in the 1880s, the records rarely indicate that families regained the property and wealth—and the strong toehold on freedom—they had lost to strikes.

Even though many white Americans embraced the cult of the Lost Cause, African Americans who lived through the revolution of Reconstruction and the ensuing counterrevolution did not forget the unmaking of their freedom, in part because it was ongoing. Frederick Douglass wrote that Black people at the end of slavery were "in a word, literally turned loose, naked, hungry, and destitute to the open sky."[12] Black Reconstruction sought to remedy this and create a more just world. Douglass and others observed how critical federal enforcement of the Constitution was to securing Black people's freedom. Without it, he said, policymakers were leaving "the lamb in the hold of the lion."[13]

Black people weren't completely powerless, of course. But the unfolding casualties from the war after the Civil War illustrate how outmatched African Americans were, without federal officials upholding the law and the principles of what Abraham Lincoln at Gettysburg had called "the new birth of freedom." Douglass was but one of many who saw the "bottomless pit" of hard-liners' transgressions—and how each violation, and the rest of white Americans' refusal of accountability, invited future ones. "The end is never reached," Douglass said.[14] The ongoing nature of mass killings and other atrocities shows how low white vigilantes and their enablers were willing to go.

The violence and the response to it made clear that the experiment in expanding American freedom and democracy was, if not over, then on a downward slope. To be sure, there were still some policy measures on the table, but Radical Reconstruction was all over but the shouting, and extremist whites knew it. So did the Black people they had targeted.

Frederick Douglass looked back on this period and wrote, in his third autobiography, *The Life and Times of Frederick Douglass*, "the wrongs of my people were not ended."[15] Douglass was speaking generally about the demise of Reconstruction but not specifically about the atrocities. He directly acknowledged oppressive policies, but not the violence that ensued when federal officials turned their backs on the cries of suffering. Douglass might have assumed his audience knew, and felt no need to state it.

By the time Douglass published those words in 1881, a mass migration of African Americans out of the Deep South was in full swing, spurred by the continued war on freedom. Election violence had seen low-level Confederates and their allies returned to political power in droves. Their return, and that of higher-level secessionists, was bolstered by a series of concessions: removal of loyalty oath requirements, restoration of land and voting rights, and pardons. With known terrorists still at large committing atrocities, the danger of removing the guardrails did not go unnoticed. Black Georgia congressman Jefferson Long had asked incredulously in a speech on southern violence a decade earlier, "Do we, then, really propose here today, . . . when those disloyal people still hate this Government, . . . to relieve from political disability the very men who have committed these Ku Klux outrages?"[16] The waves of amnesty for ex-Confederates said white Americans and the Grant administration intended to do exactly that.

In 1872, a year after the Klan hearings, President Grant signed the Amnesty Act, which ended the office disqualifications for Confederate leaders and other civil and military officials. Now, the majority of former secessionists was free to vote, hold office, and initiate laws for southern states that rolled back African Americans' new freedom. The act had some bipartisan support, including from lawmakers like Black South Carolina conservative Republican congressman Robert Carlos De Large, who voted for it. It's possible that, with a presidential election looming later that year, Republicans across government hoped to demonstrate political goodwill to conservative belligerents and their moderate Republican critics and thereby solicit their votes.

Political factions in both parties helped Grant easily win the 1872 election. But ex-Confederates' fight in Louisiana was different. The 1868 election had been marked by bloodshed, including six mass killing events, with more than two thousand Louisianians killed, wounded, or injured.[17] In 1872, Grant sent troops to the state to address disorder and to support the Republican gubernatorial candidate. This infuriated hard-liners, who intensified their effort to seize political power. Some whites formed the White League, a paramilitary group akin to the Klan that joined in on attacks of Black and white Republican voters and officeholders across the state.

The following spring, afraid that right-wingers in Grant Parish would use the White League to seize control over their evenly divided community, an all-Black militia took control of the local courthouse in Colfax, the parish seat. The men had reason to be concerned. Vigilante bands had returned. On April 5, 1873, one went to the home of Jesse M. Kinney and shot him in the head, in what one congressional report would describe as "an unprovoked, wanton, and deliberate murder."[18] Indications of future violence and white rumors about Black men run amok inspired Black residents of Grant Parish to brace for attack.

A white mob of almost two hundred—composed of Confederate soldiers, Klansmen, and White Leaguers and whites not affiliated with any group—set upon the courthouse, firing a cannon inside. After a brief exchange of gunfire, the white men set fire to the roof. Hoping to escape the fire but not wanting to be slaughtered as they fled, the Black men surrendered. The white men did not bother trying to keep up the pretense of law and order. They executed the Black men. The congressional report described the Colfax massacre as "without palliation or justification; it was deliberate, barbarous, cold-blooded murder." It saw between sixty and 150 fatalities, which lawmakers described as "a foul blot on the page of history."[19]

Authorities arrested ninety-seven members of the mob, but only nine were charged, and only with violating the Enforcement Acts. The defendants appealed their convictions, and white conservative justices on the

United States Supreme Court overturned them. Writing for the majority, Chief Justice Morrison Waite—in a radically restrictive reading of the Constitution—ruled that the Enforcement Acts had never been intended to protect individuals from attacks by private actors, only from constitutional violations by the state. Extremists staged other attacks. Celebrating their victory, they twisted the history of Colfax and folded it into the Big Lie.

"Who can but imagine the depths of the malice that is still in the breasts of these people?" *New National Era* asked of the Colfax massacre.[20] The killings and lies flowing into and out from Colfax showed, again, there was no bottom to the belligerents' vengeance.

Extremists' attacks on Black ministers and churches in the summer of 1874 illustrate again how widespread atrocities were. In August, armed men surrounded a Black church in Lee County, Alabama, during a religious service and fired a volley inside, killing four worshipping people. Armed and mounted white men in Lafayette County, Arkansas, grabbed a preacher from his church after he performed the Sunday service and shot him dead in front of his stunned congregation. White Tennesseans in Haywood County burned two churches. Black ministers were spiritual and political leaders of their communities and remained a favorite extremist target. In Texas, eight men snatched a Black minister from his home and put a rope around his neck, planning to kill him. But the minister called out to his neighbors, who rallied to his defense and scared the gang away. Whites also lynched by hanging another Texas a minister because he intervened in attacks on two Black schoolteachers.[21]

To date, waging war on freedom had been remarkably effective. And since hardly anyone but the targeted suffered any real costs, there was no reason to change the plays. Extremists ramped up the fighting in the years ahead, inscribing more bloody blots on the pages of U.S. history. Whites in Louisiana raided a federal arsenal, stealing weapons; as Black Louisianian William Murrell observed, they were now "better armed and equipped" than they had been during the Civil War and had "a better standing army," a phalanx of white men opposed to an expanded freedom and democracy. Hard-liners regularly displayed their military strength and firepower in parades with Winchester rifles and Gatling guns.[22] They even used telegraph operators to coordinate mass killing events with whites in neighboring communities.[23] "The more resistance," Murrell said, "the more colored men were killed."[24]

Henry Adams, a Louisiana freedman, veteran, Republican canvasser, and community organizer—who had witnessed his share of violence and learned of attacks on and killings of Black southerners while he was rallying votes— illuminated a well-honed extremist tactic in the war on freedom that dated back to the 1866 mass killings in Memphis and New Orleans. In both instances, white southerners had rampaged through the community destroying churches, schools, businesses, and homes, raping, torturing, and killing untold numbers of Black people. Later, authorities and the media described the rampages as "riots," misleading the American public about what had happened. In the context of the proliferation of Lost Cause false-hoods about Reconstruction, the public presumed from reports of "riots" that Black people were in open rebellion, which legitimized ongoing white aggression.

Henry Adams exposed the lie, saying, "You never hear of the Colored man raising the riot." Even if they wanted to, Black people "never [got] the chance." If one Black person killed a white person, even in self-defense, whites mobilized to "kill fifty colored men for the one white one," Adams said. Then, whites would go down "by the fifties and hundreds" to any weapons store to see whether Black people were trying to acquire arms. And when white people began rampaging through communities and Black neighborhoods, "Colored men [could not] buy ammunition" to properly defend themselves.[25]

Black Alabamans faced similar conditions of lack of protection and limited means of community defense. Edmund Turner and Jackson Turner, two tenant farmers who had been organizing to select delegates to the state Republican convention and had been targeted in extremist campaigns, appealed to Governor David Lewis for redress. They explained, "Colored men have been assaulted, threatened, driven from their homes." At least ten men were forced to hide out in the swamps of the Tombigbee River, simply because they attended a delegate meeting. The Turners wrote:

> Our property has been shamelessly destroyed . . . The present condition of affairs in Choctaw County is almost unparalleled in the history of wrong and oppression. The Colored people are in such a state of fear that life itself is almost unsupportable. We cannot have our churches, our schools, nor any social intercourse with each other . . .

Edmund and Jackson said they knew, from Lewis's prior statements, that he claimed he was "powerless" to stop white men from attacking them. Governors like Lewis insisted that if any violence was happening, it was spontaneous, random, difficult to anticipate, and impossible to prosecute with juries comprising local whites. But Edmund and Jackson trusted the governor would fulfill his responsibility to all citizens and would use his influence "to secure us, at least, in the enjoyment of our rights of life and property."[26] The Turners wanted the governor to send a state militia to suppress the violence. Their trust, however, was misplaced. Hard-liners like Lewis would not expend any effort or money to secure Black people's rights to property or to life. Edmund and Jackson's willingness to appeal to an ex-Confederate makes their desperation plain.

As Black southerners like the Turners knew, elections were one of the best ways extremists could bolster their capacity to undo freedom. By this time, many of the Radical lions of Reconstruction in Congress had died, or their health was failing. That fall, the Panic of 1873 sent the country into an extended period of economic insecurity and uncertainty. The crisis was heightened in the South, where African Americans faced pressure from planters to work harder for less, and competition from whites hit by the depression; both groups were quick with the shotgun or midnight raids if and when Black people protested. If white northerners and westerners didn't have the same objections to equality and a multiracial democracy as conservative Democratic congressman Samuel Cox did, then their belief in justice and empathy for targeted people ran dry, and they were increasingly receptive to Confederates returning to power.

In Barbour County, Alabama, right-wingers took advantage of these political winds. In November, they organized and struck the polling places in Eufaula and Spring Hill, where they drove Black voters away from the polls and burned their ballots. Continuing violence prompted a local Unionist judge to appeal to the governor to declare martial law, and to the U.S. Marshals for assistance. Later, another dispute erupted, resulting in seven deaths and upward of seventy people wounded. With Black people violently disenfranchised, Confederates took Barbour County for decades to come.[27]

A month later, right-wingers ran a similar play in Vicksburg, Mississippi. A white mob forced Peter Crosby, a Black sheriff, from office. When Black residents tried to defend Crosby's right to serve out his term, more mobs formed, killing dozens and wounding others. Authorities sent troops whose presence allowed Crosby to return to office. But a year later, a white deputy assigned to Crosby against his wishes shot Crosby in the head when he tried to fire him. Crosby lived but with debilitating injuries, completing his term through a white proxy who represented him in office.[28]

Even if Frederick Douglass could hardly imagine the "depths of the malice" right-wingers carried in their hearts, their actions amply illustrated its vast reservoir. Mass killing events remained routinized as more belligerents folded deliberate atrocities into their plans to return to power. From community to community and state to state, Black people died, and up and down the ballot, white conservatives won. In 1874, they regained control of the House of Representatives and took the governorships of Alabama, Arkansas, and Texas.

Desperate, Radical Republicans in Congress made one final push to expand freedom, just before the door of possibility for sustaining a semblance of multiracial equality was slammed and bolted shut. Even after the Reconstruction Amendments and the Civil Rights Act of 1866, African Americans still found themselves denied many privileges enjoyed by whites because of a lack of enforcement. This wasn't new. Free Black people throughout the antebellum period had suffered the denial of access and service in public establishments. They hoped Reconstruction policies would end the disrespect they faced.

But Black men and women suffered daily and often violent indignities as they moved about the world and tried to engage in activities of what one historian has called "a shared and social 'common' life."[29] State antidiscrimination laws stemming from the Reconstruction Amendments and the Civil Rights Act faced resistance. Shopkeepers and streetcar operators ignored the laws, refusing Black patrons service or charging them more for it.

Black people, including abolitionists and lawmakers, were mistreated in the very same spaces as ex-Confederates were welcomed. Harriet Tubman and Sojourner Truth were among many who found themselves denied services they had paid for. Veterans wearing their uniforms were denied rides on streetcars. Members of Congress were turned away from D.C. establishments while in session on Capitol Hill. These forms of disrespect were assaults on personal dignity, which is why African Americans saw unrestricted use of public space as a central tenet of freedom. Furthermore, if Black people defended their dignity in these situations—and especially if they fought back—it could lead to retaliatory violence and even the "riots" Henry Adams described. From Spartanburg to San Francisco, Black people had suffered these indignities and assaults, and through their Colored Conventions (state and national political meetings Black people held annually to advocate for their civil and political rights between 1830 and the 1890s), state constitutional conventions, and religious conventions, they identified this as a public wrong and pushed for change.[30]

Proponents of an 1875 supplement to the Civil Rights Act hoped to answer their call. Black Mississippi congressman John Roy Lynch saw it as a bill that "has for its object the protection of human rights."[31] Massachusetts senator Charles Sumner, the bill's author, saw it in similar terms, recognizing that the African American citizen needed affirmed rights to "travel for business, for health, or for pleasure . . . He longs, perhaps, for respite and relation at some place of amusement." Sumner believed the new law would affirm Black people's right to use public space as civic equals, free from harassment or violence.[32] "What we desire," Black congressman Richard Harvey Cain averred, "inasmuch as we have been raised to the dignity, to the honor, to the position of our manhood, we ask that laws of this country should guarantee all the rights and immunities belonging to that proud position, to be enforced all over this broad land."[33] Cain knew whereof he spoke: he lived under the regular threat of violence and had survived an assassination attempt.[34]

Upon its passage through Congress, the 1875 act applied to inns, theaters, public amusements, and more. In less than a decade, however, the mostly conservative Supreme Court would strike it down, in another of the court's many assaults on Reconstruction. But for a time, at least, some African Americans enjoyed the luxury of a sliver of access to public space without indignity.

The election year of 1876 brought more calculated atrocities, and more conservative wins in overthrowing Reconstruction. One of the largest mass killing events of that season took place in South Carolina. Historically, South Carolina had one of the largest Black populations in the South. To regain control of the state ex-Confederates had to overcome a significant Black voting bloc that cast their ballots largely, but not exclusively, for Republicans. Democrats turned increasingly to election fraud and violence.[35] In July, the Republican governor raised a state militia to corral disorder.

The militia included an eighty-four-member all-Black regiment, which was stationed in Hamburg, a hamlet in Aiken County. When members of the Black regiment attempted to conduct military exercises on a local road, two white farmers insisted on driving their carriage through the mostly Black town. The Black militiamen objected to the interruption and what they might have perceived as whites harassing the Black community. After some back-and-forth, they let the white men pass through. Infuriated by the squad's initial refusal to halt the exercise, the farmers sued. Their lawyer attempted to use the altercation to have the militia disbanded. The Black militiamen's very presence in Aiken County (to curb white election violence) and their refusal to follow the farmers' commands to halt their maneuvers maddened whites who were determined to regain political power. Four days after the clash on the road, hundreds of armed vengeful whites, including white rifle clubs, struck the armory where the Black regiment was residing and Black people from the surrounding community, announcing, "By God! We will carry South Carolina now . . . We are going to redeem South Carolina today!"[36] The Black militiamen and Black men from the community fought back, but they were outnumbered; when the fighting stopped, seven men from the regiment and one white man were dead. Right-wing whites' success in Hamburg, in turn, spurred more reactionary violence as the election drew close.[37]

White Democratic candidates tried to "persuade" South Carolina's large population of Black voters to vote for them. But as Congressman Rainey had observed when he rebuked Samuel Cox, white conservatives' "votes, actions, and constant cultivation of your cherished prejudices prove to the Negros of the entire country that the Democrats are in opposition to them," and if that party "could have sway our race would have no foothold here."[38] What is more, Confederate hard-liners' "invitation" to Black South Carolinians was laced with violence—part of the emerging "shotgun policy" of taking office by force, and in the same spirit as the pronouncements about "redeeming South Carolina" heard at Hamburg.

In Charleston, white employers threatened Black men with firing and eviction if they did not vote the white conservative ticket. Planters and shopkeepers promised to deny land rentals and provisions, too—an economic form of violence that could render families destitute and hungry. Black voters could vote for right-wingers on the Democratic ticket or suffer, one way or another.[39]

Some Black men and their families decided to vote the Democratic ticket or to not vote at all. These men tried to persuade the Black Republicans in their community to do the same, and when that didn't work, they resorted to using the same racist insults as right-wing whites used. Charleston County residents no doubt knew about the waves of night riding that had taken place in 1868–71 in the Upcountry region of the state and Hamburg to the west. Lowcountry Black folks in Charleston County had largely been spared, but now, facing menacing threats, they took no chances and were ready to fight. Black Republicans defended themselves, and white conservatives intervened. Shots were fired, and riots ensued, with Black Republicans using their numerical advantage, giving as good as they got. Tensions continued. Because attacking Black voters was proving dangerous, extremists shifted to fraud to invalidate Republicans' votes. The arrival of U.S. troops limited violence, but a dispute in the gubernatorial race, combined with local rumors, sparked the resumption of clashes. Black Charlestonians' numerical majority and preparedness enabled them to stand their ground.

Elsewhere the results of the presidential election hung in the balance, as white moderates' and conservatives' impatience for Reconstruction to end intensified. Voters on both sides were incentivized by Democrats' laser-like focus on regaining control of the southern states *and* returning to the White House, and Republicans' concerns about ex-Confederates returning to power and appeals to disaffected voters. The election, which had record turnout, was beset by wooing, fraud, and intimidation. After considerable dispute over the results of the vote, Ohioan Rutherford B. Hayes was inaugurated as president in March 1877 and largely let the white South govern its own affairs without federal intervention. He soon removed the last of the federal troops still stationed in Louisiana and South Carolina. Hayes accepted Confederates' empty promises about respecting Black people's civil rights. John Lewis spoke for many Black southerners when he lamented, "There is not a pledge a southern white man will keep . . . where a Negro is concerned."[40] The only people fooled by Reconciliation were whites who had become indifferent to—or had never cared about—the realities of the insecurity of Black life in the South.

White South Carolina Republican governor Daniel Chamberlain, who had his election stolen by what one scholar describes as "extensive fraud and intimidation" by local election officials who lifted the Democratic candidate, Wade Hampton, to victory. Chamberlain tried to contest the voting irregularities in several counties but Hayes's decision to further draw down the number of federal troops in his state left Chamberlain and South Carolina Republicans with no political course of action or military support to fight.[41]

The writing was on the wall. President Hayes had abandoned Reconstruction. In his April 10, 1877, message to his fellow Republicans, Chamberlain said:

> By order of the president whom your votes alone rescued from overwhelming defeat, the Government of the United States abandons you, and by the withdrawal of troops now protecting the State from domestic violence abandons the lawful government of the State to a struggle with insurrectionary forces too powerful to be resisted [on our own].[42]

The next day, Governor Hampton ousted all Republicans from their state cabinet posts.

With the 1876 election, reactionaries were back in charge of southern affairs. Unfortunately, their war on freedom did not end simply because they had won or stolen elections or secured the withdrawal of federal troops. That's because this war was never only about political power, any more than the reprisal violence of 1865 was only about the economics of slavery. Belligerents craved total domination, and despite the loss and upending of lives, Black people weren't vanquished.[43]

———

African Americans, especially those targeted, knew white southerners' promises were empty ones. White southerners were the same old snake with a new reconciliation skin.

Black southerners were determined to enjoy freedom—including self-determination, self-government, and community building for themselves and their children—and with no end in sight to the bloodletting all around them, they embraced another newly recognized freedom, that of mass movement. Henry Adams was one of many who surveyed their condition in the South and saw "there was no way on earth . . . we could better our condition there." With the very men who had held them in bondage holding the reins of government, "we felt we had almost as well be slaves . . . We lost all hopes."[44] Many Black people decided to get out. Adams was part of the

Exoduster Movement, the large-scale migration of several thousand African Americans from the Deep South to Kansas, Indiana, and other destinations. The mass movement peaked in 1878–80, though some survivors of night-riding attacks were already contemplating and executing moves west and north earlier.[45] Strikes and massacres had displaced many southerners from their communities, triggering migrations from night-riding zones and more rural areas to larger southern towns. But after President Hayes withdrew remaining federal troops in 1877, more families tried to seek security farther afield.

At the 1871 Klan hearings, Robert Fullerlove had testified that the war on freedom had inspired his neighbors to leave their Alabama home. Fearing reprisal violence, and having been menaced on his way to the hearings, Robert indicated he was considering giving up the four hundred acres he owned and moving to Kansas. Robert's neighbors were eager for opportunities in communities free of the grip of the plantocracy. But having experienced or witnessed the war on freedom, they were surely also intent on getting free of the slaughter. It's not clear if or when Robert, Adaline, and their children pulled up and ventured west. They are among the many families whose stories appear to have been lost. But other targeted people and witnesses to their suffering did make the journey, and the numbers of families exiting Deep South communities increased.

Kansas and other points west theoretically had frontier land "available," in areas where settlers and federal troops had displaced or marginalized Native peoples. Kansas had been a site of one of John Brown's antislavery campaigns, leading to some romanticization of the state's commitment to freedom. Black southerners had already relocated there in the 1870s, which gave rise to a promotional campaign extolling the availability of frontier land and plentiful alternatives to farming. The 1873 economic crash intensified the pressures on life and livelihood in the South. Some enterprising Black southerners and others experiencing violence were convinced enough to head west. Families started saving and packing up their things.

The coordinated movement began coming together in 1875. Migration proponent Benjamin Singleton saw that year's Colored Convention meeting in Nashville as a great opportunity to promote relocation to Kansas. Black conventioneers had been tracking freed people's progress at annual meetings for the past decade and had been writing petitions and memorials to secure relief from the war on freedom. At the Nashville meeting, Singleton and his associates developed the organizational scheme to encourage migration and establish Black colonies, with the idea that there was political power and security in numbers. Singleton initially promoted colonies in Tennessee, urging people to purchase land there, but the force of hate saw whites refusing to sell any worthwhile land to Black people. Continuing violence there made it an even harder sell, which prompted Singleton to shift his sights to Kansas, steering hopeful people there instead.

The 1878 election saw more violence and more former Confederates returning to power, eliciting greater support for migration from the Deep South. This was manifest in Louisiana. R. J. Cromwell, president of the Negro Union Cooperative Aid Association, appealed to President Hayes for relief and protection. "I write to you . . . amid a terror stricken and distressed people," he began. Cromwell wrote that he wanted to show "the condition of my race" as it pertained to voting in Shreveport. Voters had been "driven from the poll, murdered, or intimidated," he said. According to Cromwell, since the election, extremists were still actively "killing freedmen . . . The bodies are lying in the wood unburied and eaten by hogs—our town is full of refugees, most industrious men are hunted down like they were wild beasts of prey . . ."[46]

The violence Cromwell described was a repeat of the playbook hardliners had been running for more than a decade. He implored Hayes to send troops, specifically Black soldiers, who he believed could be trusted to protect Black people. Even though white Louisianians had shown they were continuing to resist the reconstruction of American freedom and democracy, Hayes did not fulfill this request. The state's new Democratic governor would not tolerate it, and Hayes was less inclined to send troops to disturb the "peace" among white people just to stop violence against Black people.

Having already experienced a significant loss of life and rollback in rights, Black Louisianians felt their insecurity acutely. The days of requesting troops were over. It was time to go. In the months following the election, the number of Black southerners loading wagons or boarding steamboats to St. Louis, and from there to points west, snowballed. The 1879 migration, which started early that year, is best characterized as a snap migration, a hurried, mass movement of significant numbers in months.[47] By the end of the year, some six thousand had left Louisiana, Mississippi, Tennessee, and Texas. Activists in the campaign described their undertaking using the language of the Israelites' flight from Egypt in the book of Exodus. The term "Exodusters" caught on as a way to describe the Black migrants fleeing southern oppression.

There were massive problems with the endeavor. The original plan was orderly, with details about what material resources families needed. But the organizers could not keep up with the demand. Best-laid plans were shredded by miscommunication; the desperate and often destitute condition of many families; and deception on the part of some speculators about the availability of free transportation, jobs, and land. Some migrants arrived in St. Louis and Indiana without adequate winter clothing, food, or shelter, triggering a public health crisis. Their lack of preparedness speaks to their desperation. Planters organized into squads to prevent Black people from leaving. This forced families to abandon their belongings and escape with whatever they could carry. Migrants' woes were compounded by outbreaks of yellow fever in the river towns they gravitated toward as final destinations or used as major transfer sites. Ignorance about how the disease spread— through mosquito bites and not by air—led many racist whites to see migrants as vectors of disease. Some town officials even established quarantines to halt the migrations.

None of that stopped the Exoduster Movement, however. All told, the state of Kansas alone drew nearly thirty thousand transplants. Others moved to the Oklahoma Territory or the Great Plains, setting up in Iowa, Idaho, and Wyoming.

None of these destinations was the "Promised Land." Much of the terrain wasn't ideal for cultivating cash crops. Only so many jobs were available. Building new communities with meager funds and few resources was challenging. There was also a bottomless supply of white animosity toward Black people trying to exercise their freedom. This manifested itself in violent attacks intended to discourage settlement, strip successful folks of their land and property, and deny new migrants political power in their new communities. Some disappointed transplants even returned home.[48] Still, African Americans' population in the West soon reached the millions because vast numbers stayed put for several more decades. For many who stayed, even a circumscribed freedom in the Midwest and Plains states was better than life in the South.

The exodus set off alarms from various sectors. Few destination or transfer towns were ready for the flood of migrants pouring in. These places lacked adequate shelter, food, and medical supplies, and in some places, the lack of jobs made it harder for migrants to support themselves. Humanitarians raised funds to provide assistance. Concerns about fraud and about unscrupulous speculators taking advantage of desperate people prompted civil and criminal inquiries. The loudest protests, of course, came from ex-Confederates and their allies seeking to continue exploiting and oppressing Black laborers.

The yelps and furious inquiries were the driving force behind another congressional investigation, this time conducted by the Senate, begun in 1879. With peace "achieved" and order "restored," why the mass exit of Black people, inquiring minds wanted to know. What could be done to address the disruption of exploited labor?

Testimonies were heard from January through April 1880. Yet on both sides of the aisle, many of the senators investigating the exodus ignored a decade of mass killing events and the cascading losses that had occurred in their wake. Indeed, the majority report from the investigation, which was published in 1880, reads like the minority report from the Klan hearings, authored by similarly conservative members aligned with extremists' goals (if not always their actions). Many of the more than one hundred Black witnesses called to testify were well-to-do critics of the migration movement who lived well outside of the terror zones, had not been targeted themselves, and felt Black migrants had been duped and were better off at home.[49]

Two of the notable exceptions, who refuted allegations of deception and exploitation, were Exoduster organizers Henry Adams and Benjamin Singleton. Both Black men had been excoriated in the white press and by Frederick Douglass for taking advantage of "ignorant" people, and they were summoned to account for their actions. Like earlier victims of and witnesses to the war on freedom, they came to set the record straight.

A central feature of both Adams's and Singleton's testimonies was the message that Confederates were violating the peace and the U.S. and state constitutions. African Americans were being persecuted in the South, and those who decided to leave felt migration was their only recourse. Both men gave accounts of the violence they themselves had experienced or had learned of from others.[50] From 1866 to 1876, Adams had canvassed Louisiana and compiled a record of assaults and killings. His report, which was entered into evidence, includes eleven affidavits and lists 683 incidents in the war on freedom in the Pelican State. Adams's report mirrors the accounts given by Freedmen's Bureau agents in 1865 about the reprisal killings and assassinations just after the end of the Civil War, and by victims of night-riding attacks at the 1871 Klan hearings.

Again, most lawmakers investigating the Exoduster Movement were interested in white politics and white people's money. The majority report concluded things had been grand until unscrupulous Black men duped gullible Black people. White Americans in power couldn't simply wish the violence to end, and since they weren't interested in enforcing agreements or even honoring the U.S. Constitution, it was easier for them to move on.

The war on freedom and the recasting of the history of the Civil War and Reconstruction did much of what its agents intended. Destroyed homes and schools and churches could be and were rebuilt. But the killings and assaults hobbled many African Americans' leap into freedom. Disenfranchisement by fraud and violence made it harder for them to protect their remaining rights and chart their destinies.

———

When it was originally published in 1854, Black abolitionist Joshua McCarter Simpson's poem "To the White People of America" was a message about the fight to end slavery.[51] But its themes proved all too timeless in 1874, when it was republished amid the dismantling of Reconstruction.

> *Hear ye that mourning?*
> *'Tis a solemn sound,*
> *O! ye wicked men take warning,*
> *For God will send his judgment down.*
> . . .
> *Hear ye that mourning?*
> *'Tis your brother's sigh,*
> *O! ye wicked men take warning,*
> *The judgment day will come by and by.*

Targeted people collectively said that being caught up in the war on freedom had smashed what progress many families had made after slavery. The horror was magnified by the improper responses of neighbors and officeholders who were spectators to the raids, failed to intervene, or refused to offer protective relief and help victims secure justice. Those failures further compromised these families' sense of security, endangering not only Black people's lives but also American freedom and democracy. Most white Americans paid no heed to "that mourning." If judgment day was coming, "by and by" wasn't soon enough to save Black people targeted in the war on freedom.

African Americans who lived through Reconstruction's revolutionary reforms looked back on this era as one of both remarkable achievement and astonishing betrayal. WPA interviews with African Americans in the 1930s are full of accounts of family reunification and plentiful schools and churches. Black print culture representing the era teemed with portrayals of Black statesmen's and their constituents' achievements. But in 1895, the Civil War veteran and former U.S. congressman Robert Smalls—who had helped spearhead the implementation of African Americans' vision of freedom—estimated that white southerners, in the process of overthrowing Reconstruction policy, had killed 53,000 African Americans.[52] It's impossible to know precisely how Smalls came up with that figure. But from the sliver of reprisal killings documented by the Freedmen's Bureau, in annual Colored Conventions reports, in Black southerners' petitions and memorials, and in congressional investigations into paramilitary strikes and mass killing events, his figures are plausible.[53]

Most Americans remained ignorant of Smalls's findings. His figures certainly didn't make it into several generations of professional historians' writings about Reconstruction. It would fall to later generations of Black freedom advocates and historians to write accurate accounts of Reconstruction, recounting violence and commenting on its erasure in the commonly accepted narrative. One of those advocates was T. Thomas Fortune, who had been a boy when the Florida Klan attacked his family, and whose father, Emanuel, testified at the 1871 hearings. Undergirding the younger Fortune's career as an activist and editor was his knowledge that this twisted history of Reconstruction had been used to justify the continuing economic exploitation of Black people and to shut them out of American political life. Fortune also saw white southerners were still using tactics perfected during Reconstruction to subjugate Black people.[54] So the violence continued through the 1880s and beyond. Extremists in the South shifted from night riding to lynching—violent, public acts of torture and killing—rape, and massacres to terrorize into submission Black people who tried to assert their dignity or to exercise their civil and political rights. Fortune and activists such as Ida B. Wells-Barnett and Mary Church Terrell not only recounted Reconstruction atrocities but also detailed their connection to contemporary ones.

As witnesses at the Klan hearings had made clear, night riding was outside the normative violence familiar to many Black southerners. This is not to say that exposure to vigilantism was not otherwise a part of their lives, because it was.[55] Rather, the atrocities committed in the war on freedom were the kinds of violent events that confronted victims with possible annihilation.[56] Having their survival threatened and their vulnerability exposed by a violent attack disintegrated some people's inner worlds.[57]

With their testimonies, witnesses tried to show lawmakers and the nation that night riding undermined their freedom. They relayed the causes and consequences of strikes. Witnesses knew—and tried to make clear to anyone who would listen—that the suffering they experienced did not end when their attackers left. Despite knowing that investigators' objectives were more limited, survivors gave extensive accounts of calamitous strikes and inadequate government responses. Their heroic testimonies evince their urgent need to communicate the unmaking of their worlds and the reversal of Reconstruction.[58] For many targeted people, the task ahead was to remember the future—to hold tightly to their kin and their deferred dreams while striding toward an uncertain horizon.

CONCLUSION

In 1885, Florida state census assessors making their way through Precinct 3 of St. Johns County landed at the home of a family with a husband and wife, and their son and daughter. The couple, Samuel and Hannah Tutson, were transplants from Clay County, just seven miles outside of Waldo, near the Santa Fe River, where their white neighbors had menaced them for their land before coordinating a raid in which both Samuel and Hannah had been tortured and savagely assaulted.[1]

When they testified at the Klan hearings in Jacksonville in November 1871, the Tutsons had been determined to make a go of it on their homestead, having, as Hannah said, "paid too much, [and] worked too much to lose it."[2] In an effort to address the wrongs that had been done to them, they had connected to a U.S. commissioner whom they described as a "reconstructionist" or pro-Reconstruction Republican who was on the Fourth Circuit. The commissioner had issued a warrant for arrests and turned it over to a U.S. marshal. The federal court in Jacksonville had held a trial in late October; the couple had traveled the sixty-mile distance to testify. Three weeks later, Hannah and Samuel had returned to Jacksonville to testify at the Klan hearings.

There, Hannah described the contentious examination she had undergone at the trial, and she did not express confidence in its outcome. And she had good reason. In many trials during the war white southerners waged on freedom, extremists went unpunished. Defendants disappeared while on bail or were released from jails. They often sought sanctuary in other communities. Trials ended with hung juries or acquittals. Even men found guilty rarely served time. Warriors against freedom were pardoned or had their sentences commuted.[3]

Although there was a criminal investigation into the raid on the Tutsons, when they testified at the Klan hearings, there had not been any legal proceeding to settle the issue regarding their homestead. For Hannah and Samuel there was no dispute; the land was rightfully theirs and they held documentation to prove it. They also had the verbal endorsements of white Republican power brokers of their entitlement to live and build on it and defend themselves. But without the force of federal or state authority to dissuade white neighbors from making claims on the Tutsons' land, even resolute homesteaders like Hannah and Samuel would think twice about rebuilding after one strike while living in constant fear of another.

The historical record is silent on when, why, or by what means the Tutsons landed in St. Johns. But their testimonies about the May 1871 raid on their family home sixty miles south—combined with what other witnesses' accounts reveal about survivors' lives one to three years after their attacks—enable us to confront the ellipses in the record. It is possible that continued threats or even attacks persuaded Hannah and Samuel to abandon their aspirations for homebuilding in Clay County. Given the power their white neighbors held in the community, it is highly unlikely the couple was even able to sell their land at a profit. If they were lucky, they were not attacked again and were able to harvest a portion of their crop. Home was no longer home, though. Samuel, Hannah, and the three younger children probably lived with the older children for a time or left the community altogether. They might have had to put distance between themselves and their dreams—and the thugs still attempting to get them.

As with most people targeted in the war on freedom, the Tutsons were violated in unthinkable ways. Try as they might to get justice or even the right to live in peace, they were far from having any satisfaction. Indeed, when the couple testified at the Klan hearings, they were still in the immediate wake of the attack, the beginning of the unraveling of the world they had made after slavery; they were losing their ability to chart their course, to shape their future and that of their young children. Their attackers and their allies appear to have gone unpunished, enjoying the rewards of their actions and feeling emboldened to steal more power from more people. What we know is that when the Tutsons testified at the hearings, they had each other, or what was left of each other, after white men came for them.

When Hannah and Samuel resurface in St. Johns County in 1885, we find them roughly aged fifty-six and sixty-seven, respectively.[4] They survived, which is more than we know about other targeted people. But census records only open a telegraphic view into a family's life. The records don't reveal how they worked through the raid's afterlives: if the couple and the three children who were with them during the raid healed physically and emotionally, whether or how they retained their property, if or how they found a degree of peace. If they were remade after their unmaking remains unknowable. The couple were in St. Johns when state assessors came through. Their youngest children were with them, too. The daughter who had spirited the little ones away to safety was not, but she might have married, which would make tracing her difficult—or she may have been dead by 1885. It's not clear whether Mary—presumably the infant injured in the raid, whose pain Hannah described—properly healed, or whether she suffered lifelong affliction and debility. We do not know whether Samuel healed from being whipped and Hannah received proper treatment for the injuries she sustained from her sexual assault, nor whether her post-traumatic distress abated. Samuel was listed as a farmer and Hannah was keeping house, but they appear to have had no property.

Given the size of the family, their older children who had left home before the raid were probably scattered throughout north central and northeast Florida or might have moved west or north. The record conceals the health of the couple's union from that horrible night up until this moment. Catastrophes, like captivity and sexual assault, often strain marriages and break affective bonds, though. Limited access to divorce might have made it difficult for them to sever ties if that's what they wanted. But it is just as likely that, as broken open as they were by the strike and repeated torment, Samuel and Hannah ultimately found refuge in each other. They knew each other and who they were after what happened, which could have bound them together. Whatever the reason, the fact that the couple remained together is significant.

Violence like the Tutsons endured is foundational. It has the power to rip families apart.[5] The loss of familial and bodily integrity from attacks combined with the aftermath of disabling injuries, dispossession, and displacement unraveled much of what families achieved in freedom.[6] Regardless of whether every member of a targeted family personally endured direct physical assaults, every person connected to them was affected by the violence perpetrated on the unit, in this generation and the next one after that. The violence unleashed on African Americans was totalizing—physical, psychological, spiritual, economic, social, and political, just as night riders intended. This was why these survivors-turned-philosophers theorized they would never get over what had happened and did not use the language of healing.

Families like Hannah and Samuel's lived. They survived on their own accord and with the assistance of their various people. The Tutsons had limited political power on their side in Clay County and therefore little protection from future harm. Families like theirs had no social safety nets sufficient to catch them in their fall. They would not have had the benefit of counseling or psychosocial care, so both adults and kids were vulnerable to emotional distress. We do not know whether this family or others later concealed what happened to them during raids from new acquaintances or the next generation, erecting a self-protective code of silence, or discussed it, using the details of that night to account for who they became in life.

Tracking the survivors of night-riding attacks a decade or more out from when their worlds were turned inside out and upside down reveals how they fared. Extending the search several more decades, one loses track of survivors who testified at the hearings but gains others: the guardians of the history of Black Reconstruction. The first line of defense was African Americans who were children during Reconstruction. These last witnesses to the war after the Civil War sat for the WPA interviews about their lives in the 1930s.[7] Their stories about what they called "Ku Klux" attacks show

how children's vivid perceptions of the horrors that befell targeted people contrast with adults' sobering perspectives. The second line of defense was the history keepers, that generation of historians who stepped forward to confront the propaganda of Reconstruction.

————

Census records, like the 1880 federal and 1885 Florida state enumeration counting the Tutsons, are imperfect tools for tracking survivors. Families were displaced by violence or left their home communities because of the 1873 financial panic. Some changed their names: women and girls married or remarried, and others started new lives with new identities for their own protection. Considering the illness frequently reported, the advanced ages of some witnesses, and the ongoing violence, some probably died within years of their testimonies. Andrew Cathcart was about seventy-seven when he testified at the Klan hearings. Patrick Tanner was sixty-three and terrified about reprisal, having named his attacker under duress at the hearings. Robert Fullerlove had been attacked on his way to the hearings. He worried about what might be happening to his family in his absence and what might happen as a result of his testimony. Others may have landed in insane asylums or been ensnared in the expanding carceral state. Alternately, assessors may simply have missed them. A fire destroyed much of the 1890 enumerations, making tracking targeted families even more difficult.

As imperfect as census records are, they nonetheless shine slivers of light into historical voids that enable efforts to trace the impact of the war on freedom. The Garrison family does appear in the records. White Georgians had killed their patriarch, Jerry, and Leanna and her son, Samuel, testified at the hearings. One of the conflict's many widows, Leanna had taken with her Jerry's bullet-ridden coat as evidence. In 1880, Leanna was alive, seventy years old, and working as a nurse. She lived in the Fulton County home of Samuel, his wife, Rosa, and several children, including the offspring of Samuel's brother.[8]

Reuben Sheets allowed his attackers to enter his Walton County, Georgia, home with the hope of deescalating an explosive situation and protecting his wife, Elizabeth, and their four children from harm. The 1880 census found Reuben and Elizabeth living in Decatur. He was a farmer and she kept house.[9]

Prosperous Clarke County, Georgia, wheat farmers Simon and Mary Elder were living so well before the raid that their harvests were large enough for them to hire laborers. Census assessors found them in Decatur, where they had fled after they were attacked. Simon, too, was listed as a farmer, and Mary kept house. They still had no children. The value of their personal estate was a mere one hundred dollars.[10]

Augustus and Letty Mills—who, along with their four children, had been beaten savagely by white men in Walton County, Georgia—were found in 1880 living in the Panthersville neighborhood of DeKalb County. Their family was larger now. Augustus was a farm laborer and Letty kept house, overseeing eight children ranging in age from fifteen to one. In 1870, the value of Augustus's personal estate had been one hundred dollars, but there was nothing in 1880.[11]

As with the Tutsons, census records don't shine much light on these families' inner lives. Some held steady. But there were reversals, some concrete—like the consequences of the loss of land—and others more abstract, though equally significant, like the distress Hannah and Samuel and the three younger children felt. The legacy of violence was a symbolic birthmark, a new identity formation passed on to their offspring.[12]

These families were among the more than four million African Americans who had sprinted off the blocks and into freedom with great expectations. Many of them achieved their dreams or were on their way to doing so when death tried to come for them in the form of white men waging war on freedom. In many ways, testimonies such as theirs about torture, disabling injuries, trauma, displacement, and dispossession serve as a moral ledger documenting the pillaging of families' freedom. Collectively, they reveal a dark history of Reconstruction and its overthrow.

Lawmakers' investigation—combined with sporadic increases in state militias and federal troops in some zones of attack—had a suppressing effect, eventually driving strikes underground, at least for the time being. But beyond capturing survivors' stories and publishing and preserving the records of the hearings, they failed to keep the memory alive. When extremists turned to new forms of violence to oppress African Americans, the findings from the Klan hearings and the Exoduster hearings could have inspired lawmakers and the larger public to press for the enforcement of civil rights legislation and the Reconstruction Amendments. It was easier for some white federal officials and citizens to unofficially pardon perpetrators, closing the book full of "foul blots" on the pages of U.S. history in the name of national healing from the Civil War and a reconciliation among white Americans.

The daily work of remembering and accounting for the lived realities of night riding's unmaking of African American victims' freedom, however, was left largely to attacked people and their descendants. For the rest of some survivors' lives, they carried with them wherever they went stories of vigilantism on their bodies and souls. In this way, attacks became new origin stories for families willing to share what had happened, moments when both lives and histories were reordered and rewritten.

Each time a survivor shared with a relative the story of what white men and their government had done to them, it was an act of memory. Each telling called into question the story white Americans told about Reconstruction's supposed "failings." In doing this work, survivors and their descendants told their stories whenever they could, chastening triumphant tales of American progress and white southern chivalry with accounts of the craven war waged on their freedom, transferring this history from one generation to the next. "I know folks think the books told the truth, but they sure don't," North Carolinian W. L. Bost said of Reconstruction violence. "[We] had to take it all."[13]

But these Black counter-histories of atrocity and betrayal were no match for the machinery of the Lost Cause and all those Americans who embraced the Big Lie of Reconstruction's "failure." They were difficult to hear amid the din of a mass propaganda campaign most white Americans were only too happy to believe. The louder, more palatable, white supremacist tale of the Civil War and Reconstruction overtook the quieter, dark, Black one.

The abundance of discussion of Reconstruction-era atrocities in the 1930s WPA collection of formerly enslaved people's stories attests to how central they were to Black family histories. Night riding's prominence throughout the collection was due, in part, to a renewed national interest in understanding this moment of history.[14] Interviewers asked former slaves about Klan violence. But survivors' answers reveal the extent to which families continued to search for witnesses who would amplify their stories.[15] And they reflect survivors' work, as the history keepers of Black Reconstruction, to combat the lies of Reconstruction's "failure."[16]

The last direct witnesses to the war on freedom were young during the strikes' zenith. But they had comprehensive insight about raids and their aftermaths, suggesting strikes left a significant impression on their lives, or that their parents or grandparents believed the stories were ones families needed to pass on. Those who had been old enough to understand what was happening revealed information about the pandemonium of strikes, their families' strategies for surviving them, and their dispossession and displacement, producing another body of knowledge about the war on freedom.

Lula Chambers was one of many interviewees who recalled the games vigilantes played with their victims. She remembered night riders coming up to their windows at night and threatening, "Your time ain't long coming." Lula told interviewers the story of a man who made an older woman who was praying "get up off her knees and dance"; this accords with witnesses' accounts of being forced to pray or perform exercises like jumping over a fence. "Of course the old soul couldn't dance," Lula said, "but he just made her hop around" to humiliate her and exercise his power over her.[17]

Ann Ulrich Evans remembered being "scared a heap more of those Ku Klux than I was of anything else." She also recalled families' survival strategies: she had helped make pallets on the floor for her family each night because "them Ku Klux just come all around our house at night time and shoot in the doors and windows." Even if the men did not shoot inside, they remained a threat. "Sometimes they come on in the house," she said, "tear up everything on the place [and] claim they were looking for somebody."

The threats were so menacing that Ann's husband had dreams of whites "coming to kill him." She said these dreams were so vivid that he felt a raid was imminent and organized a band to stand sentry. When a white posse approached, Evans's band began "shooting just up in the air," demonstrating they were prepared to fire and kill if the attackers kept advancing. The white men retreated, to the family's relief. "I was so tired of those devils," a relieved Ann said. The "Ku Klux never did bother our house no more." Ann believed that if her husband had not had the dream, and the ability to mobilize his posse, "they would have killed every one of us that night."[18]

Lorenza Ezell, who was born in Spartanburg, South Carolina, recalled his family leaving their forced labor camp shortly after slavery and having their lives broken up by night riding. "[B]y '68 we were having such an awful time with the Ku Klux," he explained. The first time Lorenza's family was struck, men dressed in sheets went to his mother's house at midnight, claiming they were soldiers who had died in the war and had returned from the dead. The family was alarmed by the raid, but not because they were afraid of ghosts. "My mama never did take up no truck with spirits," Lorenza said, "so she knew it was just a man." The men were there to force the family to return to the labor camp of the man who had held them in bondage.

The Ezells played along until the men left, then decamped to New Prospect on the Pacolet River. It was there, in the upper edge of the county, where another gang targeted them, this time with threats to kill all Radical politicians and voters. Lorenza said his father was a respected political mover and shaker who had rallied Black men in his community to vote for President Grant's first election. Threats to whip the elder Ezell forced him to lie out.[19]

Sam Kilgore, who spent much of his early years in Williams County, Tennessee, remembered, "Before we moved to Texas the Ku Kluxers done burned down my mammy's house and she lost everything." The family had saved one hundred dollars and owned a prized three-hundred-pound pig, neither of which they could save from the fire. The family sought shelter with their former enslaver before eventually migrating to Texas.[20]

Pierce Harper remembered the Klan period just outside Snow Hill, North Carolina. "After we colored folks were considered free and turned loose," he said, "the Ku Klux broke out." Black people Pierce knew had seized the initiative of freedom, just as they had envisioned during their enslavement. But "if they got so they made good money, and had a good farm, the Ku Klux would come and murder them," Pierce said.

Pierce shared other stories, including of vigilantes' raids on jails, and of violence intensifying in 1867. "The government built schoolhouses and the Ku Klux went to work and burned them down. They'd go to the jails and take the colored men out and knock their brains out and break their necks and throw them in the river," he said.[21] Pierce recalled a group of young men attending a Freedmen's Bureau school in his community. When a white woman cried theft, authorities arrested the students. "The Ku Klux went to the jail and took them out and killed them," he said.[22] In response to this kind of violence, Pierce's mother left their community on the margins and headed for Snow Hill, where they rented a house and she worked as a washerwoman. Pierce attended school and worked farms there before moving to Columbia, South Carolina.

Pierce Harper explained that, after attacks became routine, "the colored men got together and made the complaint before the law." He said the governor told law enforcement to give the men under siege the old guns southern soldiers had used, telling the colored men, "[P]rotect yourselves." Pierce said they "got together and organized the militia and had leaders like regular soldiers." The men assembled "when they heard the Ku Kluxes were coming to get some colored folks. Then they were ready for them," he said.

Pierce explained that the men would "hide in the cabins and that's when they found out who a lot of those Ku Kluxes were." He said that, because night riders killed so many of their targets, identifying them was difficult. They wore long sheets and covered the horses with sheets so captives could not always recognize them. "Men you thought was your friend was Ku Kluxes and you'd deal with them in stores in the daytime and at night they'd come to your house and kill you," he remembered. Pierce "never took part in none of the fights," he said, but he heard acquaintances discuss them—though not, he assured WPA interviewers, "anywhere the Ku Klux could hear them."[23]

Some former slaves remembered the federal government's intervention via the presence of the U.S. Army or the investigations. Mary Ellen Grandberry said, "they kept this up until some folks from the North come down and put a stop to it."[24] Jerry Moore remembered African Americans responding to night riding by flocking to Harrison County, Texas, "for protection."[25]

The WPA narratives suggest that children came to understand night riding's role in their family's makeup.[26] The loss of familial and bodily integrity from attacks, combined with their varied aftermaths, pulled targeted families back into what one historian calls the "in between space" of slavery and freedom.[27] But the last witnesses' accounts of their lives after troops arrived or their families relocated also show that the "in between space" had exit doors.

———

Black historians did their part to keep the story alive and serve as vessels for the truth of Reconstruction's overthrow, and to help more Americans witness the era through their writings and art. The abolitionist, suffragist, and teacher Frances Ellen Watkins Harper—whose poem "The Deliverance" remarked upon newly freed people living through the worst of slavery and withstanding the "gale" of emancipation—was one of many whose work was laced with remembrances of Black Reconstruction. W. E. B. Du Bois in *Black Reconstruction in America* and John Hope Franklin in *Reconstruction after the Civil War* turned to the Klan hearings to write the first histories of Reconstruction and emancipation centering African Americans. In doing so, they confronted racist propaganda of Reconstruction's "failure" by threading the war on freedom's cataclysmic effects into the tapestry of American and African American political history. James Weldon Johnson and John Rosamond Johnson even incorporated this history and its aftermath into the lyrics of "Lift Every Voice and Sing," the African American national anthem. The song's origins lie in a poem James Weldon tried to draft for an 1899 commemoration of Abraham Lincoln's birthday. Unsuccessful, he collaborated with his brother John, a musician, to produce a song for the event to be sung by Black youths. With the lines "We have come over a way that with tears has been watered / We have come, treading our path through the blood of the slaughtered," and "God of our weary years, God of our silent tears," James Weldon evoked both the history of enslavement and the killings of Reconstruction, as well as the more recent events: the Supreme Court's 1896 ruling in *Plessy v. Ferguson* (establishing the doctrine of "separate but equal"), lynchings, and the 1898 coup and massacre in Wilmington, North Carolina.[28] In writing that Black people were again "facing the rising sun of our new day begun / Let us march on till victory is won," he centered Black people's shared history of collective struggle for justice. The song acknowledged Black people's precipitous fall under Jim Crow and the struggles for freedom ahead of them as the new century arrived: "Lift every voice and sing / Till earth and heaven ring, / Ring with the harmonies of Liberty."

African Americans greeted their freedom with great expectations. Many of them had already achieved their dreams or were on their way to doing so when agents in the war on freedom came for them. Targeted families experienced the wide reach of night riding's consequences; every person absorbed some effects of the white men's blows. Captives experienced the full dragon of racial atrocities directly, but their kin felt the whips of the tail as they did what families often do—helped their loved ones attempt to reclaim their lives and recover who they had been before they were attacked.

The stories passed on, from both survivors and witnesses, to their descendants reflect African Americans' efforts to keep the memory of what they lost alive. The storytellers acted as what the poet Natasha Trethewey calls "guardians" of the history of Black Reconstruction.[29] It was in Black families, churches, and schools that the truth of how African Americans came to be after slavery was told and passed on. In time, as the generation that experienced the joy of freedom and the disastrous war waged on it passed away, and the Great Migrations separated families from elders who remained in the South, these precise memories of Black Reconstruction faded from some family histories. During Jim Crow, African Americans increasingly lacked access to the same resources and venues conservative white politicians and white media used to keep the Lost Cause mythology alive. The monuments white conservatives installed across the South, and then the nation, were celebrations of their victory—not in the Civil War, but in the war that followed it. Without adequate witnesses for the histories African Americans told, those stories of the Second Founding, Black people's roles in the experiment in a multiracial democracy, and the nation's betrayal could not travel in the circulatory system of historical knowledge, and they became lost.

This history faded from national memory and even certain segments of African American memory. Because the violence in the ongoing war against Black freedom shifted to white rampages, racial terror killings, and everyday attacks to maintain compliance with Jim Crow, the urgency of newer violence often displaced knowledge of its older forms. There were outlines of stories, of land lost to attacks, of voteless men and, after the Nineteenth Amendment, voteless women, or of ancestors running for their lives. But with no one present to fill in the details, those stories lost their meaning.

Thanks to some survivors' brave decisions to report attacks to local magistrates, testify at the Ku Klux Klan and Exoduster hearings, and pass on stories to their offspring and to the nation in WPA interviews, the history was preserved in the national record as monuments to the unrealized promise of Reconstruction. That history was waiting for anyone to claim it and tell it. It took several generations for testimonies like the ones Hannah and Samuel Tutson gave to begin to find adequate witnesses. Historians sat with the weight of their accounts and took up the task of guarding the dark history of Reconstruction, by amplifying the survivors' accounts. Many of the stories they constructed, such as W. E. B. Du Bois's *Black Reconstruction*, Kenneth M. Stampp's *The Era of Reconstruction*, John Hope Franklin's *Reconstruction after the Civil War*, Allen W. Trelease's *White Terror*, Gladys-Marie Fry's *Night Riders in Black Folk History*, Nell Irvin Painter's *Exodusters*,

Thomas C. Holt's *Black Over White*, George C. Rable's *But There Was No Peace*, Eric Foner's *Reconstruction*, Steven Hahn's *A Nation under Our Feet*, and David W. Blight's *Beyond the Battlefield*, focused primarily on electoral politics; Black officeholders and voters; the phenomenon of the Klan; and conflicts among political parties, northerners and southerners, and presidents, Congress, and the Supreme Court.[30] And those fights mattered, to be sure.

But what people targeted in the war on freedom like Andrew and Frankie Cathcart, Mary and Joseph Brown, and Eliza Lyon knew and tried to communicate to anyone who would listen was that families were the cornerstones of their individual and collective freedom. Family was the glue that bound people together. Voting, officeholding, and equal rights were a means to a future in which Black families would be free and secure. That was why Confederates struck at the very heart of freedom when they overthrew the revolutionary experiment in multiracial democracy. Understanding Black families' stories of racing into freedom and the price right-wingers made them pay in the war against it, Americans learn that the arc of our history doesn't always bend toward justice. The real story is essential to understanding why, more than a century and a half later, our struggle continues.

ACKNOWLEDGMENTS

I want to take the opportunity to acknowledge and thank some of the people who flanked me with a variety of resources I needed to write this book.

I am so very fortunate to have worked with two awesome teams, without whose support this book, in this form, would not have been possible. First, the dynamic crew at the Charlotte Sheedy Literary Agency. I am deeply appreciative of my literary agent, Charlotte Sheedy, whose faith and encouragement never wavered. I will be forever indebted to Ally Sheedy for her insight, savviness, and timely intervention. She saw the story I wanted to tell and helped me reframe it. Likewise, the extraordinary publishing brigade at Bloomsbury. I am so thankful for my editor, Ben Hyman, for his editorial acuity and care and for seeing my vision and enriching it. His meticulous support for this book was more than I could have ever asked for but exactly what I needed. I also thank publishing director Nancy S. Miller; managing editorial director Laura Phillips; associate editor Morgan Jones; cover designer Patti Ratchford; publicist Rosie Mahorter; marketer Lauren Dooley; copy editor Janet McDonald, for her eagle eye and insightful queries and comments; proofreader Katherine Kiger; indexer Cynthia Landeen; and any anonymous readers for their incisive critiques and constructive recommendations.

I am grateful to the organizations, institutions, and individuals who invited me to present and publish my research in progress. These opportunities enabled me to think through historicizing trauma and African Americans' suffering from racist violence. My deepest appreciation to discussants who commented formally or informally at Kent State University's Peace and Conflict Studies Conference, the University of Connecticut's Draper Conference: "The Greater Reconstruction," the American Studies Association, the University of Richmond's Jepson School of Leadership Studies forum on reconstruction, the Organization of American Historians, the Southern Historical Association, Stanford University's Soul Wounds conference, the George and Ann Richards Civil War Era Center at Pennsylvania State University's "The World the Civil War Made" conference, the American Civil War Museum, University of Lynchburg, Pennsylvania State University's Emerging Scholars Workshop, and the University of Detroit Mercy. I shared bits of stories from survivors who appear in this book in edited volumes and journal forums, and I thank Gregory P. Downs and Kate Masur, William D. Carrigan and Clive Webb, Kinshasha Holman Conwill and Paul Gardullo, Ed Ayers, Julian Maxwell Hayter, and George R. Goethals for the opportunity to develop the theoretical and methodological underpinnings of this book.

I enjoyed significant support from my colleagues at Wayne State University, especially Marc Kruman, Elizabeth Faue, Marilyn Vaughan, and Gayle McCreedy. Special thanks to Tracy Neumann for the workshop on visualizing data that persuaded me to map survivors' reports of attacks. At Wayne State, I have been gifted students who are receptive to the histories I teach that disrupt mythologies of innocence, exceptionalism, and progress. Their questions and feedback were a consistent affirmation of the importance of this work. Finally, I remain indebted to the sisters in the "Good Doctors" group— Lisa Ze Winters, Geralyn Gunn, Fay Martin Keys, Donyale Padgett, Shirley Thomas, and Kafi Kumasi. My life and work would be so much poorer without their communal ethic of faculty care. Spanning different cycles in life and academia, we rely on and support each other in foundational ways.

While writing this book, I had the good fortune of working with people who nurtured me as a writer. Kelly Hardcastle Jones, Ronald Young Jr., Lushik Lotus Lee, Joshua Moore, and the visionary folks at Roots. Wounds. Words. Inc. supported my passion and aided my growth as a storyteller. Elaine Frantz, Michael Pfeifer, W. Caleb McDaniel, and Carole Emberton provided helpful comments or affirmed the historical significance of African American survivors' accounts of the war on their freedom.

I am beholden to two cherished groups of women who were constant champions. These include the writers—Lisa Ze Winters, Danielle L. McGuire, Lara Langer Cohen, Paula C. Austin, LaShawn D. Harris, and Robyn C. Spencer. Their breadth of insight for reconsidering, reimagining, and reexamining often ignored parts of African American history and culture inspires me. They gave helpful, generative feedback and championed my determination to serve as an adequate witness to survivors' testimonies of their traumatic suffering. And "the girls," in no order: Pamela Taylor, Stacy Washington, Lisa Ze Winters, Barbara Kelley, Danielle L. McGuire, and the members of the Roberta's Readers Book Club. They have brightened my days, reassembled the pieces, pulled me away from work to play, and insisted that I care for myself as I tried to do right by the survivors whose stories I tell.

And finally, I must thank my family for giving me roots and wings. My mother, Janet Williams, youngest brother, Danny L. Williams, and uncle, Henry Harmon Jr., transitioned while I was writing this book. I still don't understand the world without them, but they continue to exist in my memory and my dreams. I've been graced on this new phase in my life with beloved kin who poured love and support into me as they resecured my anchor: Andrea Harmon, Sheila Harmon, Darlene Hart, Monica Mahan, Melvin Dunbar, Ethan Dunbar, Vera Stephens, Michael and Wanda Kirksy, and especially Shairon Dunbar, Shallena Dunbar, Denise Farnum, Maxine Fitzpatrick, Joyce Harmon, and Opaline Taylor.

APPENDIX

Searching for the Survivors

Only a fraction of survivors of the war on freedom left documentation of the violence they and their families endured in places that are accessible to researchers today. When one combines affidavits and other reports given to the Freedmen's Bureau from 1865 to 1868 and listed in their digitized Records of Murders and Outrages* (https://www.freedmensbureau.com/outrages.htm) with the stories of survivors who testified at the South Carolina Klan trials and the KKK hearings (both collections are digitized http://onlinebooks.library.upenn.edu/webbin /metabook?id=insurrection1872), there is more than enough evidence to validate African Americans' accounting of Reconstruction atrocities and their efforts to articulate their impact.

Even with the comparatively small number of survivors who testified at the Klan trials and hearings, there were too many targeted people to name in this book. Attending to readers' needs required excluding some witnesses' stories altogether, or using a snippet of their testimony to illustrate different aspects of the violence but muting their names in the main text. (Their names and citation information are in the endnotes.) Anonymizing any of the brave men and women who often risked their lives by testifying and whose stories I was devoted to telling, especially if any of their descendants came to this book looking for them, was difficult. I hope naming them here and including some of the additional information I learned about them suffices.

The testimonies of survivors who appeared as witnesses at the trials and hearings are filled with significant details about their lives and their people—never enough detail to satisfy my interest in who survivors were before and after white men "visited" them, but just enough to inspire more research. Survivors who testified at the Klan hearings, especially landowners, referenced recent encounters with census assessors when asked to account for valuations of their property. That was my first cue to explore the state and federal records which had been digitized and were searchable on Ancestry.

---

* "Outrages" were criminal offenses deemed outside the norms.

When I searched census records for each of the more than two hundred Black witnesses who testified at the Klan hearings, I found more than half that I could verify with two or more criteria from what survivors revealed about their lives at the hearings (name, age, location, property, employment, etc.). Census records revealed many of the people who were likely living in testifying witnesses' households when night riders struck. Take Samuel Nuckles, who declared himself a "refugee" from Union County, South Carolina. Samuel was fifty-seven, an established family head and community elder, when he testified in Columbia about his being run out of office and his and his oldest sons' being run off from their home and community. Samuel and his son Henry testified, and both referenced kin without identifying them. But the census shows that theirs was a household of *twelve*. When Samuel, Henry, and Sam Jr. fled, they left behind Siller, the family matriarch, four more children, and four other relatives, possibly adult children and their spouses and offspring. Even if some of the family escaped the physical wrath of the men targeting Samuel and the boys, they all had to live with the effects of the horror of the violence, the men's displacement, and their own increased vulnerability to future attacks without Samuel's protection. Relocating for their collective safety would have been a massive endeavor.

The census records revealed more about families, individual members, movement, and the magnitude of night-riding violence. Take their size and how they organized their family units. The Nuckleses were one of many compound families and multigenerational households. Some households, like Hamp and Susan Mitchell's, contained three generations. Families appear to have been welcoming new members into the fold about every two years. Gaps hint at possible miscarriages and child deaths. Recorded birthplaces for adults track the domestic slave trade and the separation of families as Black people were forcibly relocated south and west and people seized opportunities and located kin after the war. If one adds *all* the kin named or unnamed at the hearings who lived in witnesses' households or on their homesteads, the number of victims impacted by the atrocities *we know about* increases significantly.

The records also document states of literacy and school attendance that may or may not have been referenced in testimonies. South Carolina rock mason and patriarch Patrick Tanner could read and write. Abe and Eliza Lyon's children were attending school in Choctaw County, Alabama. William Lyon was listed as able to read and write, and Ella and Annie were learning to, at least before the white men killed Abe and the family fled.

Cultural practices are also revealed through African Americans' naming conventions. Some first names were Biblical—Mary, Rachael, Abraham, or the shortened versions like Abe and Abram. Names like Doctor, Sir, Governor, Scipio, and Prince could have been chosen to designate empowerment, or a carryover from enslavers' practice of mocking the people they held in bondage with names well above their enslaved status. Georgian John C. Calhoun's name could be a direct association with the South Carolina statesman, while Jefferson Huskins and

Washington Strong's names could be associated with past presidents or simply people with similar names. Other names reflect the merging of peoples from West and Central Africa and their new naming practices. And they indicate families' decisions to honor ancestors (Isaam); kin sold further south and west (Tennessee, Missouri); or parents. Doc and Ellen Rountree—who were driven from Live Oak, Florida, after being menaced by their former enslaver to abandon their land and apprentice their children to him—named their youngest son and daughter (of ten children total) after themselves.

The census does not fill all the ellipses in the record. But this documentation does substantiate witnesses' efforts to communicate how the war against Reconstruction undermined their freedom and changed their lives—and their families' lives—forever.

ALABAMA KLAN HEARINGS

@Alston, James H.—Oct. 17, 1871, ALKH, 1016–1022 | Tuskegee
    Nannie
    [Children]
*Barbee, Robert—Feb. 26, 1870, ALKT, 1231–1232 | Averyville, near Stevenson in Jackson County
    Manda
    Amelia
    Ann
Barry, Rina—ALKT, 1188–1189[†‡] | Near Alpine, in Cherokee County

---

@Denotes witnesses who identified themselves at the hearings as elected or appointed officials, candidates for office, Union League members, or participants in legislative sessions, including constitutional conventions.

[†] Witnesses like Rina Barry, who either gave affidavits to justices of the peace or U.S. Army official personnel or testified at the Klan trials, had their testimonies entered into evidence at the Klan hearings. Their testimonies were included in the published volume for their state alongside the testimonies of witnesses who appeared before the congressional subcommittees. Their undated testimonies are designated as ALKT or SCKT.

[‡] I've retained the original spellings of names from the congressional hearings and the census, unless noted.

[*] Indicates male witnesses at the hearings who identified themselves as veterans of the U.S. Colored Troops—the 166 mostly African American regiments in the U.S. Army—or whose name I discovered in my cursory search of National Archives' records on the Civil War Soldiers and Sailors database. I found plenty of names. But common naming conventions, including newly freed people's renaming themselves, required a deeper look and if I couldn't identify another point of reference (likely age, where the solider enlisted, theaters of the war, indications of residency), I did not indicate service here. In short, I suspect there are a few more veterans here than I can verify.

Bell, Frank—Feb. 28, 1870, ALKT, 1232 | Averyville, near Stevenson in Jackson County
    [Wife]
Bennett, Granville—Nov. 1, 1871, ALKH, 1734–1745 | Sumter County, three miles outside of Livingston
    Martha
    George
    Charlotte
    Louissianna
Blair, Augustus—Oct. 9, 1871, ALKH, 674–679 | Limestone County on Fort Hamilton Hill
    [Wife]
    William "Billy"
    Eliza Jane
    Charlotte
*Brown, Jesse—Oct. 12. 1871, ALKH, 860–861 | Madison County
Bryant, Cynthia, ALKT, 1188 | Near Alpine, in Cherokee County
Butler, John M.—July 7, 1871, ALKH, 1091–1099 | Tuskegee
    H.M.
    Frances
Campbell, Mary—Aug. 4, 1869, ALKH, 1198–1199 | Madison County
    William
    [Child]
Childers, John—Nov. 1, 1871, ALKH, 1719–1728 | Sumter County
    Julia
    John
    Amanda
    Andrew
    Robert
    Julia
    Louisa
Daniel, Sir—Oct. 14, 1871, ALKH, 993–997 | Stevenson, sixty miles from Huntsville
    [Wife]
    [Child]
Echols, Howell—Oct. 14. 1872, 957–960 | Huntsville
    Ann
    Mary
    Polly
    Green
    Letta
    Oliver
    Margaret
    Missouri
    Howell
Fenderson, Sheperd—Oct. 26, ALKH, 1395–1405 | Jefferson in Marengo County
    Martha
    Lenora
    Mary Turner

*Ford, William—Oct. 9, 1871, ALKH, 679–686 | Madison County
    [Father]
Fullerlove, Robert—Oct. 31, 1871, ALKH, 1649–1660 | Tompkinsville, Choctaw County
    Adaline
    Taylor
    Alexander
    Ary Easley
Gardiner, Major—Oct. 12, 1871, ALKH, 862–864 | Huntsville
    Brother
Giles, Henry [previously Garrett]—Oct. 17, 1871, ALKH, 1009–1016 | Nixburg beat, in Coosa County, near Watley
    [Wife]
    [Children]
Gill, Joseph—Oct. 12, 1871, ALKH, 812–815 | Briar Forks, Madison County
Hamlin, Henry—Oct. 12, 1871, ALKH, 857–859 | Trinity, below Decatur
Hargrove, Wiley—Nov. 11, 1871, ALKH, 1993–1996 | five miles outside of Columbus, Pickens County, MS
    Mahala
    Daughter
Henderson, William—Oct. 7, 1871, ALKH, 576–590 | Colbert County
    Wife
    Mack
*@Houston [or Huston], George—Oct. 17, 1871, ALKH, 997–1004 | Sumter County
    Amelia
    Monroe
    James M
    William
*Jackson, Lewis—Oct. 14, 1871, AKLH, 982–984 | Stevenson
    Sally
Johnson, Henry—Oct. 14, 1871, ALKH, 953–956 | three miles from Huntsville in Madison County
Jones, George—Oct. 26, 1871, ALKH, 1388–1395 3 | Near Jefferson, Marengo County
Judkins, Oscar [or Osker]—Oct. 18, 1871, 1042–1048 | Chambers County, between Fredonia and La Fayette
    Lucy
    Posey
    Tom Smith
    Sarah Smith
Kidd, Henry—Oct. 12, 1871, ALKH, 867–869 | Madison County
    Wife
Killens, Jane—Nov. 1, 1871, 1733–1734 | Sumter County
Lawler, Samuel—Feb. 26, 1870, ALKT, 1231–1232 | Averyville, near Stevenson in Jackson County
    Sarah
    Matt
    Mary
    Henry

     Robert Barbee
     Amanda
Mathews, William—Oct. 9, 1871, ALKH, 641–646 | Near Huntsville
     Fiancé
Lee, William—Oct. 25, 1871, ALKH, 1333–1337 | three miles from DeSotoville, a little
village in Choctaw County
     Linda
     Chaney
Leonard, Benjamin—Nov. 2, 1871, ALKH, 1785–1797 | Greene County
     Emily
     John
     Jordan
*Lipscomb, Peyton [or Paton]—Oct. 14, 1871, ALKH, 951–953 |
New Market
     Charlotte
     Washington
     Matilda
     Henry
     Becky
     Frances
     Lewis
     Ara
     Martha
@Long, Burton—Oct. 20, 1871, 1149–1154 | Russell County, near Silver Run
Low, Henry—Nov. 11, 1871, ALKH, 1996–1999 | Pickens County
Low [or Lowe], Samuel—Nov. 11, 1871, ALKH, 2005–2007 |
Pickens County
     Harriet
     John
     William
     Fenton
     Calvin
     Julia
     Amy
     Henry Tweedie
     Rachel Speed
Lyon [or Lyons], Eliza—Oct. 24, 1871, ALKH, 1262–1271 | DeSotoville
     Abe
     [Older Daughter]
     William
     Ella
     Annie
     Henn Williams
Mahone, Charles—Oct. 18, 1871, 1078–1080 | Montgomery
     Muscogee
     Missouri
Marchbanks, Alexander—Oct. 12, 1871, ALKH, 865–867 |

Madison County
  Lavenia
  Tempe
  Ben
  Robert
  Frances
  William
  Pamela
  Ann
Moore, George—Aug. 26, 1869, ALKH, 1188 | Near Alpine, in Cherokee County
  Wife
Powell, Charles—Nov. 3, 1871, ALKH, 1845–50 | Lee's Station in
Sumter County
Reese, Tiller—Oct. 28, 1871, ALKH, 1248–1251 | Marengo County
  G. Rogers
*Roper, George—Oct. 9, 1871, ALKH, 686–694 | Huntsville
Steele, Anthony—Oct. 15, 1871, ALKH, 948–950 | New Market
  Catherine
  Rutha
  Jessee
  Peggy
  Charley
  [Infant]
Strong, Washington—Oct. 14, 1871, ALKH, 956–957 | New Market
  Esther
  Malinda
Strong, Wiley—Oct. 9, 1871, ALKH, 668–674 | New Market
  Beckey
  Mary
Taylor, George—Oct. 6, 1871, ALKH, 572–576 | Cherokee in Colbert County
Tinker, Mack—Oct. 26, 1871, ALKH, 1360–1366 | Choctaw County, six miles south of
DeSotoville
  Bettie
  M.B. Pleasant
Watley, Smith—Oct. 17, 1871, ALKH, 1004–1009 | Coosa County, twenty miles north of
Wetumpka
  Caroline
  Jack
  Cilva
  Susan
  George
Westbrook, Betsy—Oct. 24, 1871, ALKH, 1242–1247 | Marengo County
  Robin
Williams, Diana—June 15, 1869, ALKH, 1194–1195 | Rodgerville,
Lauderdale County
Williams, Mary Eliza—Oct. 25, 1871, ALKH, 1356–1360 | Sumter County
  Ezekiel

FLORIDA KLAN HEARINGS & MISCELLANEOUS

TESTIMONIES AND DOCUMENTS[§]

Bryant, Homer, Nov. 14, 1871, FLKH, 302–305 | Jackson County

@Flowers, Andrew J. July 15, 1871, Washington, D.C., 41–50 | Whiteside, Tennessee

    Harriet

    Thomas

    Roxana

    Cornelius

    Manson

    Mary

@Fortune, Emanuel—Oct. 23, 1871, FLKH, 480–483 | Jackson County

    Sarah

    Timothy D

    Martha D

    Florence

    Emanuel

    Mary B

Gibbs, Jonathan C.—Nov. 13, 1871, FLKH, 220–224 | Tallahassee

    Elizabeth

    Thomas

    Amie E.

    Marry Barringon

    Isabel Barrington

    Anne Barrington

    Dalceda Barrington

    Charles Murray

@Meacham, Robert—Nov. 10, 1871, FLKH, 101–109 | Monticello in
Jefferson County

    Stella

    Margaret

    Robert

    Stella Annice

    Cornelis Hadley

    Martha Sickles

Nelson, Joseph—Nov. 11, 1871, FLKH, 136–144 | Marianna

@Pearce, Charles—Nov. 13, 1871, FLKH, 165–176 | Tallahassee

    Ellen

    Eliza Ann

    Ann Smith

@Pousser, Richard—Nov. 14, 1871, FLKH, 272–277 | Jackson County

---

[§] This volume is labeled "Florida; and Miscellaneous Testimonies and Documents." The Subcommittee
in Florida called fewer witnesses and, when binding all the records for printing, added additional
testimonies, including from witnesses who testified in legal proceedings in Washington, D.C.

Reed, Henry—Nov. 11, 1871, FLKH, 109–114 | Jackson County
  Julia
  Willie
Rountree, Doc—Nov. 14, 1871, FLKH, 279–81 | Live Oak, Suwannee County
  Ellen
  John
  Fletcher
  Sarah
  Charlotte
  Abe
  Ellen
  Doc
Tutson, Hannah—Nov. 10, 1871, FLKH, 59–65
Tutson, Samuel—Nov. 10, 1871, FLKH, 54–59
  Daughter
  Mary
  SL
White, Larry—Nov. 14, 1871, FLKH, 308–310 | Jackson County, near Marianna
  Amanda
  Louisa
  Judah
  Larra
  Martha

GEORGIA KLAN HEARINGS

@Allen, Thomas—Oct. 26, 1871, GAKH, 607–618 | Jasper County
  Sella
  Georgiana
  William
  Matilda
  Eliza
  Maria
  Susan
  Thomas
  Malinda
  [Sister]
  Emanuel
Anderson, Lewis—Nov. 1, 1871, GAKH, 864–866 | Walton County
  Baily
  Celia
  Caesar
  Albert
  Gabriel
  Barberry
  Scott

George

Felix

Manerva

Reuben Ray

Anthony, Martin—Oct. 27, 1871, 692–694 | Morgan County

Martha

John

Mary

Alford Shepard

Arnold, Rachel—Oct. 21, 1871, GAKH, 388–390 | White County

@Barnes, Eli—Nov. 2, 1871, GAKH, 954–959 | Hancock County

Wife

Family

Benafield, Jack—Oct. 27, 1871, GAKH, 683–684 | Walton County, Vinegar Hill district

Ellen

Benson, Caroline—Oct. 21, 1871, GAKH, 386–388 | White County

Jeremiah

Alford

Joseph

Thomas

James

Brown, Joseph—Oct. 24, 1871, GAKH, 501–503 | White County

Brown, Mary—Oct. 21, 1871, GAKH, 375–77 | White County

Bush, Hilliard—Oct. 27, 1871, GAKH, 684–687 | Pike County

Claiborn

Mary

Simeon

Alice

Henderson

Anna

William

Loveberry

Mary

Benjamin

Calhoun, John C.—Oct. 23, 1871, GAKH, 478–480 | Jackson County

@Campbell, Tunis—Oct. 31. 1871, GAKH, 845–864 | Darien, McIntosh

Wife

@Campbell, Tunis, Jr.—Nov. 4, 1871, GAKH, 1057–1060 | Darien, McIntosh

Harriet

TG Simpson

Harriet Taylor

Carter, Jasper—Oct. 23, 1871, GAKH, 472–477 | Haralson County, five miles from Buchanan

Maria

@Colby, Abram—Oct. 27, 1871, GAKH, 695–707 | Greene County

Anna

Minnie

Ella

Amanda

Julia

Coe, Henry—Oct. 26, 1871, GAKH, 640 | Douglas County

Davis, Warren—Oct. 28, 1871, GAKH, 727–730 | Coweta County

Patsy

Lula

Taylor Stinton

Eager, Scipio—Oct. 27, 1871, GAKH, 668–671 | Washington County

Elder, Mary—Oct. 28, 1871, GAKH, 733–735 | Clarke County

Elder, Simon—Oct. 28, 1871, GAKH, 731–733 | Clarke County

Ferrell, Anderson—Oct. 26, 1871, GAKH, 618–622 | Troup County

Lucy [Elizabeth]

Anderson

*Flannigan, Harrison—Oct. 23, 1871, GAKH, 480–483 | Jackson County

@Fleimster, George—Oct. 27, 1871, GAKH, 655–663 | Morgan County

Mary Frances

Charles

Mary Jane

Richard

Sophia

Julius Jordan

Charles Bethel

Flournoy, Hannah—Oct. 24, 1871, GAKH, 532–535 | Columbus

@Floyd, Monday—Nov. 4, 1871, GAKH, 1060–1062 | Morgan County

Dina

Harriet Reede

Garrison, Leanna—Oct. 27, 1871, GAKH, 666–668 | Cherokee County

Jerry

Cezar

Thomas

Robert

Rosa

Garrison, Samuel—Oct. 27, 1871, GAKH, 687–689 | Cherokee County

Rose

[Brother]

Goggin, Hester—Oct. 21, 1871, GAKH, 408–409 | Haralson County

@Harrison, W.H.—Oct. 23, 1871, GAKH, 576–580 | Hancock

Hayes, Henry—Nov. 1, 1871, GAKH, 866–867 | Gwinnett County

Hays, Ransom—Oct. 27, 1871, GAKH, 681–682 | Walton County, Vinegar District

@Hendricks, Charles—Oct. 24, 1871, GAKH, 515–520 | Gwinnett County near Pinckneyville District

Hendricks, Martha—Oct. 24, 1871, GAKH, 520–522 | Gwinnett County near Pinckneyville District

Minerva

Archiband

Avery

Anthony
Ann Hunnicutt
Hinton, Alexander—Oct. 27, 1871, GAKH, 694–695 | Walton County
    Brother
Ivey [or Iney], Wesley—Oct. 27, 1871, GAKH, 650–651 | Mulberry River (in Jackson County)
    Caroline
    Randel
    Ransom
    Emily
    Mariah
    Capt
    John
    Mayson Hunter
Jeter, Aury—Oct. 25, 1871, GAKH, 565–567 | Douglas County
    Emily
Jeter, Columbus—Oct. 25, 1871, GAKH, 560–655 | Douglas County
Johnson, John—Oct. 27, 1871, 664–666; recalled Nov. 1, 1871, GAKH, 867–870 | Madison, Morgan County
Jones, Warren—Oct. 27, 1871, GAKH, 689–692 | Warren County
    Lucy
    Son
Kinney, Betty—Oct. 24, 1871, 535–536 | Jackson County
Kinney, Toddy [or Lottie]—Oct. 23, 1871, GAKH, 477–478 | Jackson County
    Daughter
    Babe
    Sallie Mclester
Lane, Daniel—Oct. 27, 1871, GAKH, 653–655 | Morgan County
    Sarah
    Franklin
    Eliza
    Victoria
Little, Charles—Oct. 23, 1871, GAKH, 471–472 | Haralson County, above Buchanan, on the Tallapoosa River
    Jane
    Rery Goggans [or Goggins]
    Loutisia Goggans
    Reuben Goggans
    James Goggans
    Mary Goggans
Little, Letitia—Oct. 21, 1871, GAKH, 410–411 | Haralson County on Williams's Mills
Little, Rena—Oct. 21, 1871, GAKH, 410 | Haralson County on the Tallapoosa River
Lowther [or Lother], Henry—Oct. 20, 1871, GAKH, 356–363 | Pickens County
    Eveline
    [Son]
McEllhannon, Prince—Oct. 27, 1871, GAKH, 648–650 | Jackson County, Chandler's District

Mills, Augustus—Oct. 23, 1871, GAKH, 468–470 | Walton County
Mills, Elizabeth "Letty"—Oct. 23, 1871, GAKH, 465–468 | Walton County
 Isaiah
 Jesse
 Emma
 Mary
 Tobey
Mitchell, William Hampton "Hamp"—Oct. 26, 1871, GAKH, 641–644 | Gwinnett County
in the Laurenceville District
 Susan
 Robert
 Tilda
 Jegal
 Thomas
 George
 Eliza Allen
 Jack Allen
 Martha Allen
 Hamp Allen
 Alan Allen
 John Allen
 Lucy Allen
 Texas Allen
 Sallie Allen
 Emma Allen
 Wilton Allen
@Moore, Romulus [or Romalus]—Oct. 28, 1871, GAKH, 735–743 | Columbia County
 Mary
 William D
 Melissa
 Lizzie Jones
 Maria Gilbert
 America Gilbert
 William Alexander
 Agnes Alexander
Neal, Mary—Oct. 21, 1871, GAKH, 386 | White County
 Silas
 Selah
 Jane
 Elizabeth
 Cornelius
 Isaam
Reed, Sampson—Oct. 27, 1871, GAKH, 644–645 | Jackson County
 Lucinda
 Mitchell—Oct. 27, 1871, GAKH, 646–647
 Charles
 Andy—Oct. 27, 1871, GAKH, 645–646

Sampson
Tilda Lay
Jim Sharp
@Richardson, Alfred—July 7, 1871, GAKH, 1–19 | Clarke County
Fannie
Ella
Amanda
Laura
Sheets, Reuben—Oct. 27, 1871, GAKH, 651–653 | Walton County
Elizabeth
Nathan
Nancy
Hannah
Smith, Charles—Oct. 26, 1871, GAKH, 597–601 | Walton County
Smith, Caroline—Oct. 21, 1871, GAKH, 400–403 | Walton County
Amanda
Adaline
Daniel
R
William
H Whitworth
Sarah Ann Sturtevant
Stewart, Samuel—Oct. 26, 1871, GAKH, 591–596 | Walton County, place called Social Circle
*@Turner, Henry McNeal—Nov. 3, 1871, GAKH, 1034–1042 | Macon, Bibb County
Eliza
John
David
Victoria
Henry
Walthall, Tilda—Oct. 21, 1871, GAKH, 407–408 | Haralson County
John
Westmoreland, Greene—Oct. 28, 1871, 730–731 | Spalding County, ten miles from Griffen
Rachael
Allice
Jeff
Fannie
Thomas
William
Cicero

MISSISSIPPI KLAN HEARINGS

Anderson, Lydia—Nov. 6, 1871, MSKH, 510–513 | Macon
Beckwith, Joseph—Nov. 14, 1871, MSKH, 888–890 | Lowndes County
Lurena
Lucretia

    Amanda
    Hendly
    Mase
    Dave
    Carry
    Willy
Carter, Edward—Nov. 8, 1871, MSKH, 1083–1085 | Tuscaloosa
    Wife
    Son
    Daughter
    2 older children
Coleman, William—Nov. 6, 1871, MSKH, 482 | Winston County
    Harriet
    Mittie
    Fletcher
    Brice
    Rob Ashford
Cooper, Peter—Nov. 16, MSKH, 492–499 | Winston County
Crosby, Edward—Nov. 17, 1871, MSKH, 1133–1137 | ten miles east of Aberdeen
    [Wife]
@Davis, Alexander K.—Nov. 13, 1871, MSKH, 469–482 | Macon
Davis, Joseph—Nov. 13, 1871, MSKH, 808–819 | Aberdeen
Flint, Sanders—Nov. 13, 1871, MSKH, 803–808 | Aberdeen
    Charlotte
    Joseph
    Silva
    Willis
    Amos
    Simon
    Nathan
    Robert
    Rachel
@Gleed, Robert—Nov. 10, 1871, MSKH, 718–728 | Lowndes County
    Susan
    John
    Annie
    Virgil
    Robert
Gray, Edmund—Nov. 14, 1871, MSKH, 894–895 | Caledonia
Hairston, Joshua—Nov. 13, 1871, MSKH, 798 | Southern part of Lowndes County
    Eliza
    Alice
    Hilliard
Hicks, James—Nov. 14, 1871, MSKH, 891–893 | Caledonia
    Wife
    Daughter

Perkins, Lewis—Nov. 14, 1871, MSKH, 899–901 | Military Road in Columbus
    Wife
*Smith, Daniel H.—Nov. 7, 1871, MSKH, 570–575 | six miles east of Macon
    Angeline
    Amanda
Triplett, David—Nov. 7, 1871, MSKH, 544–548 | Winston County
    Hannah
    Judge
    Mary
    Martha
    Oby
Turner, Joseph—Nov. 11, 1871, MSKH, 769–777 | Caledonia
    Susan
    Sarah
    Josephine
@Willis, Washington—Nov. 11, 1871, MSKH, 1184–1185 | Monroe County
near Aberdeen

NORTH CAROLINA KLAN HEARINGS[**]

Harris, Essic—July 1, 1871, NCKH, 86–102 | Chatham County, near Pittsboro
    Ann
    5 children

SOUTH CAROLINA KLAN HEARINGS

Adams, Lucretia—July 27, 1871, SCKH, 1577–1580 | Clay Hill, York County
    Hezekiah
    Esther McMacken
    Rose McMacken
Bonner, Albery—July 7, 1871, SCKH, 440–446 | twenty-two miles from Spartanburg
    Sarah
    Simpson
    Alexander
    Alice
    Victoria
    William
@Bonner, Samuel—July 10, 1871, SCKH, 576–580 | Limestone Township
    Clarinda
    George

[**] North Carolina had its share of Reconstruction atrocities. However, when the subcommittee met there, they called mostly white elected or appointed officials, like U.S. Commissioner A. Webster Shaffer, who shared reports of violence he had received.

Mother
Sister
Samuel, Jr.
@Bowden, Clem—July 7, 1871, SCKH, 379–386 | Just north of Limestone Springs
Mannie [or Minerva]
Alfred
Rachael
Elizabeth
Robert
William
Lonanna
Sherman
Brumfield, Abraham—SCKT, 1947–1948 | York
Emeline—1948–1950
Butler, Willis—July 7, 1871, SCKH, 439–440 | Beech Springs, Spartanburg County
Cathcart, Andrew—July 27, 1871, SCKH, 1591–1597 | York, lower edge of county near
Charlotte Road
Frankie
Adeline
Thomas
Eliza
Cinthia
Laura
Chalk, Eliza—July 20, 1871, SCKH, 1128–1135 | Unionville
Joseph Vanlew [or Vanlue]
Thomas Vanlew
Charlie Chalk
Lizzie Vanlew
Ida Vanlew
Clowney, Jerry—SCKT, 1859–1861 | Yorkville
Daniels, Sancho—July 11, 1871, SCKH, 678–680 | Beech Springs
Dodd, Pinckney—July 7, 1871, SCKH, 416–418 | Spartanburg County, near Howard Gap
Road
Maria
Fewell, Governor—SCKT, 1956–1957 | York
Fowler, Charlotte—July 6, 1871, SCKH, 386–392 | Spartanburg Township, three miles from
Beech Springs
Wallace
Margaret
Henrietta
[Grandchild]
Gaffney, James—Oct. 10, 1871, SCKH, 616–619 | Spartanburg County, near NC border
[Wife]
Gaffney, Samuel—July 10 and July 15, 1871, SCKH, 601–604 | Spartanburg County, near
NC border
[Wife]
[Children]

Garrison, Martha—July 27, 1871, SCKH, 1574–1577 | Clay Hill, York County
    Jack
    Father
Givens, Mervin—July 12, 1871, SCKH, 698–700 | Cedar Springs
Gore, Benjamin—July 27, 1871, SCKH, 1580–1591 | Chester
    Sarah
    Walker
    Sarah
    Laura
    Jeff Davis
    John
    Mary
Hernandez, Harriet—July 10, 1871, SCKH, 585–591 | nineteen miles from town near Cowpens Furnace in Cherokee County
    Charley
    Lucy
Hill, Elias—July 25, 1871, SCKH, 1406–1414 | Clay Hill
    [Brother]
    [Sister-in-law]
Hines, John—July 12, 1871, SCKH, 690–694 | Near "Battlegrounds" perhaps Cowpens
    Rose
    Lazarus
    John
Huskie, Doctor—July 10, 1871, SCKH, 595–597 | Limestone Township
    Julia
    Emaline
    Victory
    Adalissa
    Berry
    Lottie
Huskins, Jefferson—July 10, 1871, SCKH, 580–585 | Near Limestone
    Susan
    Christina
    Nancy
    Emily
    William
    James
*Jenkins, Caleb [or Genkin]—July 12, 1871, SCKH, 696–698 | Campobello
    Cabeb
    Thaddeus
    Madora
    Malissa
    Griffin
    Jacob
    Christina
    Washington

Johnson, Jack—Nov. 1, 1871, SCKH, 1167–1170 | Laurens County
 [Wife]
Johnson, Willis—July 3, 1871, SCKH, 326–330 | Newberry County
Lancaster, Matthew—July 10, 1871, SCKH, 591–595 | Glen Springs Township
Latham, Henry—SCKT, 1858–1859 | York
Lewis, John—July 7, 1871, SCKH, 435–439 | twelve miles from Spartanburg
 Adeline
 Amelia
 Lulu
 Doctor
 Madora
 Josephine
Lindsay, William—SCKT, 1757–1762 | York district
 Sally
 Eliza
 Margaret
 Amanda
Lipscomb, Daniel—July 7, 1871, SCKH, 427–434 | Limestone
Lipscomb, Henry—July 11, 1871, SCKH, 681–687 | Spartanburg district
Lipscomb, John—July 11, 1871, SCKH, 666–675 | White Plains Township
 Julian
 Hester
 Anderson
 Laura
 Chesterfield
 Mary
 Amanda Wilkins
 Cora Wilkins
 Preston Littlejohn
McCrary, Isham—July 8, 1871, SCKH, 538–552 | Near Pacolet
McMillan, Lucy—July 10, 1871, SCKH, 604–611 | Spartanburg County
 Daughter
Miller, Joseph—July 10, 1871, SCKH, 600–601 | Downriver 8.5 miles
Montgomery, Jacob—July 12, SCKH, 695–696 | Limestone
 Freddie
 Louisa
 Nancy
 Jacob
Morehead, Thomas—SCKT, 1955–1956 | Rock Hill
@Nuckles, Samuel—July 20, 1871, SCKH, 1158–1165 | Union County
 Siller
 Rachael
 Henry
 Sam
 Cynda
 Isaiah

James
Hannibal Littlejohn
Samuel Littlejohn
Convero Littlejohn
Marietta Littlejohn
Ogelsby, Nelson—July 12, 1871, SCKH, 687–689 | Spartanburg district
    Jane
    Henry
    Lewis
    Simpson
    James
    Julia A
    Rodman
    William
    Mariah
    John
Page, Christina—July 20, 1871, SCKH, 1142–1144 | Union County
Parker, Hampton—July 10, 1871, SCKH 597–600 | Spartanburg County
Postle, Harriet—SCKT, 1951–1952 | four miles from Rock Hill
Postle, Isaac—SCKT, 1952–1955 | four miles from Rock Hill
Rice, Dennis—July 21, 1871, SCKH, 1182–1185 | Unionville
    Sally Rice
    Richard
    Robin
    Brother
Simmons, Samuel—July 7, 1871, SCKH, 402–407 | Beech Spring Township in Spartanburg
County
    Wife
    Children
Simril, Harriet—SCKT, 1861–1862 | Clay Hill in York County
    Samuel
    Caroline
    Lawson
    Neelus
    Roxana
    Lydia
Smith, Eliphaz—July 12, 1871, SCKH, 700–701 | Cedar Springs
    Sollie
    Elihu
    Catharine
    Mary
    Joanah
    Lollie
Smith, Willis—July 10, 1871, SCKH, 611–616 | Limestone
Snoddy, Spencer—July 11, 1871, SCKH, 680–681 | Beech Springs
    Caroline
    Rosalee

Henry
Bettie
Sturges, Sam—SCKT, 1950 | York
Surratt, Jackson—July 8, 1871, SCKH, 520–524 | North of Cowpens Battleground
Jane—July 8, 1871, SCKH, 524–526
[Daughter]
[Son]
[Infant]
Tanner, Patrick—July 7, 1871, SCKH, 407–410 | Spartanburg County, about 7.5 miles from town
Missouri
Adriana Moss
William Moss
Victoria
Eliza
John
Mary
Martha
Edmond
Charley
Thommason, John—SCKT, 1947–1949 | York
Mary
Hampton
Waddy
Martha
Annie
Albert
Thomson, Elias—July 7, 1871, SCKH, 410–416 | Tyger River (Spartanburg County)
Maydeen
Anna
Mary
Lois
Frank
Rosa Lee
John
Timons, Andy—SCKT, 1712–1717 | Brattonsville (Plantation in York County)
Williams, Rosy—SCKT, 1720–1723 | Brattonsville (Plantation in York County)
James
Gill
Lula
Henry
James
Minta Hubbard
Levi Hubbard
Caroline Hubbard
Vanlue, Alfred—July 20, 1871, 1135–1142 | Unionville
Wright, Alfred—July 20, 1871, SCKH, 1173–1177 | Union County, North Pacolet

Annie
Martha
Sarah
Susan Phillips
Nancy Phillips
Zachariah Phillips

EXODUSTER TESTIMONIES

Adams, Henry
Murrell, William
Singleton, Benjamin

NOTES

INTRODUCTION

1. Edward Crosby, Nov. 17, 1871, U.S. Congress, 42nd Congress, 2nd session, *Report of the Joint Select Committee to Inquire Into the Condition of Affairs in the Late Insurrectionary States: Mississippi* (Government Printing Office, 1872) [hereafter MSKH], 1133–37.

2. Elaine Frantz Parsons, "Midnight Rangers: Costume and Performance in the Reconstruction-Era Ku Klux Klan," *Journal of American History* 92, no. 3 (2005), 815.

3. For the most detailed history of the Klan's origins, see Elaine Frantz Parsons, *Ku-Klux: The Birth of the Klan During Reconstruction* (University of North Carolina Press, 2016).

4. Crosby, MSKH, 1135.

5. See Steven Hahn, *A Nation under Our Feet: Black Political Struggles in the Rural South from Slavery to the Great Migration* (Belknap Press, 2003); Herbert Shapiro, *White Violence and Black Response: From Reconstruction to Montgomery* (University of Massachusetts Press, 1988); Carole Emberton, *Beyond Redemption: Race, Violence, and the American South after the Civil War* (University of Chicago Press, 2013); and Michael W. Fitzgerald, *The Union League Movement in the Deep South: Politics and Agricultural Change During Reconstruction* (Louisiana State University Press, 2000).

6. Crosby, MSKH, 1134.

7. Crosby, MSKH, 1136.

8. Carl Schurz, "What Has Been Accomplished" in "Condition of the South" in Reports of Committees of the House of Representatives. Report on the Condition of the South, 39th Congress, Senate, 1st Session, No. 2, Message of the President of the United States, 1865, http://www.gutenberg.org/cache/epub/8872/pg8872-images.html. Hereafter "Condition of the South (1865)."

9. Schurz, "Prospective—The Reactionary Tendency," in "Condition of the South (1865)."

10. Schurz, "Returning Loyalty," in "Condition of the South (1865)."

11. General Thomas Kilby Smith to Carl Schurz, Sept. 14, 1865, Report Number 9 in "Condition of the South (1865)."

12. J. H. Weber, Freedmen's Bureau for Western District, Mississippi, to Carl Schurz, Sept. 28, 1865, in Report Number 26 in "Condition of the South (1865)."

13. Edwin M. Stanton, Message of the President of the United States and Accompanying Documents to the Two Houses of Congress at the Commencement, 40th Congress, 3rd Session, Report of the Secretary of War (Government Printing Office, 1868).

14. See Nancy Scheper-Hughes, "Small Wars and Invisible Genocides," *Social Science Medicine* 43, no. 5 (1996): 889. This is supported by research and analysis in peace and conflict studies of the violence that typically follows the clashing of armies and navies. In calling white southerners' attacks on emancipated people a war after the Civil War, I also take some guidance from George C. Rable's examination of the continuation of violence in *But There Was No Peace: The Role of Violence in the Politics of Reconstruction* (University of Georgia Press, 1984).

15. U.S. Congress, 42nd Congress, 2nd session, *Report of the Joint Select Committee to Inquire Into the Condition of Affairs in the Late Insurrectionary States* (Government Printing Office, 1872).

16. Attica Locke, *Bluebird, Bluebird* (Mulholland Books/Little, Brown 2017), 182.

17. William A. Dunning, *Reconstruction: Political and Economic, 1865–1877* (Harper and Brothers, 1907).

18. W. E. B. Du Bois called Reconstruction a "splendid failure." In doing so he acknowledged the transition from slavery to free labor, the expansion of American democracy, and the federal government and the nation's failure to enforce laws protecting Black people's lives and freedoms. Du Bois, "The Propaganda of History," in *Black Reconstruction in America: An Essay Toward a History of the Part Which Black Folk Played in the Attempt to Reconstruct Democracy in America, 1860–1880*, 1998 ed. (Free Press, 1935), 711–30.

19. To center families' stories, I performed a close textual reading of African Americans' testimonies and interviews prioritizing targeted people's accounts of "visits." Black witnesses' interviews at the Klan hearings run between half a single-spaced page to fifteen pages that include questions lawmakers asked and survivors' answers that stenographers recorded. The WPA-sponsored interviews run a bit longer but typically include less information about specific night-riding attacks, except, for example, when interviewees had experienced attacks personally and they were speaking to Black interviewers. Survivors' answers were also edited and revised by the interviewers or their supervisors at the Federal Writers' Slave Narrative Project, which aggregated and then

published the interviews. For more on the editing and internal fights over how interviewees' stories would be published, see Catherine A. Stewart, *Long Past Slavery: Representing Race in the Federal Writers' Project* (University of North Carolina Press, 2016).

20. Svetlana Alexievich, *Last Witnesses: An Oral History of the Children of World War II* (Penguin Random House, 2019); and *Voices from Chernobyl: The Oral History of a Nuclear Disaster* (Dalkey Archive Press, 2015).

21. Many survivors' stories are in fragments. Witnesses and interviewees were relying on memories of often traumatic events. Interview conditions at the hearings and with white WPA interviewers weren't always ideal. In the legal forums of the Reconstruction era, some witnesses were subpoenaed and were reluctant to provide information for fear of reprisal. They were asked invasive questions and were interrupted with often rude derailing questions. In the 1930s, some white WPA interviewers pressured vulnerable, elderly interviewees to minimize the harms white people had inflicted on them. Both record sets exist because courageous Black southerners stepped forward to tell their stories themselves. Witnesses and interviewees resisted white people's attempts to silence Black people's construction of their counternarrative of emancipation and Reconstruction.

22. I used the lens of critical trauma studies to interpret testimonies and interviews. Critical trauma studies is an interdisciplinary field with roots in psychology and anthropology that involves the examination of the human consequences of violence, namely the physical and psychological injuries or wounds that humans endure as a result of experiences that range from emotional abuse and physical attacks to war and genocide. This framework recognizes trauma as a universal experience and seeks to understand it.

Critical trauma studies showed me that individuals respond differently to traumatic events and that human recognition of psychological suffering extends back through history and predates scholarly research on it. It helped me see that Black survivors of atrocities during Reconstruction understood full well how devastating this violence was and had their own language for describing it. That knowledge helped me close the language gap between past and present descriptions of trauma. It also helped me navigate survivors' streams of consciousness and fragmented memories, and interviewers' interruptions, to understand what survivors understood about attacks and wanted known about them. This framework helped me avoid agonizing about what wasn't there. Gaps in the record were there for a reason: the survivor wasn't asked specific questions about their or their kin's psychological suffering or it did not occur to them to discuss it, they did not want to speak about it, there were gaps in their memories, or they simply did not have language to describe what happened to them. In sum, critical trauma studies scholarship has helped me understand how victims experienced racist violence, how they made sense of it and a world reshaped by it, and if and how they gave voice to what had happened to them and what they thought this violence had done to them. It persuaded me to offer careful speculation on the silences in survivors' accounts and translate survivors' descriptions using concepts of suffering that resonate with readers today.

See Judith Herman, *Trauma and Recovery: The Aftermath of Violence—From Domestic Abuse to Political Terror* (Basic Books, 1992); Bessel van der Kolk, *The Body Keeps the Score: Brain, Mind, and Body in the Healing of Trauma* (Penguin Books, 2015); Veena Das, et al., eds., *Violence and Subjectivity* (University of California Press, 2000); Arthur Kleinman, Veena Das, and Margaret Lock, eds., *Social Suffering* (University of California Press, 1997); Veena Das, et al., eds., *Remaking a World: Violence, Social Suffering, and Recovery* (University of California Press, 2001); and Cathy Caruth, *Unclaimed Experience: Trauma, Narrative, and History* (Johns Hopkins University Press, 1996).

23. When responding to questions about wealth loss from night-riding strikes, numerous witnesses mentioned census enumerators' recent assessments of their property. That inspired me to search census records for the families of people who testified at the Klan hearings. I discovered about half of the witnesses. Enumerators had visited them just before they were attacked or just afterward. There were matching names, to be sure, but other factors—age, location, etc.—were off. So I tried to only use records for people who met at least two criteria of those testifying at the hearings. The data failed to yield answers to every question I had. But, for witnesses who provided only bare details about their lives, if they had been enumerated before they were attacked, then the 1870 census filled out the complexity of their full personhood. Names, ages, color, state of literacy, birthplaces, and occupations helped me flesh out some of the pertinent details of survivors' lives. I even obtained more accurate data on property and crop cultivation. Sometimes I even found the signatures and X marks in oath books listing the names of Georgia men who had been attacked for voting. I also found a few marriage certificates, Freedman's Bank accounts, and homestead records, indicating savings accrued and property acquired. If I found them in subsequent censuses, then I was able to get a sense of survivors' displacement from their home communities.

24. For discussion of the climate that produces "state sanctioned and/or extralegal production of a group differentiated vulnerability to premature death," see Ruth Wilson Gilmore, *Golden Gulag: Prisons, Surplus, Crisis, and Opposition in Globalizing California* (University of California Press, 2007), 247; and Christina Sharpe, *In the Wake: On Blackness and Being* (Duke University Press, 2016).

25. I draw this framing of testifying as a resistance to shame and as a form of self-regard and self-respect from Toni Morrison, "The Source of Self-Regard," in *The Source of Self-Regard: Selected Essays, Speeches, and Meditations* (Vintage, 2019), 318–20; and David Shapiro, "The Tortured, Not the Torturers, Are Ashamed," *Social Research* 70, no. 4 (2003): 1141–44. Koritha A. Mitchell invokes this long history of African American protest in her concept "homemade citizenship" in *From Slave Cabins to the White House: Homemade Citizenship in African American Culture* (University of Illinois Press, 2020).

26. For a larger discussion of testimonies' circulatory networks and survivors' search for adequate witnesses to their testimonies, see Leigh Gilmore, *Tainted Witness: Why We Doubt What Women Say About Their Lives* (Columbia University Press, 2017), 2–6, 16.

27. Saidiya V. Hartman discusses "the time of slavery" being the period when chattel slavery was protected by law and its afterlife. See *Lose Your Mother: A Journey Along the Atlantic Slave Route* (Farrar, Straus, and Giroux, 2008), 133.

CHAPTER 1: WE HAD TO PICK OURSELVES UP

1. Francis S. Lyon, Oct. 26, 1871, U.S. Congress, 42nd Congress, 2nd session, *Report of the Joint Select Committee to Inquire Into the Condition of Affairs in the Late Insurrectionary States: Alabama* (Government Printing Office, 1872) [hereafter ALKH], 1412.

2. The census records this family as Lyons but at the hearings, they were identified as Lyon. Eliza Lyon, Oct. 24, 1871, ALKH, 1262–71; Abe and Eliza Lyon, U.S. Census, Choctaw County, Alabama, population schedule, 1870. Digital Image. Ancestry.com. April 1, 2015.

3. Andrew Cathcart, July 27, 1871, U.S. Congress, 42nd Congress, 2nd session, *Report of the Joint Select Committee to Inquire Into the Condition of Affairs in the Late Insurrectionary States: South Carolina* (Government Printing Office, 1872) [hereafter SCKT for trials and SCKH for the Klan hearings], 1591–97; 1870 U.S. Census, York County, South Carolina, population schedule. Digital Image. Ancestry.com. April 1, 2015.

4. Joseph Brown, Oct. 24, 1871, U.S. Congress, 42nd Congress, 2nd session, *Report of the Joint Select Committee to Inquire Into the Condition of Affairs in the Late Insurrectionary States: Georgia* (Government Printing Office, 1872) [hereafter GAKH], 860–61; Mary Brown, Oct. 21, 1871, GAKH, 375–77; Caroline Benson, Oct. 21, 1871, GAKH, 386–88; and 1870 U.S. Census, White County, Georgia, population schedule. Digital Image. Ancestry.com. April 1, 2015.

5. Eric Foner, *The Second Founding: How the Civil War and Reconstruction Remade the Constitution* (W. W. Norton, 2019).

6. Enslaved people had to learn what being enslaved meant and societies in which enslaved people lived had to be reorganized to accommodate nearly absolute deference to the master's will. See Orlando Patterson, *Slavery and Social Death: A Comparative Study* (Harvard University Press, 1982). See the "chattel principle" in Walter Johnson, *Soul by Soul: Life Inside the Antebellum Slave Market* (Harvard University Press, 1999), 21.

7. Frederick Douglass, *Narrative of the Life of Frederick Douglass, an American Slave* (Barnes & Noble Classics Series, 2003), 51–52.

8. Ashraf Rushdy and others have pushed against Sigmund Freud's limitation of primal scenes to sexual situations. "The primal scene need not be sexual," he explains. "[I]t need only be of such significance that an individual would recollect an episode, and not another, at a critical moment when driven to re-evaluate her or his life." Ashraf H. A. Rushdy, "'Rememory': Primal Scenes and Constructions in Toni Morrison's Novels," *Contemporary Literature* 31, no. 3 (1990): 303. See also Saidiya V. Hartman, *Scenes of Subjection: Terror, Slavery, and Self-Making in Nineteenth-Century America* (Oxford University Press, 1997). These scenes play out in the WPA narratives, too. The difference is that most interviewees were asked direct questions about Ku Klux.

9. Peter Bruner, Federal Writers' Slave Narrative Project, Volume 7, Kentucky. Kindle edition.

10. John Finnely, Federal Writers' Slave Narrative Project, Volume 16, Part 2, Texas. Kindle edition.

11. Mary Anderson, Federal Writers' Slave Narrative Project, Volume 11, Part 1, North Carolina. Kindle edition.

12. Robert Falls, Federal Writers' Slave Narrative Project, Volume 15, Tennessee. Kindle edition.

13. Jeffrey Kauffman, ed., *Loss of the Assumptive World: A Theory of Traumatic Loss* (Routledge, 2013), 1.

14. Samuel Childress to Robert Hamilton, Nov. 29, 1865, in C. Peter Ripley, ed., *The Black Abolitionist Papers, Volume 5: The United States, 1859–1865* (University of North Carolina Press, 2015), 405.

15. Hannah Tutson, Nov. 10, 1871, U.S. Congress, 42nd Congress, 2nd session, *Report of the Joint Select Committee to Inquire Into the Condition of Affairs on the Late Insurrectionary States: Florida* (Government Printing Office, 1872) [hereafter FLKH], 60.

16. Jim Downs, *Sick from Freedom: African-American Illness and Suffering During the Civil War and Reconstruction* (Oxford University Press, 2012), 3. See also Leslie A. Schwalm, "Surviving Wartime Emancipation: African Americans and the Cost of Civil War," *Journal of Law, Medicine & Ethics* 39, no. 1 (2011): 21–27.

17. Andrew F. Smith, *Starving the South: How the North Won the Civil War* (St. Martin's, 2011).

18. John Cameron, Federal Writers' Slave Narrative Project, Volume 9, Mississippi. Kindle edition.

19. See David Blight, *Race and Reunion: The Civil War in American Memory* (Belknap Press, 2002); and Caroline Janney, *Remembering the Civil War: Reunion and the Limits of Reconciliation* (University of North Carolina Press, 2013). The historian Manisha Sinha has detailed white northerners' and westerners' apathy toward enslaved people and disinterest in their plight during the antebellum period. See Sinha, Part I: The First Wave, in *The Slave's Cause: A History of Abolition* (Yale University Press, 2017), 9–191. This white indifference did not completely dissipate after the war despite some white northerners' support for civil rights. In many instances it intensified during the rights revolution. See also Stacey L. Smith, *Freedom's Frontier: California and the Struggle for over Unfree Labor, Emancipation, and Reconstruction* (University of North Carolina Press, 2013) and Kate Masur, *Until Justice Be Done: America's First Civil Rights Movement, from the Revolution to Reconstruction* (W. W. Norton, 2021).

20. H. R. Brinkerhoff, 52nd U.S. Colored Infantry, July 8, 1865, Report Number 24, in Carl Schurz, Report on the Condition of the South, 39th Congress, Senate, 1st Session, No. 2, Message of the President of the United States, 1865, http://www.gutenberg.org/cache /epub/8872/pg8872-images.html. Hereafter "Condition of the South (1865)."

21. Tom Holland, Federal Writers' Slave Narrative Project, Volume 16, Part 2, Texas. Kindle edition.

22. Anna Parkes, Federal Writers' Slave Narrative Project, Volume 4, Part 3, Georgia. Kindle edition.

23. Nancy Smith, Federal Writers' Slave Narrative Project, Volume 4, Part 3, Georgia. Kindle edition.

24. Rhody Holsell, Federal Writers' Slave Narrative Project, Volume 10, Missouri. Kindle edition.

25. Richard H. Steckel, "A Peculiar Population: The Nutrition, Health, and Mortality of American Slaves from Childhood to Maturity," *Journal of Economic History* 46, no. 3 (September 1986): 721–41; and Walter Johnson, *River of Dark Dreams: Slavery and Empire in the Cotton Kingdom* (Belknap Press, 2013), 219–20, 342.

26. Falls, Federal Writers' Slave Narrative Project, Tennessee.

27. Downs, *Sick from Freedom*.

28. Holland, Federal Writers' Slave Narrative Project, Texas.

29. For my framework for using and interpreting the WPA narratives, see Stephanie Shaw, "Using the WPA Ex-Slave Narratives to Study the Impact of the Great Depression," *Journal of Southern History* 69, no. 3 (2003): 623–58.

30. Falls, Federal Writers' Slave Narrative Project, Tennessee.

31. "Newspaper Account of a Meeting between Black Religious Leaders and Union Military Authorities," January 12, 1865, http://www.freedmen.umd.edu/savmtg.htm, accessed February 2020.

32. Paul A. Cimbala and Randall M. Miller, eds., *The Freedmen's Bureau and Reconstruction: Reconsiderations* (Fordham University Press, 1999); and Michael Perman, *Emancipation and Reconstruction, 1862–1879* (Harlan Davidson, 1987).

33. "Committee of Freedmen on Edisto Island, South Carolina, to the Freedmen's Bureau Commissioner, October 20 or 21, 1865," in *Freedom: A Documentary History of Emancipation, 1861–1867, Series 3: Volume I: Land and Labor, 1865*, ed. Steven Hahn, et al. (University of North Carolina Press, 2017), 442–44.

34. Samuel Childress to Robert Hamilton, Nov. 29, 1865, in Ripley, *Black Abolitionist*, 405.

35. W. A. Poillon, Captain, Assistant Superintendent, Mobile Freedmen's Bureau, to Carl Schurz, Sept. 9, 1865, Report Number 22 in "Condition of the South (1865)."

36. For details on this process, see Laura F. Edwards, *A Legal History of the Civil War and Reconstruction: A Nation of Rights* (Cambridge University Press, 2015), 131.

37. Childress to Hamilton, 405.

38. "Committee of Freedmen on Edisto Island."

39. William Lawrence, Civil Rights Speech, Congressional Globe, House of Representatives, April 7, 1866, 2, http://onlinebooks.library.upenn.edu/webbin/book/lookupid?key =ha012504195, accessed February 2022.

40. See V. P. Franklin, *Black Self-Determination: A Cultural History of African-American Resistance* (Lawrence Hill Books, 1992).

41. H. R. Brinkeroff, July 8, 1865, in Schurz, "Condition of the South (1865)."

42. Samuel Thomas, Mississippi Bureau Agent, to Carl Schurz, Sept. 28, 1865, Report Number 27 in "Condition of the South (1865)."

43. Poillon to Schurz.

44. General Thomas Kilby Smith to Carl Schurz, Sept. 14, 1865, Report Number 9 in "Condition of the South (1865)."

45. Hannah Davidson, Federal Writers' Slave Narrative Project, Volume 12, Ohio. Kindle edition. For similar cases, see Karin L. Zipf, "Reconstructing 'Free Woman': African-American Women, Apprenticeship, and Custody Rights During Reconstruction," *Journal of Women's History* 12, no. 1 (2000): 8–31; and Mary Niall Mitchell, *Raising Freedom's Child: Black Children and Visions of the Future after Slavery* ((New York University Press, 2008).

46. Georgia Telfair, Federal Writers' Slave Narrative Project, Volume 4, Part 4, Georgia. Kindle edition.

47. Tera W. Hunter, *Bound in Wedlock: Slave and Free Black Marriage in the Nineteenth Century* (Belknap Press, 2017). Research on families reveals them to be incredibly violent institutions, filled with tensions and rivalries that rarely fit in the frames of people drawing portraits of them or appear in archival records. See Marianne Hirsch, *Family Frames: Photography, Narrative, and Postmemory* (Harvard University Press, 1997); and Patricia Hill Collins, "It's All in the Family: Intersections of Gender, Race, and Nation," *Hypatia* 13, no. 3 (1998): 62–82.

48. To understand the depths of the domestic slave trade and its implications for African American families, capitalism, and the nation, see Edward E. Baptist, "'Stol' and Fetched Here': Enslaved Migration, Ex-Slave Narratives, and Vernacular History," in *New Studies in the History of American Slavery*, eds. Edward E. Baptist and Stephanie M. H. Camp (University of Georgia Press, 2006), 243–74; and Edward E. Baptist, *The Half Has Never Been Told: Slavery and the Making of American Capitalism* (Basic Books, 2014).

49. Documentation of antebellum and wartime freedom seekers' endeavors to return south or use abolitionist networks to recover kin can be found in Sydney Nathans, *To Free a Family: The Journey of Mary Walker* (Harvard University Press, 2012).

50. For African Americans' search for family, see Heather Andrea Williams, *Help Me to Find My People: The African American Search for Family Lost in Slavery* (University of North Carolina Press, 2012). See also Dylan C. Penningroth, *The Claims of Kinfolk: African American Property and Community in the Nineteenth-Century South* (University of North Carolina Press, 2003); and Anthony Kaye, *Joining Places: Slave Neighborhoods in the Old South* (University of North Carolina Press, 2007).

51. Mary Armstrong, Federal Writers' Slave Narrative Project, Volume 16, Part 1, Texas. Kindle edition; and Abigail Cooper, "'Away I'm Goin' to Find My Mamma': Self-Emancipation, Migration, and Kinship in Refugee Camps in the Civil War Era," *Journal of African American History* 102, no. 4 (2017): 444–67.

52. John William De Forest, *A Union Officer in the Reconstruction*, quoted in Williams, *Help Me to Find My People*, 141.

53. "A Long Lost Mother," *Evansville Journal*, republished in the *Owensboro Monitor*, May 6, 1874, Information Wanted, https://informationwanted.org/items/show/3544, accessed February 26, 2022.

54. "Wedding after Forty-Three Years of Separation," *Highland Weekly News* (Hillsboro, Ohio), Aug. 14, 1873; Information Wanted, https://informationwanted.org/items/show/3565, accessed February 26, 2022.

55. Quoted in Williams, *Help Me to Find My People*, 161.

56. Poillon to Carl Schurz.

57. See, for example, Rebecca J. Fraser, *Courtship and Love among the Enslaved in North Carolina* (University Press of Mississippi, 2007); and Hunter, *Bound in Wedlock.*

58. Kaye, *Joining Places*, 51–82.

59. African Americans' fight for social rights involved gaining unrestricted access to public spaces and public services, including schools, leisure spaces, and public transportation. Civil rights, when read through the lens of the Civil Rights Act of 1866, involved universal guarantees for all citizens to "handle their business, primarily economic business, of their own lives." Political rights were of a higher order, denoting privileges like equal protection, due process, and privileges and immunities, as indicated by the Fourteenth Amendment. For discussions on the relationship between civil, political, and social rights and the accompanying protections, see Edwards, *A Legal History*, 108–9 and 31–32; Kate Masur, *An Example for All The Land: Emancipation and the Struggle over Equality in Washington, D. C.* (University of North Carolina Press, 2010); and Masur, *Until Justice Be Done.*

60. The history of citizenship protections for African Americans being linked to marriage dates back to the Civil War with congressional debates over enlisting male freedom seekers in the Union Army. See Amy Dru Stanley, "Instead of Waiting for the Thirteenth Amendment: The War Power, Slave Marriage, and Inviolate Human Rights," *The American Historical Review* 115, no. 3 (2010): 732–65.

61. Mary J. Farmer, "'Because They Are Women': Gender and the Virginia Freedmen's Bureau's 'War on Dependency,'" in Cimbala and Miller, eds., *The Freedmen's Bureau and Reconstruction*; Tera W. Hunter, *To 'Joy My Freedom: Southern Black Women's Lives and Labors after the Civil War* (Harvard University Press, 1997); Gerald David Jaynes, *Branches Without Roots: Genesis of the Black Working Class in the American South, 1862–1882* (Oxford University Press, 1986); and Leslie A. Schwalm, *A Hard Fight for We: Women's Transition from Slavery to Freedom in South Carolina* (University of Illinois Press, 1997).

62. See Laura F. Edwards, "Status Without Rights: African Americans and the Tangled History of Law and Governance in the Nineteenth-Century U.S. South," *American Historical Review* 112, no. 2 (2007): 365–93. Edwards argues that African Americans "turned issues that had been considered social rights into civil rights." Edwards, *A Legal History*, 131.

63. Elizabeth Regosin, *Freedom's Promise: Ex-Slave Families and Citizenship in the Age of Emancipation* (University of Virginia Press, 2002). For additional work on gendered transitions, see Jessica Millward, "'The Relics of Slavery': Interracial Sex and Manumission in the American South," *Frontiers: A Journal of Women Studies* 31, no. 3 (2010): 22–30; Thelma Jennings, "'Us Colored Women Had to Go Through a Plenty':

Sexual Exploitation of African-American Slave Women," *Journal of Women's History* 1, no. 3 (1990): 45–74; and Jim Cullen, "'I's a Man Now': Gender and African-American Men," in *Divided Houses: Gender and the Civil War*, eds. Catherine Clinton and Nina Silber (Oxford University Press, 1992), 76–91.

64. Hunter, *Bound in Wedlock*, 215.
65. See Brenda E. Stevenson, *Life in Black and White: Family and Community in the Slave South* (Oxford University Press, 1996), 161–62. For discussion of this shift to patrifocal and patrilocal, see Sylviane A. Diouf, *Dreams of Africa in Alabama: The Slave Ship Clotilda and the Story of the Last Africans Brought to America* (Oxford University Press, 2007).
66. Self-reported carpenters included Henry Reed, Nov. 11, 1871, FLKH, 112; Joseph Nelson, Nov. 11, 1871, FLKH, 136–38; and Monday Floyd, Nov. 4, 1871, GAKH, 1060.
67. Samuel Stewart, October 26, 1871, GAKT, 591.
68. Other men who identified as blacksmiths included Alfred Wright, July 20, 1871, SCKH, 1173–75, and U.S. Census, Union County, South Carolina, population schedule, 1880. Digital Image. Ancestry.com. April 1, 2015; and Smith Watley, Oct. 17, 1871, ALKH, 1004–06, and U.S. Census, Coosa County, Alabama, population schedule, 1870. Digital Image. Ancestry.com. April 1, 2015.
69. Patrick W. Tanner, July 7, 1871, SCKH, 407.
70. Columbus Jeter, Oct. 25, 1871, GAKH, 561.
71. Many people sharecropped but not all of them self-reported this at the Klan hearings. Scipio Eager was one witness who specified in his testimony that he was sharecropping. Oct. 27, 1871, GAKH, 670.
72. Henry Hamlin, Oct. 12, 1871, ALKH, 857; Essic Harris, July 1, 1871, U.S. Congress, 42nd Congress, 2nd session, *Report of the Joint Select Committee to Inquire Into the Condition of Affairs in the Late Insurrectionary States: North Carolina* (Government Printing Office, 1872) [hereafter NCKH], 86–102; and Isham McCrary, July 8, 1871, SCKH, 538–39.
73. See Pinckney Dodd, July 7, 1871, SCKH, 416–18; and Eager, 670.
74. Hannah Flournoy, Oct. 24, 1871, GAKH, 533.
75. Joshua Hairston, Nov. 13, 1871, MSKH, 798.
76. Mary Brown, Oct. 21, 1871, GAKH, 375–77.
77. Hunter, *To 'Joy My Freedom*; and Thavolia Glymph, *Out of the House of Bondage: The Transformation of the Plantation Household* (Cambridge University Press, 2008).
78. Historical fiction was helpful for reminding me of the seemingly mundane functions of how African Americans transitioned to freedom. See Margaret Walker, *Jubilee* (Mariner Books, 1999); J. California Cooper, *Family* (Anchor Books, 1991) and *The*

Wake of the Wind (Random House, 1999); Leonard Pitts Jr., *Freeman* (Agate Bolden, 2012); Lalita Tademy, *Red River* (Grand Central Publishing, 2008) and *Citizens Creek* (Atria Books, 2014). See also Toni Morrison, *Beloved: A Novel*, 2nd ed. (Vintage, 2004); and Sherley Anne Williams, *Dessa Rose* (Harper Perennial, 1986; reprinted, 2010). Also, literary historians threw needed light on literary and historical imaginations. See Angelyn Mitchell, *The Freedom to Remember: Narrative, Slavery, and Gender in Contemporary Black Women's Fiction* (Rutgers University Press, 2002); and Karla Holloway's work on the literary imagination, *Private Bodies, Public Texts: Race, Gender, and a Cultural Bioethics* (Duke University Press, 2011), 107.

79. "Forty Years in the Wilderness," in Margaret Walker's 1966 novel *Jubilee*, was useful for reminding me of the details of post-emancipation life and helping me stretch the field of view. Walker, 327, 30.

80. Daniel Lipscomb, July 7, 1871, SCKH, 430.

81. Wright, SCKH, 1176.

82. Simon Elder, Oct. 28, 1871, GAKH, 731; Mary Elder, Oct. 28, 1871, GAKH, 733–4. The Measuring Worth tool calculates the relative worth for an 1870 wage or income of $2,370 as ranging between $434,336 and $719,389 in labor earnings and $887,285 in relative income in today's dollars.

83. For overviews of these fights, see, for example, Leon F. Litwack, *Been in the Storm So Long: The Aftermath of Slavery* (Vintage, 1980); Eric Foner, *Nothing but Freedom: Emancipation and Its Legacy* (Louisiana State University Press, 1983) and *Reconstruction: America's Unfinished Revolution, 1863–1877* (Harper and Row, 1988); and Du Bois, *Black Reconstruction*. For debates about land, see Steven Hahn, et al., eds., *Freedom: A Documentary History of Emancipation, 1861–1867 Series 3, Volumes 1 & 2* (University of North Carolina Press, 2008); and Penningroth, *The Claims of Kinfolk*. For fights over labor, see Schwalm, *A Hard Fight for We*; James L. Roark, *Masters Without Slaves: Southern Planters in the Civil War and Reconstruction* (W. W. Norton, 1977); and Julie Saville, *The Work of Reconstruction: From Slave to Wage Laborer in South Carolina, 1860–1870* (Cambridge University Press, 1994).

84. W. B. Stickney, Lieutenant and Assistant Superintendent of Freedmen (Shreveport), to Carl Schurz, Aug. 26, 1865, Report Number 33 in "Condition of the South (1865)."

85. Stickney, "Condition of the South (1865)."

86. Hunter, *To 'Joy My Freedom*.

87. Hunter, *To 'Joy My Freedom*.

88. Hunter, *To 'Joy My Freedom*; Amy Dru Stanley, *From Bondage to Contract: Wage Labor, Marriage, and the Market in the Age of Slave Emancipation* (Cambridge University Press, 1998); Glymph, *Out of the House of Bondage*; Susan E. O'Donovan, *Becoming Free in*

the Cotton South (Harvard University Press, 2007); Litwack, *Been in the Storm So Long*, 336–86.

89. See Sharla M. Fett, *Working Cures: Healing, Health, and Power on Southern Slave Plantations* (University of North Carolina Press, 2002); Harriet A. Washington, *Medical Apartheid: The Dark History of Medical Experimentation on Black Americans from Colonial Times to the Present*, 1st ed. (Doubleday, 2006); Gretchen Long, *Doctoring Freedom: The Politics of African American Medical Care in Slavery and Emancipation* (University of North Carolina Press, 2012); and Adam Rothman, *Beyond Freedom's Reach: A Kidnapping in the Twilight of Slavery* (Harvard University Press, 2015), 36, 57–58.

90. Pauline Grice, Federal Writers' Slave Narrative Project, Volume 16, Part 2, Texas. Kindle edition.

91. For more, see Roger L. Ransom and Richard Sutch, *One Kind of Freedom: The Economic Consequences of Emancipation* (Cambridge University Press, 2001); and Edward Royce, *The Origins of Southern Sharecropping* (Temple University Press, 1993; reprinted 2010).

92. This was part of a longer process of returning land to Confederates. For more information about this process and its impact on African Americans, see Eric Foner, *A Short History of Reconstruction, 1863–1877*, 1st ed. (Harper & Row, 1990), 72–75, 78, 85.

93. See Adam Rothman, *Slave Country: American Expansion and the Origins of the Deep South* (Harvard University Press, 2005), "Jefferson's Horizon," 1–36.

94. See Claude F. Oubre, *Forty Acres and a Mule: The Freedmen's Bureau and Black Land Ownership* (Louisiana State University Press, 1978); and Walter Lynwood Fleming, *The Freedmen's* [sic] *Savings Bank: A Chapter in the Economic History of the Negro Race* (University of North Carolina Press, 1927; reprinted 2013).

95. Samuel Tutson, Nov. 10, 1871, FLKH, 54–59 and Hannah Tutson, FLKH, 59–65; Samuel and Hannah Tutson, 1885 Florida Census, St. Johns County, Florida, population schedule. Digital Image. Ancestry.com. April 1, 2015; Emanuel Fortune, Nov. 10, 1871, FLKH, 94–101; Emanuel and Sarah Fortune, 1870 U.S. Census, Duval County, Florida, population schedule. Digital Image. Ancestry.com. April 1, 2015.

96. Addie Vinson, Federal Writers' Slave Narrative Project, Volume 4, Part 4, Georgia. Kindle edition.

97. See Michael L. Lanza, *Agrarianism and Reconstruction Politics: The Southern Homestead Act* (Louisiana State University, 1990); and Keri Leigh Merritt, *Masterless Men: Poor Whites and Slavery in the Antebellum South* (Cambridge University Press, 2017).

98. Samuel Thomas, Mississippi Bureau Agent, to Carl Schurz, Sept. 28, 1865, Report Number 27 in "Condition of the South (1865)."

99. Vinson, Federal Writers' Slave Narrative Project, Georgia.

100. Hannah Tutson, FLKH, 60.

101. See Samuel Lawler, Feb. 26, 1870, ALKH, 1231; Robert Barbee, Feb. 26, 1870, ALKH, 1232; and Frank Bell, Feb. 28, 1870, ALKH, 1232.

102. bell hooks, "Homeplace," in *Yearning: Race, Gender, and Cultural Politics* (South End Press, 1990), 42–43; and Nell Irvin Painter, "Soul Murder and Slavery: Toward a Fully Loaded Cost-Accounting," in *Southern History Across the Color Line* (University of North Carolina Press, 2002), 15–35.

103. John Michael Vlach, " 'Snug Li'l House with Flue and Oven': Nineteenth-Century Reforms in Plantation Slave Housing," *Perspectives in Vernacular Architecture* 5, Gender, Class, and Shelter (1995): 118–29.

104. George Houston, Oct. 17, 1871, ALKH, 999–1000.

105. James H. Alston, Oct. 17, 1871, ALKH, 1018.

106. Anderson Ferrell, GAKH, Oct. 26, 1871, 618–22.

107. Farah Jasmine Griffin, *Read Until You Understand: The Profound Wisdom of Black Life and Literature* (W. W. Norton, 2021), 154.

108. Kiese Laymon, "The Worst of White Folks," in *How to Slowly Kill Yourself and Others in America* (Scribner, 2020), 139–49. For more on African Americans' belief in and work toward "racial destiny" after slavery, see Michele Mitchell, *Righteous Propagation: African Americans and Politics of Racial Destiny after Reconstruction* (University of North Carolina Press, 2004). Mitchell's book focuses on the post-Reconstruction period, but she makes clear that Black people's notions of their collective fate predate it.

109. Griffin, *Read Until You Understand*, 162–63.

110. Henry Giles, Oct 17, 1871, AKLH, 1010.

111. Telfair, Federal Writers' Slave Narrative Project, Georgia.

112. See Earl Lewis, *In Their Own Interests: Race, Class, and Power in Twentieth-Century Norfolk, Virginia* (University of California Press, 1991), 5, 90. In doing this work, Black southerners after slavery modeled their work on that of earlier free Black communities. See Ira Berlin, *Many Thousands Gone: The First Two Centuries of Slavery in North America* (Belknap Press, 1998); Leslie M. Harris, *In the Shadow of Slavery: African Americans in New York City, 1626–1863* (University of Chicago Press, 2004); James Oliver Horton and Lois E. Horton, *In Hope of Liberty: Culture, Community, and Protest among Northern Free Blacks* (Oxford University Press, 1996); and hooks, "Homeplace," 46–47.

113. Crosby, 1133; Jeter, 561.

114. I take this idea of community care from Griffin, *Read until You Understand*, 203.

115. See Wilma King, *Stolen Childhood: Slave Youth in Nineteenth-Century America*, 2nd ed., Blacks in the Diaspora (Indiana University Press, 2011), xx; Robin Bernstein, *Racial*

Innocence: Performing American Childhood from Slavery to Civil Rights (New York University Press, 2011).

116. For more about enslaved people's recollections of their childhoods, see King, *Stolen Childhood*; and Anya Jabour, *Topsy-Turvy: How the Civil War Turned the World Upside Down for Southern Children* (Rowman & Littlefield, 2010).

117. Telfair, Federal Writers' Slave Narrative Project, Georgia.

118. See Heather Andrea Williams, *Self-Taught: African American Education in Slavery and Freedom: African American Education in Slavery and Freedom* (University of North Carolina Press, 2009); Janet Cornelius, "'We Slipped and Learned to Read': Slave Accounts of the Literacy Process, 1830–1865," *Phylon* 44, no. 3 (1983): 171–86; James D. Anderson, *The Education of Blacks in the South, 1860–1935* (University of North Carolina Press, 1988); and Hilary Green, *Educational Reconstruction: African American Schools in the Urban South, 1865–1890* (Fordham University Press, 2016).

119. For a discussion on slaveholders' value of enslaved children, see Jennifer L. Morgan, *Laboring Women: Reproduction and Gender in New World Slavery* (University of Pennsylvania Press, 2004); Marie Jenkins Schwartz, *Birthing a Slave: Motherhood and Medicine in the Antebellum South* (Harvard University Press, 2006); and Daina Ramey Berry, *The Price for Their Pound of Flesh: The Value of the Enslaved from Womb to Grave in the Building of a Nation* (Beacon Press, 2017).

120. Doc Rountree, Nov. 14, 1871, FLKH, 280. Doc and Ellen Rountree, U.S. Census, Suwannee County, Florida, population schedule, 1870. Digital Image. Ancestry.com. April 1, 2015.

121. Rountree, FLKH, 280.

122. See Noralee Frankel, *Freedom's Women: Black Women and Families in Civil War Era Mississippi* (Indiana University Press, 1999), 79–122; Nancy Bercaw, *Gendered Freedoms: Race, Rights, and the Politics of Household in the Delta, 1861–1875* (University Press of Florida, 2003), 19–50 and 99–116; O'Donovan, *Becoming Free in the Cotton South*.

123. See Thomas C. Holt, *Black over White: Negro Political Leadership in South Carolina During Reconstruction* (University of Illinois Press, 1977); Howard N. Rabinowitz, *Southern Black Leaders of the Reconstruction Era* (University of Illinois Press, 1982); Foner, *Reconstruction*, 110–18 and 271–90; Leon F. Litwack and August Meier, *Black Leaders of the Nineteenth Century* (University of Illinois Press, 1991).

124. Frances Ellen Watkins Harper, "The Deliverance," https://www.poetrynook.com/poem/deliverance-1.

125. Laymon, "The Worst of White Folks."

126. See Carol Anderson, *White Rage: The Unspoken Truth of Our Racial Divide* (Bloomsbury, 2016).

127. See also Richard White, *The Republic for Which It Stands: The United States During Reconstruction and the Gilded Age, 1865–1896* (Oxford University Press, 2017).

CHAPTER 2: THE DEVIL WAS TURNED LOOSE

1. Caroline Benson, Oct. 21, 1871, U.S. Congress, 42nd Congress, 2nd session, *Report of the Joint Select Committee to Inquire Into the Condition of Affairs in the Late Insurrectionary States: Georgia* (Government Printing Office, 1872) [hereafter GAKH], 386–87; Pinckney Dodd, July 7, 1871, U.S. Congress, 42nd Congress, 2nd session, *Report of the Joint Select Committee to Inquire Into the Condition of Affairs in the Late Insurrectionary States: South Carolina* (Government Printing Office, 1872) [hereafter SCKH], 416–17; Jackson Surratt, July 8, 1871, SCKH, 520–21; and George Taylor, Oct. 6, 1871, U.S. Congress, 42nd Congress, 2nd session, *Report of the Joint Select Committee to Inquire Into the Condition of Affairs in the Late Insurrectionary States: Alabama* (Government Printing Office, 1872) [hereafter ALKH], 572–74.

2. James H. Alston, Oct. 17, 1871, ALKH, 1019; Essic Harris, July 1, 1871, U.S. Congress, 42nd Congress, 2nd session, *Report of the Joint Select Committee to Inquire Into the Condition of Affairs in the Late Insurrectionary States: North Carolina* (Government Printing Office, 1872) [hereafter NCKH], 87; Hannah Tutson, Nov. 10, 1871, U.S. Congress, 42nd Congress, 2nd session, *Report of the Joint Select Committee to Inquire Into the Condition of Affairs in the Late Insurrectionary States: Florida; and Miscellaneous Testimonies and Documents* (Government Printing Office, 1872) [hereafter FLKH], 59–65; Augustus Blair, Oct. 9, 1871, ALKH, 675–76; and Charlotte Fowler, July 6, 1871, SCKH, 388.

3. See Elaine Frantz Parsons, "The Roots of the Ku-Klux Klan in Pulaski, Tennessee," in *Ku-Klux: The Birth of the Klan During Reconstruction* (University of North Carolina Press, 2016), 27–71.

4. In his research on societies after conflict, Michael J. Boyle has identified three categories of violence that occur after episodes like war that I find useful for understanding anti-Black violence. Boyle, *Violence after War: Explaining Instability in Post-Conflict States* (Johns Hopkins University Press, 2014), 23–44.

5. John William De Forest, quoted in William A. Blair, *The Record of Murders and Outrages: Racial Violence and the Fight Over Truth at the Dawn of Reconstruction* (University of North Carolina Press, 2021), 31.

6. United Nations Definition of Genocide, https://www.un.org/en/genocideprevention /genocide.shtml.

7. In considering the UN definition of genocide, we cannot ignore the reality that this is a political and legal definition that on the one hand avoids trivializing mass atrocities but

on the other hand risks obscuring meaningful redress for those that don't rise to the level of a state-sponsored campaign like the Holocaust. The political bar is supposed to trigger international intervention and the legal bar means charges of intent need to stand up in an international court. So just because the international community doesn't intervene in mass killing events and just because mass murderers aren't tried before an international court does not mean state-sponsored or state-supported, if not state-directed, mass atrocities or genocidal violence has not happened. The UN definition is imperfect but it provides a framework to understand what mass atrocities and genocidal violence can look like, including events that predate the Holocaust like the deliberate targeting of the Native peoples across North America and the targeting of self-emancipating Black people during the Civil War and Black people during Reconstruction. For more on the legal and political debates about genocide and mass violence in the present day, see, Martha Minow, *Between Vengeance and Forgiveness: Facing History after Genocide and Mass Violence* (Beacon, 1998); Michael P. Broache and Kate Cronin-Fruman, "Does Type of Violence Matter for Interventions to Mitigate Mass Atrocities?" *Journal of Global Security Studies* 6, no. 1 (2021): 1–9; William Schabas, "National Courts Finally Begin to Prosecute Genocide, the 'Crime of Crimes,'" *Journal of International Criminal Justice* 1, no. 1 (2003), 39–63; and Erik Linstrum, "Facts about Atrocity: Reporting on Colonial Violence in Postwar Britain," *History Workshop Journal* 84 (2017): 108–27.

8. See Nancy Scheper-Hughes, "Small Wars and Invisible Genocides," *Social Science and Medicine* 43, no. 5 (1996): 889–90.

9. For a deconstruction of each of the components of "the right to have rights", see Stephanie DeGooyer, Alastair Hunt, Lida Maxwell, and Samuel Moyn, *The Right to Have Rights* (Verso, 2018).

10. Edwin M. Stanton, Message of the President of the United States and Accompanying Documents to the Two Houses of Congress at the Commencement, 40th Congress, 3rd Session, Report of the Secretary of War (Government Printing Office, 1868).

11. In her analysis of U.S. Army campaigns against the Native peoples of the Old Northwest, Barbara Alice Mann writes about the "fractal nature of successive waves of attacks" and how they can collectively point to genocide. See Mann, "Fractal Massacres in the Old Northwest: The Example of the Miamis," *Journal of Genocide Research* 15, no. 2 (2010): 167.

12. See Boyle, *Violence after War*; Mann, "Fractal Massacres in the Old Northwest"; and Scheper-Hughes, "Small Wars." For a history of military occupation of the South after the Civil War and what the historian Gregory P. Downs calls the "false peace" and "quasi-peace," see Downs, *After Appomattox: Military Occupation and the Ends of War* (Harvard University Press, 2015).

13. Mann analyzes the small-scale patterns of violence, specifically incessant waves of small massacres, that when seen in aggregate reveal a tidal wave of killing. Mann, "Fractal Massacres in the Old Northwest."

14. See Boyle, *Violence after War*. Because there does not appear to be evidence that night-riding strikes were coordinated across a state or even the former slaveholding region, it is probably best to think of right-wing whites' larger war as what Nancy Scheper-Hughes called a "small war." See Scheper-Hughes, "Small Wars." For the cumulative effect of successive attacks and how they can collectively point to geno-cide, see Mann, "Fractal Massacres in the Old Northwest." For a history of military occupation, debates over deployments, and changing troop levels, see Downs, *After Appomattox*.

15. Carl Schurz, "Prospective—The Reactionary Tendency," in "Condition of the South" in Report on the Condition of the South, 39th Congress, Senate, 1st Session, No. 2, Message of the President of the United States, 1865, http://www.gutenberg.org/cache /epub/8872/pg8872-images.html. Hereafter "Condition of the South (1865)."

16. Robert Dale Owen, *New York Tribune*, June 24, 1865, quoted in Blair, *The Record of Murders and Outrages*, 8.

17. I take my use of the language of "*Disunion*" from the Disunion series published in the Opinion section of the *New York Times* from 2011 to 2015, which marked the sesqui-centennial of the Civil War, https://www.nytimes.com/interactive/2014/opinion /disunion.html and from historian David Blight, who drew parallels between white Americans' resistance to Reconstruction's expansion of American democracy and the January 6, 2021, riot at the Capitol by calling the perpetrators "disunionists." "Impeachment: Catharsis and Impunity," *The United States of Anxiety* (podcast), February 15, 2021, https://www.wnycstudios.org/podcasts/anxiety/episodes/impeachment -catharsis-and-impunity

18. Poillon to Schurz, July 29, 1865.

19. Schurz, "The Freedman," in "Condition of the South (1865)."

20. Poillon to Schurz. See also Michael W. Fitzgerald, *Reconstruction in Alabama: From Civil War to Redemption in the Cotton South* (Louisiana State University Press, 2017).

21. Kenneth L. Marcus, "Accusation in a Mirror," *Loyola University Chicago Law Journal* 43 (2012): 359 and 361.

22. Marcus, quoting Catharine MacKinnon on the International Criminal Tribunal for Rwanda, "Accusation in a Mirror," 378.

23. Poillon to Carl Schurz, July 29, 1865.

24. Poillon to Carl Schurz, July 29, 1865.

25. Poillon to Carl Schurz, July 29, 1865.

26. J. M. Phipps, Acting Staff Surgeon at Post Hospital, to Carl Schurz, Aug. 21, 1865, Report Number 26 in "Condition of the South (1865)."

27. J. P. Houston, Provost Marshall U.S. forces at Selma, Alabama, to Carl Schurz, Aug. 22, 1865, Report Number 21 in "Condition of the South (1865)."

28. Weber to Carl Schurz, Report Number 26 in "Condition of the South (1865)."

29. Blair, *The Record of Murders and Outrages*, especially 6–29.

30. Daina Ramey Berry, *The Price for Their Pound of Flesh: The Value of the Enslaved from Womb to Grave in the Building of a Nation* (Beacon Press, 2017).

31. Schurz, "The True Problem.—Difficulties and Remedies," in "Condition of the South (1865)," http://www.gutenberg.org/cache/epub/8872/pg8872-images.html.

32. Schurz, "The Effects of Such Opinions, and General Treatment of the Negro," in "Condition of the South (1865)."

33. For a discussion of the vicious cycles spurred by revenge, see Minow, *Between Vengeance and Forgiveness*, 10.

34. See Beverly Greene Bond and Susan Eva O'Donovan, eds., *Remembering the Memphis Massacre: An American Story* (University of Georgia Press, 2020); Stephen Ash, *A Massacre in Memphis: The Race Riot that Shook the Nation One Year After the Civil War* (Hill and Wang, 2013); Hannah Rosen, *Terror in the Heart of Freedom: Citizenship, Sexual Violence, and the Meaning of Race in the Postemancipation South* (University of North Carolina Press, 2009); James G. Hollandsworth Jr., *An Absolute Massacre: The New Orleans Race Riot of July 30, 1866* (Louisiana State University Press, 2001); and Gilles Vandal, *The New Orleans Riot of 1866: Anatomy of a Tragedy* (University of Louisiana at Lafayette Press, 1983).

35. David Remnick, "How Henry Louis Gates, Jr., Helped Remake the Literary Canon," *The New Yorker*, February 19, 2022.

36. Thavolia Glymph, " 'I Could Not Come in Unless over Their Dead Bodies': Dignitary Offenses," *Law and History Review* 38, no. 3 (2020): 585–98.

37. See Allen W. Trelease, *White Terror: The Ku Klux Klan Conspiracy and Southern Reconstruction* (Louisiana State University Press, 1995).

38. Michael W. Fitzgerald, *The Union League Movement in the Deep South: Politics and Agricultural Change During Reconstruction* (Louisiana University Press, 2000).

39. Blair, "The Killing Fields of 1868," in *The Record of Murders and Outrages*, 80–105.

40. U.S. Congress, 43rd Congress, 2nd session, House of Representatives Report Number 261, Louisiana Affairs. Report of the Select Committee on that Portion of the President's Message Relating to the Condition of the South (Government Printing Office, 1875), 11–14, https://babel.hathitrust.org/cgi/pt?id=nyp.33433081764296&view=1up&seq=22&skin=2021. Hereafter House Report on the Condition of the South (1875).

41. Daniel Dennett, October 10, 1868, reprinted in Henry Clay Warmoth, *War, Politics, and Reconstruction: Stormy Days in Louisiana* (University of South Carolina Press, 2009), 68. For more on the Opelousas Massacre, see Michael J. Pfeifer, *Rough Justice: Lynching and American Society, 1874–1947* (University of Illinois Press, 2004).

42. House Report on the Condition of the South (1875), 11–14.

43. Anderson Ferrell, registry date, August 7, 1867, Georgia, Returns of Qualified Voters, and Reconstruction Oath Books, 1867–69, Digital Image. Ancestry.com. May 13, 2015; William Hampton Mitchell, registry date, July 9, 1867, Georgia, Returns of Qualified Voters, and Reconstruction Oath Books, 1867–69, Digital Image. Ancestry.com. May 13, 2015; Sampson Reed, registry date, August 1, 1867, Georgia, Returns of Qualified Voters, and Reconstruction Oath Books, 1867–69, Digital Image. Ancestry.com. May 13, 2015; Martin Anthony, registry date, June 22, 1867, Georgia, Returns of Qualified Voters, and Reconstruction Oath Books, 1867–69, Digital Image. Ancestry.com. May 13, 2015.

44. Essic Harris, NCKH, 86–102; A. Webster Shaffer, June 15, 1871, NCKH, 50; and Edward Carter, U.S. Congress, 42nd Congress, 2nd session, *Report of the Joint Select Committee to Inquire Into the Condition of Affairs in the Late Insurrectionary States: Mississippi* (Government Printing Office, 1872) [hereafter MSKH], 1083–85.

45. Thomas C. Holt, *Black over White: Negro Political Leadership in South Carolina During Reconstruction* (University of Illinois Press, 1977).

46. Robert Gleed, Nov. 10, 1871, MSKH, 718–28.

47. Charles Pearce, Nov. 13, 1871, FLKH, 165–76.

48. J. C. Gibbs, Nov. 13, 1871, FLKH, 220–24.

49. Boyle, *Violence after War*, 7. For more on the political dimensions of the postwar conflict over freedom, see Du Bois, *Black Reconstruction*; Foner, *Reconstruction*; Gregory P. Downs, *Declarations of Dependence: The Long Reconstruction of Popular Politics in the South, 1861–1908* (University of North Carolina Press, 2011); Heather Cox Richardson, *The Death of Reconstruction: Race, Labor, and Politics in the Post–Civil War North, 1865–1901* (Harvard University Press, 2001); Mark Wahlgren Summers, *The Ordeal of the Reunion: A New History of Reconstruction* (University of North Carolina Press, 2014), and *A Dangerous Stir: Fear, Paranoia, and the Making of Reconstruction* (University of North Carolina Press, 2009); Kenneth M. Stampp, *The Era of Reconstruction, 1865–1877* (Vintage Books, 1965); and Michael J. Pfeifer, *The Roots of Rough Justice: Origins of American Lynching* (University of Illinois Press, 2011).

50. Isaac Stier, Federal Writers' Slave Narrative Project, Volume 9, Mississippi, Kindle edition.

51. Hannah Arendt noted the paradox and danger of assuming human rights were a stand-in for citizenship rights. See Arendt, *The Origins of Totalitarianism* (Shocken Books, 1951), 179.

52. Laura F. Edwards, *A Legal History of the Civil War and Reconstruction: A Nation of Rights* (Cambridge University Press, 2015), 131.

53. Edwards, *A Legal History*, 143–45.

54. Du Bois, *Black Reconstruction*, 674.

55. W. B. Stickney, Lieutenant and Assistant Superintendent of Freedmen (Shreveport), to Carl Schurz, Aug. 26, 1865, Report Number 33 in "Condition of the South (1865)."

56. General Thomas Kilby Smith to Carl Schurz, Sept. 14, 1865, Report Number 9 in "Condition of the South (1865)."

57. Samuel Thomas, Mississippi Bureau Agent, to Carl Schurz, Sept. 28, 1865, Report Number 27 in "Condition of the South (1865)."

58. Tutson, FLKH, 64.

59. For information on the southern occupation, see Gregory P. Downs, *After Appomattox*. To learn more about Black defensive and offensive activities securing their freedom, start with Steven Hahn, *A Nation under Our Feet: Black Political Struggles in the Rural South, from Slavery to the Great Migration* (Belknap Press, 2003); and Fitzgerald, *The Union League Movement*.

60. Leanna Garrison, Oct. 27, 1871, GAKH, 666–67.

61. Philip Gourevitch, *We Wish to Inform You That Tomorrow We Will Be Killed with Our Families* (Farrar, Straus and Giroux, 1998), 95.

62. Keri Leigh Merritt, *Masterless Men: Poor Whites and Slavery in the Antebellum South* (Cambridge University Press, 2017).

63. Historians have discussed the diversity of the violence and the motives behind it. See, for example, Douglas R. Egerton, *The Wars of Reconstruction: The Brief, Violent History of America's Most Progressive Era* (Bloomsbury, 2013); and Carole Emberton, *Beyond Redemption: Race, Violence, and the American South after the Civil War* (University of Chicago Press, 2013). Elaine Frantz Parsons has revealed the hazards of relying solely on white conservative southern newspaper reports to understand why Klan groups attacked. They inserted a lot of misinformation about the Klan into the public spheres. See Parsons, *Ku-Klux*. See also Stephen W. Berry II, *All That Makes a Man: Love and Ambition in the Civil War South* (Oxford University Press, 2002). Michael Boyle has also argued that the mixing of political violence with criminal violence reflects the new factions that emerged following war. Boyle, *Violence after War*, 5–8.

64. Gleed, MSKH, 721.

65. Charlotte Fowler, July 6, 1871, SCKH, 386–92.

66. Fowler, 386.

67. Warren Jones, Oct. 27, 1871, GAKH, 689.

68. See Donald G. Nieman, *Black Freedom/White Violence, 1865–1900* (Garland, 1994); Hahn, *A Nation under Our Feet*; and George C. Rable, *But There Was No Peace: The Role of Violence in the Politics of Reconstruction* (University of Georgia Press, 1984).

69. Samuel Simmons, July 7, 1871, SCKH, 403–4.

70. Henry Latham, SCKT, 1859. Latham testified at the trials but not the hearings.

71. Clem Bowden, July 7, 1871, SCKH, 383.

72. For more on white women's violence, see Thavolia Glymph, *Out of the House of Bondage: The Transformation of the Plantation Household* (Cambridge University Press, 2008).

73. Diana Williams, June 15, 1869, ALKH, 1195.

74. Williams, 1195.

75. Elias Hill, July 25, 1871, SCKH, 1406–1414.

76. Henry Reed, Nov. 11, 1871, FLKH, 110.

77. Peter Cooper, Nov. 16, 1871, MSKH, 493.

78. Willis Smith, July 10, 1871, SCKH, 612.

79. Anderson Ferrell, Oct. 26, 1871, GAKH, 619.

80. U.S. Department of Justice, "Special Report: National Crime Victimization Survey: Victimization During Household Burglary," ed. Bureau of Justice Statistics (2010).

81. For a discussion of the limits of escaping captivity, see Roberta Culbertson, "Embodied Memory, Transcendence, and Telling: Recounting Trauma, Re-Establishing the Self," *New Literary History* 26, no. 1 (1995): 169–95; and Irene Rafanell and Hugo Gorringe, "Consenting to Domination?: Theorising Power, Agency and Embodiment with Reference to Caste," *The Sociological Review* 58, no. 4 (2010): 604–22.

82. Rosen, *Terror in the Heart of Freedom*, 179–221.

83. Edwards, *A Legal History*, 144.

84. See Marcelo M. Suárez-Orozco, "The Treatment of Children in the 'Dirty War': Ideology, State Terrorism, and the Abuse of Children in Argentina," in Nancy Scheper-Hughes and Philippe I. Bourgois, eds., *Violence in War and Peace* (Blackwell, 2003), 384.

85. William Coleman, Nov. 6, 1871, MSKH, 488.

86. Benson, GAKH, 387–88.

87. For more on the paradigms of captivity and coercion, see Judith Herman, *Trauma and Recovery: The Aftermath of Violence—From Domestic Abuse to Political Terror* (Basic Books, 1992), 74–96; Elaine Scarry, *The Body in Pain: The Making and Unmaking of the World* (Oxford University Press, 1985); and Marilyn Frye, "In and Out of Harm's Way: Arrogance and Love," in *The Politics of Reality: Essays in Feminist Theory* (The Crossing Press, 1983), 55–57.

88. Essic Harris, NCKH, 87.

89. Carol Anderson, *The Second: Race and Guns in a Fatally Unequal America* (Bloomsbury, 2021).

90. Harris, NCKH, 89.

91. Harris, NCKH, 89.

92. Harris, NCKH, 89.

93. Harris, NCKH, 90.

94. Augustus Blair, ALKH, 675.

95. Essic Harris, NCKH, 92.

96. Augustus Blair, ALKH, 675.

97. John Thommason, SCKT, 1947–49.

98. Peyton Lipscomb, Oct. 14, 1871, ALKH, 952.

99. Jerry Clowney, SCKT, 1859.

100. Henry Low, Nov. 11, 1871, ALKH, 1997.

101. Patrick W. Tanner, July 7, 1871, SCKH, 407.

102. William Henderson, Oct. 7, 1871, ALKH, 578–79.

103. Andy Reed, Oct. 27, 1871, GAKH, 645–46.

104. George Roper, Oct. 9, 1871, ALKH, 688.

105. Herman, *Trauma and Recovery*, 75.

106. Elias Thomson, July 7, 1871, SCKH, 410–16.

107. See Rosen, *Terror in the Heart of Freedom*; Lisa Cardyn, "Sexualized Racism/Gendered Violence: Outraging the Body Politic in the Reconstruction South," *Michigan Law Review* 100, no. 4 (2002): 675–867; Sharon Block, *Rape and Sexual Power in Early America* (University of North Carolina Press, 2006); Kim Murphy, *I Had Rather Die: Rape in the Civil War* (Coachlight Press, 2014); Estelle B. Freedman, *Redefining Rape: Sexual Violence in the Era of Suffrage and Segregation* (Harvard University Press, 2013); Adrienne Davis, "'Don't Let Nobody Bother Yo' Principle': The Sexual Economy of American Slavery," in *Sister Circle: Black Women and Work*, ed. Sharon Harley (Rutgers University Press, 2002), 103–27; and Catherine Clinton, "Bloody Terrain: Freedwomen, Sexuality, and Violence During Reconstruction," *Georgia Historical Quarterly* 76, no. 2 (Summer 1992): 313–32.

108. For analysis of the rape of Black girls and women during the Civil War and Reconstruction, see Crystal N. Feimster, "'What if I Am a Woman?': Black Women's Campaigns for Sexual Justice and Citizenship," in *The World the Civil War Made*, eds. Gregory P. Downs and Kate Masur (University of North Carolina Press, 2015), 249–68; Crystal N. Feimster, "Rape and Mutiny at Fort Jackson: Black Laundresses Testify in Civil War Louisiana," *Labor: Studies in Working-Class History* 19, no. 1 (2022): 11–31; and Kaisha Esty, "'I Told Him to Let Me Alone, That He Hurt Me': Black Women

and Girls and the Battle over Labor and Sexual Consent in Union-Occupied Territory," *Labor: Studies in Working-Class History* 19, no. 1 (2022): 32–51.

In 1951, when the Civil Rights Congress, under the leadership of William L. Patterson, penned "We Charge Genocide," a book-length petition to the United Nations charging the U.S. with genocide against Black Americans, racism-based sexual assault featured prominently in their presentation of evidence of genocidal violence and government inaction. See William L. Patterson, *We Charge Genocide: The Crime of Government against the Negro People* (International Publishers, 1970; reprinted 2020). For analysis of racism-based rape in the petition, see Denise Lynn, "Gender Violence as Genocide: The Rosa Lee Ingram Case and *We Charge Genocide* petition," *Radical Americas* 7, no. 1 (2022): 1–15.

109. See Claudia Card, "Rape as a Weapon of War," *Hypatia* 11, no. 4 (1996): 5–18.

110. Shaffer, NCKH, 36–37.

111. Harriet Hernandez, July 10, 1871, SCKH, 587.

112. Eli Barnes, Nov. 2, 1871, GAKH, 958. Eli and Juliann Barnes, 1880 U.S. Census, Hancock County, Georgia, population schedule.

113. For more on the racialized sexual economy tied to and extending out from slavery, see Davis, " 'Don't Let Nobody Bother Yo' Principle': The Sexual Economy of American Slavery," 115–16.

114. Card, "Rape as a Weapon of War," 7, 10.

115. Henry Hamlin, Oct. 12, 1871, ALKH, 857.

116. Hamlin, ALKH, 857.

117. Wiley Hargrove, Nov. 11, 1871, MSKH, 1993.

118. See Booker T. Washington, *Up from Slavery* (Penguin, 1986), 4. See also Julius S. Scott, *The Common Wind: Afro-American Currents in the Age of the Haitian Revolution* (Verso, 2018); and Manisha Sinha, *The Slave's Cause: A History of Abolition* (Yale University Press, 2017*).

119. Jennifer Harford Vargas, "Novel Testimony: Alternative Archives in Edwidge Danticat's *The Farming of Bones*," *Callaloo* 37, no. 5 (2014): 1162, 1166–67.

120. Marcelo M. Suárez-Orozco, "Speaking of the Unspeakable: Toward a Psychosocial Understanding of Responses to Terror," *Ethos* 18, no. 1 (1990): 353–83.

121. Hilliard Bush, Oct. 27, 1871, GAKH, 685.

122. Barbara Alice Mann, in "Fractal Massacres in the Old Northwest" (by which she means the Miami people of Indiana in what was known from 1787 to 1803 as the Northwest Territory), writes that genocidal violence takes place in multiple forms—bursts of killing as seen in the Holocaust and Rwanda and in miniature where the killing occurs all the same but is often dispersed and therefore easy to miss. "Taken singly, each massacre

can appear negligible, even innocuous. Some are so small that they might easily be missed in the rush of the larger events, yet were each fractal massacre not present, the wave of genocide as a whole would collapse." See Mann, 167.

CHAPTER 3: I DIDN'T KNOW HOW SOON THEY MIGHT COME TO SEND ME UP

1. See Marilyn Frye, "In and Out of Harm's Way: Arrogance and Love," in *The Politics of Reality: Essays in Feminist Theory* (Crossing Press, 1993), 66–72; Mariana Ortega, "Being Lovingly, Knowingly Ignorant: White Feminism and Women of Color," *Hypatia* 21, no. 3 (2006): 58. For scholarly research on the complexity of fear, see Joel S. Brown, John W. Laundré, and Mahesh Gurung, "The Ecology of Fear: Optimal Foraging, Game Theory, and Trophic Interactions," *Journal of Mammalogy* 80, no. 2 (May 1999): 385–99; John W. Laundré, Lucina Hernández, and William J. Ripple, "The Landscape of Fear: Ecological Implications of Being Afraid," *The Open Ecology Journal* 3 (2010): 1–7; and Michel T. Kohl, et al., eds., "Diel Predator Activity Drives a Dynamic Landscape of Fear," *Ecological Monographs* 88, no. 4 (2018): 638–52.

2. Hannah Tutson, Nov. 10, 1871, U.S. Congress, 42nd Congress, 2nd session, *Report of the Joint Select Committee to Inquire Into the Condition of Affairs in the Late Insurrectionary States: Florida; and Miscellaneous Testimonies and Documents* (Government Printing Office, 1872) [hereafter FLKH], 54–65; Hannah and Samuel Tutson, 1885 U.S. Census, St. Johns County, Florida, population schedule, Digital Image. Ancestry.com. April 1, 2015. I could not locate a record of the Tutsons in the 1870 census. But the 1885 state census lists the family. The older daughter possibly married and left home or died.

3. Bessel van der Kolk, *The Body Keeps the Score: Brain, Mind, and Body in the Healing of Trauma* (Penguin, 2015), 61.

4. Freedmen's Bureau records are filled with dozens of reports of killings from different locales each year. Because of a lack of systematic reporting and, in some cases, no documentation, historians examining the reports of "Murders and Outrages" agree they barely scratch the surface of the killings. And that surface only includes the reports taken while the bureau was documenting some of the violence. See, for example, "Types of Murders and Outrages by State, 1865–1868," in William A. Blair, *The Record of Murders and Outrages: Racial Violence and the Fight Over Truth at the Dawn of Reconstruction* (University of North Carolina Press, 2021).

5. Michael Taussig calls this state a "space of death." Taussig, "Culture of Terror—Space of Death: Roger Casement's Putumayo Report and the Explanation of Torture," *Comparative Studies in Society and History* 26, no. 3 (1984): 467–97. Robert Jay Lifton refers to similar

situations as "death encounters." He notes one cannot have survivors unless there has been a literal death, a close encounter with death, or a figurative one wherein the survivor's previous sense of himself or herself and the world was fractured by their encounter with death. Cathy Caruth, "An Interview with Robert Jay Lifton," in *Trauma: Explorations in Memory*, ed. Cathy Caruth (Johns Hopkins University Press, 1995), 128–47.

6. Van der Kolk, "Running for Your Life," in *The Body Keeps the Score*, 51–73.
7. Jasper Carter, Oct. 23, 1871, U.S. Congress, 42nd Congress, 2nd session, *Report of the Joint Select Committee to Inquire Into the Condition of Affairs in the Late Insurrectionary States: Georgia* (Government Printing Office, 1872) [hereafter GAKH], 473.
8. William Hampton Mitchell, Oct. 26, 1871, GAKH, 641.
9. Mitchell, GAKH, 641.
10. William Hampton and Susan Mitchell, 1870 U.S. Census, Gwinnett County, Georgia, population schedule, Digital Image. Ancestry.com. April 1, 2015. The transcribed version of the census lists Hamp Mitchell as being W for white but the scanned version suggests M for mulatto. I list this Mitchell's family among my subjects because he identified Jack Allen, his brother-in-law, as living "within hollering distance of each other," which is supported by the census report. Additionally, the 1880 census lists a Hampton Mitchell born in Georgia around the same time as living in Alabama.
11. Jack and Eliza Allen, 1870 U.S. Census, Gwinnett County, Georgia, population schedule, Digital Image. Ancestry.com. April 1, 2015. Neither Jack nor Eliza testified at the hearings, but William Hampton Mitchell reported their whipping.
12. Tutson, FLKH, 59–64.
13. They lived within a quarter mile of the former governor, Joseph Brown, who put up two $6,000 rewards for the capture and then return to prison of Jerry's killers.
14. Leanna Garrison, Oct. 27, 1871, GAKH, 666–67 and Samuel Garrison, Oct. 27, 1871, GAKH, 687.
15. Doc and Ellen Rountree, 1870 U.S. Census, Suwanee County, Florida, population schedule, Digital Image. Ancestry.com. April 1, 2015.
16. Doc Rountree, Nov. 14, 1871, FLKH, 279–81.
17. Hannah Tutson, FLKH, 59–64.
18. Columbus Jeter, Oct. 25, 1871, GAKH, 560.
19. Henry Reed, Nov. 11, 1871, FLKH, 111.
20. Henry Reed, FLKH, 109–10.
21. See John Leach, "Why People 'Freeze' in an Emergency: Temporal and Cognitive Constraints on Survival Responses," *Aviation, Space, and Environmental Medicine* 75, no. 6 (2004): 539–42.
22. Maria Carter, Oct. 21, 1871, GAKH, 411.

23. Van der Kolk, *The Body Keeps the Score*, 61.

24. Charles Smith, Oct. 26, 1871, GAKH, 597; and Caroline Smith, Oct. 21, 1871, GAKH, 400.

25. Elaine Scarry, *The Body in Pain: The Making and Unmaking of the World* (Oxford University Press, 1985), 35. Jennifer Harford Vargas argues that Edwidge Danticat's novel *The Farming of Bones* "imagines the body as an expressive and cognitive agent" that knows its pain and acts on it, revealing a capacity to produce "resistant consciousness." The body can be used as a corporeal text for understanding conflict. Harford Vargas, "Novel Testimony: Alternative Archives in Edwidge Danticat's *The Farming of Bones*," *Callaloo* 37, no. 5 (2014), 1173–74.

26. Barbara Baumgartner discusses the ways in which victims can have an "obsessive focus on the physical" tied up in their "struggle to survive." Baumgartner, "The Body as Evidence: Resistance, Collaboration, and Appropriation in *The History of Mary Prince*," *Callaloo* 24, no. 1 (2001): 256–57.

27. Charles Smith, GAKH, 597–8.

28. Charles Smith, 597.

29. Sarah Ann Sturtevant, Oct. 23, 1871, GAKH, 463.

30. Charles Smith, 599.

31. Jasper Carter, Oct. 23, 1871, GAKH, 472–73.

32. Tilda Walthall, Oct. 21, 1871, GAKH, 407–8.

33. Carter, GAKH, 472–73.

34. For a larger discussion of testimonial bodies, testimonies' circulatory networks, and survivors' search for adequate witnesses to their testimonies, see Leigh Gilmore, *Tainted Witness: Why We Doubt What Women Say about Their Lives* (Columbia University Press, 2017), 74–76, 2–6, and 16.

35. Charlotte Fowler, July 6, 1871, U.S. Congress, 42nd Congress, 2nd session, *Report of the Joint Select Committee to Inquire Into the Condition of Affairs in the Late Insurrectionary States: South Carolina* (Government Printing Office, 1872) [hereafter SCKH], 392.

36. Robert Fullerlove, Oct. 31, 1871, U.S. Congress, 42nd Congress, 2nd session, *Report of the Joint Select Committee to Inquire Into the Condition of Affairs in the Late Insurrectionary States: Alabama* (Government Printing Office, 1872) [hereafter ALKH], 1653.

37. Alfred Wright, July 20, 1871, SCKH, 1173; Alfred and Elmira Wright, 1880 U.S. Census, Union County, South Carolina, population schedule, Digital Image. Ancestry.com. April 1, 2015.

38. Major Gardiner, Oct. 12, 1871, ALKH, 862.

39. Gardiner, ALKH, 862.

40. Henry Kidd, Oct. 12, 1871, ALKH, 867–68.

41. Hampton Parker, July 10, 1871, SCKH 598–99.

42. Jasper Carter, GAKH, 477.

43. John Lipscomb, July 11, 1871, SCKH, 699.

44. Matthew Lancaster, July 10, 1871, SCKH, 592.

45. Lancaster, SCKH, 594.

46. Lancaster, SCKH, 594.

47. In her two novels, *Red River* (which re-presents the Colfax Massacre) and *Citizens Creek* (which re-presents Afro-Native peoples living through the Civil War and horrors of Indian Removal), Lalita Tademy reconstructs what life was like for families that took to the woods or fled for their lives. These novels enabled me to fill in some of the outlines of night-riding survivors' accounts.

48. William Coleman, Nov. 6, 1871, U.S. Congress, 42nd Congress, 2nd session, *Report of the Joint Select Committee to Inquire Into the Condition of Affairs in the Late Insurrectionary States: Mississippi* (Government Printing Office, 1872) [hereafter MSKH], 488.

49. Abraham Brumfield, SCKT, 1947; and Emeline Brumfield, SCKT, 1949. See also Mack Tinker, Oct. 26, 1871, ALKH, 1363; and Benjamin Gore, July 27, 1871, SCKH, 1583.

50. Elias Hill, July 25, 1871, SCKH, 1409.

51. Jackson Surratt, July 8, 1871, SCKH, 521.

52. Jane Surratt, July 8, 1871, SCKH, 525.

53. Harriet Hernandez, July 10, 1871, SCKH, 585–91.

54. The details of Harriet's and Lucy's victimization are sketchy. Harriet mentions being beaten herself and that Lucy was too, and most historians examining the testimony believe the details point to the men sexually assaulting both mother and daughter.

55. Steven Hahn, *A Nation under Our Feet: Black Political Struggles in the Rural South, from Slavery to the Great Migration* (Belknap Press, 2003), 265–311; and Michael W. Fitzgerald, *The Union League Movement in the Deep South: Politics and Agricultural Change During Reconstruction* (Louisiana State University Press, 2000).

56. Lewis Jackson, Oct. 14, 1871, AKLH, 982–83.

57. Jackson, AKLH, 982–83.

58. Jackson, ALKH, 983.

59. Reuben Sheets, Oct. 27, 1871, GAKH, 651.

60. Elias Thomson, July 7, 1871, SCKH, 411.

61. Joseph Nelson, Nov. 11, 1871, SCKH, 137.

62. Charles Hendricks, Oct. 24, 1871, GAKH, 516–17.

63. Willis Johnson, July 3, 1871, SCKH, 327.

64. Columbus Jeter, GAKH, 560.

65. Jeter, GAKH, 560.

66. Jeter, GAKH, 561.
67. Jeter, GAKH, 560.
68. Edmund Gray, Nov. 14, 1871, MSKH, 894.
69. Gray, MSKH, 894.
70. James Hicks, Nov. 14, 1871, MSKH, 891.
71. Governor Fewell, SCKT, 1956.
72. Sir Daniel, Oct. 14, 1871, ALKH, 994.
73. Tiller Reese, Oct. 28, 1871, ALKH, 1248.
74. Reese, ALKH, 1248.
75. Alfred Richardson, July 7, 1871, GAKH, 2, 8.
76. Mitchell Reed, Oct. 27, 1871, GAKH, 646.
77. George Fleimster, Oct. 27, 1871, GAKH, 655.
78. Fleimster, GAKH, 656.

CHAPTER 4: THEY DEVILED US A WHILE

1. Robert Fullerlove, Oct. 31, 1871, U.S. Congress, 42nd Congress, 2nd session, *Report of the Joint Select Committee to Inquire Into the Condition of Affairs in the Late Insurrectionary States: Alabama* (Government Printing Office, 1872) [hereafter ALKH], 1652–54.
2. For more on covert resistance, see W. Fitzhugh Brundage, "The Roar on the Other Side of Silence: Black Resistance and White Violence in the American South, 1880–1940," in *Under Sentence of Death: Lynching in the South*, ed. W. Fitzhugh Brundage (University of North Carolina Press, 1997), 271–91. Farah Jasmine Griffin's work on Malcolm X and the "promise of protection" wherein Black men, freed from the constraints of fearing Jim Crow, offered Black women and girls the promise that they would protect them from the sexually predatory behavior of white men helped me reevaluate this idea. See Griffin, " 'Ironies of the Saint': Malcolm X, Black Women, and the Price of Protection," in *Sisters in the Struggle: African American Women in the Civil Rights–Black Power Movement*, eds. Bettye Collier-Thomas and V. P. Franklin (New York University Press, 2001), 214–29. See also Kali N. Gross, "African American Women, Mass Incarceration, and the Politics of Protection," *Journal of American History* 102, no. 1 (2015): 25–33.
3. Emily West, *Chains of Love: Slave Couples in Antebellum South Carolina* (University of Illinois Press, 2004).
4. Koritha Mitchell, "The Resilience of Black Love in Black History," Black Perspectives blog, February 12, 2021, https://www.aaihs.org/the-resilience-of-black-love-in-black-history/, accessed February 14, 2021.
5. Smith Watley, Oct. 17, 1871, ALKH, 1004.

3 of 388)

6. Watley, ALKH, 1004.

7. Watley, ALKH, 1004.

8. Watley, ALKH, 1005.

9. Watley, ALKH, 1005.

10. Thomas Allen, Oct. 26, 1871, U.S. Congress, 42nd Congress, 2nd session, *Report of the Joint Select Committee to Inquire Into the Condition of Affairs in the Late Insurrectionary States: Georgia* (Government Printing Office, 1872) [hereafter GAKH], 608.

11. Allen, GAKH, 608.

12. Allen, GAKH, 608.

13. Emeline Brumfield, U.S. Congress, 42nd Congress, 2nd session, *Report of the Joint Select Committee to Inquire Into the Condition of Affairs in the Late Insurrectionary States: South Carolina* (Government Printing Office, 1872) [hereafter SCKT for trials or SCKH for the Klan hearings], 1949.

14. Abraham Brumfield, SCKT, 1947.

15. Harriet Postle, SCKT, 1951–52.

16. John Lewis, July 7, 1871, SCKH, 436.

17. Mary Brown, Oct. 21, 1871, GAKH. 375.

18. Caroline Benson, Oct. 21, 1871, GAKH, 387.

19. Benson, 387.

20. Joseph Brown, Oct. 24, 1871, GAKH, 502.

21. Mary Brown, GAKH, 375.

22. Eliza Lyon, Oct. 24, 1871, ALKH, 1263. Here, Eliza seemed to be describing Abe as entering a trancelike state. See also Bessel van der Kolk, *The Body Keeps the Score: Brain, Mind, and Body in the Healing of Trauma* (Penguin, 2015); and John Leach, "Why People 'Freeze' in an Emergency: Temporal and Cognitive Constraints on Survival Responses," *Aviation, Space, and Environmental Medicine* 75, no. 6 (2004): 539–42.

23. Roberta Culbertson, "Embodied Memory, Transcendence, and Telling: Recounting Trauma, Re-Establishing the Self," *New Literary History* 26, no. 1 (1995): 169–195.

24. Van der Kolk, *The Body Keeps the Score*, 54.

25. Lyon, ALKH, 1263.

26. Lyon, 1263.

27. Lyon, 1263. Eliza's description of Abe's behavior suggests he experienced altered moments of consciousness in which he dissociated from the attack. This altered state of consciousness might be regarded as what Judith Herman called "one of nature's small mercies, a protection against unbearable pain." See Judith Herman, *Trauma and Recovery: The Aftermath of Violence—From Domestic Abuse to Political Terror* (Basic Books, 1992), 43.

28. Lyon, 1263.
29. Lyon, 1263. Eliza testified that a Dr. McCall had counted thirty-three holes they shot in him.
30. Lyon, 1263.
31. Lyon, 1263.
32. Wiley Strong, Oct. 9, 1871, ALKH, 668.
33. Strong, ALKH, 672.
34. Jackson Surratt, July 8, 1871, SCKH, 521.
35. Jackson Surratt, SCKH, 521.
36. Jackson Surratt, SCKH, 521.
37. Jane Surratt, July 8, 1871, SCKH, 524.
38. Jane Surratt, SCKH, 524.
39. Jane Surratt, SCKH, 524.
40. Augustus Blair, Oct. 9, 1871, ALKH, 674.
41. Blair, 674.
42. Blair, 675.
43. Blair, 675.
44. Blair, 675–76.
45. Abram Colby, Oct. 27, 1871, GAKH, 695–99.
46. William Henderson, Oct. 7, 1871, ALKH, 588–89.
47. Columbus Jeter, GAKH, 560.
48. Joseph Brown, GAKH, 502.
49. Jackson Surratt, SCKH, 522.
50. Harriet Hernandez, July 10, 1871, SCKH, 586.
51. John Hamilton affidavit, August 29, 1869, ALKH, 1189–90.
52. Martin Anthony, Oct. 27, 1871, GAKH, 692.
53. Sir Daniel, Oct. 14, 1871, ALKH, 993–94.
54. Augustus Mills, Oct. 23, 1871, GAKH, 468; Augustus and Elizabeth (Letty) Mills, U.S. Census, Walton County, Georgia, population schedule, 1870. Digital Image. Ancestry .com. April 12, 2015; Augustus and Elizabeth (Letty) Mills, U.S. Census, DeKalb County, Georgia, population schedule, 1880. Digital Image. Ancestry.com. April 12, 2015.
55. Letty Mills, Oct. 23, 1871, GAKH, 465.
56. Augustus Mills, GAKH, 466.
57. Charlotte Fowler, July 6, 1871, SCKH, 387.
58. Historians have not ignored children and youths amid postwar violence as much as we have tended to lump casualties together as composite "victims." The scholars who have made significant strides are the ones studying sexual assault and gender-based violence.

Catherine Clinton, "Bloody Terrain: Freedwomen, Sexuality, and Violence During Reconstruction," *Georgia Historical Quarterly* 76, no. 2 (Summer (1992): 313–32; Lisa Cardyn, "Sexualized Racism/Gendered Violence: Outraging the Body Politic in the Reconstruction South," *Michigan Law Review* 100, no. 4 (2002): 675–867; Thavolia Glymph, *Out of the House of Bondage: The Transformation of the Plantation Household* (Cambridge University Press, 2008); and Crystal N. Feimster, *Southern Horrors: Women and the Politics of Rape and Lynching* (Harvard University Press, 2009). Some of this work is being done, to be sure, but we still need more, especially after, or outside the context of, slavery. See, for example, LaKisha Michelle Simmons, *Crescent City Girls: The Lives of Young Black Women in Segregated New Orleans* (University of North Carolina Press, 2015); and Marcia Chatelain, *South Side Girls: Growing Up in the Great Migration* (Duke University Press, 2015).

59. Jill E. Korbin, "Children, Childhoods, and Violence," *Annual Review of Anthropology* 32 (2003), 433.

60. Dea H. Boster, *African American Slavery and Disability: Bodies, Property, and Power in the Antebellum South, 1800–1860* (Routledge, 2013); Jim Downs, "The Continuation of Slavery: The Experience of Disabled Slaves During Emancipation," *Disability Studies Quarterly* 28, no. 3 (2008), http://dsq-sds.org/article/view/112/112; Jenifer L. Barclay, "Mothering the 'Useless': Black Motherhood, Disability, and Slavery," *Women, Gender, and Families of Color* 2, no. 2 (2014): 115–40; and Lennard J. Davis, *The Disability Studies Reader*, 3rd ed. (Routledge, 2010).

61. Wiley Hargrove, Nov. 11, 1871, ALKH, 1994.

62. Elias Hill, July 25, 1871, SCKH, 1406.

63. Hill, SCKH, 1406.

64. Hill, SCKH, 1406.

65. For a brief discussion of the social and legal conventions regarding the care and sales of disabled slaves, see Jeff Forret, "Deaf & Dumb, Blind, Insane, or 'Idiotic': The Census, Slaves, and Disability in the Antebellum South," *Journal of Southern History* 82, no. 3 (2016), 504–7.

66. Hill, SCKH, 1407.

67. Hill, SCKH, 1407.

68. Hill, SCKH, 1407.

69. Hill, SCKH, 1407.

70. Augustus Mills, GAKH, 468.

71. Patrick W. Tanner, July 7, 1871, SCKH, 407; Patrick and Missouri Tanner, U.S. Census, Spartanburg County, South Carolina, population schedule, 1870. Digital Image. Ancestry.com. May 18, 2015.

72. Harriet Postle, SCKT, 1951–52.

73. Maria Carter, Oct. 21, 1871, GAKH, 412.

74. James Alston, Oct. 17, 1871, ALKH, 1018.

75. Sir Daniel, ALKH, 994.

76. Most histories of the insurgency against Reconstruction contain only superficial acknowledgments of some differences between terrorized Blacks. See Kimberlé Crenshaw, "Mapping the Margins: Intersectionality, Identity Politics, and Violence Against Women of Color," *Stanford Law Review* (1991): 1241–99. My larger point, here, is that we need to dig deeper into African Americans' multiple subject positions. See Earl Lewis, "To Turn As on a Pivot: Writing African Americans into a History of Overlapping Diasporas," *American Historical Review* 100, no. 3 (1995): 765–87.

CHAPTER 5: I DON'T EVER EXPECT IN THIS LIFE
TO GET OVER IT

1. Andrew Cathcart, July 27, 1871, U.S. Congress, 42nd Congress, 2nd session, *Report of the Joint Select Committee to Inquire Into the Condition of Affairs in the Late Insurrectionary States: South Carolina* (Government Printing Office, 1872) [hereafter SCKT for trials or SCKH for Klan hearings], 1592.

2. Judith Herman, *Trauma and Recovery: The Aftermath of Violence—From Domestic Abuse to Political Terror* (Basic Books, 1992), 93.

3. Federal Writers' Slave Narrative Project, Volume 9, Mississippi. Kindle edition.

4. William Freudenberg, "Contamination, Corrosion and the Social Order: An Overview," *Current Sociology* 45, no. 3 (1997), 23.

5. Anthony Wallace, "Mazeway Disintegration: The Individual's Perception of Socio-Cultural Disorganization," *Human Organization* 16, no. 2 (1957): 24.

6. Harriet Simril, Dec. 19, 1871, SCKT, 1861–62. When lawmakers at the Klan hearings asked her about the details of her sexual assault, including the things her attackers said, the transcript of Harriet Simril's testimony reads "witness here detailed the conversation on the part of her tormenters, but it was of too obscene a nature to permit publication," SCKT, 1862.

7. Freudenberg, "Contamination, Corrosion and the Social Order," 28.

8. Clem Bowden, July 7, 1871, SCKH, 381.

9. Clem Bowden, 383.

10. Veena Das discusses the tentacle-like nature of conflict. See Veena Das, *Life and Words: Violence and the Descent into the Ordinary* (University of California Press, 2007), 1.

11. Tiya Miles, "In Anxious Times, Black History Can Be a Blueprint for Survival," *New York Times*, February 14, 2022.

12. Rob Nixon discusses what he calls "slow violence." See Nixon, *Slow Violence and the Environmentalism of the Poor* (Harvard University Press, 2011).

13. Hannah Tutson, Nov. 10, 1871, U.S. Congress, 42nd Congress, 2nd session, *Report of the Joint Select Committee to Inquire Into the Condition of Affairs in the Late Insurrectionary States: Florida; and Miscellaneous Testimonies and Documents* (Government Printing Office, 1872) [hereafter FLKH], 59–64.

14. Eliza Lyon, Oct. 24, 1871, U.S. Congress, 42nd Congress, 2nd session, *Report of the Joint Select Committee to Inquire Into the Condition of Affairs in the Late Insurrectionary States: Alabama* (Government Printing Office, 1872) [hereafter ALKH], 1262–71. Eliza Lyon did not identify the waterway she crossed but Demopolis sits at a confluence of the Black Warrior and Tombigbee Rivers.

15. Lyon, 1263.

16. See Vincent Brown, *The Reaper's Garden: Death and Power in the World of Atlantic Slavery* (Harvard University Press, 2010); Karla F. C. Holloway, *Passed On: African American Mourning Stories: A Memorial* (Duke University Press, 2002); Fred Moten, "Black Mo'nin'," in *Loss: The Politics of Mourning*, eds. David L. Eng and David Kazanjian (University of California Press, 2003), 59–76; and Allan Amanik and Kami Fletcher, eds., *Till Death Do Us Part: American Ethnic Cemeteries as Borders Uncrossed* (University Press of Mississippi, 2020).

17. George Houston, Oct. 17, 1871, ALKH, 1001.

18. Bowden, SCKH, 381.

19. Letty Mills, Oct. 23, 1871, U.S. Congress, 42nd Congress, 2nd session, *Report of the Joint Select Committee to Inquire Into the Condition of Affairs in the Late Insurrectionary States: Georgia* (Government Printing Office, 1872) [hereafter GAKH], 465.

20. Jane Surratt, July 8, 1871, SCKH, 524.

21. Augustus Blair, Oct. 9, 1871, ALKH, 676.

22. Augustus Blair, ALKH, 676.

23. Augustus Blair, ALKH, 676.

24. Daniel Lipscomb, July 7, 1871, SCKH, 428.

25. Daniel Lipscomb, SCKH, 429.

26. James Alston, Oct. 17, 1871, ALKH, 1017.

27. Eliphaz Smith, July 12, 1871, SCKH, 701.

28. Sharla M. Fett, *Working Cures: Healing, Health, and Power on Southern Slave Plantations* (University of North Carolina Press, 2002); and Gretchen Long, *Doctoring Freedom:*

The Politics of African American Medical Care in Slavery and Emancipation (University of North Carolina Press, 2012).

29. See Herbert C. Covey, *African American Slave Medicine: Herbal and Non-Herbal Treatments* (Lexington Books, 2007).

30. See Long, *Doctoring Freedom.*

31. Charles Powell, Nov. 3, 1871, ALKH, 1146.

32. Matthew Lancaster did not testify to his treatment, but a neighbor did. See Charlotte Fowler, July 6, 1871, SCKH, 388. Jesse Brown, October 12, 1871, ALKH, 861.

33. Columbus Jeter, Oct. 25, 1871, GAKH, 562.

34. Harriet A. Washington, *Medical Apartheid: The Dark History of Medical Experimentation on Black Americans from Colonial Times to the Present*, 1st ed. (Doubleday, 2006).

35. Columbus Jeter, GAKH, 563.

36. Henry Lowther, Oct. 20, 1871, GAKH, 357.

37. Lowther, GAKH, 357.

38. Lowther, 357.

39. Lowther, 357.

40. Lowther, 357.

41. Bessel van der Kolk, *The Body Keeps the Score: Brain, Mind, and Body in the Healing of Trauma* (Penguin, 2015), 54. See also Cathy Caruth, *Unclaimed Experience: Trauma, Narrative, and History* (Johns Hopkins University Press, 1996), 4.

42. Roberta Culbertson writes of survivors being stuck in the "unreality" of "violation," which she defines as "violence from which there is no escape" and how that can lead to existential crises. Culbertson, "Embodied Memory, Transcendence, and Telling: Recounting Trauma, Re-Establishing the Self," *New Literary History* 26, no. 1 (1995), 171.

43. Herman, *Trauma and Recovery*, 51.

44. The Impact of Events Scale. See a sample here, https://compassionworks.com/wp-content/uploads/2019/12/impact-of-events-scale-1.pdf; accessed December 20, 2020.

45. Daniel Lipscomb, SCKH, 430.

46. Jane Surratt, SCKH, 525.

47. William Ford, Oct. 9, 1871, ALKH, 685.

48. Edward Crosby, Nov. 17, 1871, U.S. Congress, 42nd Congress, 2nd session, *Report of the Joint Select Committee to Inquire Into the Condition of Affairs in the Late Insurrectionary States: Mississippi* (Government Printing Office, 1872) [hereafter MSKH], 1135.

49. Daniel Lipscomb, SCKH, 429–30.

50. Joseph Miller, July 10, 1870, SCKH, 601.

51. Charles Powell, Nov. 3, 1871, ALKH, 1848.

52. Herman, *Trauma and Recovery*, 52. Vincent Brown discusses our responsibility to the dead and the dead's ownership over us. See also *The Reaper's Garden*, chapter 3, especially.

53. Abram Colby, Oct. 27, 1871, GAKH, 697.

54. Karl Sallin, et al., "Resignation Syndrome: Catatonia? Culture-Bound?" *Frontiers in Behavioral Neuroscience* 10, no. 7 (2016), 10.3389/fnbeh.2016.00007.

55. John Thommason, SCKT, 1947.

56. The hormones include epinephrine, norepinephrine, and cortisol and they can trigger heart attacks or strokes. In extreme cases, organs can fail. See Ilan S. Wittstein, et al., "Neurohumoral Features of Myocardial Stunning Due to Sudden Emotional Stress," *New England Journal of Medicine* 352, no. 6 (2005): 539–48.

57. Colby, GAKH, 697.

58. Colby, 695–99. Guilt, David Shapiro writes, "is concerned with what one does; shame has to do with what one is." Shapiro, "The Tortured, Not the Torturers, Are Ashamed," *Social Research* 70, no. 4 (2003): 1134.

59. Colby, 695–99.

60. "To be spared oneself in the knowledge that others have met a worse fate," writes Judith Herman, "creates a severe burden of consciousness," especially if the survivor is related to the deceased. Herman, *Trauma and Recovery*, 54.

    The transcripts of the Klan hearings indicate some witnesses cried during their testimonies and needed a moment to get their emotions under control to continue.

61. George Taylor, Oct. 6, 1871, ALKH, 573.

62. Harriet Hernandez, July 10, 1871, SCKH, 590.

63. See Kenneth J. Doka, "How We Die: Stigmatized Death and Disenfranchised Grief," in Doka, ed., *Disenfranchised Grief: New Directions, Challenges, and Strategies for Practice* (Research Press, 2002), 323–36; and Tanya L. Sharpe, "Understanding the Sociocultural Context of Coping for African American Family Members of Homicide Victims: A Conceptual Model," *Trauma, Violence and Abuse* 16, no. 1 (2015): 48–59.

64. Farah Jasmine Griffin, "'Ironies of the Saint': Malcolm X, Black Women, and the Price of Protection," in *Sisters in the Struggle: African American Women in the Civil Rights—Black Power Movement*, eds. Bettye Collier-Thomas and V. P. Franklin (New York University Press, 2001), 214–29.

65. Nell Irvin Painter discussed what she calls "testimonies of desolation," those clear indicators of psychological injury. See Painter, "Soul Murder and Slavery: Toward a Fully Loaded Cost-Accounting," in *Southern History Across the Color Line* (University of North Carolina Press, 2002), 29; bell hooks, "Homeplace" in *Yearning: Race, Gender,*

and Cultural Politics (South End Press, 1990), 41–49; Albert J. Raboteau, *Slave Religion: The 'Invisible Institution' in the Antebellum South* (Oxford University Press, 1980); and James H. Cone, *God of the Oppressed* (Orbis, 1977).

66. Barbara Christian argued that Black people "have always theorized," especially on conditions relating to their subjection under slavery or its aftereffects. Although Black people's theorizations have been ignored by the larger society, survivors' theorizations on the likely outcomes of strikes are historically significant and merit acknowledgment. Christian, "The Race for Theory," *Feminist Studies* 14, no. 1 (1988): 68. David Kazanjian notes that sometimes this theorization can be subsumed by what he calls archival "quotidiana," seemingly useless data and expectations that Black people's theorization occurs in the same form as a treatise by the likes of Frederick Douglass, Anna Julia Cooper, or W. E. B. Du Bois. Kazanjian, "Scenes of Speculation," *Social Text* 33, no. 4 (125) (2015): 78–79 and 81.

 For more on corrosive community, see Kai Erikson, *A New Species of Trouble: The Human Experience of Modern Disasters* (W. W. Norton, 1995); William R. Freudenberg, "Contamination, Corrosion and the Social Order," 19–39; and J. Steven Picou and Cecelia G. Martin, Report to the National Science Foundation, "Long-Term Community Impacts of the *Exxon Valdez* Oil Spill: Patterns of Social Disruption and Psychological Stress Seventeen Years after the Disaster," https://www.arlis.org/docs/vol1/B/243478793.pdf.

67. Since the publication of Stanley Elkins's *Slavery*, in 1959, historians have avoided examining African Americans' psychic wounds resulting from histories of subjection lest they contribute to arguments of Black people's racial inferiority. Elkins, *Slavery: A Problem in American Institutional and Intellectual Life* (University of Chicago Press, 1959). The result is that historians have tended to give short shrift to African Americans' articulations of their own emotional injuries and theorization of their effects in archival sources.

68. Judith Herman writes, "the damage to the survivor's faith and sense of community is particularly severe when the traumatic events themselves involve the betrayal of important relationships." Herman, *Trauma and Recovery*, 55.

69. Julia Kristeva, *Powers of Horror: An Essay on Abjection* (Columbia University Press, 1982), 4.

70. Alfred Wright, July 20, 1871, SCKH, 1174.

71. Anthony Wallace called this stupor "disaster syndrome." It is marked by "an initial stage of stunned disbelief, inability to express emotion, random movement; a stage of passivity, dependence, acceptance of sympathy and help from family and friends; and finally a stage of joining with the community in burying the departed and taking up a new life more or less free of disability grief over the deceased." Wallace, "Mazeway Disintegration," 24.

72. Miriam Greenspan argues that we fear what she calls "dark emotions"—despair, fear, grief, and anger—because they are overwhelming and we believe that if we lean into them we will lose ourselves. Greenspan, *Healing Through the Dark Emotions: The Wisdom of Grief, Fear, and Despair* (Shambhala, 2003).

73. Essic Harris, July 1, 1871, NCKH.

74. Elaine Scarry, *The Body in Pain: The Making and Unmaking of the World* (Oxford University Press, 1985).

75. Hernandez, SCKH, 586.

76. These gaps present their own challenges for historians attempting to reconstruct attacks.

77. Jane Surratt, SCKH, 524.

78. Samuel Low, Nov. 11, 1871, MSKH, 2005.

79. Clem Bowden, SCKH, 383.

80. Letty Mills, Oct. 23, 1871, GAKH, 466.

81. See Laura F. Edwards, "Status Without Rights: African Americans and the Tangled History of Law and Governance in the Nineteenth-Century U.S. South," *American Historical Review* 112, no. 2 (2007), and *The People and Their Peace: Legal Culture and the Transformation of Inequality in the Post-Revolutionary South* (University of North Carolina Press, 2009); as well as Lea VanderVelde, *Redemption Songs: Suing for Freedom before Dred Scott* (Oxford University Press, 2014), and Melissa Milewski, *Litigating Across the Color Line: Civil Cases Between Black and White Southerners from the End of Slavery to Civil Rights* (Oxford University Press, 2017).

82. Edwards, "Status Without Rights," 366.

83. Edwards, "Status Without Rights," 366.

84. Edwards, "Status Without Rights," 377.

85. Smith Watley, Oct. 17, 1871, ALKH, 1006–07.

86. Robert Fullerlove, Oct. 31, 1871, ALKH, 1652–53.

87. Edwards, "Status Without Rights," 382–83.

88. Cathcart, SCKH, 1592.

89. William Henderson, Oct. 7, 1871, ALKH, 588–589.

90. Columbus Jeter, GAKH, 560.

91. Willis Johnson, Nov. 17, 1871, SCKH, 328.

92. Thomas Allen, Oct. 26, 1871, GAKH, 608.

93. Augustus Mills, Oct. 23, 1871, GAKH, 469.

94. Isham McCrary, July 8, 1871, SCKH, 540.

95. James Gaffney, July 10, 1871, SCKH, 617.

96. Mervin Givens, July 12, 1871, SCKH, 699.

97. Mary Brown, Oct. 21, 1871, GAKH, 376.

98. Watley, ALKH, 1005–6.

99. Fullerlove, ALKH, 1653.

100. Wright, SCKH, 1176–1177.

101. Wright, 1176.

102. Lowther, GAKH, 357.

CHAPTER 6: THEY NEVER INTENDED TO DO ME JUSTICE

1. Eliza Lyon, Oct. 24, 1871, U.S. Congress, 42nd Congress, 2nd session, *Report of the Joint Select Committee to Inquire Into the Condition of Affairs in the Late Insurrectionary States: Alabama* (Government Printing Office, 1872) [hereafter ALKH], 1264.

2. Warsan Shire, "Home," in *Bless the Daughter Raised by a Voice in Her Head: Poems* (Random House, 2002), 24–25.

3. Shire, "Home."

4. Daniel Lane, Oct. 27, 1871, U.S. Congress, 42nd Congress, 2nd session, *Report of the Joint Select Committee to Inquire Into the Condition of Affairs in the Late Insurrectionary States: Georgia* (Government Printing Office, 1872) [hereafter GAKH], 654.

5. Doc Rountree, Nov. 14, 1871, U.S. Congress, 42nd Congress, 2nd session, *Report of the Joint Select Committee to Inquire Into the Condition of Affairs in the Late Insurrectionary States: Florida; and Miscellaneous Testimonies and Documents* (Government Printing Office, 1872) [hereafter FLKH], 279–81.

6. Rountree, FLKH, 279–81.

7. Clem Bowden, July 7, 1871, U.S. Congress, 42nd Congress, 2nd session, *Report of the Joint Select Committee to Inquire Into the Condition of Affairs in the Late Insurrectionary States: South Carolina* (Government Printing Office, 1872) [hereafter SCKT for trials and SCKH for Klan hearings], 385–86.

8. Bowden, SCKH, 385–86.

9. Bowden, 386.

10. Jack Johnson, Nov. 1, 1871, SCKH, 1168.

11. A. Webster Shaffer, June 15, 1871, U.S. Congress, 42nd Congress, 2nd session, *Report of the Joint Select Committee to Inquire Into the Condition of Affairs in the Late Insurrectionary States: North Carolina* (Government Printing Office, 1872) [hereafter NCKH], 31–51.

12. See Gregory P. Downs, *After Appomattox: Military Occupation and the Ends of War* (Harvard University Press, 2015).

13. Shaffer, NCKH, 32, 51.

14. Augustus Blair, Oct. 9, 1871, ALKH, 675–77.

15. Thomas Allen, Oct. 26, 1871, GAKH, 608.

16.   Robert Fullerlove, Oct. 31, 1871, ALKH, 1653.

17.   Charles Smith, Oct. 26, 1871, GAKH, 600.

18.   William Henderson, Oct. 7, 1871, ALKH, 588.

19.   Anderson Ferrell, Oct. 26, 1871, GAKH, 620–21.

20.   Matthew Lancaster, July 10, 1871, SCKH, 594.

21.   Alfred Wright, July 20, 1871, SCKH, 1177.

22.   For a comprehensive study see Lou Falkner Williams, *The Great South Carolina Ku Klux Klan Trials, 1871–1872* (University of Georgia Press, 1996).

23.   Mack Tinker, Oct. 26, 1871, ALKH, 1363.

24.   Hampton Parker, July 10, 1871, SCKH, 598.

25.   Clem Bowden, SCKH, 381.

26.   Mary Brown, Oct. 21, 1871, GAKH, 377.

27.   Mary Brown, GAKH, 377.

28.   Joseph Brown, Oct. 24, 1871, GAKH, 502.

29.   Henry Lowther, Oct. 20, 1871, GAKH, 361.

30.   Abram Colby, Oct. 27, 1871, GAKH, 697.

31.   Colby, GAKH, 699.

32.   Colby, 698.

33.   Jasper Carter, Oct. 23, 1871, GAKH, 477.

34.   Thomas Allen, Oct. 26, 1871, GAKH, 609.

35.   Smith Watley, Oct. 17, 1871, ALKH, 1006.

36.   Watley, 1007.

37.   Henry Giles, Oct. 17, 1871, ALKH, 1010.

38.   Giles, ALKH, 1012–14.

39.   Giles, 1013.

40.   Giles, 1013.

41.   Giles, 1013.

42.   Giles, 1013.

43.   Giles, 1013.

44.   Giles, 1012.

45.   Mary Elder, Oct. 28, 1871, GAKH, 734.

46.   Charles Little, Oct. 23, 1871, GAKH, 471.

47.   Jack Johnson, Nov. 1, 1871, SCKH, 1167.

48.   Johnson, SCKH, 1168.

49.   James H. Alston, Oct. 17, 1871, ALKH, 1018.

50.   Alston, ALKH, 1017.

51.   Mary Elder, GAKH, 732.

52. Simon Elder, Oct. 28, 1871, GAKH, 733.

53. Gabe Hines, Federal Writers' Slave Narrative Project, Volume 1, Alabama. Kindle edition.

54. Letty Mills, Oct. 23, 1871, GAKH, 467.

55. Columbus Jeter, Oct. 25, 1871, GAKH, 562.

56. Anderson Ferrell, GAKH, 620–621.

57. Robert Gleed, Nov. 10, 1871, U.S. Congress, 42nd Congress, 2nd session, *Report of the Joint Select Committee to Inquire Into the Condition of Affairs in the Late Insurrectionary States: Mississippi* (Government Printing Office, 1872) [hereafter MSKH], 720–21.

58. Gleed, MSKH, 720.

59. Elias Hill, July 25, 1871, SCKH, 1410. Hill's cohort was not the only group of African Americans contemplating emigration to Liberia during Reconstruction. See, for example, Claude A. Clegg III, *The Price of Liberty: African Americans and the Making of Liberia* (University of North Carolina Press, 2004).

60. Elias Hill.

61. Henry McNeal Turner, Nov. 3, 1871, GAKH, 1040.

62. Thomas Allen, GAKH, 611.

63. Emanuel Fortune, Nov. 10, 1871, FLKH, 94.

64. Fortune, 94.

65. Fortune, 95.

66. Fullerlove, ALKH, 1656.

67. Samuel Nuckles, July 20, 1871, SCKH, 1161.

68. Nuckles, SCKH,1158.

69. Nuckles, 1159.

70. Nuckles, 1158.

71. Alston, ALKH, 1021.

72. Andrew Cathcart, July 27, 1871, SCKH, 1592.

73. Samuel Tutson, Nov. 10, 1871, FLKH, 56.

74. Wiley Hargrove, Nov. 11, 1871, ALKH, 1994.

75. Rountree, FLKH, 279–81.

76. Tinker, ALKH, 1363.

77. Warren Jones, Oct. 27, 1871, GAKH, 690.

78. Jones, GAKH, 690, 692. Jones's wealth loss was significant. He explained that cotton was running $0.14 per pound. MeasuringWorth.com calculates the real price of $1,052 in 2014 dollars as being worth $21,000. But the tool calculates the relative labor value of this income or wealth at $179,000 (for unskilled wage) and $371,000 (for skilled wage) today.

79. Clem Bowden, SCKH, 381.

80. Sir Daniel, Oct. 14, 1871, ALKH, 996.

81. Major Gardiner, Oct. 12, 1871, ALKH, 863.

82. Augustus Blair, Oct. 9, 1871, ALKH, 676. MeasuringWorth.com calculates the real price of Blair's stated $500 loss as $11,400. But the tool calculates the relative labor value of this income or wealth at $83,800 (for unskilled wage) and $144,000 (for skilled wage) today.

83. Augustus Blair, ALKH, 677.

84. George Houston, Oct. 17, 1871, ALKH, 1001.

85. Houston, ALKH, 1001 and 1003.

86. Fullerlove, ALKH, 1653.

87. Fullerlove, ALKH, 1656.

88. Fullerlove, 1653.

89. Fullerlove, 1653.

90. Lyon, ALKH, 1263–64.

91. Lyon, 1270.

92. Lyon, 1270.

93. Columbus Jeter, GAKH, 563.

94. Augustus Mills, Oct. 23, 1871, GAKH, 470.

95. Samuel Nuckles, July 20, 1871, SCKH, 1162.

96. Daniel Lane, Oct. 27, 1871, GAKH, 655.

97. Caleb Jenkins, July 12, 1871, SCKH, 697–98.

98. Henry McNeal Turner, Nov. 3, 1871, GAKH, 1040.

99. Studying the devastating and multigenerational effects of urban renewal upon mostly African American families, psychiatrist Mindy Thompson Fullilove coined the phrase "root shock," by which she means the "traumatic stress reaction to the destruction of all or part of one's emotional ecosystem" that resembles physiological shock from physical injuries. Fullilove, *Root Shock: How Tearing Up City Neighborhoods Hurts America, and What We Can Do About It* (One World/Ballantine, 2009), 11, 14.

In her 1997 novel *Paradise*, Toni Morrison explored the multigenerational impact of a striving Black community's betrayal of displaced people seeking sanctuary from racist violence in ways that reflect the corrosion of community and the disastrous effects of violence articulated by survivors at the Klan hearings. Morrison, *Paradise: A Novel* (A. A. Knopf, 1997).

CHAPTER 7: WHAT THEY DID IS HURTING MY FAMILY

1. Hannah Tutson, Nov. 10, 1871, U.S. Congress, 42nd Congress, 2nd session, *Report of the Joint Select Committee to Inquire Into the Condition of Affairs in the Late Insurrectionary*

States: Florida; and Miscellaneous Testimonies and Documents (Government Printing Office, 1872) [hereafter FLKH], 64.

2. "Telegraphic Summary," *The Elevator*, March 19, 1869.

3. Albion Tourgée quoted in Elaine Frantz Parsons, "Midnight Rangers: Costume and Performance in the Reconstruction-Era Ku Klux Klan," *Journal of American History* 92, no. 3 (2005), 814.

4. 42nd Congress, 1st Session, Senate, Memorial of a Committee Appointed at a Meeting of Colored Citizens of Frankfort, KY, and Vicinity, Praying for the Enactment of Laws for the Better Protection of Life, April 11, 1871 (Government Printing Office, 1871).

5. "Answer the Question," *The Elevator*, July 3, 1868.

6. "New Outrage," *New Orleans Tribune*, February 7, 1869.

7. "Ku-Klux Homicides," *The Elevator*, June 18, 1869.

8. William A. Blair, *The Record of Murders and Outrages: Racial Violence and the Fight Over Truth at the Dawn of Reconstruction* (University of North Carolina Press, 2021), 54.

9. Edwin Stanton, Message of the President of the United States and Accompanying Documents to the Houses of Congress at the Commencement of the Third Session of the Fortieth Congress, Report of the Secretary of War (Government Printing Office, 1868).

10. For a detailed discussion on the Johnson administration's role in casting doubt on white extremist violence in the South, see Blair, "The Battle for Credibility," in *The Record of Murders and Outrages*, 6–28.

11. For more on the role of the courts, see Blair, *The Record of Murders and Outrages;* and Gregory P. Downs, *After Appomattox: Military Occupation and the Ends of War* (Harvard University Press, 2015).

12. Lisset Marie Pino and John Fabian Witt, "The Fourteenth Amendment As an Ending: Constitutional Beginnings and the Demise of the War Power," *Journal of the Civil War Era* 10, no. 1 (March 2020): 5–28; and John Fabian Witt, "Elias Hill's Exodus: Exit and Voice in the Reconstruction Nation," in *Patriots and Cosmopolitans: Hidden Histories of American Law* (Harvard University Press, 2007), 85–154.

13. Congressional Globe, 42nd Congress, House of Representatives, 1st Session, 468.

14. Congressional Globe, 42nd Congress, House of Representatives, 1st Session, 180.

15. Congressional Globe, 42nd Congress, House of Representatives, 1st Session, 189.

16. Dori Laub writes that testimony is needed when there is a crisis of knowledge caused by doubt that has been cast on claims or reports of crimes or atrocities. See Laub, "Bearing Witness, or the Vicissitudes of Listening," in Shoshana Felman and Dori Laub, *Testimony: Crises of Witnessing in Literature, Psychoanalysis, and History* (Routledge, 1991), 17.

17. William Ford, Oct. 9, 1871, U.S. Congress, 42nd Congress, 2nd session, *Report of the Joint Select Committee to Inquire Into the Condition of Affairs in the Late Insurrectionary States: Alabama* (Government Printing Office, 1872) [hereafter ALKH], 683.
18. Wiley Hargrove, Nov. 11, 1871, ALKH, 1995.
19. See Elaine Frantz Parsons, *Ku-Klux: The Birth of the Klan During Reconstruction* (University of North Carolina Press, 2016), 181–214.
20. For speech acts and the discursive practice of testifying, see Shoshana Felman, "Education and Crisis, or the Vicissitudes of Teaching," in *Trauma: Explorations in Memory*, ed. Cathy Caruth (Johns Hopkins University Press, 1995), 17.
21. Charles Pearce, Nov. 13, 1871, FLKH, 165.
22. Pierce Harper, Federal Writers' Slave Narrative Project, Volume 16, Texas, Part 2. Kindle edition.
23. Elias Thomson, July 7, 1871, U.S. Congress, 42nd Congress, 2nd session, *Report of the Joint Select Committee to Inquire Into the Condition of Affairs in the Late Insurrectionary States: South Carolina* (Government Printing Office, 1872) [hereafter SCKT for trials and SCKH for Klan hearings], 415.
24. Pinckney Dodd, July 7, 1871, SCKH, 417.
25. Essic Harris, July 1, 1871, U.S. Congress, 42nd Congress, 2nd session, *Report of the Joint Select Committee to Inquire Into the Condition of Affairs in the Late Insurrectionary States: North Carolina* (Government Printing Office, 1872) [hereafter NCKH], 92.
26. Augustus Blair, Oct. 9, 1871, ALKH, 678.
27. Charlotte Fowler, July 6, 1871, SCKH, 392.
28. Laura F. Edwards, *A Legal History of the Civil War and Reconstruction: A Nation of Rights* (Cambridge University Press, 2015), 142.
29. Richard Pousser, Nov. 14, 1871, FLKH, 273.
30. Larry White, Nov. 14, 1871, FLKH, 810.
31. Roberta Culbertson, "Embodied Memory, Transcendence, and Telling: Recounting Trauma, Re-Establishing the Self," *New Literary History* 26, no. 1 (1995): 171.
32. See Steven Hahn, *A Nation under Our Feet: Black Political Struggles in the Rural South, from Slavery to the Great Migration* (Belknap Press, 2003); and Witt, "Elias Hill's Exodus."
33. Elias Hill, July 25, 1871, SCKH, 1411.
34. Samuel Gaffney, July 15, 1871, SCKH, 604.
35. See Farah Jasmine Griffin, "'Ironies of the Saint': Malcolm X, Black Women, and the Price of Protection," in *Sisters in the Struggle: African American Women in the Civil Rights–Black Power Movement*, eds. Bettye Collier-Thomas and V. P. Franklin (New York University Press, 2001), 214–29; and V. P. Franklin, *Black Self-Determination: A Cultural History of African-American Resistance* (Lawrence Hill Books, 1992).

36. Andy Reed, Oct. 27, 1871, U.S. Congress, 42nd Congress, 2nd session, *Report of the Joint Select Committee to Inquire Into the Condition of Affairs in the Late Insurrectionary States: Georgia* (Government Printing Office, 1872) [hereafter GAKH], 645–46.

37. Harriet Hernandez, July 10, 1871, SCKH, 591.

38. Mervin Givens, July 12, 1871, SCKH, 700.

39. Andrew Cathcart, July 27, 1871, SCKH, 1596.

40. Patrick W. Tanner, July 7, 1871, SCKH, 409.

41. Tanner, SCKH, 408.

42. Tanner, 408. Thulani Davis discusses Black people's "right" to tell their stories as they understood them and to have them heard and not dismissed or trivialized. Davis, "Recovering Fugitive Freedoms," *Social Text* 33, no. 4 125 (2015): 66.

43. Benjamin Leonard, Nov. 2, 1871, ALKH, 1792, 1785.

44. Leonard, ALKH, 1792.

45. John Childers, Nov. 1, 1871, ALKH, 1722.

46. Robert Fullerlove, Oct. 31, 1871, ALKH, 1657.

47. Alexander K. Davis, Nov. 6, 1871, U.S. Congress, 42nd Congress, 2nd session, *Report of the Joint Select Committee to Inquire Into the Condition of Affairs in the Late Insurrectionary States: Mississippi* (Government Printing Office, 1872) [hereafter MSKH], 478.

48. This is evident in witnesses' discussion of terror and violence as temporal markers in their lives. See Kidada E. Williams, *They Left Great Marks on Me: African American Testimonies of Racial Violence from Emancipation to World War I* (New York University Press, 2006), 7; Sasanka Perera, "Spirit Possessions and Avenging Ghosts: Stories of Supernatural Activity as Narratives of Terror and Mechanisms of Coping and Remembering," in *Remaking a World: Violence, Social Suffering, and Recovery*, eds. Veena Das, et al. (University of California Press, 2001), 159.

49. Henry Latham, SCKT, 1859.

50. Barbara Baumgartner discusses the ways in which people can use their bodies as supporting, corporeal evidence of verbal claims. See Baumgartner, "The Body as Evidence: Resistance, Collaboration, and Appropriation in *The History of Mary Prince*," *Callaloo* 24, no. 1 (2001): 264.

51. George Roper, Oct. 9, 1871, ALKH, 688.

52. For more on bodies as evidence, see Kathleen Kennedy, "On Writing the History of the Body in Pain," *Cultural History* 4, no. 1 (2015): 88. See also Robert I. Goler, "Loss and the Persistence of Memory: 'The Case of George Dedlow' and Disabled Civil War Veterans," *Literature and Medicine* 23, no. 1 (2004): 160–83; and Larry M. Logue and Peter Blanck, "'Benefit of the Doubt': African-American Civil War Veterans and Pensions," *Journal of Interdisciplinary History* 38, no. 3 (2008): 377–99.

53. Jennifer Harford Vargas, "Novel Testimony: Alternative Archives in Edwidge Danticat's *The Farming of Bones*," *Callaloo* 37, no. 5 (2014): 1173–74.

54. Leanna Garrison, Oct. 27, 1871, GAKH, 666–67.

55. Charlotte Fowler, SCKH, 390.

56. Investigators summoned a Robert D. Webb, a physician from Sumter County, to examine Robert Fullerlove. Dr. Webb told lawmakers that Fullerlove's story of being assaulted on his way to the hearings did not sync with his bodily examination. Progressives on the committee, however, drilled down into the doctor's report, arguing that the kind of injuries Fullerlove described were not extensive enough to break the skin but that did not mean he was lying about what had happened. Robert D. Webb, Nov. 1, 1871, ALKH, 1728.

57. Scipio Eager, Oct. 27, 1871, GAKH, 671.

58. Jesse Brown, Oct. 12. 1871, ALKH, 861.

59. Samuel Stewart, Oct. 26, 1871, GAKH, 93.

60. Stewart, GAKH, 594.

61. Jack Johnson, July 20, 1871, SCKH, 1169.

62. Columbus Jeter, Oct. 25, 1871, GAKH, 563.

63. Roger L. Ransom and Richard Sutch, *One Kind of Freedom: The Economic Consequences of Emancipation* (Cambridge University Press, 2001); and Leon F. Litwack, *Been in the Storm So Long: The Aftermath of Slavery* (Vintage, 1980), 292–502.

64. John Lewis, July 7, 1871, SCKH, 438.

65. Stewart, GAKH, 592–93.

66. Hannah Flournoy, Oct. 24, 1871, GAKH, 534.

67. People who experience repeated traumatic events are at greater risk for suffering from PTSD. Rachel Yehuda, "Post-Traumatic Stress Disorder," *New England Journal of Medicine* 346, no. 2 (2002), 109; and Ronnie Janoff-Bulman, *Shattered Assumptions: Towards a New Psychology of Trauma* (Free Press, 1992), 54. Robert J. Lifton wrote that events wherein victims experience "a jarring awareness of the fact of death" can leave a "death imprint." Lifton is quoted in Janoff-Bulman, *Shattered Assumptions*, 56–57. See also Elaine Scarry, *The Body in Pain: The Making and Unmaking of the World* (Oxford University Press, 1985); and Arthur Kleinman, Veena Das, and Margaret Lock, eds., *Social Suffering* (University of California Press, 1997). Witnesses did not name what psychologists call "moral injuries," which come as a result of enduring or witnessing "acts that transgress deeply held moral beliefs and expectations." But their testimonies point them. See Brett T. Litz, Nathan Stein, Eileen Delaney, Leslie Lebowitz, William P. Nash, Caroline Silva, and Shira Maguen, "Moral Injury and Moral Repair in War Veterans: A Preliminary Model and Intervention Strategy," *Clinical Psychology Review* 29, no. 8 (2009): 695–706.

68. Faith Lichen, letter to *New National Era*, March 30, 1871, reprinted in *The Trouble They Seen: The Story Of Reconstruction In The Words Of African Americans*, ed. Dorothy Sterling (Da Capo Press, 1994), 395.

69. For more on the Georgia militias, see Gregory Mixon, *Show Thyself a Man: Georgia State Troops, Colored, 1865–1905* (University of Florida Press, 2016).

70. Anonymous letter to the editor from Columbia, South Carolina, to *New National Era*, July 15, 1874, reprinted in *The Trouble They Seen*, 401–2.

71. Mindy Thompson Fullilove, *Root Shock: How Tearing Up City Neighborhoods Hurts America, and What We Can Do About It* (One World/Ballantine, 2009). See also Ta-Nehisi Coates, "The Case for Reparations," *The Atlantic* (June 2014).

72. Clem Bowden, July 7, 1871, SCKH, 385.

73. See Nell Irvin Painter's discussions of "testimonies of desolation" in "Soul Murder and Slavery: Toward a Fully Loaded Cost-Accounting," in *Southern History Across the Color Line* (University of North Carolina Press, 2002), 29.

74. Report of the Joint Select Committee (1872), the Minority Report, 289, 515, https://quod.lib.umich.edu/cgi/t/text/text-idx?c=moa;idno=ACA4911.0001.001;cc=moa; accessed March 1, 2022.

75. Report of the Joint Select Committee (1872), the Majority Report, 3, 18, https://quod.lib.umich.edu/m/moa/ACA4911.0001.001?rgn=main;view=fulltext; accessed March 1, 2022.

76. Report of the Joint Select Committee (1872), the Majority Report, 28.

77. Report of the Joint Select Committee (1872), the Majority Report, 22.

78. Report of the Joint Select Committee (1872), the Majority Report, 28.

79. Report of the Joint Select Committee (1872), the Majority Report, 98.

80. Report of the Joint Select Committee (1872), the Majority Report, 99.

CHAPTER 8: A REVOLUTION IN REVERSE

1. Thomas Wentworth Higginson, *Army Life in a Black Regiment* (Fields, Osgood, 1870), 47.

2. Arundhati Roy, "Peace and the New Corporate Liberation Theology," 2004 Sydney Peace Prize Lecture, November 4, 2004, http://sydney.edu.au/news/84.html?newsstoryid=279, accessed May 2017.

3. J. Steven Picou and Cecelia G. Martin, Report to the National Science Foundation, "Long-Term Community Impacts of the Exxon Valdez Oil Spill: Patterns of Social Disruption and Psychological Stress Seventeen Years after the Disaster," https://www.arlis.org/docs/vol1/B/243478793.pdf.

4. Speech of Hon. Samuel S. Cox on Miscegenation and Slavery, *The Daily Ohio Statesman*, February 23, 1864.

5.   Joseph Rainey, Congressional Globe, 42nd Congress, 2nd Session (1872) 1442–43.

6.   See Melinda Meek Hennessey, *Political Terrorism in the Black Belt: The Eutaw Riot* (University of Alabama Press, 1980).

7.   See, for example, Adam H. Domby, *The False Cause: Fraud, Fabrication, and White Supremacy in Confederate Memory* (University of Virginia Press, 2020); W. Fitzhugh Brundage, *The Southern Past: A Clash of Race and Memory* (Harvard University Press, 2005); and Karen L. Cox, *No Common Ground: Confederate Monuments and the Ongoing Fight for Racial Justice* (University of North Carolina Press, 2021) and *Dreaming of Dixie: How the South Was Created in American Popular Culture* (University of North Carolina Press, 2011).

8.   Frederick Douglass, *The Life and Times of Frederick Douglass, from 1817 to 1882* (Park Publishing Company, 1881; reprinted (London: Christian Age Office, 1882), 359, accessed January 2021, https://oll.libertyfund.org/title/lobb-the-life-and-times-of -frederick-douglass-from-1817-1882.

9.   For a discussion of this framework of refusing to punish and forgetting the unforgivable following mass atrocities in which specific groups are targeted, see Hannah Arendt, *The Origins of Totalitarianism* (Shocken Books, 1951).

10. For a comprehensive discussion of this concept, see Nicole McClure, "Injured Bodies, Silenced Voices: Reclaiming Personal Trauma and the Narration of Pain in Northern Ireland," *Peace and Change* 40, no 4 (2015): 497–516.

11. See *Inquiry into the Alleged Frauds in the Late Elections*, Senate Report 855, in Senate Reports, vol. 2, 45th Congress, 3rd Session (1878–79) and Senate Report 693, *Report and Testimony of the Select Committee of the United States Senate to Investigate the Causes of the Removal of the Negroes from the Southern States to the Northern States*, 46th Congress, 2nd Session (1880). Hereafter referred to as Exoduster Testimony.

12. Frederick Douglass, *The Life and Times*, 332.

13. Douglass, *The Life and Times*, 334.

14. Douglass, *The Life and Times*, 336.

15. Douglass, *The Life and Times*, 331.

16. Jefferson F. Long, Congressional Globe, 41st Congress, 3rd Session, (1872), 881–82.

17. U.S. Congress, 43rd Congress, 2nd session, House of Representatives Report Number 261, Louisiana Affairs. Report of the Select Committee on that Portion of the President's Message Relating to the Condition of the South (Government Printing Office, 1875) [hereafter House Report on the Condition of the South (1875)], 11–14.

18. House Report on the Condition of the South (1875), 13.

19. For a comprehensive account, see LeeAnna Keith, *The Colfax Massacre: The Untold Story of Black Power, White Terror and the Death of Reconstruction* (Oxford University Press,

2009); Charles Lane, *The Day Freedom Died: The Colfax Massacre, the Supreme Court, and the Betrayal of Reconstruction* (Henry Holt, 2009); and House Report on the Condition of the South (1875), 14.

20. *New National Era*, May 29, 1873.

21. "White League Outrages," *The Elevator*, October 17, 1874.

22. William Murrell, William Murrell, April 2 and April 3, 1880, Washington, D.C., U.S. Congress Report and Testimony of the United States Senate to Investigate the Cause of the Removal of Negroes from the Southern States to the Northern States, Senate Report 693, Part II, 46th Congress, 2nd Session (1880) [hereafter Exoduster Testimony Part II], 521.

23. Murrell, Exoduster Testimony Part II, 522.

24. Murrell, Exoduster Testimony Part II, 522.

25. Henry Adams, March 12–March 13, 1880, Exoduster Testimony, Part II, 113.

26. Edmund Turner and Jackson Turner to Governor David P. Lewis, August 21, 1874, Alabama Department of Archives and History, quoted in *The Trouble They Seen: The Story Of Reconstruction In the Words Of African Americans*, ed. Dorothy Sterling (Da Capo Press, 1994), 434.

27. Steven Hahn, "Of Paramilitary Politics," in *A Nation under Our Feet: Black Political Struggles in the Rural South, from Slavery to the Great Migration* (Belknap Press, 2003).

28. See Hahn's discussion of the Vicksburg Massacre, in "Of Paramilitary Politics," *A Nation under Our Feet.*

29. Rebecca J. Scott, "Discerning a Dignitary Offense: The Concept of Equal 'Public Rights' During Reconstruction," *Law and History Review* 38, no. 3 (August 2020): 519–53.

30. To access some of the Colored Conventions movement's records, visit https://coloredconventions.org/. For more on the movement's history, see P. Gabrielle Foreman, Jim Casey, and Sarah Lynn Patterson, eds., *The Colored Conventions Movement: Black Organizing in the Nineteenth Century* (University of North Carolina Press, 2021).

31. John Roy Lynch, Congressional Record, 43rd Congress, 2nd Session (1875), 947.

32. Charles Sumner, Congressional Globe, 42nd Congress, 2nd Session (1872), 381, quoted in Amy Dru Stanley, "Slave Emancipation and the Revolutionizing of Human Rights," in *The World the Civil War Made*, eds. Gregory P. Downs and Kate Masur (University of North Carolina Press, 2015), 271.

33. Richard Harvey Cain, Congressional Record, 43rd Congress, 1st Session, (1874), 565–67; For more on African Americans' articulation of civil rights as human rights, see Stanley, "Slave Emancipation and the Revolutionizing of Human Rights"; and Thavolia Glymph, "'I Could Not Come in Unless over their Dead Bodies': Dignitary Offenses," *Law and History Review* 38, no. 3 (2020): 585–98.

34. Cain's adopted daughter, Ann J. Edwards, shared this story. Quoted in *We Are Your Sisters: Black Women in the Nineteenth Century*, ed. Dorothy Sterling (W. W. Norton, 1984), 346–47.

35. The history of slavery in South Carolina played a significant role in shaping the political landscape of Reconstruction. See Manisha Sinha, *The Counterrevolution of Slavery: Politics and Ideology in Antebellum South Carolina* (University of North Carolina Press, 2000).

36. Dock Adams, quoted in Dorothy Sterling, ed., *The Trouble They Seen: The Story of Reconstruction in the Words of African Americans* (Da Capo Press, 1994), 463–64.

37. For more on the Hamburg massacre, see Stephen Budiansky, *The Bloody Shirt: Terror After Appomattox* (Viking Penguin, 2008); Thomas Holt, *Black over White: Negro Political Leadership in South Carolina during Reconstruction* (University of Illinois Press, 1979); and Richard Zuczek, *State of Rebellion: Reconstruction in South Carolina* (University of South Carolina Press, 1966).

38. Joseph Rainey, Congressional Globe, 42nd Congress, 2nd Session, (1872), 1442–43.

39. U.S. Congress Report of the Testimony Taken by the Select Committee on the Recent Election in South Carolina, House Report 174, 44th Congress, 2nd Session (1877), quoted from Hennessey, *Political Terrorism in the Black Belt*, 103.

40. John Lewis, March 30 and April 1, 1880, Exoduster Testimony, Part II, 436.

41. For more details on the 1876 election's outcome in South Carolina, see Ronald F. King, "Counting the Votes: South Carolina's Stolen Election of 1876," *Journal of Interdisciplinary History* 32, no. 2 (2001), 190–91. For a new and compelling interpretation on the election, see Michael F. Holt, *By One Vote: The Disputed Presidential Election of 1876* (University of Kansas Press, 2008).

42. "Address to the Republicans of South Carolina," reported by Walter Allen, Governor Chamberlain's Administration, quoted in Sterling, *The Trouble They Seen*, 475–76.

43. For a comprehensive examination of African Americans' ongoing fight, see Hahn, "The Unvanquished," in *A Nation under Our Feet*.

44. Henry Adams, Exoduster Testimony, Part II, 108.

45. See Nell Irvin Painter, *Exodusters: Black Migration to Kansas after Reconstruction* (New York: W. W. Norton, 1979).

46. R. J. Cromwell to President Rutherford B. Hayes, Nov. 10, 1878, quoted in Painter, *Exodusters*, 98.

47. Nell Painter wrote the definitive history; see *Exodusters*. See also Kendra T. Field, "No Such Thing as Stand Still": Migration and Geopolitics in African American History," *Journal of American History* 102, no. 3 (December 2015): 693–718, and *Growing Up with the Country: Family, Race, and the Nation after the Civil War* (Yale University Press, 2018).

48. See Brent M. S. Campney, *This Is Not Dixie: Racist Violence in Kansas, 1861–1927* (University of Illinois Press, 2017), and *Hostile Heartland: Racism, Repression, and Resistance in the Midwest* (University of Illinois Press, 2019).

49. Mingo Simmons was one critic who testified. Mingo Simmons, February 13, 1880, Washington, D.C., U.S. Congress Report and Testimony of the United States Senate to Investigate the Cause of the Removal of Negroes from the Southern States to the Northern States, Senate Report 693, Part I, 46th Congress, 2nd Session (1880) [hereafter Exoduster Testimony Part I], 371–78.

50. Henry Adams, Exoduster Testimony Part II, 101–214; and Benjamin Singleton, April 17, 1880, Washington, D.C., U.S. Congress Report and Testimony of the United States Senate to Investigate the Cause of the Removal of Negroes from the Southern States to the Northern States, Senate Report 693, Part III, 46th Congress, 2nd Session (1880), 379–405.

51. Joshua McCarter Simpson, "To the White People of America," https://www.poemhunter .com/poem/to-the-white-people-of-america/, accessed March 1, 2021.

52. Robert Smalls, Speech Before the South Carolina Constitutional Convention, 1895. Text of the speech is available at "A Word of Warning: A Former Slave Urges Constitutional Caution," http://historymatters.gmu.edu/d/5468, accessed September 1, 2019.

53. Historian Douglas Egerton finds this figure plausible. See "Terrorized African-Americans Found Their Champion in Civil War Hero Robert Smalls," *Smithsonian Magazine*, September 2018, https://www.smithsonianmag.com/history/terrorized -african-americans-champion-civil-war-hero-robert-smalls-180970031, accessed September 1, 2019.

    The Equal Justice Initiative initially documented 4,500 lynchings from 1877 to 1950. More recently, they examined the Freedmen's Bureau's "Record of Murders and Outrages" and testimonies from the Klan hearings, and added 2,000 lynchings to their tally. See Reconstruction in America: Racial Violence after the Civil War, https://eji.org /report/reconstruction-in-america/documenting-reconstruction-violence/. Accounting for racism-based killings of African Americans is beset with challenges, including those of definition and documentation. In the late 1800s, Americans understood "lynching" as a particular kind of killing: it often involved organized murders where groups of perpetrators were purported to be "exacting justice" for "crimes" they claimed local, state, and federal governments could not punish sufficiently. Across U.S. history, lynching victims came from different racial and ethnic backgrounds, but the vast majority of victims in the late nineteenth and early twentieth century were Black men, women, and children white southerners punished for resisting racist oppression. Most white southerners' killings of African Americans, however, fell outside the recognized framework of lynching as organized group murders. Local and state criminal cases and the massive Department of Justice records, which have not yet been digitized, are filled with reports of white-on-Black violence, including U.S. Marshals Service reports of attacks and killings from 1870 to the mid 1880s as well as affidavits from victims of and witnesses to this violence. These data sets would help approximate how many Black people white southerners killed and why. And even those murders would have been underreported because victims were disappeared (grabbed, thrown in waterways or transported to other locations and buried), agents of the state did not always care enough to document white-on-Black killings, or they lacked the resources to do it. We do not know how Smalls calculated this figure, but the records we do have and our understanding of how he likely deduced that many, if not most, white southerners' killings of Black people was part of their resistance to emancipation and Reconstruction makes it worthy of inclusion here.

54. See Timothy Thomas Fortune, *Black and White: Labor, Land, and Politics in the South* (1884), https://www.gutenberg.org/files/16810/16810-h/16810-h.htm, accessed March 5, 2022.

55. Elaine Frantz Parsons, *Ku-Klux: The Birth of the Klan During Reconstruction* (University of North Carolina Press, 2016), 220. See also Michael J. Pfeifer, *The Roots of Rough Justice: Origins of American Lynching* (University of Illinois Press, 2011).

56. Robert J. Lifton wrote that events wherein victims experience "a jarring awareness of the fact of death" can leave a "death imprint." Quoted in Janoff-Bulman, *Shattered Assumptions*, 56–57.

57. Janoff-Bulman, *Shattered Assumptions*, 63.

58. Elaine Scarry has written about the ways in which physical pain can unmake victims' worlds, but the accounts of survivors of night-riding attacks suggest their social pain has a similar effect. Elaine Scarry, *The Body in Pain: The Making and Unmaking of the World* (Oxford University Press, 1985). For a more comprehensive analysis of the multi-faceted social suffering generated by conflict, see also Arthur Kleinman, Veena Das, and Margaret Lock, eds., *Social Suffering* (University of California Press, 1997). Brett T. Litz, Nathan Stein, Eileen Delaney, Leslie Lebowitz, William P. Nash, Caroline Silva, and Shira Maguen, "Moral Injury and Moral Repair in War Veterans: A Preliminary Model and Intervention Strategy," *Clinical Psychology Review* 29, no. 8 (2009): 695–706.

CONCLUSION

1. Samuel and Hannah Tutson, Florida Census, St. Johns County, population schedule, 1885. Digital Image. Ancestry.com. April 1, 2015.

2. Hannah Tutson, Nov. 10, 1871, U.S. Congress, 42nd Congress, 2nd session, *Report of the Joint Select Committee to Inquire Into the Condition of Affairs in the Late Insurrectionary*

States: Florida; and Miscellaneous Testimonies and Documents (Government Printing Office, 1872) [hereafter FLKH], 64.

3. Lou Falkner Williams, *The Great South Carolina Ku Klux Klan Trials, 1871–1872* (University of Georgia Press, 1996); and Elaine Frantz Parsons, *Ku-Klux: The Birth of the Klan During Reconstruction* (University of North Carolina Press, 2016).

4. State assessors recorded Hannah and Samuel's ages as sixty-five and seventy-five, respectively. But when they testified at the Klan hearings in 1871, they informed lawmakers they were forty-two or forty-three and fifty-three or fifty-four, respectively. It is possible that when assessors came through, someone other than the couple provided their information. Hannah Tutson, FLKH, 59; and Samuel Tutson, Nov. 10, 1871, FLKH, 54.

5. Psychologists and sociologists who work with survivors note that some situations, especially those in which people have death encounters together, can result in a certain type of "knowing." In a fellowship of survivors, members rarely need a context; they understand what each other went through and how they were transformed by the event without having it explained to them. In the Tutsons' case, it is possible they remained together because they went through the space of death together and came out the other side. See Kai Erikson, "Notes on Trauma and Community," in *Trauma: Explorations in Memory*, ed. Cathy Caruth (Johns Hopkins University Press, 1995), 186–87.

6. Thavolia Glymph, "'Invisible Disabilities': Black Women in War and in Freedom," *Proceedings of the American Philosophical Society* 160, no. 3 (2016): 239.

7. I take the concept of "last witnesses" from Svetlana Alexievich, *Last Witnesses: An Oral History of the Children of World War II* (Penguin Random House, 2019).

8. Samuel and Rose Garrison, U.S. Census, Fulton County, Georgia, population schedule, 1880. Digital Image. Ancestry.com. April 1, 2015.

9. Reuben and Elizabeth Sheets, U.S. Census, Walton County, Georgia, population schedule, 1880. Digital Image. Ancestry.com. April 1, 2015.

10. Simon and Mary Elder, U.S. Census, DeKalb County, Georgia, population schedule, 1880. Digital Image. Ancestry.com. April 1, 2015.

11. Augustus and Elizabeth Mills, U.S. Census, DeKalb County, Georgia, population schedule, 1880. Digital Image. Ancestry.com. April 1, 2015.

12. Destiny O. Birdsong, "'Memories that are (n't) mine: Matrilineal Trauma and Defiant Reinscription in Natasha Trethewey's *Native Guard*," *African American Review* 48, no. 1 (2015): 97–98.

13. W. L. Bost, Federal Writers' Slave Narrative Project, Volume 11, North Carolina, Part 1. Kindle edition.

14. See John Ernest, ed., *The Oxford Handbook of the African American Slave Narrative* (Oxford University Press, 2014); Lynda M. Hill, "Ex-Slave Narratives: The WPA Federal

Writers' Project Reappraised," *Oral History* 26, no. 1 (1998): 64–72; and John W. Blassingame, "Using the Testimony of Ex-Slaves: Approaches and Problems," *The Journal of Southern History* 41, no. 4 (1975): 473–92.

15. Catherine A. Stewart, *Long Past Slavery: Representing Race in the Federal Writers' Project* (University of North Carolina Press, 2016).

16. Natasha Trethewey, *Native Guard: Poems* (Mariner Books, 2007).

17. Lula Chambers, Federal Writers' Slave Narrative Project, Volume 10, Missouri. Kindle edition.

18. Ann Ulrich Evans, Federal Writers' Slave Narrative Project, Volume 10, Missouri. Kindle edition.

19. Lorenza Ezell, Federal Writers' Slave Narrative Project, Volume 16, Texas, Part 2. Kindle edition.

20. Sam Kilgore, Federal Writers' Slave Narrative Project, Volume 16, Texas, Part 2. Kindle edition.

21. Pierce Harper, Federal Writers' Slave Narrative Project, Volume 16, Texas, Part 2. Kindle edition.

22. Harper, Federal Writers' Slave Narrative Project, Texas.

23. Harper, Federal Writers' Slave Narrative Project, Texas.

24. Mary Ellen Grandberry, Federal Writers' Slave Narrative Project, Volume 1, Alabama. Kindle edition.

25. Jerry Moore, Federal Writers' Slave Narrative Project, Volume 16, Texas, Part 3. Kindle edition.

26. Erikson, "Notes on Trauma and Community," 186–87.

27. Glymph, "'Invisible Disabilities.'"

28. See Blair L. M. Kelley, *Right to Ride: Streetcar Boycotts and African American Citizenship in the Era of Plessy v. Ferguson* (University of North Carolina Press, 2010); David Zucchino, *Wilmington's Lie: The Murderous Coup of 1898 and the Rise of White Supremacy* (Grove Atlantic, 2020); and David S. Cecelski and Timothy Tyson, eds., *Democracy Betrayed: The Wilmington Race Riot of 1898 and Its Legacy* (University of North Carolina Press, 1998).

29. See Trethewey, *Native Guard*, especially "Native Guard," 41–52; "Southern History," 63–64; and "Elegy for the Native Guards," 75–77.

30. W. E. B. Du Bois, *Black Reconstruction in America: An Essay Toward a History of the Part Which Black Folk Played in the Attempt to Reconstruct Democracy in America, 1860–1880*, 1998 ed. (Free Press, 1935); Kenneth Stampp, *The Era of Reconstruction, 1865–1877* (Vintage, 1965); John Hope Franklin, *Reconstruction after the Civil War* (University of Chicago Press, 1966); Allen W. Trelease, *White Terror: The Ku Klux Klan*

Conspiracy and Southern Reconstruction (Harper & Row, 1971); Gladys-Marie Fry, *Night Riders in Black Folk History* (University of Tennessee Press, 1975); Nell Irvin Painter, *Exodusters: Black Migration to Kansas after Reconstruction* (New York: W. W. Norton, 1979); Thomas C. Holt, *Black over White: Negro Political Leadership in South Carolina During Reconstruction* (University of Illinois Press, 1977); George C. Rable, *But There Was No Peace: The Role of Violence in the Politics of Reconstruction* (University of Georgia Press, 1984); Eric Foner, *Reconstruction: America's Unfinished Revolution, 1863–1877* (Harper & Row, 1988); Steven Hahn, *A Nation under Our Feet: Black Political Struggles in the Rural South from Slavery to the Great Migration* (Belknap Press, 2003); and David W. Blight, *Beyond the Battlefield: Race, Memory, and the American Civil War* (University of Massachusetts Press, 2002).

Black novelists were more likely to produce representations of ordinary people's experiences of Reconstruction era violence, likely using Klan testimonies, Federal Writers' Slave Narrative Project interviews, and family stories. See Margaret Walker, *Jubilee* (Houghton Mifflin, 1966); J. California Cooper, *The Wake of the Wind* (Doubleday, 1998); and Lalita Tademy, *Red River* (Warner Books, 2006) and *Citizens Creek* (Simon and Schuster, 2014).

INDEX

The letter *f* following a page locator denotes a figure.

A NOTE ON THE AUTHOR

Kidada E. Williams is Associate Professor of History at Wayne State University. She is the author of *They Left Great Marks on Me*, coauthor of *Charleston Syllabus*, and creator of the podcast *Seizing Freedom*. Williams has been interviewed on NPR's *Morning Edition* and *On Point*, and her essays have appeared in the *New York Times*, *Slate*, and multiple scholarly journals. She lives in Detroit.